Natural Language Processing with AWS AI Services

Derive strategic insights from unstructured data with Amazon Textract and Amazon Comprehend

Mona M

Premkumar Rangarajan

BIRMINGHAM—MUMBAI

Natural Language Processing with AWS AI Services

Publishing Product Manager: Sunith Shetty
Senior Editor: David Sugarman
Content Development Editor: Priyanka Soam
Technical Editor: Devanshi Ayare
Copy Editor: Safis Editing
Project Coordinator: Aparna Ravikumar Nair
Proofreader: Safis Editing
Indexer: Pratik Shirodkar
Production Designer: Sinhayna Bais

First published: November 2021

Production reference: 2191121

Published by Packt Publishing Ltd.
Livery Place
35 Livery Street
Birmingham
B3 2PB, UK.

978-1-80181-253-5

www.packt.com

Dr. Arun Kumar
August 23, 1960 – March 9, 2016

Shri T. Rangarajan
June 15, 1947 – May 4, 2021

Wisdom is knowing I am nothing. Love is knowing I am everything.
Between the two, my life moves. – Shri Nisargadatta Maharaj

We dedicate this book to our dear fathers, for it is their wisdom and love
that guides us from within. We may miss their physical presence, but we are
blessed with the light of their true essence in every moment of our lives.

Acknowledgments

We also wanted to take a few moments to express our sincere gratitude to our families, friends, and well-wishers for their continued support, without whom this book would not have been possible.

I, Premkumar Rangarajan, would like to thank my wife, Sapna Mohan Kumar, for her patience with me, her words of encouragement during creative blocks, and her skillful ability to know exactly when to leave me alone; my son, Harivatsa Premkumar, for his faith in me; my mother, Prabhavathy Rangarajan, for her constant love and guidance; my brother, Arun Rangarajan, for his unwavering support; my niece Anya Arun and my nephew Satvik Arun for their playful encouragement; and all my family and friends, for being there for me during this very tough 2021.

I, Mona M, would like to thank my grandparents, Nawal Kishore Prasad and Indu Kumari Sinha, for their constant encouragement to write this book; my mother, Punam Kumari, for never losing faith in me even in the most difficult situation of my life. Also, to my aunts (Nirupama Kaushik and Anupama Kunwar), for always giving me the strength to stay positive, and all the rest of my family and friends, for being there for me during this very tough 2021

Foreword

For decades, very few organizations could master the arcane field of **Machine Learning (ML)**. A fascinating mix of math, computer science, software engineering, and IT, ML required a collection of skills and resources that were simply not available outside of very large companies or research labs.

This all changed about 10 years ago with the availability of commodity compute and storage, open source libraries, and the omnipresence of digital data. Indeed, the near-simultaneous emergence of tools such as Amazon EC2, Amazon S3, scikit-learn, and Theano quickly made ML much more accessible and cost-effective. Just a few years later, research teams demonstrated that **Graphical Processing Units (GPUs)** could be used to massively accelerate neural networks, giving this ancient and impractical technology a new lease of life, and kicking off a **Deep Learning (DL)** frenzy that has yet to slow down.

Initially, **Computer Vision (CV)** stole the limelight, amazing us all with ever more sophisticated applications. Meanwhile, **Natural Language Processing (NLP)** progressed as well, although in a quieter manner. For a while, tasks such as translation, sentiment analysis, and searching didn't look as exciting and flashy as autonomous driving. And then, transformer models burst onto the scene, delivering stunning, state-of-the-art results on NLP tasks and rejuvenating the whole field.

Today, NLP use cases are ubiquitous. Many organizations have accumulated mountains of text documents, including invoices, contracts, forms, reports, emails, web pages, and more. The sheer volume and diversity of these documents make it very challenging to process them efficiently so as to extract precious business insights that can help improve business performance and customer experience.

Some teams decide to build their own NLP solutions using ML libraries and their preferred flavor of IT infrastructure. On top of the ML work, this also requires deploying and managing production environments, with their cohort of challenges: security, monitoring, high availability, scaling, and so on. All of this is important work (who wants to skimp on security?), but it takes valuable time and resources away from the project without creating any actual business value.

This is precisely the problem that AWS AI Services solves. You can extract business insights from your text documents without having to train models or manage any infrastructure. In fact, you don't even need to know the first thing about ML! The answer is literally an API call away, and any developer can start using these services in minutes. Many AWS customers have deployed these services in production in a couple of days, if not hours. They're that simple, and they provide the out-of-the-box security and robustness that is commonly associated with AWS infrastructure.

Authors Mona and Prem have worked with diverse AWS customers for years, and they've distilled this experience in their book, the first of its kind. Not only will you learn how AWS APIs work, but you'll also and, most importantly, learn how to combine them to implement powerful NLP workflows, such as automating document processing, understanding the voice of your customers, or building a solution to monetize content. I highly recommend this book to every developer interested in adding NLP capabilities to their applications with just a few lines of code. So, turn the page, start learning, and build great apps!

Julien Simon

Global AI and ML Evangelist, AWS

Contributors

About the authors

Mona M is an AI/ML customer engineer at Google. She is a highly skilled IT professional, with more than 10 years' experience in software design, development, and integration across diverse work environments. As an AWS solutions architect, her role is to ensure customer success in building applications and services on the AWS platform. She is responsible for crafting a highly scalable, flexible, and resilient cloud architecture that addresses customer business problems. She has published multiple blogs on AI and NLP on the AWS AI channel along with research papers on AI-powered search solutions.

Premkumar Rangarajan is an enterprise solutions architect, specializing in AI/ML at Amazon Web Services. He has 25 years of experience in the IT industry in a variety of roles, including delivery lead, integration specialist, and enterprise architect. He has significant architecture and management experience in delivering large-scale programs across various industries and platforms. He is passionate about helping customers solve ML and AI problems.

About the reviewers

Hitesh Hinduja is an ardent AI enthusiast working as a Senior Manager in AI at Ola Electric, where he leads a team of 20+ people in the areas of ML, statistics, CV, NLP, and reinforcement learning. He has filed 14+ patents in India and the US and has numerous research publications to his name. Hitesh has been associated in research roles at India's top B-schools: the Indian School of Business, Hyderabad, and the Indian Institute of Management, Ahmedabad. He is also actively involved in training and mentoring and has been invited to be a guest speaker by various corporations and associations across the globe.

Egor Pushkin is a technical leader responsible for natural language processing and understanding efforts within the AWS Languages organization. His specialty is the design of highly scalable and reliable services backed by ML/NLP tech. Before joining AWS, he focused on location-sharing technology and built systems deployed to over a billion devices worldwide. Prior to his years in the industry, he pursued an academic career, studying the processing of multispectral satellite images with the use of neural networks.

Table of Contents

3

Introducing Amazon Comprehend

Section 2: Using NLP to Accelerate Business Outcomes

4

Automating Document Processing Workflows

5
Creating NLP Search

6
Using NLP to Improve Customer Service Efficiency

7
Understanding the Voice of Your Customer Analytics

8
Leveraging NLP to Monetize Your Media Content

9
Extracting Metadata from Financial Documents

10
Reducing Localization Costs with Machine Translation

11
Using Chatbots for Querying Documents

12

AI and NLP in Healthcare

Section 3: Improving NLP Models in Production

13

Improving the Accuracy of Document Processing Workflows

14

Auditing Named Entity Recognition Workflows

15

Classifying Documents and Setting up Human in the Loop for Active Learning

16

Improving the Accuracy of PDF Batch Processing

17
Visualizing Insights from Handwritten Content

18
Building Secure, Reliable, and Efficient NLP Solutions

Preface

Authors are a quirky lot; almost like the weather in London. The sky is overcast, you want to go for a walk in Trafalgar Square, you wear your raincoat, pick up your umbrella just in case, and you think you are ready for anything. But you are woefully unaware of the sinister plan nature has for you. You walk a mile or so, and suddenly, without warning, the sky clears, the sun pours its brightest song upon your face, and lo and behold, you are caught unaware (like a deer in headlights) with your raincoat and umbrella and you are too far from home to go back and get rid of them. This is exactly what happens to the best of us when we set out to write a book. You set out with a clear objective, focus your thoughts, write a fantastic outline, get it approved, and start formulating your chapters, but unbeknown to you, the book has other plans on how it wants to write itself.

When this happens, as in life, there are always choices. You can let the creative stream express itself through your hands onto the pages of the book, or you can resist and follow the preconceived pattern you laid out. There is, of course, also a third choice, which is to follow the overall structure for what you want to convey, but allow creativity to take control when it wants to. This is what we did for this book. But it was not as easy as we thought at first, because creativity doesn't take no for an answer. The famous Sufi poet Jalaluddin Rumi said: "In silence, there is eloquence. Stop weaving and see how the pattern improves." The most difficult part was to stop "weaving" or to stop being inspired by the content that we had already published as AWS authors. This was also a hard requirement for the book, and so it was a strong motivation for us to be creative and come up with original, in-demand, and fresh content for the book.

So, we stopped "weaving." The next logical step was for the pattern to improve. But nothing happened. The deadline for the first chapter was looming, and our editors were very politely reminding us of the due date. Still nada. We used this "no weaving" time to storyboard and architect the technical chapters, but the glue that was to hold together the book, the main narrative, continued to elude us. And then suddenly, one day, without warning it struck. We had totally missed the important first part of Rumi's saying: "In silence, there is eloquence." A walk in nature at a trail nearby took care of the daily quota of silence, during which time a faint thought appeared, a memory of a story that my father (Shri T. Rangarajan) had narrated to me when I was a kid called *Ali Baba and the Forty Thieves*. It dawned on me that the famous sequence from the story was in fact my first recollection of using voice to perform a task (please refer to *Chapter 1, NLP in the Business Context and Introduction to AWS AI Services*, in the book). And from then on, the floodgates opened. They never stopped until the book was written in its entirety. And that is how this book came about.

An interesting fact about life we all know is that change is the only constant thing. And this was true when writing this book as well. One of the best things about AWS is the pace of innovation with which new features are introduced. The AWS product roadmap is based on direct customer feedback and features are improved iteratively with new features launched continuously. So, as we were writing this book, **Amazon Comprehend** and **Amazon Textract** added new features, the console experience was changed, and so on. For example, Amazon Comprehend modified its console experience, added support for custom entity recognition training from PDF documents directly, and improved its custom entity recognition model framework to support training with just 100 annotations per entity and 250 documents. Amazon Textract reduced pricing by 32% for the **AnalyzeDocument** and **DetectDocumentText** APIs in eight global AWS Regions, announced support for the automated processing of invoices, and so on. A full list of what's new in AWS in 2021 can be reviewed at this link: `https://aws.amazon.com/about-aws/whats-new/2021/`.

You will notice these changes as you build the solutions for the various NLP use cases in this book. *Please note that since the Amazon Textract and Amazon Comprehend consoles have changed, the instructions in the book may not be a word-for-word match with your experience in the AWS Management Console; however, they are accurate and adequate for your needs.*

For example, the **Train Recognizer** button in the Amazon Comprehend console for custom entity recognition has now changed to **Create new model**. Similarly, **Train Classifier** in the Amazon Comprehend console for custom classification has now also changed to **Create new model**. When you specify **Training and test dataset** for custom entity recognition, a new option will now appear in the console for selecting **PDF, Word documents**. Amazon Textract has changed and it now reflects **AnalyzeExpense** as an option to view the results for your document in the console.

In the majority of the book however we have used APIs to build the solutions and the best thing about AWS is that the APIs do not change. You get consistent responses and requests. You just need to upgrade the version of Python Boto3 if you want to use the latest one. Moreover, our goal is to make sure this book remains relevant and up to date.

Who this book is for

If you're an NLP developer or data scientist looking to get started with AWS AI services to implement various NLP scenarios quickly, this book is for you. It will show you how easy it is to integrate AI in applications with just a few lines of code. A basic understanding of machine learning concepts is necessary to understand the concepts covered. Experience with Jupyter Notebooks and Python will be helpful.

What this book covers

Chapter 1, NLP in the Business Context and Introduction to AWS AI Services, introduces the NLP construct and the business value of using NLP, leading to an overview of the AWS AI stack along with the key NLP services.

Chapter 2, Introducing Amazon Textract, provides a detailed introduction to Amazon Textract, what its functions are, what business challenges it was created to solve, what features it has, what types of user requirements it can be applied to, and how easy it is to integrate Textract with other AWS services, such as AWS Lambda for building business applications.

Chapter 3, Introducing Amazon Comprehend, provides a detailed introduction to Amazon Comprehend, what its functions are, what business challenges it was created to solve, what features it has, what types of user requirements it can be applied to, and how easy it is to integrate Comprehend with other AWS services, such as AWS Lambda for building business applications.

Chapter 4, Automating Document Processing Workflows, dives deep into the several types of use cases prevalent across industries that can benefit from NLP based on our collective experience and the usage trends we have observed. We will provide detailed code samples, a design and development approach, and a step-by-step guide on how to set up and run these examples along with access to the GitHub repository.

Chapter 5, Creating NLP Search, dives deep into the several types of use cases prevalent across industries that can benefit from NLP based on our collective experience and the usage trends we have observed. We will provide detailed code samples, a design and development approach, and a step-by-step guide on how to set up and run these examples along with access to the GitHub repository.

Chapter 6, Using NLP to Improve Customer Service Efficiency, dives deep into the several types of use cases prevalent across industries that can benefit from NLP based on our collective experience and the usage trends we have observed. We will provide detailed code samples, a design and development approach, and a step-by-step guide on how to set up and run these examples along with access to the Github repository.

Chapter 7, Understanding the Voice of Your Customer Analytics, dives deep into the several types of use cases prevalent across industries that can benefit from NLP based on our collective experience and the usage trends we have observed. We will provide detailed code samples, a design and development approach, and a step-by-step guide on how to set up and run these examples along with access to the Github repository.

Chapter 8, Leveraging NLP to Monetize Your Media Content, dives deep into the several types of use cases prevalent across industries that can benefit from NLP based on our collective experience and the usage trends we have observed. We will provide detailed code samples, design and development approach, and a step-by-step guide on how to set up and run these examples along with access to the Github repository.

Chapter 9, Extracting Metadata from Financial Documents, dives deep into the several types of use cases prevalent across industries that can benefit from NLP based on our collective experience and the usage trends we have observed. We will provide detailed code samples, a design and development approach, and a step-by-step guide on how to set up and run these examples along with access to the Github repository.

Chapter 10, Reducing Localization Costs with Machine Translation, dives deep into the several types of use cases prevalent across industries that can benefit from NLP based on our collective experience and the usage trends we have observed. We will provide detailed code samples, a design and development approach, and a step-by-step guide on how to set up and run these examples along with access to the Github repository.

Chapter 11, Using Chatbots for Querying Documents, dives deep into the several types of use cases prevalent across industries that can benefit from NLP based on our collective experience and the usage trends we have observed. We will provide detailed code samples, a design and development approach, and a step-by-step guide on how to set up and run these examples along with access to the Github repository.

Chapter 12, AI and NLP in Healthcare, dives deep into the use case of how AWS NLP solutions can help achieve operational efficiency in healthcare with an automated claims adjunction use case.

Chapter 13, Improving the Accuracy of Document Processing Workflows, talks about why we need **humans in the loop** (**HITLs**) in document processing workflows, and how setting up HITL processes with Amazon **Augmented AI** (**A2I**) can help improve the accuracy of your existing document processing workflows with Amazon Textract.

Chapter 14, Auditing Named Entity Recognition Workflows, walks through an extension of the previous approach by including Amazon Comprehend for text-based insights, thereby demonstrating an end-to-end process for setting up an auditing workflow for your custom named entity recognition use cases.

Chapter 15, Classifying Documents and Setting up Human in the Loop for Active Learning, talks about how you can use Amazon Comprehend custom classification to classify documents and then how you can set up active learning feedback with your custom classification model using Amazon A2I.

Chapter 16, Improving the Accuracy of PDF Batch Processing, tackles an operational need that has been around for a while and is ubiquitous, and yet organizations struggle to address it efficiently – known as PDF batch processing.

Chapter 17, Visualizing Insights from Handwritten Content, is all about how to visualize insights from text – that is, handwritten text – and make use of it to drive decision-making.

Chapter 18, Building Secure, Reliable, and Efficient NLP Solutions, reviews the best practices, techniques, and guidance on what makes a good NLP solution great.

To get the most out of this book

You will need access to an AWS account, so before getting started, we recommend that you create one.

Software/hardware covered in the book	Operating system requirements/Account creation requirements
Access and signing up to an AWS account	`https://portal.aws.amazon.com/billing/signup`
Creating a SageMaker Jupyter notebook	
Creating an Amazon S3 bucket	

If you are using the digital version of this book, we advise you to type the code yourself. Doing so will help you avoid any potential errors related to the copying and pasting of code.

Download the example code files

You can download the example code files for this book from GitHub at `https://github.com/PacktPublishing/Natural-Language-Processing-with-AWS-AI-Services`. In case there's an update to the code, it will be updated on the existing GitHub repository.

We also have other code bundles from our rich catalog of books and videos available at `https://github.com/PacktPublishing/`. Check them out!

Download the color images

We also provide a PDF file that has color images of the screenshots and diagrams used in this book. You can download it here: `https://static.packt-cdn.com/downloads/9781801812535_ColorImages.pdf`.

Code in Action

The Code in Action videos for this book can be viewed at `https://bit.ly/3vPvDkj`.

Conventions used

There are a number of text conventions used throughout this book.

`Code in text`: Indicates code words in text, database table names, folder names, filenames, file extensions, pathnames, dummy URLs, user input, and Twitter handles. Here is an example: "Copy the created bucket name, open `Chapter 05/Ch05-Kendra Search.ipynb`, and paste it in the following cell in place of '`<your s3 bucket name>`' to get started."

A block of code is set as follows:

```
# Define IAM role
role = get_execution_role()
print("RoleArn: {}".format(role))
sess = sagemaker.Session()
s3BucketName = '<your s3 bucket name>'
prefix = 'chapter5'
```

When we wish to draw your attention to a particular part of a code block, the relevant lines or items are set in bold:

```
<body>
        <h1>Family Bank Holdings</h1>
        <h3>Date: <span id="date"></span></h3>
        <div id="home">
          <div id="hometext">
        <h2>Who we are and what we do</h2>
```

Bold: Indicates a new term, an important word, or words that you see onscreen. For instance, words in menus or dialog boxes appear in **bold**. Here is an example: "You will see that the page has a few headings and then a paragraph talking about **Family Bank**, a subsidiary of **LiveRight Holdings**."

> **Tips or Important Notes**
> Appear like this.

Get in touch

Feedback from our readers is always welcome.

General feedback: If you have questions about any aspect of this book, email us at customercare@packtpub.com and mention the book title in the subject of your message.

Errata: Although we have taken every care to ensure the accuracy of our content, mistakes do happen. If you have found a mistake in this book, we would be grateful if you would report this to us. Please visit www.packtpub.com/support/errata and fill in the form.

Piracy: If you come across any illegal copies of our works in any form on the internet, we would be grateful if you would provide us with the location address or website name. Please contact us at copyright@packt.com with a link to the material.

If you are interested in becoming an author: If there is a topic that you have expertise in and you are interested in either writing or contributing to a book, please visit authors.packtpub.com.

Share Your Thoughts

Once you've read *Natural Language Processing with AWS AI Services*, we'd love to hear your thoughts! Scan the QR code below to go straight to the Amazon review page for this book and share your feedback.

https://packt.link/r/1-801-81253-5

Your review is important to us and the tech community and will help us make sure we're delivering excellent quality content.

Section 1: Introduction to AWS AI NLP Services

In this section, we introduce the NLP construct and the business value of using NLP, leading to an overview of the AWS AI stack, along with the key NLP services.

This section comprises the following chapters:

- *Chapter 1, NLP in the Business Context and Introduction to AWS AI Services*
- *Chapter 2, Introducing Amazon Textract*
- *Chapter 3, Introducing Amazon Comprehend*

1

NLP in the Business Context and Introduction to AWS AI Services

Natural language processing, or **NLP**, is quite popular in the scientific community, but the value of using this **Artificial Intelligence** (**AI**) technique to gain business benefits is not immediately obvious to mainstream users. Our focus will be to raise awareness and educate you on the business context of NLP, provide examples of the proliferation of data in unstructured text, and show how NLP can help derive meaningful insights to inform strategic decisions within an enterprise.

In this introductory chapter, we will be establishing the basic context to familiarize you with some of the underlying concepts of AI and **Machine Learning** (**ML**), the types of challenges that NLP can help solve, common pitfalls when building NLP solutions, and how NLP works and what it's really good at doing, with examples.

In this chapter, we will cover the following:

- Introducing NLP

- Overcoming the challenges in building NLP solutions

- Understanding why NLP is becoming mainstream

- Introducing the AWS ML stack

Introducing NLP

Language is as old as civilization itself and no other communication tool is as effective as the spoken or written word. In their childhood days, the authors were enamored with *The Arabian Nights*, a centuries-old collection of stories from India, Persia, and Arabia. In one famous story, *Ali Baba and the Forty Thieves*, Ali Baba is a poor man who discovers a thieves' den containing hordes of treasure hidden in a cave that can only be opened by saying the magic words *open sesame*. In the authors' experience, this was the first recollection of a voice-activated application. Though purely a work of fiction, it was indeed an inspiration to explore the art of the possible.

Recently, in the last two decades, the popularity of the internet and the proliferation of smart devices has fueled significant technological advancements in digital communications. In parallel, the long-running research to develop AI made rapid strides with the advent of ML. Arthur Lee Samuel was the first to coin the term *machine learning*, in 1959, and helped make it mainstream in the field of computer science by creating a checkers playing program that demonstrated how computers can be *taught*.

The concept that machines can be taught to mimic human cognition, though, was popularized a little earlier in 1950 by Alan Turing in his paper *Computing Machinery and Intelligence*. This paper introduced the *Turing Test*, a variation of a common party game of the time. The purpose of the test was for an interpreter to ask questions and compare responses from a human participant and a computer. The trick was that the interpreter was not aware which was which, considering all three were isolated in different rooms. If the interpreter was unable to differentiate the two participants because the responses matched closely, the *Turing Test* had successfully validated that the computer possessed AI.

Of course, the field of AI has progressed leaps and bounds since then, largely due to the success of ML algorithms in solving real-world problems. An algorithm, at its simplest, is a programmatic function that converts inputs to outputs based on conditions. In contradiction to regular programmable algorithms, ML algorithms have learned the ability to alter their processing based on the data they encounter. There are different ML algorithms to choose from based on requirements, for example, **Extreme Gradient Boosting (XGBoost)**, a popular algorithm for regression and classification problems, **Exponential Smoothing (ETS)**, for statistical time series forecasting, **Single Shot MultiBox Detector (SSD)**, for computer vision problems, and **Latent Dirichlet Allocation (LDA)**, for topic modeling in NLP problems.

For more complex problems, ML has evolved into deep learning with the introduction of **Artificial Neural Networks (ANNs)**, which have the ability to solve highly challenging tasks by learning from massive volumes of data. For example, AWS DeepComposer (`https://aws.amazon.com/deepcomposer/`), an ML service from **Amazon Web Services (AWS)**, educates developers with music as a medium of instruction. One of the ML models that DeepComposer uses is trained with a type of neural network called the **Convolutional Neural Network (CNN)** to create new and unique musical compositions from a simple input melody using **AutoRegressive (AR)** techniques:

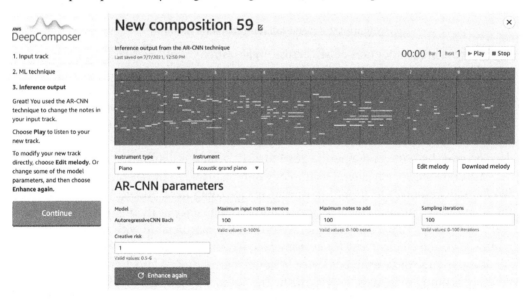

Figure 1.1 – Composing music with AWS DeepComposer and ML

A piano roll is an image representation of music, and AR-CNN considers music generation as a sequence of these piano roll images:

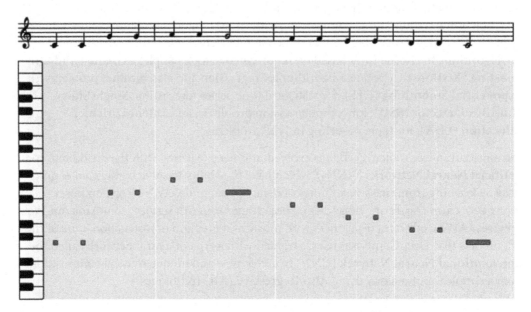

Figure 1.2 – Piano roll representation of music

While there is broad adoption of ML across organizations of all sizes and industries spurred by the democratization of advanced technologies, the potential to solve many types of problems, and the breadth and depth of capabilities in AWS, ML is only a subset of what is possible today with AI. According to one report (`https://www.gartner.com/en/newsroom/press-releases/2019-01-21-gartner-survey-shows-37-percent-of-organizations-have`, accessed on March 23, 2021), AI adoption grew by 270% in the period 2015 to 2019. And it is continuing to grow at a rapid pace. AI is no longer a peripheral technology only available to those enterprises that have the economic resources to afford high-performance computers. Today, AI is a mainstream option for organizations looking to add cognitive intelligence to their applications to accelerate business value. For example, ExxonMobil in partnership with Amazon created an innovative and efficient way for customers to pay at gas stations. The *Alexa pay for gas* skill uses the car's Alexa-enabled device or your smartphone's Alexa app to communicate with the gas pump to manage the payment. The authors paid a visit to a local ExxonMobil gas station to try it out, and it was an awesome experience. For more details, please refer to `https://www.exxon.com/en/amazon-alexa-pay-for-gas`.

AI addresses a broad spectrum of tasks similar to human intelligence, both sensory and cognitive. Typically, these are grouped into categories, for example, computer vision (mimics human vision), NLP (mimics human speech, writing, and auditory processes), conversational interfaces (such as chatbots, mimics dialogue-based interactions), and personalization (mimics human intuition). For example, **C-SPAN**, a broadcaster that reports on proceedings at the US Senate and the House of Representatives, uses **Amazon Rekognition** (a computer vision-based image and video analysis service) to tag who is speaking/on camera at each time. With Amazon Rekognition, C-SPAN was able to index twice as much content compared to what they were doing previously. In addition, AWS offers AI services for intelligent search, forecasting, fraud detection, anomaly detection, predictive maintenance, and much more, which is why AWS was named the leader in the first Gartner Magic Quadrant for Cloud AI.

While language is inherently structured and well defined, the usage or interpretation of language is subjective, and may inadvertently cause an unintended influence that you need to be cognizant of when building natural language solutions. Consider, for example, the *Telephone Game*, which shows how conversations are involuntarily embellished, resulting in an entirely different version compared to how it began. Each participant repeats exactly what they think they heard, but not what they actually heard. It is fun when played as a party game but may have more serious repercussions in real life. Computers, too, will repeat what they heard, based on how their underlying ML model interprets language.

To understand how small incremental changes can completely change the meaning, let's look at another popular game: *Word Ladder* (`https://en.wikipedia.org/wiki/Word_ladder`). The objective is to convert one word into a different word, often one with the opposite meaning, in as few steps as possible with only one letter in the word changing in one step.

An example is illustrated in the following table:

Starting Word	CATS
Step 1	MATS
Step 2	MATE
Step 3	MACE
Ending Word	MICE

Figure 1.3 – The Word Ladder game

Adapting AI to work with natural language resulted in a group of capabilities that primarily deal with computational emulation of cognitive and sensory processes associated with human speech and text. There are two main categories that applications can be grouped into:

- **Natural Language Understanding** (**NLU**), for voice-based applications such as Amazon Alexa, and speech-to-text/text-to-speech conversions
- **NLP**, for the interpretation of context-based insights from text

With NLU, applications that hitherto needed multiple and sometimes cumbersome interfaces, such as a screen, keyboard, and a mouse to enable computer-to-human interactions, can work as efficiently with just voice.

In Stanley Kubrick's 1968 movie *2001: A Space Odyssey*, (spoiler alert!!) an artificially intelligent computer known as the *HAL 9000* uses vision and voice to interact with the humans on board, and in the course of the movie, develops a personality, does not accept when it is in error, and attempts to kill the humans when it discovers their plot to shut it down. Fast forward to now, 20 years after the future depicted in the movie, and we have made significant progress in language understanding and processing, but not to the extreme extent of the dramatization of the plot elements used in the movie, thankfully.

Now that we have a good understanding of the context in which NLP has developed and how it can be used, let's try examining some of the common challenges you might face while developing NLP solutions.

Overcoming the challenges in building NLP solutions

We read earlier that the main difference between the algorithms used for regular programming and those used for ML is the ability of ML algorithms to modify their processing based on the input data fed to them. In the NLP context, as in other areas of ML, these differences add significant value and accelerate enterprise business outcomes. Consider, for example, a book publishing organization that needs to create an intelligent search capability displaying book recommendations to users based on topics of interest they enter.

In a traditional world, you would need multiple teams to go through the entire book collection, read books individually, identify keywords, phrases, topics, and other relevant information, create an index to associate book titles, authors, and genres to these keywords, and link this with the search capability. This is a massive effort that takes months or years to set up based on the size of the collection, the number of people, and their skill levels, and the accuracy of the index is prone to human error. As books are updated to newer editions, and new books are added or removed, this effort would have to be repeated incrementally. This is also a significant cost and time investment that may deter many unless that time and those resources have already been budgeted for.

To bring in a semblance of automation in our previous example, we need the ability to digitize text from documents. However, this is not the only requirement, as we are interested in deriving context-based insights from the books to power a recommendations index for a reader. And if we are talking about, for example, a publishing house such as Packt, with 7,500+ books in its collection, we need a solution that not only scales to process large numbers of pages, but also understands relationships in text, and provides interpretations based on semantics, grammar, word tokenization, and language to create smart indexes. We will cover a detailed walkthrough of this solution, along with code samples and demo videos, in *Chapter 5, Creating NLP Search*.

Today's enterprises are grappling with leveraging meaningful insights from their data primarily due to the pace at which it is growing. Until a decade or so, most organizations used relational databases for all their data management needs, and some still do even today. This was fine because the data volume need was in single-digit terabytes or less. In the last few years, the technology landscape has witnessed a significant upheaval with smartphones becoming ubiquitous, the large-scale proliferation of connected devices (in the billions), the ability to dynamically scale infrastructure in size and into new geographies, and storage and compute costs becoming cheaper due to the democratization offered by the cloud. All of this means applications get used more often, have much larger user bases, more processing power, and capabilities, can accelerate their pace of innovation with faster go-to-market cycles, and as a result, have a need to store and manage petabytes of data. This, coupled with application users demanding faster response times and higher throughput, has put a strain on the performance of relational databases, fueling a move toward purpose-built databases such as Amazon DynamoDB, a key-value and document database that delivers single-digit millisecond latency at any scale.

While this move signals a positive trend, what is more interesting is how enterprises utilize this data to gain strategic insights. After all, data is only as useful as the information we can glean from it. We see many organizations, while accepting the benefits of purpose-built tools, implementing these changes in silos. So, there are varying levels of maturity in properly harnessing the advantages of data. Some departments use an S3 data lake (`https://aws.amazon.com/products/storage/data-lake-storage/`) to source data from disparate sources and run ML to derive context-based insights, others are consolidating their data in purpose-built databases, while the rest are still using relational databases for all their needs.

You can see a basic explanation of the main components of a data lake in the following *Figure 1.5, An example of an Amazon S3 data lake*:

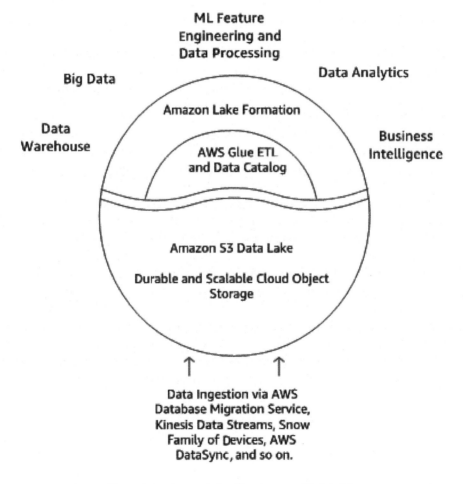

Figure 1.4 – An example of an Amazon S3 data lake

Let's see how NLP can continue to add business value in this situation by referring back to our book publishing example. Suppose we successfully built our smart indexing solution, and now we need to update it with book reviews received via Twitter feeds. The searchable index should provide book recommendations based on review sentiment (for example, don't recommend a book if reviews are negative > 50% in the last 3 months). Traditionally, business insights are generated by running a suite of reports on behemoth data warehouses that collect, mine, and organize data into marts and dimensions. A tweet may not even be under consideration as a data source. These days, things have changed and mining social media data is an important aspect of generating insights. Setting up business rules to examine every tweet is a time-consuming and compute-intensive task. Furthermore, since a tweet is unstructured text, a slight change in semantics may impact the effectiveness of the solution.

Now, if you consider model training, the infrastructure required to build accurate NLP models typically uses the deep learning architecture called **Transformers** (please see `https://www.packtpub.com/product/transformers-for-natural-language-processing/9781800565791`) that use sequence-to-sequence processing without needing to process the tokens in order, resulting in a higher degree of parallelization. Transformer model families use billions of parameters with the training architecture using clusters of instances for distributed learning, which adds to time and costs.

AWS offers AI services that allow you, with just a few lines of code, to add NLP to your applications for the sentiment analysis of unstructured text at an almost limitless scale and immediately take advantage of the immense potential waiting to be discovered in unstructured text. We will cover AWS AI services in more detail from *Chapter 2, Introducing Amazon Textract,* onward.

In this section, we reviewed some challenges organizations encounter when building NLP solutions, such as complexities in digitizing paper-based text, understanding patterns from structured and unstructured data, and how resource-intensive these solutions can be. Let's now understand why NLP is an important mainstream technology for enterprises today.

Understanding why NLP is becoming mainstream

According to this report (`https://www.marketsandmarkets.com/Market-Reports/natural-language-processing-nlp-825.html`, accessed on March 23, 2021), the global NLP market is expected to grow to USD 35.1 billion by 2026, at a **Compound Annual Growth Rate (CAGR)** of 20.3% during the forecast period. This is not surprising considering the impact ML is making across every industry (such as finance, retail, manufacturing, energy, utilities, real estate, healthcare, and so on) in organizations of every size, primarily driven by the advent of cloud computing and the economies of scale available.

This article about *Emergence Cycle* (`https://blogs.gartner.com/anthony_bradley/2020/10/07/announcing-gartners-new-emergence-cycle-research-for-ai/`), a research into emerging technologies in NLP (based on patents submitted, and looking at technology still in labs or recently released), shows the most mature usage of NLP is multimedia content analysis. This trend is true based on our experience, and content analysis to gain strategic insights is a common NLP requirement based on our discussions with a number of organizations across industries:

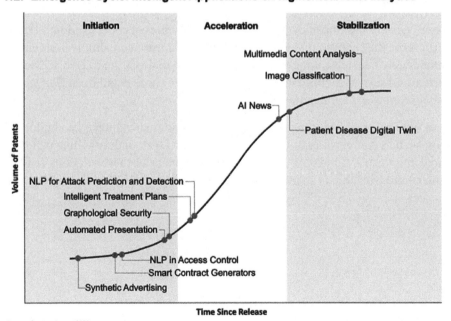

Figure 1.5 – Gartner's NLP Emergence Cycle 2020

For example, in 2020, when the world was struggling with the effects of the pandemic, a number of organizations adopted AI and specifically NLP to power predictions on the virus spread patterns, assimilate knowledge on virus behavior and vaccine research, and monitor the effectiveness of safety measures, to name a few. In April 2020, AWS launched an NLP-powered search site called `https://cord19.aws/` using an AWS AI service called **Amazon Kendra** (`https://aws.amazon.com/kendra/`). The site provides an easy interface to search the **COVID-19 Open Research Dataset** using natural language questions. As the dataset is constantly updated based on the latest research on COVID-19, CORD-19 Search, due to its support for NLP, makes it easy to navigate this ever-expanding collection of research documents and find precise answers to questions. The search results provide not only specific text that contains the answer to the question but also the original body of text in which these answers are located:

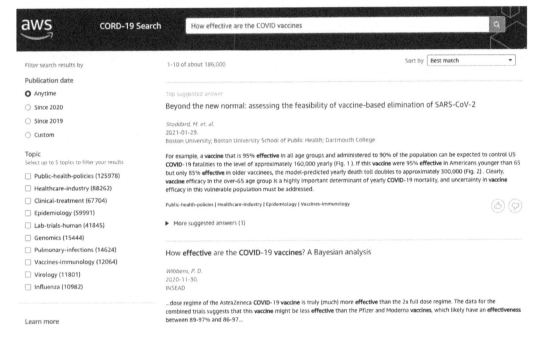

Figure 1.6 – CORD-19 search results

Fred Hutchinson Cancer Research Center is a research institute focused on curing cancer by 2025. *Matthew Trunnell, Chief Information Officer of Fred Hutchinson Cancer Research Center*, has said the following:

> *"The process of developing clinical trials and connecting them with the right patients requires research teams to sift through and label mountains of unstructured clinical record data. Amazon Comprehend Medical will reduce this time burden from hours to seconds. This is a vital step toward getting researchers rapid access to the information they need when they need it so they can find actionable insights to advance lifesaving therapies for patients."*

For more details and usage examples of Amazon Comprehend and Amazon Comprehend Medical, please refer to *Chapter 3, Introducing Amazon Comprehend*.

So, how can AI and NLP help us cure cancer or prepare for a pandemic? It's about recognizing patterns where none seem to exist. Unstructured text, such as documents, social media posts, and email messages, is similar to the treasure waiting in Ali Baba's cave. To understand why, let's briefly look at how NLP works.

NLP models train by learning what are called *word embeddings*, which are vector representations of words in large collections of documents. These embeddings capture semantic relationships and word distributions in documents, thereby helping to map the context of a word based on its relationship to other words in the document. The two common training architectures for learning word embeddings are **Skip-gram** and **Continuous Bag of Words** (CBOW). In Skip-gram, the embeddings of the input word are used to derive the distribution of the related words to predict the context, and in CBOW, the embeddings of the related words are used to predict the word in the middle. Both are neural network-based architectures and work well for context-based analytics use cases.

Now that we understand the basics of NLP (analyzing patterns in text by converting words to their vector representations), when we look at training models using text data from disparate data sources, unique insights are often derived due to patterns that emerge that previously appeared hidden when looked at within a narrower context, because we are using numbers to find relationships in text. For example, *The Rubber Episode* in the Amazon Prime TV show *This Giant Beast That Is The Global Economy* shows how a fungal disease has the potential to devastate the global economy, even though at first it might appear there is no link between the two. According to the *US National Library of Medicine*, natural rubber accounts for 40% of the world's consumption, and the **South American Leaf Blight (SALB)** fungal disease has the potential to spread worldwide and severely inhibit rubber production. Airplanes can't land without rubber, and its uses are so myriad that it would have unprecedented implications on the economy. This an example of a pattern that ML and NLP models are so good at finding specific items of interest across vast text corpora.

Before AWS and cloud computing revolutionized access to advanced technologies, setting up NLP models for text analytics was challenging to say the least. The most common reasons were as follows:

- **Lack of skills**: Expertise in identifying data, feature engineering, building models, training, and tuning are all tasks that require a unique combination of skills, including software engineering, mathematics, statistics, and data engineering, that only a few practitioners have.

- **Initial infrastructure setup cost**: ML training is an iterative process, often requiring a trial-and-error approach to tune the models to get the desired accuracy. Further training and inference may require GPU acceleration based on the volume of data and the number of requests, requiring a high initial investment.

- **Scalability with the current on-premises environment**: Running ML training and inference from on-premises servers constrains the elasticity required to scale compute and storage based on model size, data volumes, and inference throughput needed. For example, training large-scale transformer models may require massively parallel clusters, and capacity planning for such scenarios is challenging.

- **Availability of tools to help orchestrate the various moving parts of NLP training**: As mentioned before, the ML workflow comprises many tasks, such as data discovery, feature engineering, algorithm selection, model building, which includes training and fine-tuning the models several times, and finally deploying those models into production. Furthermore, getting an accurate model is a highly iterative process. Each of these tasks requires purpose-built tools and expertise to achieve the level of efficiency needed for good models, which is not easy.

Not anymore. The AWS AI services for natural language capabilities enable adding speech and text intelligence to applications using API calls rather than needing to develop and train models. NLU services provide the ability to convert speech to text with **Amazon Transcribe** (`https://aws.amazon.com/transcribe/`) or text to speech with **Amazon Polly** (`https://aws.amazon.com/polly/`). For NLP requirements, **Amazon Textract** (`https://aws.amazon.com/textract/`) enables applications to read and process handwritten and printed text from images and PDF documents, and with **Amazon Comprehend** (`https://aws.amazon.com/comprehend/`), applications can quickly analyze text and find insights and relationships with no prior ML training. For example, Assent, a supply chain data management company, used Amazon Textract to read forms, tables, and free-form text, and Amazon Comprehend to derive business-specific entities and values from the text. In this book, we will be walking you through how to use these services for some popular workflows. For more details, please refer to *Chapter 4, Automating Document Processing Workflows*.

In this section, we saw some examples of NLP's significance in solving real-world challenges, and what exactly it means. We understood that finding patterns in data can bring new meaning to light, and NLP models are very good at deriving these patterns. We then reviewed some technology challenges in NLP implementations and saw a brief overview of the AWS AI services. In the next section, we will introduce the AWS ML stack, and provide a brief overview of each of the layers.

Introducing the AWS ML stack

The AWS ML services and features are organized into three layers of the stack, keeping in mind that some developers and data scientists are expert ML practitioners who are comfortable working with ML frameworks, algorithms, and infrastructure to build, train, and deploy models.

For these experts, the bottom layer of the AWS ML stack offers powerful CPU and GPU compute instances (the `https://aws.amazon.com/ec2/instance-types/p4/` instances offer the highest performance for ML training in the cloud today), support for major ML frameworks including **TensorFlow**, **PyTorch**, and **MXNet**, which customers can use to build models with **Amazon SageMaker** as a managed experience, or using **deep learning** AMIs and containers on Amazon EC2 instances.

You can see the three layers of the AWS ML stack in the next figure. For more details, please refer to `https://aws.amazon.com/machine-learning/infrastructure/`:

To make ML more accessible and expansive, at the middle layer of the stack, **Amazon SageMaker** is a fully managed ML platform that removes the undifferentiated heavy lifting at each step of the ML process. Launched in 2018, SageMaker is one of the fastest-growing services in AWS history and is built on Amazon's two decades of experience in building real-world ML applications. With SageMaker Studio, developers and data scientists have the first fully integrated development environment designed specifically for ML. To learn how to build ML models using Amazon SageMaker, refer to Julien Simon's book, *Learn Amazon SageMaker*, also published by Packt (`https://www.packtpub.com/product/learn-amazon-sagemaker/9781800208919`):

Prepare	Build	Train & Tune	Deploy & Manage
SageMaker Ground Truth	SageMaker Studio	One-Click Training	One-Click Deployment
SageMaker Data Wrangler	Built-In and Bring-Your-Own-Algorithms	SageMaker Experiments	Kubernetes and Kubeflow Integration
SageMaker Processing	Local Mode	Automatic Model Tuning	Multi-Model Endpoints
SageMaker Feature Store	SageMaker Autopilot	Distributed Training Libraries	SageMaker Model Monitor
SageMaker Clarify	SageMaker JumpStart	SageMaker Debugger	SageMaker Edge Manager
		Managed Spot Training	SageMaker Pipelines

Figure 1.7 – A tabular list of Amazon SageMaker features for each step of the ML workflow

For customers who are not interested in dealing with models and training, at the *top layer* of the stack, the AWS AI services provide pre-trained models with easy integration by means of API endpoints for common ML use cases including speech, text, vision, recommendations, and anomaly detection:

Health AI	Industrial AI	Fraud	Anomaly Detection	Contact Centers	Code and DevOps
• Amazon HealthLake • Amazon Transcribe Medical • Amazon Comprehend Medical	• AWS Panorama • Amazon Monitron • Amazon Lookout for Equipment • Amazon Lookout for Vision	• Amazon Fraud Detector	• Amazon Lookout for Metrics	• Contact Lens for Amazon Connect	• DevOps Guru • Code Guru

Vision	Speech	Text	Search	Chatbots	Personalization	Forecasting
• Amazon Rekognition	• Amazon Polly • Amazon Transcribe	• Amazon Textract • Amazon Translate • Amazon Comprehend	• Amazon Kendra	• Amazon Lex	• Amazon Personalize	• Amazon Forecast

Figure 1.8 – AWS AI services

Alright, it's time that we started getting technical. Now that we understand how cloud computing played a major role in bringing ML and AI to the mainstream and how adding NLP to your application can accelerate business outcomes, let's deep dive into the NLP services Amazon Textract for document analysis and Amazon Comprehend for advanced text analytics.

Ready? Let's go!!

Summary

In this chapter, we introduced NLP by tracing the origins of AI, how it evolved over the last few decades, and how the application of AI became mainstream with the significant advances made with ML algorithms. We reviewed some examples of these algorithms, along with an example of how they can be used. We then pivoted to AI trends and saw how AI adoption grew exponentially over the last few years and has become a key technology in accelerating enterprise business value.

We read a cool example of how ExxonMobil uses Alexa at their gas stations and delved into how AI was created to mimic human cognition, and the broad categories of their applicability, such as text, speech, and vision. We saw how AI in natural language has two main areas of usage *NLU for voice-based uses* and *NLP for deriving insights from text*.

In analyzing how enterprises are building NLP models today, we reviewed some of the common challenges and how to mitigate them, such as digitizing paper-based text, collecting data from disparate sources, and understanding patterns in data, and how resource-intensive these solutions can be.

We then reviewed NLP industry trends and market segmentation and saw with an example how important NLP was and still continues to be during the pandemic. We dove deep into the philosophy of NLP and realized it was all about converting text to numerical representations and understanding the underlying patterns to decipher new meanings. We looked at an example of this pattern with how SALB could impact the global economy.

Finally, we reviewed the technology implications in setting up NLP training and the associated challenges. We reviewed the three layers of the AWS ML stack and introduced AWS AI services that provided pre-built models and ready-made intelligence.

In the next chapter, we will introduce Amazon Textract, a fully managed ML service that can read both printed and handwritten text from images and PDFs without having to train or build models and can be used without the need for ML skills. We will cover the features of Amazon Textract, what its functions are, what business challenges it was created to solve, what types of user requirements it can be applied to, and how easy it is to integrate Amazon Textract with other AWS services such as AWS Lambda for building business applications.

Further reading

- *This Giant Beast that Is The Global Economy* (https://www.amazon.com/This-Giant-Beast-Global-Economy/dp/B07MJDD22F)

- *Learn Amazon SageMaker* by Julien Simon (https://www.packtpub.com/product/learn-amazon-sagemaker/9781800208919)

- *AWS CORD-19 Search: A Neural Search Engine for COVID-19 Literature* (https://arxiv.org/abs/2007.09186)

- *Transformers and Natural Language Processing* (https://aws.amazon.com/blogs/machine-learning/aws-and-hugging-face-collaborate-to-simplify-and-accelerate-adoption-of-natural-language-processing-models/)

- *Training NLP models with Amazon SageMaker's model parallelism library*
  (`https://aws.amazon.com/blogs/machine-learning/how-latent-space-used-the-amazon-sagemaker-model-parallelism-library-to-push-the-frontiers-of-large-scale-transformers/`)

- Oppy, Graham and David Dowe, "The Turing Test", *The Stanford Encyclopedia of Philosophy* (Winter 2021 Edition), Edward N. Zalta (ed.), forthcoming URL
  (`https://plato.stanford.edu/archives/win2021/entries/turing-test/`)

2
Introducing Amazon Textract

In the previous chapter, you read how businesses can harness the benefits of applying NLP to derive insights from text, and you were briefly introduced to the *AWS ML stack*. We will now provide a detailed introduction to **Amazon Textract**, along with do-it-yourself code samples and instructions. Amazon Textract is an AWS AI service that can be used to extract text from documents and images with little to no prior ML skills. But before we get to what Textract can do, we will first cover some of the challenges with document processing. Then we will cover how Textract can help in overcoming the challenges. We will also talk about the benefits of using Amazon Textract, along with its product features. Lastly, we will cover how you can integrate Amazon Textract quickly into your applications.

We will navigate through the following sections in this chapter:

- Setting up your AWS environment
- Overcoming challenges with document processing
- Understanding how Amazon Textract can help
- Presenting Amazon Textract's product features
- Using Amazon Textract with your applications

Technical requirements

For this chapter, you will need access to an AWS account at `https://aws.amazon.com/console/`. Please refer to the *Signing up for an AWS account* sub-section within the *Setting up your AWS environment* section for detailed instructions on how you can sign up for an AWS account and sign in to the **AWS Management Console**.

The Python code and sample datasets for the solution discussed in this chapter are available at `https://github.com/PacktPublishing/Natural-Language-Processing-with-AWS-AI-Services/tree/main/Chapter%2002`.

Check out the following video to see the Code in Action at `https://bit.ly/3be9eUh`.

Setting up your AWS environment

> **Important Note**
>
> Please do not execute the instructions in this section on their own. This section is a reference for all the basic setup tasks needed throughout the book. You will be guided to this section when building your solution in this chapter and the rest of the chapters in this book. Only execute these tasks when so guided.

Depending on the chapter you are in, you will be running tasks using the AWS Management Console, an Amazon SageMaker Jupyter notebook, from your command line, or a combination of any of these. Either way, you need the right AWS **Identity and Access Management** (**IAM**) permissions, resources, and, in most cases, one or more Amazon **Simple Storage Service** (**S3**) buckets, as prerequisites for your solution builds. This section provides instructions for setting up these basic tasks. We will be referring to this section throughout the rest of the chapters in the book as needed.

Signing up for an AWS account

In this chapter and all subsequent chapters in which we run code examples, you will need access to an AWS account. Before getting started, we recommend that you create an AWS account by going through the following steps:

> **Note**
>
> Please use the AWS Free Tier, which enables you to try services free of charge based on certain time limits or service usage limits. For more details, please see `https://aws.amazon.com/free`.

1. Open `https://portal.aws.amazon.com/billing/signup`.

2. Click on the **Create a new AWS account** button at the bottom left of the page

3. Enter your email address and a password, confirm the password, and provide an AWS account name (this can be a reference for how you will use this account, such as **sandbox**, for example).

4. Select the **usage type** (**Business or Personal**), provide your contact information, read and agree to the terms of the AWS Customer Agreement, and click **Continue**.

5. Provide credit card information and a billing address and click **Continue**.

6. Go through the rest of the steps to complete your AWS account signup process. Please make a note of your user ID and password; this is your root access to your AWS account.

7. Once the AWS account is created, go to the **AWS Management Console –** `console.aws.amazon.com` – and sign in using the root credentials you created in the previous steps.

8. Type `IAM` in the services search bar at the top of the console and select **IAM** to navigate to the IAM console. Select **Users** from the left pane in the IAM console and click on **Add User**.

9. Provide a username, then select **Programmatic access** and **AWS Management Console access** for **Access Type**. Keep the password as **Autogenerated** and keep **Required Password reset** as selected.

10. Click **Next: Permissions**. On the **Set Permissions** page, click on **Attach existing policies directly** and select the checkbox to the left of **AdministratorAccess**. Click **Next** twice to go to the **Review** page. Click **Create user**.

11. Now go back to the AWS Management Console (`console.aws.amazon.com`) and click **Sign In**. Provide the IAM username you created in the previous step, the temporary password, and enter a new password to log in to the console.

12. Log in to your AWS account when prompted in the various chapters and sections.

You now have access to the AWS Management Console (`https://aws.amazon.com/console/`). In the next section, we will show how to create an S3 bucket and upload your documents.

Creating an Amazon S3 bucket and a folder and uploading objects

In this book, we will use Amazon S3 as the storage option for our solutions. So, we will need to create an S3 bucket, create folders within the bucket, and upload documents for use within the solution. Please follow these instructions to learn how to do this:

1. Log in to the AWS Management Console (`https://aws.amazon.com/console/`) and, in the search bar at the top, type `S3`.

2. Select **S3** from the results and navigate to the Amazon S3 console. Click on **Create Bucket**.

3. On the **Create Bucket** page, provide a **bucket name** (it cannot contain spaces or uppercase characters; for more details, see `https://docs.aws.amazon.com/console/s3/bucket-naming`), and select an **AWS Region** from the list (for more details on AWS Regions, please see `https://docs.aws.amazon.com/AmazonRDS/latest/UserGuide/Concepts.RegionsAndAvailabilityZones.html`).

4. Accept the defaults for the rest of the options and click on **Create Bucket**. For more details on what these options mean, please see `https://docs.aws.amazon.com/AmazonS3/latest/userguide/UsingBucket.html`.

5. Now that our S3 bucket is successfully created, either search using your bucket name on the **Buckets** pane or click the bucket name if it is displayed in the list of buckets on the **Buckets** pane. On the bucket page, click the **Create folder** button on the right of the page.

6. On the **Create folder** page, provide a name for the folder, accept the defaults for the rest of the fields, and click **Create folder** at the bottom right of the page.

7. On the **Objects** page, either search for the folder you created in the search bar underneath the **Objects** heading or click on the folder name.

8. Now you can select either the **Add files** or **Add folder** button on the right to bring up an option to select files or folders from your computer to add to the S3 bucket in the folder we created.

    Please note that the AWS Management Console is not the only option to upload objects to S3. You can do it using the AWS **Command-Line Interface (CLI)** (for more details, see `https://docs.aws.amazon.com/cli/latest/reference/s3/`) or you can also upload files programmatically using the Python SDK, for example (`https://boto3.amazonaws.com/v1/documentation/api/latest/reference/services/s3.html`). AWS provides SDKs for programming in several languages (`https://aws.amazon.com/tools/`).

And that concludes the instructions for creating an S3 bucket, creating a folder, and uploading objects to the bucket. In the next section, let's see how we can add IAM permissions policies for our Amazon SageMaker Jupyter notebook role.

Creating an Amazon SageMaker Jupyter notebook instance

In this section, we will see how to create a notebook instance in Amazon SageMaker. This is an important step, as most of our solution examples are run using notebooks. After the notebook is created, please follow the instructions to use the notebook in the specific chapters based on the solution being built. Please follow these steps to create an Amazon SageMaker Jupyter notebook instance:

1. Log in to the AWS Management Console if you haven't already. Type `SageMaker` in the services search bar at the top of the page, select **SageMaker** from the list, and click on it to go to the Amazon SageMaker management console.

2. In the SageMaker console, on the left pane, click on **Notebook** to expand the option, and click **Notebook instances**.

3. On the **Notebook instances** page, click the **Create notebook instance** button at the top right.

4. Type a name for the notebook instance and select a suitable notebook instance type. For most of the solution builds in this book, an AWS Free Tier (`https://aws.amazon.com/free`) instance such as `ml.t2.medium` should suffice.

5. In the **Permissions and encryption** section, click the **IAM role** list and choose **Create a new role**, and then choose **Any S3 bucket.**

6. Accept defaults for the rest of the fields and click **Create notebook instance.**

> **Note**
>
> By default, each notebook instance is provided internet access by SageMaker. If you want to disable internet access for this notebook instance, you can attach it to your **Virtual Private Cloud** (**VPC**), a highly secure virtual network in the cloud for launching AWS resources (`https://docs.aws.amazon.com/sagemaker/latest/dg/appendix-notebook-and-internet-access.html`), and select to disable internet access. We need internet access for this notebook instance, so if you are planning to attach a VPC and disable internet access through SageMaker, please either configure a **Network Address Translation** (**NAT**) gateway, which allows instances in a subnet within the VPC to communicate with resources outside the VPC but not the other way around (`https://docs.aws.amazon.com/vpc/latest/userguide/vpc-nat-gateway.html`), or an interface VPC endpoint (`https://docs.aws.amazon.com/sagemaker/latest/dg/interface-vpc-endpoint.html`), which allows a private connection through the AWS backbone between the notebook instance and your VPC. This allows you to manage access to the internet for your notebook instance through the controls you have implemented within your VPC.

Your notebook instance will take a few minutes to be provisioned; once it's ready, the status will change to **InService**. Please follow the instructions in the *Using Amazon Textract with your applications* section to find out how you can use your notebook instance. In the next few sections, we will walk through the steps required to modify the IAM role we attached to the notebook.

Changing IAM permissions and trust relationships for the Amazon SageMaker notebook execution role

> **Note**
>
> You cannot attach more than 10 managed policies to an IAM role. If your IAM role already has a managed policy from a previous chapter, please detach this policy before adding a new policy as per the requirements of your current chapter.

When we create an **Amazon SageMaker** Jupyter notebook instance (like we did in the previous section), the default role creation step includes permissions to either an S3 bucket you specify or any S3 bucket in your AWS account. But often, we need the notebook to have more permissions that that. For example, we may need permission to use **Amazon Textract** or **Amazon Comprehend** APIs, and/or other services as required.

In this section, we will walk through the steps needed to add additional permissions policies to our Amazon SageMaker Jupyter notebook role:

1. Open the Amazon SageMaker console by typing `sagemaker` in the services search bar at the top of the page in your AWS Management Console, and select **Amazon SageMaker** from the list.

2. In the **Amazon SageMaker** console, on the left pane, expand **Notebook** and click **Notebook instances**.

3. Click the name of the notebook instance you need to change permissions for.

4. On the **Notebook instance settings** page, scroll down to **Permissions and encryption**, and click **IAM role ARN**.

5. This will open the **IAM management console** and your role **summary** will be displayed along with the **permissions** and other details for your role. Click **Attach policies**.

6. On the **Add permissions to <your execution role name>** page, type `textract` in the search bar, select the checkbox next to the policy you are interested in, and click **Attach policy** at the bottom right. You should now see the policy attached to your role.

7. In some cases, we may need a custom policy for our requirement rather than a managed policy provided by AWS. Specifically, we add an inline policy (`https://docs.aws.amazon.com/IAM/latest/UserGuide/id_roles_use_passrole.html`) to allow `PassRole` of our SageMaker notebook execution role to services that can assume this role (added in **Trust relationships**) for actions needed to be performed from the notebook. Click **Add inline policy** on the right of your SageMaker notebook execution role summary page.

8. Now click the **JSON** tab and paste the following JSON statement in the input area:

```
{ "Version": "2012-10-17", "Statement": [ {
  "Action": [
      "iam:PassRole"
  ],
  "Effect": "Allow",
  "Resource": "<IAM ARN of your current SageMaker
notebook execution role>"
  }
 ]
}
```

9. Click **Review policy**.

10. On the **Review policy** page, type a name for your policy and click **Create policy** at the bottom right of the page.

11. Now that you know how to attach permissions and an inline policy to your role, let's go to the last step of this section, updating **trust relationships** (`https://docs.aws.amazon.com/directoryservice/latest/admin-guide/edit_trust.html`) for your role. On the **Summary** page for your SageMaker notebook execution role, click the **Trust relationships** tab, and click **Edit trust relationship**.

12. Copy the following JSON snippet and paste it in the **Policy Document** input field. This statement allows Amazon SageMaker, Amazon S3, and Amazon Comprehend the ability to assume the SageMaker notebook execution role permissions. Depending on the chapter and the use case we are building, the services that will need to assume the role will vary and you will be instructed accordingly. For now, please consider the following JSON snippet as an example to understand how to edit trust relationships:

```
{ "Version": "2012-10-17", "Statement": [
  { "Effect": "Allow",
    "Principal":
      { "Service":
        [ "sagemaker.amazonaws.com",
          "s3.amazonaws.com",
          "comprehend.amazonaws.com" ]
      },
      "Action": "sts:AssumeRole" }
  ]
}
```

13. Click the **Update Trust Policy** button at the bottom right of the page.

14. You should see the **trusted entities** updated for your role.

And you are all set. In this section, you learned how to update the IAM role for your Amazon SageMaker notebook instances to add permissions policies, add a custom inline policy, and, finally, edit the trust relationships to add the trusted entities you needed for your solution build. You may now go back to the chapter you navigated to here from and continue your solution build task.

Overcoming challenges with document processing

Automating operational activities is very important for organizations looking to minimize costs, increase productivity, and enable faster go-to-market cycles. Typically, operations that are at the core of these businesses are prioritized for automation. Back-office support processes, including administrative tasks, are often relegated to the bottom of the priority list because they may not be deemed *mission critical*. According to this *Industry Analysts* report (https://www.industryanalysts.com/111015_konica/, *written in 2015, with data collected from sources such as Gartner Group, AIIM, the US Department of Labor, Imaging Magazine, and Coopers and Lybrand, and accessed on March 30, 2021*), organizations continue to be reliant on paper-based documents, and the effort required to maintain these documents poses significant challenges due to the lack of automation and inefficiencies in the document workflow.

Many organizations, such as financial institutions, healthcare, manufacturing, and other small-to-medium-sized enterprises, have a large number of scanned and handwritten documents. These documents can be in various formats, such as invoices, receipts, resumes, application forms, and so on. Moreover, these documents are not kept in one place; instead, they are in silos, which makes it really difficult to uncover useful insights from these documents. Suppose that you have an archive of documents that you would like to extract data from. And let's say we build an application that makes it easy for you to search across the vast collection of documents in these archives. Extracting data from these documents is really important for you as they contain a lot of useful information that is relevant for your organization. Once you extract the information you need (of course, we first have to determine what is useful and what is not), you can do so many things, such as discover business context, set up compliance, design search and discovery for important keywords, and automate your existing business processes.

As time progresses, we see more organizations embracing digital media for their business processes due to the ease of integration with their operational systems, but paper-based documents are not going away anytime soon. According to this article (https://medium.com/high-peak-ai/real-time-applications-of-intelligent-document-processing-993e314360f9, *accessed on March 30, 2021*), there is in fact an increase in the usage of paper documents in organizations. And that's why it's really important to automate document processing workflows.

So, what is the problem with paper documents? The problem is the cost and time required to extract the data from documents using traditional approaches. One of the most common approaches is **manual processing** of these documents. What is manual processing? A human will read the documents and then key all the values into an application or copy and paste them into another document. This approach is highly inefficient and expensive: not only do you need to invest time and effort to train the human workforce to understand the data domain they are working with, but also there may be errors in data entry due to human nature. For example, when working with tax forms and financial forms, you would need an experienced **Certified Public Accountant (CPA)** to do that manual entry, as this would require accounting knowledge to extract the details needed. So, we can see that a traditional approach with manual processing of documents is time consuming, error prone, and expensive.

Another approach that we have seen organizations use is rule-based formatting templates along with **Optical Character Recognition (OCR)** systems to extract data from these documents. The challenge with this method is that these rule-based systems are not intelligent enough to adapt to evolving document formats, and often break with even minor template changes. As businesses grow and expand, their underlying processes need the flexibility to adapt, and this often leads to working with multiple document structures, often running to hundreds or even thousands of formats. Trying to set up and manage these formats for each document type can turn into a huge maintenance overhead pretty quickly and it can become challenging to update these formats in rule-based systems once the document format changes. Another challenge to consider is the provisioning of infrastructure and the scaling required to handle millions of such documents and the associated costs.

That's why we have **Amazon Textract**, a fully managed ML and AI service, built with out-of-the-box features to extract handwritten and printed text in forms, tables, and pages from images and PDF documents. Textract provides **Application Programming Interfaces (APIs)** behind which run powerful ML models trained on millions of documents to provide a highly effective solution for intelligent text extraction.

So, we covered the challenges with processing documents in this section and why we need Amazon Textract. In the next section, we will talk about how Amazon Textract can quickly help organizations solve this pain point.

Understanding how Amazon Textract can help

We covered *AWS AI Services* briefly in *Chapter 1, NLP in the Business Context and Introduction to AWS AI Services,* when introducing the *business context for NLP.* Amazon Textract is an OCR-based service in the AWS AI Services stack that comes with ready-made intelligence, enabling you to use it without any prior ML experience for your document processing workflows. It is interesting to note that Amazon Textract has its origins in the deep learning ML models built for Amazon.com. It comes with a pre-trained model and provides APIs where you can send your documents in PDF or image format and get a response as text/tables and key/value pairs along with a confidence score.

> **Note**
> Amazon Textract currently supports PNG, JPEG, and PDF formats.

Amazon Textract provides serverless APIs without you needing to manage any kind of infrastructure, enabling you to quickly automate document management and scale to process millions of documents. Once the document content is extracted, you can leverage it within your business applications for a variety of document processing use cases for your industry and operational requirements. Amazon Textract models learn as they go, so they become more intelligent in understanding your documents as you continue to use them. Please refer to the following list for a subset of Amazon Textract usage examples we will be covering in the upcoming chapters:

- **Natural language processing (NLP)** *for text extraction* – This use case will show an end-to-end example of how to use Textract to get text from documents and then perform NLP techniques on the text to derive insights. We will cover some of these key concepts with an example in *Chapter 3, Introduction to Amazon Comprehend.*

- *Quickly set up automated document processing workflows* – In this use case we will see how to build a solution using Textract and other AWS services to automate common document management tasks, such as a loan application approval workflow, resulting in cost and time savings. This use case will be covered as part of *Chapter 4, Automating Document Processing Workflows.*

- *Building a scalable intelligent centralized search index* – Amazon Textract enables you to extract data from scanned documents and store it in Amazon *S3.* Amazon S3 is a cost-effective and scalable object storage solution. The data in Amazon S3 can be indexed using **Amazon Elasticsearch** and you can make your archives searchable. You can also create a centralized search solution for your data sitting in silos by moving them into Amazon S3. We will cover this use case in *Chapter 5, Creating NLP Search.*

- *Implementing compliance in archival documents* – Because of Textract's inherent ML capabilities, it can identify text in pages, tables, and forms automatically. This feature is especially helpful when you want to build intelligent systems that depend on document metadata for determining compliance with business processes. We will look at an example of this use case in *Chapter 6, Using NLP to Improve Customer Service Efficiency.*

- *Building automated data capture from forms into existing apps/chatbots* – Amazon Textract provides APIs that you can use within your applications with a diverse collection of document types. For example, you may need to query receipts from your vendors and use that to make decisions as part of your operations. In this use case we will see how to use a chatbot with your document processing application using **Amazon Lex** (`https://aws.amazon.com/lex/`). This will be covered in detail in *Chapter 8, Leveraging NLP to Monetize Your Media Content.*

As you can see, Amazon Textract can be used for various types of document processing use cases and provides several advanced benefits that you would not find in traditional rule-based systems or OCR solutions. You can read some of these benefits here:

- *Text? Structured? Unstructured? Textract to the rescue*: Amazon Textract uses AI and ML to detect structured text in tables and unstructured text such as textual data from documents in pages, lines, and words. Amazon Textract first determines the layout of the document, then detects the types of content in the document, along with their relationships and context, prior to extraction. It also provides a confidence score with each detected text, table, and key/value pair. We will see some examples in the next section.

- *Amazon Textract overcomes the limitations of OCR*: While Amazon Textract uses OCR implicitly, that is not the only benefit. You do not have to worry about maintaining various templates and formats as it uses ML rather than a template-based approach. So, it works for all kinds of document templates used across industries, for example invoices, receipts, employment forms, resumes, tax preparation docs, medical claim forms, technical specifications, and more.

- *Security and compliance*: Security is the highest priority at AWS. Amazon Textract conforms to the Shared Responsibility Model (`https://aws.amazon.com/compliance/shared-responsibility-model/`).

To understand the security and compliance features of Amazon Textract, please refer to `https://docs.aws.amazon.com/textract/latest/dg/security.html`. Amazon Textract is covered in multiple AWS compliance programs, including **System and Organizational Control (SOC)**, **International Organization for Standardization (ISO)**, as well as **PCI** and **HIPAA**. For more details, please refer to `https://docs.aws.amazon.com/textract/latest/dg/SERVICENAME-compliance.html`.

- *APIs for easy integration with your applications*: Amazon Textract provides APIs in Java, Python, and other languages. Behind these APIs run powerful ML models to easily extract text from your documents. For a detailed walk-through of the APIs, please refer to the section titled *Using Amazon Textract with your applications*.

- *Amazon Textract is serverless and scalable*: Amazon Textract is a fully managed and serverless service that will automatically scale based on the volumes of documents you need to process. It will scale up to handle additional demand and will scale down once the demand subsides.

- *Cost effective*: Amazon Textract pricing is similar to other fully managed AWS services. Customers pay only for what they use. For example, the cost to process one page of a document in the us-east-1 region is $0.0015. There is a free tier available for you to get started quickly. For more details, please refer to `https://aws.amazon.com/textract/pricing/`.

In this section, we briefly listed some interesting document-processing use cases that Amazon Textract can help solve and reviewed some of the key benefits of Amazon Textract, such as pre-built intelligence, cost effectiveness, scalability, and ease of use. In the next section, we will use the AWS Management Console (`https://console.aws.amazon.com/`) to walk through Amazon Textract's product features, such as table detection, form detection, handwriting detection, text detection, and multi-language support.

Presenting Amazon Textract's product features

Alright, it's time to start exploring the cool features we have been talking about so far. We will start by seeing how you can quickly upload the sample documents provided in our GitHub repository (https://github.com/PacktPublishing/Natural-Language-Processing-with-AWS-AI-Services) to your Amazon Textract AWS console. Then, we will walk through the key features of Amazon Textract, along with multi-language support by using a French COVID-19 form. We will also cover Amazon Textract's integration with Amazon A2I, which will quickly help set up a human review workflow for the text, which needs to be highly accurate, such as an invoice amount (https://aws.amazon.com/augmented-ai/) at a high level. We will cover the following:

1. Sign in to your AWS Management Console.

2. Upload sample document(s).

3. Raw text or text extraction.

4. Key value extraction or form values.

5. Table extraction.

6. Multiple language support.

7. Handwriting extraction.

8. Amazon Augmented AI or A2I support for human in the loop.

As a first step, please refer to the *Technical requirements* section to sign up for an AWS account and sign in to get started.

Uploading sample document(s)

Now, let's see how to upload a document to Textract:

1. Download the sample documents from the GitHub repository (https://github.com/PacktPublishing/Natural-Language-Processing-with-AWS-AI-Services/blob/main/Chapter%2002/employment_history.png).

2. In your AWS Management Console, in the **Services** search window, start typing Textract, and select **Amazon Textract**.

3. Now click on **Try Amazon Textract** and click the **Upload Document** button to select the document you downloaded in *step 1*:

Figure 2.1 – Click the Upload document button on Amazon Textract console

This will upload the document to Amazon Textract:

Employment Application

Application Information

Full Name: Jane Doe

Phone Number: 555-0100

Home Address: 123 Any Street, Any Town, USA

Mailing Address: same as above

Previous Employment History				
Start Date	End Date	Employer Name	Position Held	Reason for leaving
1/15/2009	6/30/2011	Any Company	Assistant baker	relocated
7/1/2011	8/10/2013	Example Corp.	Baker	better opp.
8/15/2013	Present	AnyCompany	head baker	N/A, current

Figure 2.2 – Employment application.png

Raw text or text extraction

The following analysis is displayed in the Amazon Textract console:

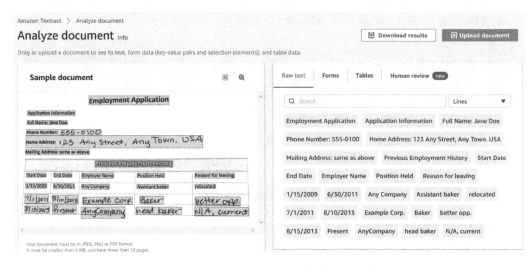

Figure 2.3 – Amazon Textract console for text extraction

Click on the **Raw text** tab to see the extracted text:

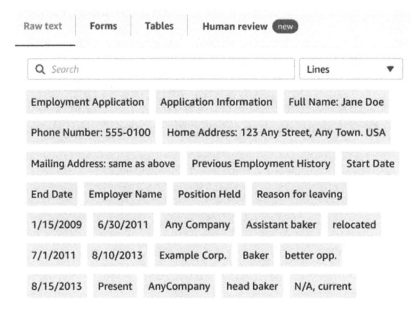

Figure 2.4 – Amazon Textract text response as lines and words

> **Note**
>
> Amazon Textract provides support for rotated documents. Please refer to `https://docs.aws.amazon.com/textract/latest/dg/limits.html` for more details on Textract service limits.

Working with multi-page documents

Amazon Textract has the intelligence to recognize that some documents have multiple formats in them and is able to extract content accordingly. For example, you may be working with reports or a request for proposal document with multiple segments. Please download the image shown in *Figure 2.4* (`https://github.com/PacktPublishing/Natural-Language-Processing-with-AWS-AI-Services/blob/main/Chapter%2002/two-column-image.jpeg`) and upload it to the Amazon Textract console to try this out:

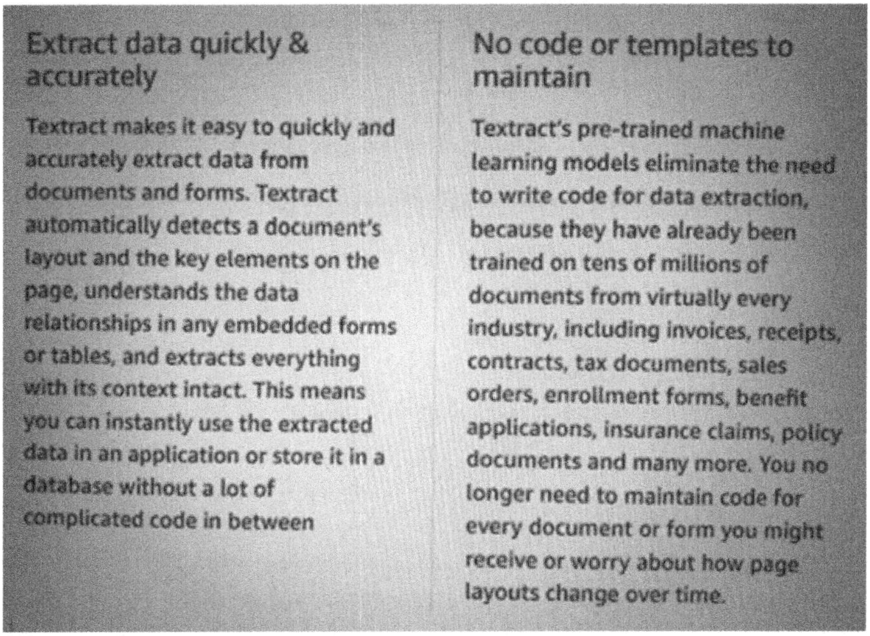

Extract data quickly & accurately

Textract makes it easy to quickly and accurately extract data from documents and forms. Textract automatically detects a document's layout and the key elements on the page, understands the data relationships in any embedded forms or tables, and extracts everything with its context intact. This means you can instantly use the extracted data in an application or store it in a database without a lot of complicated code in between

No code or templates to maintain

Textract's pre-trained machine learning models eliminate the need to write code for data extraction, because they have already been trained on tens of millions of documents from virtually every industry, including invoices, receipts, contracts, tax documents, sales orders, enrollment forms, benefit applications, insurance claims, policy documents and many more. You no longer need to maintain code for every document or form you might receive or worry about how page layouts change over time.

Figure 2.5 – Multi-page scanned image sample

Amazon Textract will extract the pages and the paragraphs, along with the lines and the words. Also, it will give you the exact positions of these words and paragraphs in the document, which is very important for context. See the following screenshot to understand the bounding box or geometry derived using Textract:

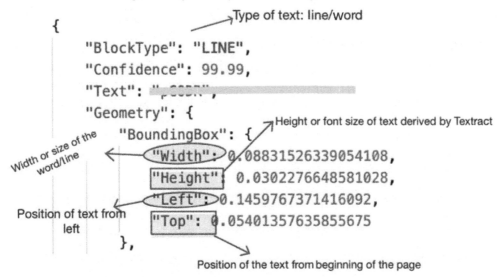

Figure 2.6 – Textract bounding box response for detected text

Here is a screenshot of this document in the AWS console:

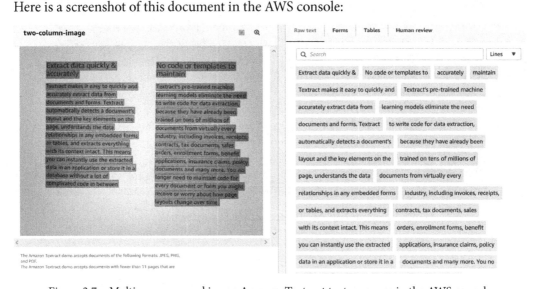

Figure 2.7 – Multi-page scanned image Amazon Textract text response in the AWS console

Form data and key/value pairs

Amazon Textract segments documents to identify forms so it can return your key/value pairs from these forms. We will use the employment application sample document template (`https://github.com/PacktPublishing/Natural-Language-Processing-with-AWS-AI-Services/blob/main/Chapter%2002/emp_app_printed.png`), which you downloaded from the GitHub repository:

1. Click on the **Upload document** button in the Amazon Textract console:

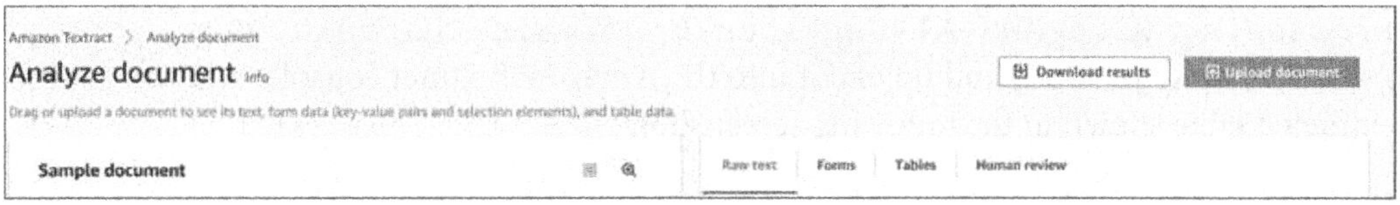

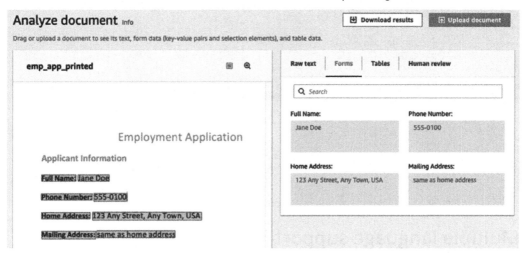

Figure 2.8 – Upload document button in the Textract console

2. Click on the **Forms** tab. You will see the extracted key/value pairs, as shown:

Figure 2.9 – Sample document form and key/value pair extraction in the Amazon Textract console

Table extraction

Amazon Textract can recognize if your document has content structured in tables, for example, receipts, or a listing of technical specifications, pharmacy prescription data, and so on. Textract provides you with the ability to specify whether it should look for tables in your documents when using the API. Along with the table and its contents, Textract returns metadata and indexing information of the table contents, which you can find out more about in the API walk-through later. For this demo, you can download this sample receipt (`https://github.com/PacktPublishing/Natural-Language-Processing-with-AWS-AI-Services/blob/main/Chapter%2002/receipt-image.png`) and upload it into the Amazon Textract console. You will get the extracted table shown in the following screenshot:

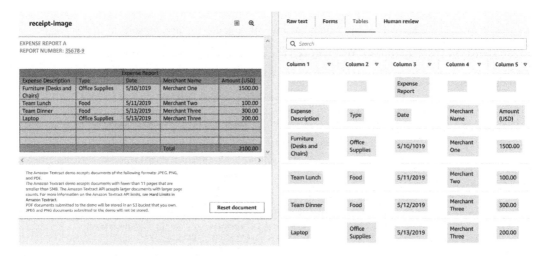

Figure 2.10 – Table extraction of sample receipt in the Amazon Textract console.

Multiple language support

Amazon Textract provides support for extracting text in multiple languages. For the latest list of languages supported, please refer to this link: `https://aws.amazon.com/textract/faqs/`.

> **Note**
> Handwriting support is available only in English at the time of writing (*April 2021*).

During the COVID lockdown in France, anyone wishing to leave their house had to fill in a declaration form to explain why they were outside. We will use this sample form to demo the Amazon Textract language detection feature for the French language. The form is available at `https://www.connexionfrance.com/French-news/Covid-19-in-France-Your-questions-on-declaration-form-needed-to-leave-the-house`.

You can also download this form from `https://github.com/PacktPublishing/Natural-Language-Processing-with-AWS-AI-Services/blob/main/Chapter%2002/form-derogatoire.jpg` and upload it to the Amazon Textract console. Click on the **Raw text** tab, then **Forms**:

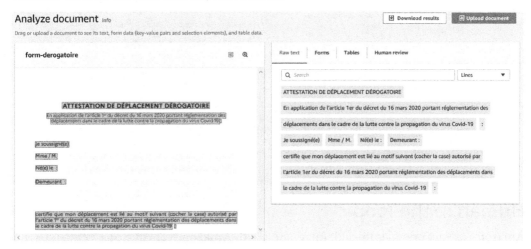

Figure 2.11 – French data extraction from a sample scanned COVID form in French

Amazon Textract is able to detect both key/value pairs and raw text from this form in French.

Handwriting detection

Another very common challenge customers face with data extraction is when you have mixed content documents, such as handwritten text along with printed text. This could be, for example, a prescription form that doctors write for their patients on paper printed with the doctor's name and address. This brings us to another key feature of Amazon Textract: detecting handwritten content from documents:

1. Download the sample handwritten invoice from the GitHub repository (`https://github.com/PacktPublishing/Natural-Language-Processing-with-AWS-AI-Services/blob/main/Chapter%2002/sample-invoice.png`).

2. Upload the sample into the Amazon Textract console, as shown in *Figure 2.12*. Amazon Textract is able to extract handwritten as well as printed key/value pairs (form data), tables, and text from the sample document:

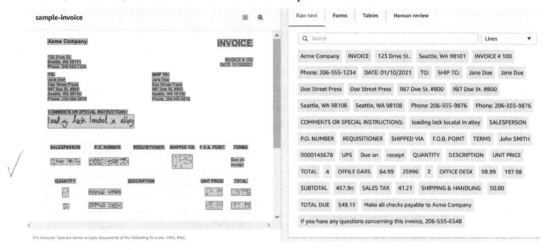

Figure 2.12 – Handwritten as well as printed text extracted from a sample invoice

3. You can change tabs to **Forms** and **Tables** to see how Amazon Textract is able to quickly extract this handwritten and printed content from this sample document.

Human in the loop

Amazon Textract provides in-built integration with **Amazon A2I** (https://aws. amazon.com/augmented-ai/). Using Amazon A2I, you can build human workflows to manage certain documents that require further review by a human for auditing purposes, or just to review the ML predictions. For example, social security numbers or monetary amounts may need to be highly accurate. It is similar to having a first pass of getting text from AI and then using human teams to double-check what the AI has predicted for you.

We will cover handwriting and human in the loop in detail when we get to *Chapter 17, Visualizing Insights from Handwritten Content*.

Lastly, the Textract console provides you the option to download and review the JSON documents that are the result of the API responses that were invoked for the various Textract features we walked through:

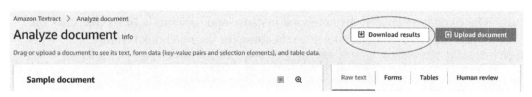

Figure 2.13 – Download Textract results from console

In this section, we walked through Amazon Textract's key product features to extract text, forms, tables, and handwritten content from PDF and image documents, including support for documents in multiple languages. In the next section, we will review how to use Amazon Textract APIs, walk through the JSON responses in detail, and understand how to use Textract with your applications.

Using Amazon Textract with your applications

In this section, we will introduce and walk through the Amazon Textract APIs for real-time analysis and batch processing of documents. We will show these APIs in action using Amazon SageMaker Jupyter notebooks. For this section, you will need to create an Amazon SageMaker Jupyter notebook and set up **IAM** permissions for that notebook role to access Amazon Textract. After that you will need to clone the notebook from our GitHub repository (https://github.com/PacktPublishing/Natural-Language-Processing-with-AWS-AI-Services), download the sample images, create an Amazon S3 (https://aws.amazon.com/s3/) bucket, upload these images to the S3 bucket, and then refer to this location in the notebook for processing.

Let's get started:

1. For instructions to create an Amazon SageMaker notebook instance, please refer to the *Creating an Amazon SageMaker Jupyter notebook instance* sub-section in the *Setting up your AWS environment* section at the beginning of this chapter. Alternatively, you can refer to the Amazon SageMaker documentation to create a notebook instance: https://docs.aws.amazon.com/sagemaker/latest/dg/gs-setup-working-env.html.

> **IAM role permissions while creating Amazon SageMaker Jupyter notebooks**
>
> First, accept the default for the IAM role at notebook creation time to allow access to any S3 bucket. After the notebook instance is created, follow the instructions in the *sub-section Changing IAM permissions and trust relationships for the Amazon SageMaker notebook execution role* under the section, *Setting up your AWS environment* at the beginning of this chapter to add **AmazonTextractFullAccess** as a permissions policy to the notebook's IAM role.

2. Once you have created the notebook instance and its status is **InService**, click on **Open Jupyter** in the **Actions** menu heading for the notebook instance:

Figure 2.14 – Open the Jupyter notebook

This will take you to the home folder of your notebook instance.

3. Click on **New** and select **Terminal**, as shown in the following screenshot:

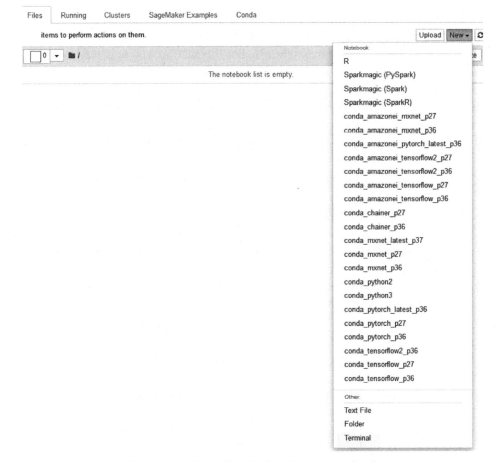

Figure 2.15 – Open Terminal in a Jupyter notebook

4. In the terminal window, first type `cd SageMaker` and then type `git clone https://github.com/PacktPublishing/Natural-Language-Processing-with-AWS-AI-Services`, as shown in the following screenshot:

```
sh-4.2$ pwd
/home/ec2-user
sh-4.2$ cd SageMaker/
sh-4.2$ git clone https://github.com/PacktPublishing/Natural-Language-Processing-with-AWS-AI-Services
```

Figure 2.16 – git clone command

5. Now, exit the terminal window, go back to the home folder, and you will see a folder called `Chapter 02`. Open the folder and you should see a notebook called **Amazon Textract API Sample.ipynb**. Open this notebook by clicking it.

6. Follow through the steps in this notebook that correspond to the next few subheadings in this section by executing one cell at a time. Please read the descriptions provided above each notebook cell.

Textract APIs

Before jumping into a notebook demo of how you can use the Textract APIs, we will explore the APIs and their features. Amazon Textract APIs can be classified into synchronous APIs for real-time processing and asynchronous APIs for batch processing. Let's now examine the functions of these APIs.

Synchronous APIs for real-time processing

These APIs take single-page scanned images (JPG or PNG) from your existing filesystem, which is local to your computer, or in an Amazon S3 bucket. There are two APIs for real-time analysis:

*   **Detect Document Text API**: This API will extract words and lines from scanned images. You can use this API for use cases where you just want the text content from the scans, and your data does not have forms or tables, such as story books, student exam papers, and scanned news articles. You can use this API in web or mobile applications to quickly scan text from documents in real time. Another way to use this API is to extract the text data and perform further NLP on this data, such as to identify paragraphs and headers, perform further data labeling for key/value pairs, or use it for downstream processing.

> **Key/value pairs**
>
> Key/value pairs in the case of a form means the key will be the name and the value will be "Jane Doe."

- **Analyze Document API**: This API is much more comprehensive in its function and can help you extract text from scanned images and identify forms (key/value pairs) and tables from documents. You can use this API with various types of documents, such as invoices, receipts, medical intake forms, resumes, tax forms, and all types of financial forms. You can create an application where a user can take pictures of receipts and use this API to do a quick analysis of the invoice to retrieve the amount or the invoice ID.

Asynchronous APIs for batch processing

These APIs accept single-page or multi-page images (JPG/PNG) and PDFs that are uploaded to an Amazon S3 bucket. It runs a batch analysis to extract content from these images and documents:

- **StartDocumentAnalysis**: This API is similar to the `AnalyzeDocument` synchronous API in function, as it will extract text, tables, and form data from the input documents. The difference is this API also supports PDF documents. Input documents should be stored in an Amazon S3 bucket, and its S3 URL should be provided to this API. This API will start the batch job for document analysis.

- **GetDocumentAnalysis**: This API will receive the results for an Amazon Textract `StartDocumentAnalysis` operation in the form of key/value pairs, tables, and text. This also returns the job ID and their success or failure status.

- **StartDocumentTextDetection**: This API is similar to the real-time `DetectDocumentText` API in functionality as it detects text from documents in batches that have been uploaded to an Amazon S3 bucket. We will see this API demo in the Python notebook example.

- **GetDocumentTextDetection**: This API is used to retrieve the results of an Amazon Textract `StartDocumentTextDetection` operation in the form of lines and words. This also returns the job ID and its success or failure status.

> **Note**
> Batch APIs can be used with JPEG, PNG, and PDF documents stored in an Amazon S3 bucket.

In this section, we covered batch and real-time APIs of Amazon Textract. In the next section, we will see the implementation of these APIs through the Jupyter notebook you set up in the previous section.

Textract API demo with a Jupyter notebook

In this section, we will provide Textract APIs' implementation through a Jupyter notebook. We will execute the code cells in the Jupyter notebook you set up at `https://github.com/PacktPublishing/Natural-Language-Processing-with-AWS-AI-Services/blob/main/Chapter%2002/Amazon%20Textract%20API%20Sample.ipynb`, which you cloned in a previous step in a Jupyter notebook environment. The notebook contains the prerequisite steps, and we will walk through the complete code for all the APIs here. We provide only important code snippets in the book, as follows:

- `DetectText API` with a document passed from a local filesystem in the form of image bytes
- `AnalyzeText API` with a document passed from S3 to detect text, forms, and tables from invoices
- Batch processing with an employment application form using the `StartDocumentText` and `GetDocumentText` APIs

DetectText API

Let's begin:

1. Open the notebook and execute the first cell to import the `boto3` libraries to set up the Amazon Textract `boto3` Python SDK.
2. Refer to the notebook to set up and install `boto3`:

   A. Setting up an Amazon S3 Python SDK `boto3` client: `https://boto3.amazonaws.com/v1/documentation/api/latest/reference/services/s3.html`:

   ```
   s3 = boto3.client('s3')
   ```

    B. Setting up an Amazon Textract Python SDK boto3 client: https://boto3.
amazonaws.com/v1/documentation/api/latest/reference/
services/textract.html:

```
textract = boto3.client('textract')
```

3.   Download the sample documents from https://github.com/
PacktPublishing/Natural-Language-Processing-with-AWS-AI-
Services/blob/main/Chapter%2002/sample-invoice.png. If you
have already cloned this GitHub repository, you don't have to download the sample
again, you can directly refer to them from your notebook under Chapter 02.

4.   Follow the instructions in the *Creating an Amazon S3 bucket and a folder and
uploading objects* sub-section in the *Setting up your AWS environment* section to
create an S3 bucket and upload your sample documents.

5.   Copy the name of the Amazon S3 bucket you created and to which you uploaded
the sample documents and paste it in the notebook:

```
s3BucketName = "<your amazon s3 bucket>"
```

6.   Here is the image we are going to use in this notebook:

```
documentName = "sample-invoice.png"
display(Image(filename=documentName))
```

That displays the following image:

Acme Company

INVOICE

123 Drive St.
Seattle, WA 98101
Phone: 206-555-1234

INVOICE # 100
DATE: 01/10/2021

TO:
Jane Doe
Doe Street Press
987 Doe St. #800
Seattle, WA 98108
Phone: 206-555-9876

SHIP TO:
Jane Doe
Doe Street Press
987 Doe St. #800
Seattle, WA 98108
Phone: 206-555-9876

COMMENTS OR SPECIAL INSTRUCTIONS:

loading back located in alley

SALESPERSON	P.O. NUMBER	REQUISITIONER	SHIPPED VIA	F.O.B. POINT	TERMS
JOHN SMITH	0000145078		UPS		Due on receipt

QUANTITY	DESCRIPTION	UNIT PRICE	TOTAL
4	OFFICE CHAIRS	64.99	259.96
2	OFFICE DESK	98.99	197.98

SUBTOTAL	457.94
SALES TAX	41.21
SHIPPING & HANDLING	50.00
TOTAL DUE	549.15

Make all checks payable to Acme Company
If you have any questions concerning this invoice, 206-555-6548

Figure 2.17 – A sample receipt

7. Let's get back to the notebook and run the following code to see how Amazon Textract's `DetectText` API works.

    The following code will read the document's content in the form of image bytes:

    ```
    with open(documentName, 'rb') as document:
        imageBytes = bytearray(document.read())
    ```

8. The following code will call Amazon Textract by passing image bytes from your local file in your filesystem:

```
response = textract.detect_document_
text(Document={'Bytes': imageBytes})
```

You are passing the image bytes directly to this API and getting a JSON response. This JSON response has a structure that contains blocks of identified text, pages, lines, a bounding box, form key values, and tables. In order to understand the Amazon Textract JSON structure and data types, refer to this link: https://docs.aws.amazon.com/textract/latest/dg/API_Block.html.

9. Now we will import the JSON Python package so we can print our API responses:

```
import json
print (json.dumps(response, indent=4, sort_keys=True))
```

10. The following shows a sample JSON response for a line from the document. It consists of blocks, the block type, the confidence score of detecting this block type line, and the geometrical location of the line using bounding boxes, along with the identified text:

```
{
        "BlockType": "LINE",
        "Confidence": 99.96764373779297,
        "Geometry": {
            "BoundingBox": {
                "Height": 0.013190358877182007,
                "Left": 0.5149770379066467,
                "Top": 0.16227620840072632,
                "Width": 0.06892169266939163
            },
```

> **Note**
>
> This API will not give you forms and tables. It gives only lines, words, and corresponding bounding boxes. This API will be helpful for use cases such as paragraph detection in audit documents and extracting text from scanned books.

Execute the rest of the cells in the notebook to explore the JSON response in detail.

DetectDocument API   *PROBLEM! IN THIS INSTRUCTION*

Now, we will show you how you can use the DetectDocument API to detect text in two-column documents in a reading order, with your data in stored in an Amazon S3 bucket:

1. Download the sample documents from https://github.com/
   PacktPublishing/Natural-Language-Processing-with-AWS-AI-
   Services/blob/main/Chapter%2002/two-column-image.jpeg. If you
   have already cloned this GitHub repository, you don't have to download the sample
   again, you can directly refer to it under Chapter 02. ← *??*

2. Upload these documents to your Amazon S3 bucket under the textract-
   samples prefix using the instructions here: https://docs.aws.amazon.
   com/AmazonS3/latest/user-guide/upload-objects.html.

3. Display the input document from the Amazon S3 bucket:

```
documentName = "textract-samples/two-column-image.jpg"
display(Image(url=s3.generate_presigned_url('get_object',
Params={'Bucket': s3BucketName, 'Key': documentName})))
```

4. Invoke the DetectDocumentText API by specifying the Amazon S3 bucket and
   the filename, as shown in the following code snippet. Let's also print the response to
   review the results:

```
Response = textract.detect_document_text(
    Document={
        'S3Object': {
            'Bucket': s3BucketName,
            'Name': documentName
        }
    })
print(response)
```

> **Note**
>
> For more details about the DetectDocumentText API, refer to this link:
> https://boto3.amazonaws.com/v1/documentation/api/
> latest/reference/services/textract.html#Textract.
> Client.detect_document_text.

5. Once we have the response, we will use the following code to parse documents in reading order for multi-page documents. We will use the Amazon Textract JSON response parser to get the lines in reading order. Please run this command to install this library:

```
python -m pip install amazon-textract-response-parser
```

6. Now, run the following code to see the results printed line by line for multi-column format documents:

```
doc = Document(response)
for page in doc.pages:
    for line in page.getLinesInReadingOrder():
        print(line[1])
```

You get the following response:

```
Acme Company
123 Drive St.
Seattle, WA 98101
Phone: 206-555-1234
TO:
Jane Doe
Doe Street Press
987 Doe St. #800
Seattle, WA 98108
Phone: 206-555-9876
COMMENTS OR SPECIAL INSTRUCTIONS:
loading lack locatal in alley
SALESPERSON
John SMITH
QUANTITY
4
2
Make all checks payable to Acme Company
If you have any questions concerning this invoice, 206-555-6548
INVOICE
INVOICE # 100
DATE: 01/10/2021
TERMS
Due on
receipt
```

Figure 2.18 – Textract response for lines in reading order

AnalyzeDocument API

Now we will analyze invoices with the `AnalyzeDocument` API to extract forms and tables:

1. Call the Amazon Textract `AnalyzeDocument` API:

```
response = textract.analyze_document(
    Document={
        'S3Object': {
            'Bucket': s3BucketName,
            'Name': documentName
        }
    },
    FeatureTypes=["FORMS","TABLES"])
```

2. Run the following code to parse the key/value pairs and search for keys. To make it easy to parse the Textract response, you can use the Amazon Textract Response Parser library. We will use this to extract the data and search for some keys:

```
doc = Document(response)
for page in doc.pages:
    print("Fields:")
    for field in page.form.fields:
        print("Key: {}, Value: {}".format(field.key,
field.value))
```

3. In the following code, we are looking for the `Phone  Number` ikey n the document:

```
    print("\nGet Field by Key:")
    key = "Phone Number:"
    field = page.form.getFieldByKey(key)
    if(field):
        print("Key: {}, Value: {}".format(field.key,
field.value))
```

4. In the following code, we are looking for the `Address` key in the document:

```
print("\nSearch Fields:")
key = "address"
fields = page.form.searchFieldsByKey(key)
for field in fields:
    print("Key: {}, Value: {}".format(field.key,
field.value))
```

You will get the following output:

```
Fields:
Key: Phone:, Value: 206-555-1234
Key: Phone:, Value: None
Key: Phone:, Value: None
Key: COMMENTS OR SPECIAL INSTRUCTIONS:, Value: loading
lack locatal in alley
Key: SALES TAX, Value: 41.21
Key: SHIPPING and HANDLING, Value: 50.00
Key: REQUISITIONER, Value: None
Key: SUBTOTAL, Value: 457.9n
Key: TOTAL DUE, Value: 549.15
Key: SALESPERSON, Value: John SMITH
Key: SHIP TO:, Value: Jane Doe Doe Street Press 987 Doe
St. #800 Seattle, WA 98108 206-555-9876
Key: P.O. NUMBER, Value: 0000145678
Key: TO:, Value: Jane Doe Doe Street Press 987 Doe St.
#800 Seattle, WA 98108 206-555-9876
Key: DATE:, Value: 01/10/2021
```

5. To parse tables from the JSON response, please refer to the following code snippet:

```
doc = Document(response)
for page in doc.pages:
    # Print tables
    for table in page.tables:
        for r, row in enumerate(table.rows):
            for c, cell in enumerate(row.cells):
                print("Table[{}][{}] = {}".format(r, c,
cell.text))
```

6. You will see the following response:

```
Table[0][0] = QUANTITY
Table[0][1] = DESCRIPTION
Table[0][2] = UNIT PRICE
Table[0][3] = TOTAL
Table[1][0] = 4
Table[1][1] = OFFILE GARS
Table[1][2] = 64.99
Table[1][3] = 25996
Table[2][0] = 2
Table[2][1] = OFFICE DESX
Table[2][2] = 98.99
Table[2][3] = 197.98
```

> **Note**
>
> You can convert these values into a pandas DataFrame, which we will cover in *Chapter 16, Improving the Accuracy of PDF Batch Processing.*
>
> To find out more about the API JSON responses, refer to this link: `https://docs.aws.amazon.com/textract/latest/dg/how-it-works-tables.html`.

Processing PDF documents using Textract Asynchronous APIs

In this section, you will see how to analyze PDF documents using Textract async APIs for a sample job application form:

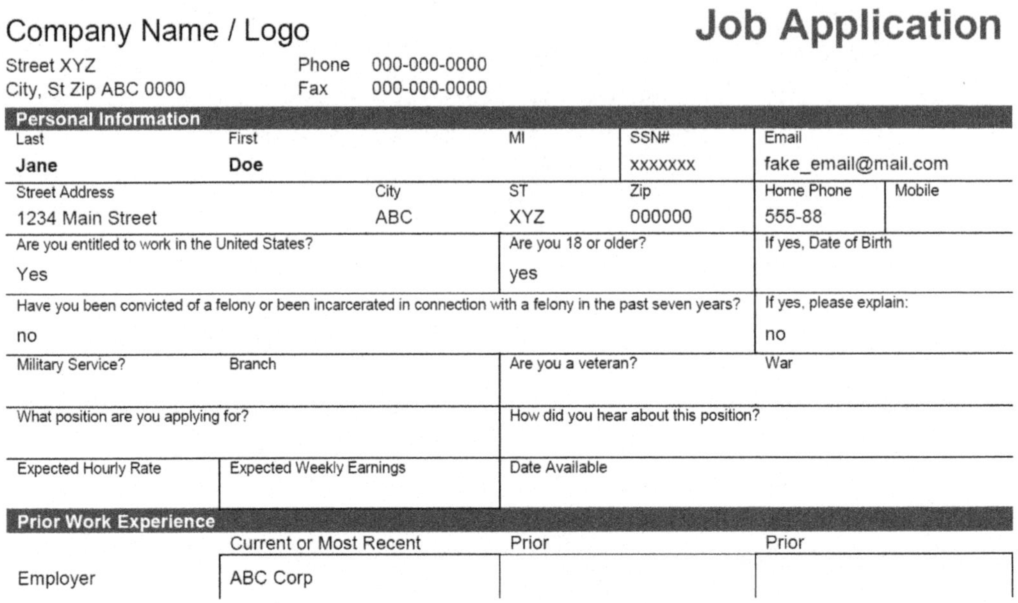

Company Name / Logo

Job Application

Street XYZ
City, St Zip ABC 0000

Phone 000-000-0000
Fax 000-000-0000

Personal Information

Last	First	MI	SSN#	Email
Jane	**Doe**		XXXXXXX	fake_email@mail.com

Street Address	City	ST	Zip	Home Phone	Mobile
1234 Main Street	ABC	XYZ	000000	555-88	

Are you entitled to work in the United States?	Are you 18 or older?	If yes, Date of Birth
Yes	yes	

Have you been convicted of a felony or been incarcerated in connection with a felony in the past seven years?	If yes, please explain:
no	no

Military Service?	Branch	Are you a veteran?	War

What position are you applying for?	How did you hear about this position?

Expected Hourly Rate	Expected Weekly Earnings	Date Available

Prior Work Experience

	Current or Most Recent	Prior	Prior
Employer	ABC Corp		

Figure 2.19 – A sample job application file

1. The following code will help you get started with the `StartDocumentText` API and the `GetDocumentText` API:

```
jobID = startTextAnalysis(s3Bucket, docName)
print("Started text analysis for: {}".format(jobID))
if(isAnalysisComplete(jobID)):
    response = getAnalysisResults(jobID)
```

2. In this `startTextAnalysis` method, you call the `StartDocumentTextDetection` API to start the text analysis job:

```
def startTextAnalysis(s3Bucket, doc):
    response = None
    response = textract.start_document_text_detection(
    DocumentLocation={
        'S3Object': {
            'Bucket': s3Bucket,
            'Name': doc
```

```
            }
    })
    return response["JobID"]
```

3. Once you start the analysis, you use the following method to check whether the analysis is complete:

```
def isAnalysisComplete(jobID):
    response = textract.get_document_text_
detection(JobId=jobID)
    status = response["JobStatus"]
    print("Text Analysis status: {}".format(status))
    while(status == "IN_PROGRESS"):
        time.sleep(2)
        response = textract.get_document_text_
detection(JobId=jobID)
        status = response["JobStatus"]
        print("Status of Text Analysis is: {}".
format(status))
    return status
```

4. Once the job is completed, you can use the GetDocumentTextDetection API to get the results:

```
def getAnalysisResults(jobID):
    pages = []
    response = textract.get_document_text_
detection(JobId=jobID)
    pages.append(response)
    print("We received results for: {}".
format(len(pages)))
    nextToken = None
    if('NextToken' in response):
        nextToken = response['NextToken']
    while(nextToken):
        response = textract.get_document_text_
detection(JobId=jobId, NextToken=nextToken)
        pages.append(response)
        print("We got the results for: {}".
format(len(pages)))
```

```
            nextToken = None
        if('NextToken' in response):
            nextToken = response['NextToken']
    return pages
```

And we are done with the demo. Hopefully, you have had an opportunity to review and work with the different Textract APIs for real-time and batch processing and have successfully completed your notebook. In the next section, we will see how you can use these APIs to build serverless applications.

Building applications using Amazon Textract APIs

We have spoken about both synchronous (or real-time) APIs and asynchronous (or batch) APIs. Now, the question is how to integrate these APIs into an application. You can quickly integrate these APIs into a web application or any batch processing systems by using AWS Lambda. AWS Lambda runs any code in a serverless manner, be it Java or Python. It's an event-based trigger or programming technique in which you trigger a Lambda function based on an event. For example, you upload your documents to Amazon S3, which can trigger a Lambda function. In that Lambda function, you can call the Amazon Textract APIs and save the results in Amazon S3:

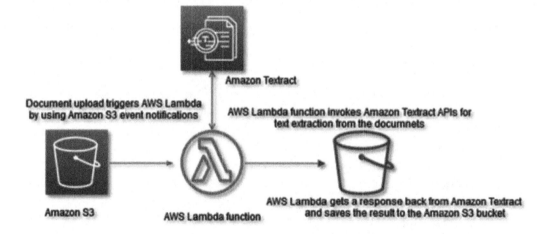

Figure 2.20 – Building serverless architecture with Amazon Textract to use with your apps

We will cover the architecture in detail in upcoming chapters, where we will talk about how you can build applications using the synchronous versus asynchronous APIs of Amazon Textract. We will also talk about using AWS API Gateway to create RESTful APIs to integrate into your web applications or mobile applications.

Summary

In this chapter, we saw a detailed introduction to Amazon Textract and its product features, along with a console walk-through, as well as running code samples using Textract APIs for different types of documents using both real-time and batch analysis.

We started by introducing the ready-made intelligence that Amazon Textract offers with powerful pre-trained ML models, and the ability to use its capabilities in your applications with just an API call. We also read about some popular use cases that Textract can be used for, along with references to some of the following chapters, where we will review those use cases in greater detail. We also read about Textract's benefits as compared to traditional OCR applications and rule-based document processing.

We covered various examples on how you can use Amazon Textract with different types of scanned images and forms. We reviewed different functions of Textract, such as detecting raw text, detecting form values that are stored as key/value pairs, detecting text in tables, detecting pages of text, detecting lines and words, detecting handwritten text and printed text, and detecting text in multiple languages, as well as detecting text that is written in two-column styles in documents. We covered both synchronous processing and asynchronous processing using Textract APIs. We also saw how to set up an Amazon SageMaker Jupyter notebook, clone the GitHub repository, and get started with running a Jupyter notebook. We were able to use an Amazon S3 bucket to store input documents and use them with Textract, and we were able to extract data from unstructured documents and store them in an Amazon S3 bucket.

In this chapter, we also covered Amazon Textract real-time APIs such as the **AnalyzeDocument** API and the **DetectDocumentText** API. We discussed the expected input document formats for these APIs and their limitations. We then spoke about how you can scale document processing for use cases where you need to extract data in batches. We read about **batch processing APIs** along with a Python SDK demo. Finally, we introduced an architecture to integrate Textract into your applications using AWS Lambda.

In the next chapter, you will be introduced to Amazon Comprehend, an AI service that uses ML to uncover insights in text. You will learn about different NLP techniques, review the features for Amazon Comprehend, read about its APIs, learn how you can set up a custom NLP model using Comprehend to detect entities unique to your business, and, like we did in this chapter, you will see Comprehend in action for different use cases.

3
Introducing Amazon Comprehend

In the previous chapter, we covered how you can use **Amazon Textract** for **Optical Character Recognition** (**OCR**) and deep dive into its features and specific API implementations. In this chapter, you will get a detailed introduction to **Amazon Comprehend** and **Amazon Comprehend Medical**, what their functions are, what business challenges they were created to solve, what features they have, what types of user requirements they can be applied to, and how easy it is to integrate Comprehend with different **AWS** services, such as **AWS Lambda**, to build business applications.

In this chapter, we will go through the following sections:

- Understanding Amazon Comprehend and Amazon Comprehend Medical
- Exploring Amazon Comprehend and Amazon Comprehend Medical product features
- Using Amazon Comprehend with your applications

Technical requirements

For this chapter, you will need access to an **AWS account**. Before getting started, we recommend that you create an AWS account by referring to *AWS account setup* and *Jupyter notebook creation steps* in *Technical requirements* in *Chapter 2, Introducing Amazon Textract*. While creating an **Amazon SageMaker Jupyter notebook**, make sure you input ~~Amazon~~ComprehendFullAccess to the **IAM** role attached with your notebook instance, and follow these steps:

1. Once you create the notebook instance and its status is **InService**, click on **Open Jupyter** in the **Actions** menu heading for the notebook instance.

2. In the terminal window, type first cd SageMaker and then type git clone https://github.com/PacktPublishing/Natural-Language-Processing-with-AWS-AI-Services. The Python code and sample datasets for Amazon Comprehend examples are in this repository: https://github.com/PacktPublishing/Natural-Language-Processing-with-AWS-AI-Services. Once you navigate to the repository, please select *Chapter 3, Introducing Amazon Comprehend – Sample Code*.

Check out the following video to see the Code in Action at https://bit.ly/3G-kd1Oi.

Understanding Amazon Comprehend and Amazon Comprehend Medical

In this section, we will talk about the challenges associated with setting up **ML (ML)** preprocessing for **NLP (NLP)**. Then, we will talk about how Amazon Comprehend and Amazon Comprehend Medical can help solve these pain points. Finally, we will talk about how you can use Amazon Comprehend to analyze the extracted text from documents by using Amazon Textract to extract the data.

Challenges associated with setting up ML preprocessing for NLP

Some of the key challenges while setting up NLP preprocessing are that documents can be semi-structured, unstructured, or can be in various languages. Once you have a large amount of unstructured data, you would probably like to extract insights from the data using some NLP techniques for most common use cases such as **sentiment analysis**, **text classification**, **NER (NER)**, **machine translation**, and **topic modeling**.

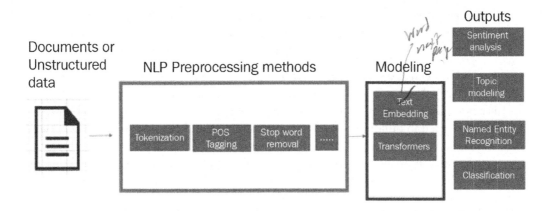

Figure 3.1 – NLP modeling

The challenge with applying these techniques is that the majority of the time is spent in data preprocessing. This applies whether you are doing ML, for example, sentiment analysis, or deep learning to apply key NLP techniques to find insights. If you are doing ML, some of the key preprocessing techniques you would use include the following:

- **Tokenization**: This simply means you are dividing unstructured text into words or sentences. For example, for the sentence: "This book is focusing on NLP", the tokenized word output will be "This", "book", "is", "focusing", "on", and "NLP". Similarly, if it is a complex text, you can tokenize it by sentences rather than words.

- **Stop word removal**: Stop words are words that do not have primary meaning in a sentence, for example, "and" "a", "is", "they", and so on, but they have a meaningful impact when we use them to communicate. An example of the stop words in the following text: "This book is focusing on NLP", would be "is" and "on", and these would be removed as part of preprocessing. A use case where you would not remove a stop word would be in certain sectors, such as healthcare, where removing stop words would be a blunder as it will completely change the meaning of the sentence.

- **Stemming**: Stemming means removing the last few characters of a given word to obtain a shorter form, even if that form doesn't have any meaning. For instance, the words "focusing", "focuses", and "focus" convey the same meaning, and can be clubbed under one stem for computer analysis. So instead of having them as different words, we can put them together under the same term: "focus."

- **Lemmatization**: This, on the other hand, means converting the given word into its base form according to the dictionary definition of the word. For example, focusing → focus. This takes more time than stemming and is a compute-intensive process.

- **Part-of-speech (PoS) tagging:** After tokenizing it, this method tags each word as a part of speech. Let's stick with the "This book is focusing on NLP" example. "Book" is a noun and "focusing" is a verb. PoS tags are useful for building **parse trees**. Parse trees are used in building named entity recognizers and extracting relations between words. PoS tagging is used for building lemmatizers. Lemmatizers will reduce a word to its root form. Moreover, there are various techniques to do PoS tagging, such as lexical-based methods, rule-based methods, and more.

Even after these preprocessing steps, you would still need to apply advanced NLP techniques if you are doing deep learning on top of the preprocessed steps. Some popular techniques are the following:

- **Word embedding**: These are vector representations of strings with similar semantic meanings. Word embeddings are used as a starting technique for most deep learning NLP tasks and are a popular way of **transfer learning** in NLP. Some of the common word embeddings are **Word2vec**, **Doc2Vec** for documents, **GloVe**, **Continuous Bag of Words (CBOW)**, and **Skip-gram**.

- **Transformers**: In 2017, there was a paradigm shift from the standard way NLP applications were built upon with transformers, for example, using **RNNs**, **LSTMs**, or **GRUs** initialized with word embedding. Transformers have led to the development of pretrained systems such as **Bidirectional Encoder Representations from Transformers (BERT)** and **Generative Pretrained Transformer (GPT)**. BERT and GPT have been trained with huge general language datasets, such as **Wikipedia Corpus** and **Common Crawl**, and can be fine-tuned to specific language tasks.

Some of the challenges with setting up these NLP models include the following:

- Compute-intensive process and requires GPUs and CPUs

- Requires large, labeled datasets for training

- Set up infrastructure for managing the compute and scaling the models in production

- Time-intensive and ML skills are needed to perform modeling

To overcome these challenges, we have Amazon SageMaker, which helps with removing all the infrastructure-heavy lifting of building, training, tuning, and deploying NLP models from idea to execution quickly.

> **Amazon SageMaker**
>
> You can learn more about how to get started with Amazon SageMaker NLP techniques in the book *Learn Amazon SageMaker* by Julien Simon.

Moreover, talking specifically about implementing transformers in your NLP models, Amazon SageMaker also supports transformer implementation in **PyTorch**, **TensorFlow**, and **HuggingFace**.

The **Hugging Face transformers** package is an immensely popular Python library providing pretrained models that are useful for a variety of NLP tasks. Refer to this blog to learn more: `https://aws.amazon.com/blogs/machine-learning/aws-and-hugging-face-collaborate-to-simplify-and-accelerate-adoption-of-natural-language-processing-models/`.

So, we have covered some of the key challenges with preprocessing NLP techniques and modeling. With AWS AI services such as Amazon Comprehend, you don't need to worry about spinning up servers or setting up complex infrastructure for NLP training. You also don't need to worry about all the preprocessing techniques we've covered, for example, tokenization, PoS tagging, and so on.

You also don't need to think about implementing transformers to set up deep learning models to accomplish some of the key NLP tasks, such as text classification, topic modeling, NER, key phrase detection, and a lot more.

Amazon Comprehend and Comprehend Medical give you APIs to accomplish some key NLP tasks (such as sentiment analysis, text classification, or topic modeling) on a variety of unstructured texts (such as emails, chats, social media feeds, or healthcare notes).

In the next section, we will cover how Comprehend and Comprehend Medical can detect insights in text with no preprocessing.

Exploring the benefits of Amazon Comprehend and Comprehend Medical

In this section, we will cover some of the key benefits of Amazon Comprehend and Comprehend Medical by discussing the following examples:

- Integrates NLP APIs that use a pretrained deep learning model under the hood. These APIs can be added to your apps to make them intelligent as you do not need textual analysis expertise to use them.

- Provides scalable NLP processing, as its serverless APIs enable you to analyze several documents or unstructured textual data for NLP without worrying about spinning up servers and managing them.

- Both of these services integrate with other AWS services: **AWS IAM**, for identity and access management; **Amazon S3**, for storage; **AWS Key Management Service (KMS)**, to manage security keys during encryption; **AWS Lambda**, to create serverless architecture. You can perform real-time analysis both from streaming data coming from **Amazon Kinesis** or a batch of data in Amazon S3, then use the NLP APIs to gain insights on this data and display it in a dashboard using **Amazon Quicksight**, which is a visualization tool similar to **Tableau**.

- These services provide encryption of output results and volume data in Amazon S3. With Amazon Comprehend, you can use KMS keys to encrypt the output results of the jobs, as well as the data attached on the storage volume of the compute instance that processes the analysis job under the hood.

- It's cost-effective, as you only have to pay for the text that you will analyze.

Detecting insights in text using Comprehend and Comprehend Medical without preprocessing

Amazon Comprehend and Amazon Comprehend Medical are AWS AI services, similar to Amazon Textract (which we covered in *Chapter 2, Introducing Amazon Textract*), where you do not need to set up complex models. You call the Amazon Comprehend and Amazon Comprehend Medical APIs and send a text request, and you will get a response back with the detected confidence score. The difference between Amazon Comprehend and Amazon Comprehend Medical is that Comprehend Medical is specific to healthcare NLP use cases. Comprehend Medical uses ML to extract health-related, meaningful insights from unstructured medical text, while Amazon Comprehend uses NLP to extract meaningful information about the content of unstructured text by recognizing the **entities**, **key phrases**, **language**, **sentiments**, and other common elements in the text.

Some of the key use cases of Amazon Comprehend are as follows:

- *Using topic modeling to search documents based on topics*: With Amazon Comprehend topic modeling, you have the ability to configure the number of topics you are looking for in your documents or text files. With topic modeling, you can search the documents attached with each topic.

- *Using sentiment analysis to analyze the sentiment of what customers think of your product*: With Amazon Comprehend sentiment analysis APIs, you can find out how customers feel (such as positive, negative, neutral, or mixed) about their products. For example, suppose you find a restaurant on Yelp. It's a pizza place. You go there, try the pizza, and do not like it, so you post a comment: "The pizza here was not great." Business owners using Comprehend sentiment analysis can quickly analyze the sentiment of this text and act in real time on improving user satisfaction before their business goes down.

- *Quick discovery of customer feelings based on topics and entities*: You can combine multiple features of Amazon Comprehend, such as topic modeling, with entity recognition and sentiment analysis to discover the topics that your end users are talking about in various forums.

- *Bring your own data to perform custom classification and custom entity recognition*: Amazon Comprehend provides you with the capability to quickly get started with custom entities. For example, if you are a manufacturing firm and you are looking for certain product codes in the documents, such as PR123, it should be detected as the product code using ML.

    You can bring a sample of your data and use Amazon Comprehend Custom entity recognition to get started without needing to worry about writing a complex model. You also do not need to worry about labeling large datasets to get started, as Amazon Comprehend **Custom** uses transfer learning under the hood. You can get started with a small set of labeled data to create custom entities specific to your use case. Similarly, you can bring your own data and perform custom classification to perform multi-class and multi-label classification to identify classes.

In the case of healthcare records, you can use Amazon Comprehend Medical. You can use Comprehend Medical for the following healthcare applications:

- Using Comprehend Medical APIs to analyze case documents for patient case management and outcomes.

- Using Comprehend Medical APIs to detect useful information in clinical texts to optimize the matching process and drug safety for life sciences and research organizations.

- Using Comprehend Medical to extract billing codes which can decrease the time to revenue for insurance payers involved in medical billing.

- Comprehend Medical also supports ontology linking for **ICD-10-CM (International Classification of Diseases – 10th Version – Clinical Modification)** and **RxNorm**. Ontology linking means detecting entities in clinical text and linking those entities to concepts in standardized medical ontologies, such as the RxNorm and ICD-10-CM knowledge bases.

- Detecting **PHI** data, such as age, date from clinical documents, and set controls, to implement PHI compliance in the medical organization.

We will cover Amazon Comprehend Medical use cases in detail in *Chapter 12, AI and NLP in Healthcare.*

Using these services to gain insights from OCR documents from Amazon Textract

If you have documents in the form of scanned images or PDFs, you can use Amazon Textract to extract data quickly from these documents and then use Amazon Comprehend to gain meaningful insights from the extracted text, such as entities, key phrases, and sentiment. You can further classify these documents using Amazon Comprehend text classification, and also perform topic modeling to identify key topics within the documents. We will cover how you can use Amazon Textract with Amazon Comprehend together in an architecture in *Chapter 4, Automating Document Processing Workflows for Financial Institutions*, and in *Chapter 5, Creating NLP Search* in the section *Creating NLP-powered smart search indexes*. Moreover, for the healthcare industry, if you have lots of scanned documents such as medical intake forms, patient notes, and so on, you can use Amazon Textract to extract data from these documents and then use Amazon Comprehend Medical to extract key insights from this unstructured text data.

In this section, we first covered the challenges associated with setting up NLP modeling. Then we discussed how Amazon Comprehend and Comprehend Medical can address the pain points associated with setting up NLP models, such as scalability, preprocessing steps, and infrastructure setup. Lastly, we covered how you can automate your documents and enrich them with NLP by combining Amazon Textract and Amazon Comprehend. We have covered how Comprehend and Comprehend Medical can provide rich APIs for building intelligent NLP applications, which are also scalable to process large numbers of documents or unstructured data. In the next section, we will talk about some of the product features of these services using an AWS Console demo.

Exploring Amazon Comprehend and Amazon Comprehend Medical product features

In this section, we will talk about Amazon Comprehend and Amazon Comprehend Medical product features using an AWS Console demo. We will start with Amazon Comprehend, and then move to Amazon Comprehend Medical.

Discovering Amazon Comprehend

Amazon Comprehend enables you to examine your unstructured data, for example, social media feeds, posts, emails, web pages, data extracted from Amazon Textract, phone transcripts, call center records, or really any kind of unstructured textual data. It can help you gain various insights about its content by using a number of pretrained models. *Figure 3.2* is a diagram of how Amazon Comprehend actually works:

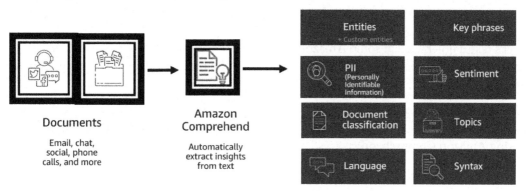

Figure 3.2 – Amazon Comprehend features

With Amazon Comprehend, you can perform the following on your input unstructured textual data by using the following **text analysis** APIs:

- **Detect Entities**
- **Detect Key Phrases**
- **Detect the Dominant Language**
- **Detect Personally Identifiable Information (PII)**
- **Determine Sentiment**
- **Analyze Syntax**
- **Topic Modeling**

These text analysis APIs can be used both in real-time and in a batch manner, while topic modeling is a batch job or asynchronous process and cannot be used for real-time use cases.

There are two modes in which you can use these APIs:

- *Real-time in any application*: You can use these APIs for real-time use cases by sending one document at a time, or in batch real-time operations by sending 15 documents in a batch and getting a response immediately.

- *Batch or asynchronous manner*: Where you bring your large batch of data into Amazon S3, point to a dataset, and run any of the preceding analyses in the form of a batch job. The results of the batch job are saved to an S3 bucket.

> **Note**
> For synchronous APIs, your text has to be UTF-8 encoded and 5,000 bytes.

Let's take a quick look at some Amazon Comprehend features on the AWS Console. Please refer to the *Technical requirements* section if you have not already set up your AWS account.

Since we all forget to set up autopay messages to pay our credit card bills, in this demo we will show you a quick analysis of a sample autopay message to extract some key insights using Amazon Comprehend:

1. Go to Amazon Comprehend. Click on **Launch Amazon Comprehend**:

Figure 3.3 – Amazon Comprehend Console

2. We will use the following sample autopay text to analyze all of the features of Amazon Comprehend available through the AWS Console:

> Hi Alex. Your NoNameCompany Financial Services, LLC credit card account 1111-0000-1111-0010 has a minimum payment of $25.00 that is due by Sunday, June 19th. Based on your autopay settings, we are going to withdraw your payment on the due date from your bank account XXXXXX1121 with the routing number XXXXX0000.

> Your latest statement was mailed to 100 XYZ Street, Anytown, WA 98121.

> After your payment is received, you will receive a confirmation text message at 555-0100-0000.

> If you have questions about your bill, NoNameCompany Customer Service is available by phone at 206-555-0199 or email at support@nonamecompany.com.

3. Copy the preceding text and insert it into **Real-time analysis** → **Input text**, as shown in *Figure 3.4*, and click on **Built-in**, and then **Analyze**:

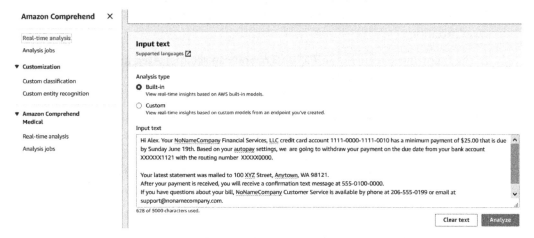

Figure 3.4 – Real-time analysis Input text in AWS Console

4. Scroll down to see the insights.

Now, we will walk through each **Insights** API by changing each tab.

Detecting entities

You can see from the screenshot in *Figure 3.5* that Amazon Comprehend was able to detect the highlighted entities from the text you entered:

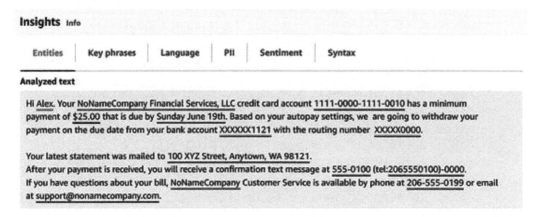

Figure 3.5 – Detect entities insights

1. Scroll down to the results to understand more about these entities and what is identified as an entity by Amazon Comprehend's built-in APIs without any customization.

    In the following screenshot in *Figure 3.6*, you can see that **Alex** has been identified as a **Person**, and **NoNameCompany**, the sender of the autopay message, has been identified as an **Organization**. The date by which Alex's amount is due (**June 19th**) has been identified as a **Date** entity, along with their specific confidence scores. The **confidence score** means how likely a match is to be found by the ML model, which is in a range from 0 to 100. The higher the score, the greater the confidence in the answer. A score of 100 is likely an exact match, while a score of 0 means that no matching answer was found:

▼ **Results**

Entity	⏷	Type	⏷	Confidence	⏷
Alex		—— Person		0.99+	
NoNameCompany Financial Services, LLC		—— Organization		0.99+	
1111-0000-1111-0010		—— Other		0.97	
$25.00		—— Quantity		0.99+	
Sunday June 19th		—— Date		0.99+	
XXXXXX1121		—— Other		0.96	
XXXXX0000		—— Other		0.89	
100 XYZ Street, Anytown, WA 98121		—— Location		0.99+	
555-0100-0000		—— Other		0.99+	
NoNameCompany		—— Organization		0.93	

Figure 3.6 – Detect entities results

> **Note**
>
> Out of the box, Amazon Comprehend's built-in APIs can detect Person, Location, Quantity, Organization, Date, Commercial Item, Quantity, and Title from any text.

2. Let's quickly scroll down to **Application integration** to see what type of request it expects, and what type of response it gives based on this request for the API:

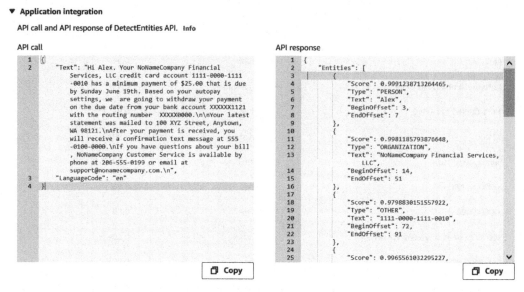

Figure 3.7 – Comprehend Detect Entities request and response

In the last section of this chapter, we will see how to call these APIs using `python boto 3` **SDK**s and integrate them into your applications.

Detecting key phrases

Change the tab to **key phrases** to understand what the key phrases are and what Amazon Comprehend has predicted:

Insights Info

| Entities | Key phrases | Language | PII | Sentiment | Syntax |

Analyzed text

Hi Alex. Your NoNameCompany Financial Services, LLC credit card account 1111-0000-1111-0010 has a minimum payment of $25.00 that is due by Sunday June 19th. Based on your autopay settings, we are going to withdraw your payment on the due date from your bank account XXXXXX1121 with the routing number XXXXX0000.

Your latest statement was mailed to 100 XYZ Street, Anytown, WA 98121.
After your payment is received, you will receive a confirmation text message at 555-0100-0000.
If you have questions about your bill, NoNameCompany Customer Service is available by phone at 206-555-0199 or email at support@nonamecompany.com.

▼ Results

Q Search   ‹ 1 2 3 › ⚙

Key phrases	Confidence
Hi Alex	0.99+
Your NoNameCompany Financial Services	0.99+
LLC credit card account 1111-0000-1111-0010	0.90

Figure 3.8 – Detect key phrases

In English, a key phrase consists of a noun phrase (noun plus modifier) that describes a particular thing. For example, in the text in *Figure 3.8*, "**Hi Alex**", "**Your NoNameCompany Financial Services**", and "**minimum payment**" are some of the key phrases identified by the Amazon Comprehend API. Without reading the text and just looking at these keywords a person can know it is about a finance company and something to do with a payment, which is really useful when you have large amounts of unstructured text.

Language detection

Change the tab to see the dominant language identified by Amazon Comprehend, as shown in *Figure 3.9*:

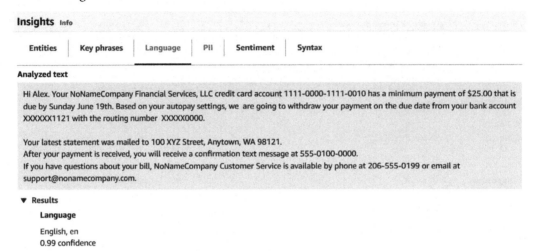

Figure 3.9 – Detect language console demo

Similar to other Comprehend APIs, Amazon Comprehend detects the language of the given text and provides a confidence score along with it. You can use this feature for a book written in multiple different languages, such as both French and Hindi. Using language detection APIs, you can detect the language and classify the percentage of each language the book consists of, and then you can use **Amazon Translate**, which is an AWS service that translates the text from one language to another. We will see this example in future chapters in order to translate it.

PII detection

Change the tab to PII to see what you will get using the Amazon Comprehend out-of-the-box PII detection API as follows:

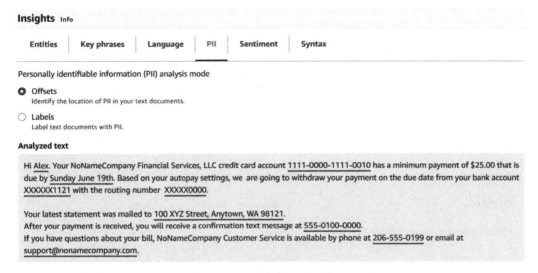

Insights Info

| Entities | Key phrases | Language | PII | Sentiment | Syntax |

Personally identifiable information (PII) analysis mode

● Offsets
Identify the location of PII in your text documents.

○ Labels
Label text documents with PII.

Analyzed text

Hi Alex. Your NoNameCompany Financial Services, LLC credit card account 1111-0000-1111-0010 has a minimum payment of $25.00 that is due by Sunday June 19th. Based on your autopay settings, we are going to withdraw your payment on the due date from your bank account XXXXXX1121 with the routing number XXXXX0000.

Your latest statement was mailed to 100 XYZ Street, Anytown, WA 98121.
After your payment is received, you will receive a confirmation text message at 555-0100-0000.
If you have questions about your bill, NoNameCompany Customer Service is available by phone at 206-555-0199 or email at support@nonamecompany.com.

Figure 3.10 – PII detection demo

As you can see in *Figure 3.10*, Amazon Comprehend provides you with **Offsets** and **Labels** with its real-time or sync PII APIs. If you want to redact the PII data from your text, you can use an asynchronous job. Amazon Comprehend can detect these PII entities: age, address, AWS access key, AWS secret key, bank-related details (such as bank account and bank routing number), credit card details (such as credit card number and expiry date), identification details (such as driving license ID and passport number), network-related details (such as emails, IP address, and MAC address), URLs; passwords; and usernames.

With this understanding of types of PII entities detected by Amazon Comprehend, let's scroll down to see the entities or results of Offsets detected by PII for the text you entered:

▼ **Results**

Q Search		‹ 1 › ⚙
Entity ▽	**Type** ▽	**Confidence** ▽
Alex	Name	0.99+
1111-0000-1111-0010	Credit debit number	0.99+
Sunday June 19th	Date time	0.99+
XXXXXX1121	Bank account number	0.99+
XXXXX0000	Bank routing	0.99+
100 XYZ Street, Anytown, WA 98121	Address	0.99+
555-0100-0000	Phone	0.99+
206-555-0199	Phone	0.99+
support@nonamecompany.com	Email	0.99+

Figure 3.11 – Detect PII results

You also get a confidence score along with the entity and the type of PII entity.

In case you do not want to identify the specific entities and just want to know what type of PII your documents have, you can use the Labels PII feature.

Select the **Labels** button to see this feature in action:

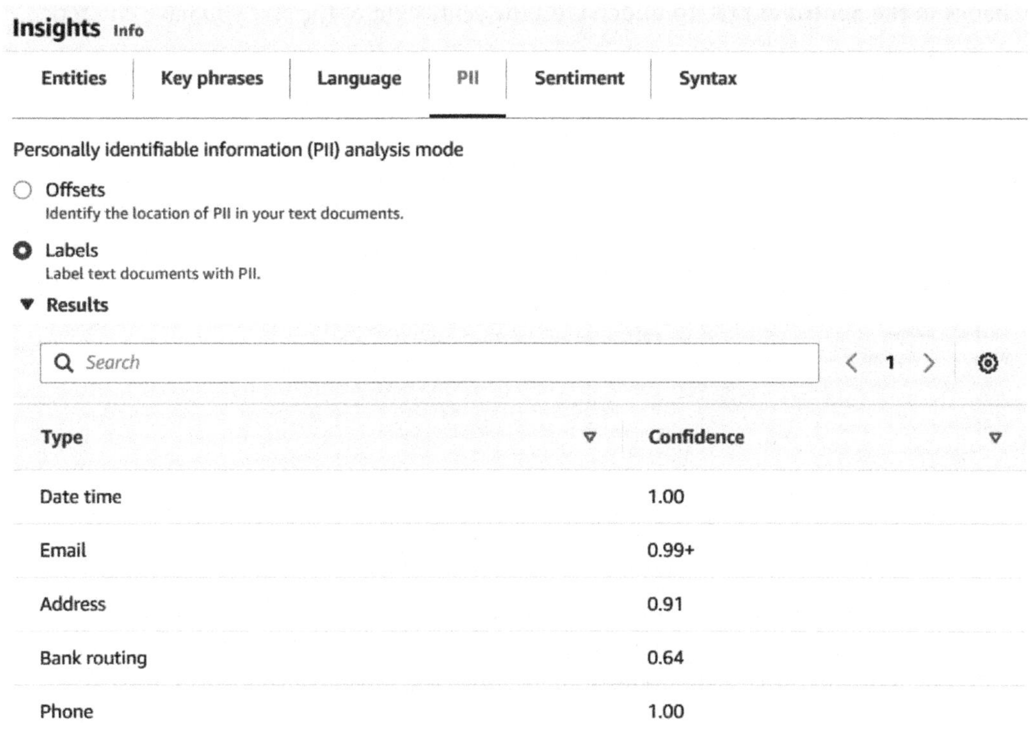

Insights Info

| Entities | Key phrases | Language | PII | Sentiment | Syntax |

Personally identifiable information (PII) analysis mode

○ **Offsets**
Identify the location of PII in your text documents.

● **Labels**
Label text documents with PII.

▼ **Results**

Q Search   ‹ **1** ›   ⚙

Type ▽	Confidence ▽
Date time	1.00
Email	0.99+
Address	0.91
Bank routing	0.64
Phone	1.00

Figure 3.12 – Detect PII Labels result

From the results shown in *Figure 3.12*, you can clearly see that **Date time**, **Email**, **Name**, **Address**, and **Phone** are some of the pieces of PII related to a person in the text you entered.

Detecting sentiment

Change to the **Sentiment** tab to understand the sentiment of the text you have entered:

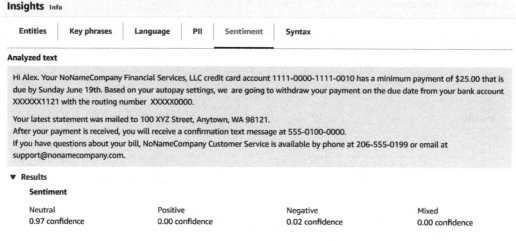

Insights Info

| Entities | Key phrases | Language | PII | Sentiment | Syntax |

Analyzed text

Hi Alex. Your NoNameCompany Financial Services, LLC credit card account 1111-0000-1111-0010 has a minimum payment of $25.00 that is due by Sunday June 19th. Based on your autopay settings, we are going to withdraw your payment on the due date from your bank account XXXXXX1121 with the routing number XXXXX0000.

Your latest statement was mailed to 100 XYZ Street, Anytown, WA 98121.
After your payment is received, you will receive a confirmation text message at 555-0100-0000.
If you have questions about your bill, NoNameCompany Customer Service is available by phone at 206-555-0199 or email at support@nonamecompany.com.

▼ Results

Sentiment

| Neutral | Positive | Negative | Mixed |
| 0.97 confidence | 0.00 confidence | 0.02 confidence | 0.00 confidence |

Figure 3.13 – Detect sentiment results

Since the text was related to an autopay message, a neutral sentiment was detected by Amazon Comprehend's Detect Sentiment real-time API. The Amazon Comprehend sentiment analysis feature helps determine whether the sentiment is positive, negative, neutral, or mixed. You can use this feature for various use cases, such as determining the sentiments of an online book review, Twitter sentiment analysis, or any social media sentiment handles, such as Reddit or Yelp reviews sentiment analysis.

Detecting syntax

Click on the last tab, **Syntax**, to see what type of responses you can get with Amazon Comprehend's Detect Syntax feature:

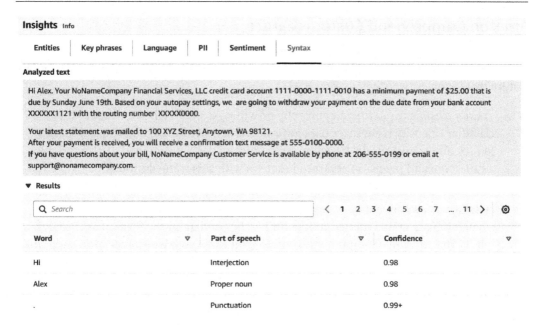

Figure 3.14 – Detect syntax or part of speech results

Amazon Comprehend is able to identify nouns, verbs, and adjectives, and can identify 17 types of parts of speech overall. This feature can be really useful for data preprocessing for NLP models that require PoS tagging.

> **Note**
>
> We covered all the Amazon Comprehend text analysis real-time APIs in detail. You can perform batch real-time operations with all of these APIs we covered and send 25-5,000 bytes (`https://docs.aws.amazon.com/comprehend/latest/dg/guidelines-and-limits.html`) UTF-8 text documents at once to get real-time results. Comprehend custom has now the ability to bring pdf documents directly for analysis and custom training.

Amazon Comprehend Custom feature

With Amazon Comprehend Custom you can bring your own datasets, quickly create custom entities, and perform custom classification. This feature is a batch or asynchronous feature that involves two steps:

1. *Train a classifier or entity recognizer* by providing a small, labeled dataset. This classifier or entity recognizer uses **automated ML (AutoML)** and transfer learning to pick and train a model based on your training dataset provided. It also provides an F1 score and precision and recall metrics with this trained model.

2. *Run batch or real-time analysis on this trained model* after you have trained a custom classifier or custom entity recognizer model. You again have two choices to create a batch job using this trained model for batches of data in the form of an "Analysis job" in the Amazon Comprehend console. You can also create a real-time endpoint that can be used for classifying use cases such as live Twitter feeds, news feed or customer service requests, and so on, using this model in near-real-time.

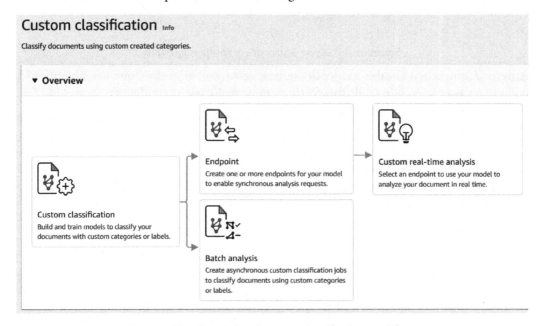

Figure 3.15 – Comprehend custom classification workflow

We will cover Comprehend custom entity features in *Chapter 14, Auditing Named Entity Recognition Workflows*, and Comprehend custom classification features in *Chapter 15, Classifying Documents and Setting up Human in the Loop for Active Learning*.

We will cover topic modeling product features in detail in *Chapter 6, Using NLP to Improve Customer Service Efficiency*.

Amazon Comprehend Events

Amazon Comprehend **Events** has a specific use case for financial organizations, where you can use this API to see the relationships between various entities extracted through Amazon Comprehend in the case of any important financial events such as press releases, mergers, and acquisitions. You can use this Events batch API to detect events over large documents to answer who, what, when, and where the event happened. To learn more about Comprehend Events, refer to this blog: `https://aws.amazon.com/blogs/machine-learning/announcing-the-launch-of-amazon-comprehend-events/`.

Deriving diagnoses from a doctor-patient transcript with Comprehend Medical

Amazon Comprehend Medical provides two types of analysis:

- **Text analysis APIs**: Similar to Amazon Comprehend text analysis APIs, Comprehend Medical has APIs to detect medical entities and detect PHI.

- **Oncology detection APIs**: These APIs help link the entities with either RxNorm or ICD-10-CM linking. According to the **National Institutes of Health** (**NIH**) (`https://www.nlm.nih.gov/research/umls/rxnorm/index.html`), RxNorm provides normalized names for clinical drugs and links its names to many of the drug vocabularies commonly used in pharmacy management and drug interaction software. By providing links between these vocabularies, RxNorm can mediate messages between systems not using the same software and vocabulary. ICD-10-CM (The ICD-10 Clinical Modification) is a modification of the ICD-10, authorized by the World Health Organization, and used as a source for diagnosis codes in the United States of America. To learn more, refer to its Wikipedia entry: `https://en.wikipedia.org/wiki/ICD-10-CM`.

Now, we will quickly cover Amazon Comprehend Medical features through the AWS Console again:

1. Open the AWS Console: `https://console.aws.amazon.com/comprehend/v2/home?region=us-east-1#try-comprehend-medical`.

2. Click on the **Real-time analysis** feature in Amazon Comprehend Medical, and enter the following sample text:

```
Pt is 35 yo woman, IT professional with past medical
history that includes
- status post cardiac catheterization in may 2019.
```

```
She haspalpitations and chest pressure today.

HPI : Sleeping trouble for present dosage of Catapres.
Severe rash on thighs, slightly itchy

Meds : Xanax100 mgs po at lunch daily,

Catapres 0.2 mgs -- 1 and 1 / 2 tabs po qhs

Lungs : clear

Heart : Regular rhythm

Next follow up as scheduled on 06/19/2021
```

3.   Copy this text and paste it into **Input text**, as shown in *Figure 3.16*, and click on
Analyze:

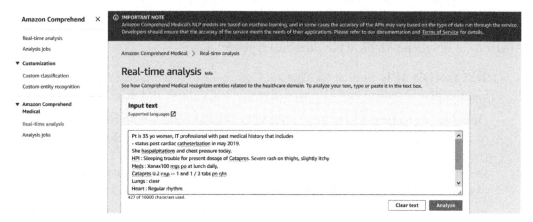

Figure 3.16 – Input text for real-time Amazon Comprehend Medical analysis

> **Note**
> With Comprehend Medical real-time APIs, you can analyze up to 200,000
> characters.

4.   Scroll down to see the result of Comprehend Medical entities real-time APIs:

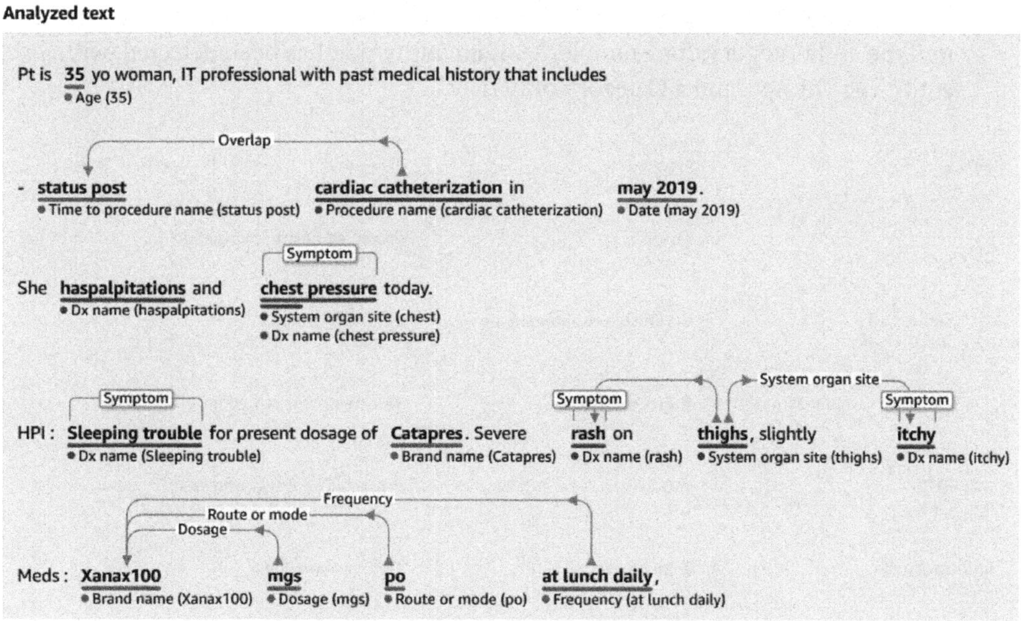

Analyzed text

Figure 3.17 – Comprehend Medical detect entities

You can see that Comprehend Medical also provides relationships within these entities, such as **Catapres** dosage, and the frequency at which the drug should be administered. Amazon Comprehend Medical detects Entity, Type, and Category, such as whether the entity is PHI or treatment or time expression and traits, along with a confidence score.

5. Scroll down further to see detected entities in **Results**. This detects the entity with its Type and Category; for example, 35 is an entity that has been detected, with an entity Type of Age, and a Category of PHI.

Entity	Type	Category	Traits
35 0.9969 score	● Age	Protected health information	-
⊟ status post 0.6577 score	● Time to procedure name	Time expression	-
cardiac catheterization 0.9182 score	● Procedure name	Test treatment procedure	-
may 2019 0.9997 score	● Date	Protected health information	-
haspalpitations 0.4688 score	● Dx name	Medical condition	-
chest 0.9425 score	● System organ site	Anatomy	-
chest pressure 0.5286 score	● Dx name	Medical condition	Symptom 0.5457 score
Sleeping trouble 0.8365 score	● Dx name	Medical condition	Symptom 0.6399 score
Catapres 0.7436 score	● Brand name	Medication	-
⊟ rash 0.9967 score	● Dx name	Medical condition	Symptom 0.7731 score
thighs 0.9688 score	● System organ site	Anatomy	-

Figure 3.18 – Comprehend Medical detect entities results

RxNorm concepts

Use this feature to identify medication as entities:

1. Switch tabs to **RxNorm**. You'll see a screen like the following screenshot:

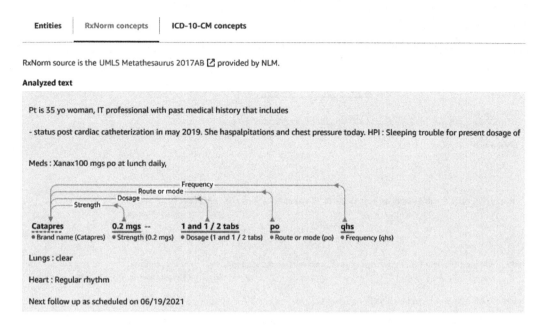

| Entities | RxNorm concepts | ICD-10-CM concepts |

RxNorm source is the UMLS Metathesaurus 2017AB ⧉ provided by NLM.

Analyzed text

Pt is 35 yo woman, IT professional with past medical history that includes

- status post cardiac catheterization in may 2019. She haspalpitations and chest pressure today. HPI : Sleeping trouble for present dosage of

Meds : Xanax100 mgs po at lunch daily,

Catapres   0.2 mgs --   1 and 1 / 2 tabs   po   qhs
● Brand name (Catapres)   ● Strength (0.2 mgs)   ● Dosage (1 and 1 / 2 tabs)   ● Route or mode (po)   ● Frequency (qhs)

Lungs : clear

Heart : Regular rhythm

Next follow up as scheduled on 06/19/2021

Figure 3.19 – Comprehend Medical InferRxNorm results

If you scroll down to **Results**, Comprehend Medical shows the **RXCUI**s for each medication, along with a confidence score. An RXCUI is a machine-readable code that refers to a unique name for a particular drug, and drugs having the same RXCUI are considered to be the same drug. This Comprehend Medical feature provides RxNorm information such as strength, frequency, dose, dose form, and route of administration. You can use this RxNorm feature for scenarios such as the following:

- Patient screening for medications.

- Preventing probable negative reactions, which can be caused by new prescription drugs interacting with drugs the patient is already taking.

- Screening based on drug history, using the RXCUI for inclusion in clinical trials.

- Checking for appropriate frequency and dosage of a drug and drug screening.

ICD-10-CM concepts

Let's change the tab to **ICD-10-CM concepts** and you will get the following analysis:

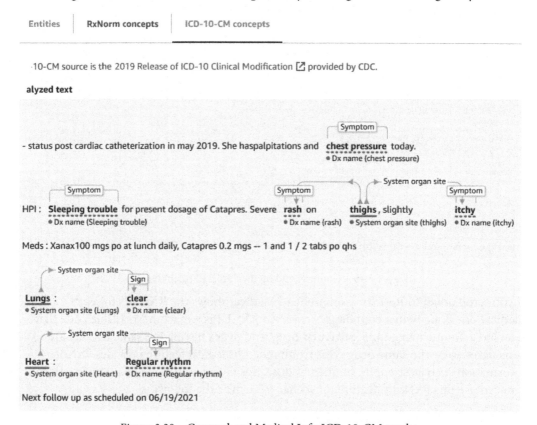

Figure 3.20 – Comprehend Medical InferICD-10-CM results

The **InferICD10CM** API detects possible medical conditions as entities and links them to codes from the ICD-10-CM, along with a confidence score. In healthcare, these codes are standard medical transaction codes, set for diagnostic purposes to comply with the **Health Insurance Portability and Accountability Act (HIPAA)**, and used for classifying and reporting diseases. You can use these ICD-10-CM codes for downstream analysis as the signs, symptoms, traits, and attributes.

InferICD10CM is well-suited to scenarios such as professional medical coding assistance for patient records, clinical trials and studies, integration with an existing medical software system, early detection and diagnosis, and population health management.

In the next section, we will see these APIs in action by performing a walkthrough of a Jupyter notebook.

Using Amazon Comprehend with your applications

In this section, you will see a detailed walkthrough of broad categories of APIs available for Amazon Comprehend and Comprehend Medical through a Jupyter notebook example, which you can run in your AWS account. To set up the notebook, refer to the *Technical requirements* section of this chapter.

We will be showing you a subset of key APIs in Comprehend along with their functions, and then will talk about how you can build applications integrating with AWS Lambda, **API Gateway**, and Comprehend.

> **Note**
>
> We will cover Amazon Comprehend Medical APIs in *Chapter 12, AI and NLP in Healthcare.*

Let's start with the Amazon Comprehend APIs first. Amazon Comprehend provides three types of API.

- **Real-time APIs**: For all the text analysis features we covered and Comprehend Custom model endpoints.

- **Batch real-time APIs**: For all the text analysis features.

- **Batch or analysis job APIs**: For all text analysis features, topic modeling features, and Comprehend Custom model training.

In the notebook `https://github.com/PacktPublishing/Natural-Language-Processing-with-AWS-AI-Services/blob/main/Chapter%2003/Chapter%203%20Introduction%20to%20Amazon%20Comprehend.ipynb`, we will cover real-time APIs and batch real-time APIs.

> **Note**
>
> You can implement the same features in other supported APIs such as Java, Ruby, .NET, AWS CLI, Go, C++, JavaScript, and PHP. For more information on Comprehend APIs, refer to the Amazon documentation: `https://docs.aws.amazon.com/comprehend/latest/dg/API_Reference.html`.

2. Let's start with setting up the Python `boto3` APIs for Amazon Comprehend:

    ```
    import boto3
    comprehend = boto3.client('comprehend')
    ```

3. Let's see how we can perform entity extraction using sync or real-time APIs of `detect_entities`. I am sure you have been reading a lot of Packt books; let's see the following sample text about Packt Publications and what entities we can find from this:

    ```
    SampleText="Packt is a publishing company founded in 2003
    headquartered in Birmingham, UK, with offices in Mumbai,
    India. Packt primarily publishes print and electronic
    books and videos relating to information technology,
    including programming, web design, data analysis and
    hardware."
    ```

4. We will call the `detect_entities` API (`comprehend.detect_entities`) to extract entities from the sample text:

    ```
    response = comprehend.detect_entities(
    Text=SampleText,
        LanguageCode='en')
    ```

5. The following is the response for extracted entities from the blurb about Packt Publications:

    ```
    import json
    print (json.dumps(response, indent=4, sort_keys=True))
    ```

    This gives us the following output:

```json
{
    "Entities": [
        {
            "BeginOffset": 0,
            "EndOffset": 5,
            "Score": 0.995110809803009,
            "Text": "Packt",
            "Type": "ORGANIZATION"
        },
        {
            "BeginOffset": 41,
            "EndOffset": 45,
            "Score": 0.9951934218406677,
            "Text": "2003",
            "Type": "DATE"
        },
        {
            "BeginOffset": 63,
            "EndOffset": 77,
            "Score": 0.9813098311424255,
            "Text": "Birmingham, UK",
            "Type": "LOCATION"
        },
        {
            "BeginOffset": 95,
            "EndOffset": 108,
            "Score": 0.9864111542701721,
            "Text": "Mumbai, India",
            "Type": "LOCATION"
        },
        {
            "BeginOffset": 110,
            "EndOffset": 115,
            "Score": 0.9877771139144897,
            "Text": "Packt",
            "Type": "ORGANIZATION"
        }
    }
```

Figure 3.21 – JSON results screenshot

Comprehend was able to successfully detect entities along with their type, and give a response that Packt Publications is an organization located in Birmingham, UK, and Mumbai, India.

6. Now we know what Packt Publications is, let's identify some key phrases about this organization using the `detect_key_phrases` API, but when the text is in French.

> **Note**
>
> Amazon Comprehend supports analysis in multiple languages using these APIs. The supported languages are French, Japanese, Korean, Hindi, Arabic, and Chinese.

Here is a sample text about Packt Publications (`https://en.wikipedia.org/wiki/Packt`), translated into French using **Amazon Translate**:

```
SampleText="Packt est une société d'édition fondée
en 2003 dont le siège est à Birmingham, au Royaume-
Uni, avec des bureaux à Mumbai, en Inde. Packt publie
principalement des livres et des vidéos imprimés et
électroniques relatifs aux technologies de l'information,
y compris la programmation, la conception Web, l'analyse
de données et le matériel"
```

7. We are going to use the `detect_key_phrases` API with `fr` as a parameter to `LanguageCode` to detect key phrases from the preceding French text:

```
response = comprehend.detect_key_phrases(
    Text= SampleText,
    LanguageCode='fr'
)
```

8. Let's see the response from Amazon Comprehend:

```
print (json.dumps(response, indent=4, sort_keys=True))
```

This returns the following:

```json
{
    "KeyPhrases": [
        {
            "BeginOffset": 0,
            "EndOffset": 5,
            "Score": 1.0,
            "Text": "Packt"
        },
        {
            "BeginOffset": 10,
            "EndOffset": 31,
            "Score": 0.9999998211860657,
            "Text": "une soci\u00e9t\u00e9 d'\u00e9dition"
        },
        {
            "BeginOffset": 42,
            "EndOffset": 46,
            "Score": 0.9999995231628418,
            "Text": "2003"
        },
        {
            "BeginOffset": 47,
            "EndOffset": 60,
            "Score": 0.9999982714653015,
            "Text": "dont le si\u00e8ge"
        },
        {
            "BeginOffset": 67,
            "EndOffset": 93,
            "Score": 0.9880826473236084,
            "Text": "Birmingham, au Royaume-Uni"
        },
        {
            "BeginOffset": 100,
            "EndOffset": 121,
            "Score": 0.8736910223960876,
            "Text": "des bureaux \u00e0 Mumbai,"
        },
        {
            "BeginOffset": 125,
            "EndOffset": 129,
            "Score": 0.9220616221427917,
            "Text": "Inde"
        },
```

Figure 3.22 – Comprehend Detect Key Phrase response

Amazon Comprehend is able to identify key phrases along with the location of the text.

Now, what if you wanted to buy a book from Packt Publications, you might want to read the reviews and determine whether they are positive or not.

Using the `batch_detect_sentiment` API, we will show you how you can analyze multiple reviews at once. For this demo, we will pick some sample reviews from the book *40 Algorithms Every Programmer Should Know* (`https://www.packtpub.com/product/40-algorithms-every-programmer-should-know/9781789801217`):

1. We are going to analyze some of the reviews of this book using `batch_detect_sentiment`:

```
response = comprehend.batch_detect_sentiment(
    TextList=[
        'Well this is an area of my interest and this
book is packed with essential knowledge','kinda all
in one With good examples and rather easy to follow',
'There are good examples and samples in the book.', '40
Algorithms every Programmer should know is a good start
to a vast topic about algorithms'
    ],
    LanguageCode='en'
)
```

2. Now, let's see the response for this by running the following code:

```
print (json.dumps(response, indent=4, sort_keys=True))
```

This produces the following output:

```
        },
        "ResultList": [
            {
                "Index": 0,
                "Sentiment": "POSITIVE",
                "SentimentScore": {
                    "Mixed": 0.004781718365848064,
                    "Negative": 0.00489041255787015,
                    "Neutral": 0.028603093698620796,
                    "Positive": 0.9617248177528381
                }
            },
            {
                "Index": 1,
                "Sentiment": "POSITIVE",
                "SentimentScore": {
                    "Mixed": 0.043538015335798264,
                    "Negative": 0.0020733894780278206,
                    "Neutral": 0.005934751592576504,
                    "Positive": 0.9484539031982422
                }
            },
            {
                "Index": 2,
                "Sentiment": "POSITIVE",
                "SentimentScore": {
                    "Mixed": 0.006463758181780577,
                    "Negative": 0.001142512890510261,
                    "Neutral": 0.00479789637029171,
                    "Positive": 0.9875959157943726
                }
            },
            {
                "Index": 3,
                "Sentiment": "NEUTRAL",
                "SentimentScore": {
                    "Mixed": 0.00010260937415296212,
                    "Negative": 0.004924369975924492,
                    "Neutral": 0.6275114417076111,
                    "Positive": 0.36746159195899963
                }
            }
        ]
    }
```

Figure 3.23 – Comprehend Sentiment Analysis response

Out of these four reviews analyzed, we can definitely see that, overall, it's a positive review for this book. Now, while reading the reviews, there were some reviews in different languages which, being an English reader, I did not understand. Unfortunately, I don't know which languages these reviews use, and therefore what to choose for translation.

3. Let's use the batch_detect_dominant_language API of Comprehend to identify what languages these reviews are in before we translate them:

```
response = comprehend.batch_detect_dominant_language(
    TextList=[
```

```
            'It include recenet algorithm trend. it is very
helpful.','Je ne lai pas encore lu entièrement mais
le livre semble expliquer de façon suffisamment claire
lensemble de ces algorithmes.'
    ]
)
```

4. Now, let's see the response from Comprehend to figure out the review languages:

```
print (json.dumps(response, indent=4, sort_keys=True))
```

This gives us the following output:

```
{
    "ErrorList": [],
    "ResponseMetadata": {
        "HTTPHeaders": {
            "content-length": "179",
            "content-type": "application/x-amz-json-1.1",
            "date": "Tue, 13 Apr 2021 16:03:59 GMT",
            "x-amzn-requestid": "88d1ffc8-13c3-4cde-9c2b-ba47aba8d360"
        },
        "HTTPStatusCode": 200,
        "RequestId": "88d1ffc8-13c3-4cde-9c2b-ba47aba8d360",
        "RetryAttempts": 0
    },
    "ResultList": [
        {
            "Index": 0,
            "Languages": [
                {
                    "LanguageCode": "en",
                    "Score": 0.9827539324760437
                }
            ]
        },
        {
            "Index": 1,
            "Languages": [
                {
                    "LanguageCode": "fr",
                    "Score": 0.99605792760849
                }
            ]
        }
    ]
}
```

Figure 3.24 – Comprehend Detect Language response

It's interesting to find out that out of the two reviews sent to this batch detect the dominant language, one is in English, and one is in French.

We have now covered some of the key APIs, such as `detect_entities`, `detect_key_phrases`, `batch_detect_sentiment`, and `batch_detect_dominant_languages`.

Now, we will see how we can use these APIs in building an application.

Architecting applications with Amazon API Gateway, AWS Lambda, and Comprehend

In a previous section, we covered Amazon Comprehend's text analysis API. You can easily call these APIs in a serverless manner using a Lambda function. Amazon Lambda is a serverless event-based trigger that can be integrated with Amazon API Gateway and triggered for **GET** and **POST** requests. Amazon API gateway is a serverless **REST**-based service, which allows you to build GET/POST APIs to easily integrate with any application, be it mobile or web app.

You can create an API to be embedded in your application where you send a text to be analyzed using API Gateway; then the API Gateway calls the Amazon Lambda function, based on the type of request it receives. Amazon Lambda can further call Amazon Comprehend APIs (real-time or batch detect real-time APIs). It then passes the Comprehend response to API Gateway, as shown in the architecture diagram in *Figure 3.25*:

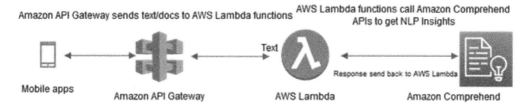

Figure 3.25 – Building real-time application with Amazon Comprehend

Summary

In this chapter, we covered why you would need to use Amazon Comprehend and Amazon Comprehend Medical. We also discussed the challenges associated with setting NLP pipelines.

Then, we introduced these services, and covered some key benefits they provide, for example, not needing ML skills, or easily using the APIs to build scalable NLP solutions. After that, we showed some key product features of Amazon Comprehend and Amazon Comprehend Medical through a Console demo. Some of Amazon Comprehend's features are identifying entities, key phrases, and sentiment, as well as detecting dominant language, topic modeling, and so on. For Amazon Comprehend Medical, we covered how you can use both text analysis APIs and oncology APIs to enrich and extract key information from medical notes. Then we gave you a quick walkthrough of these APIs using a Jupyter notebook and covered sync and batch sync APIs. We gained a basic theoretical understanding of creating a serverless application using these APIs.

In the next chapter, we will talk about how you can integrate Amazon Textract with Amazon Comprehend for automating financial documents.

Section 2: Using NLP to Accelerate Business Outcomes

In this section, we dive deep into the several types of use cases prevalent across industries that can benefit from NLP based on our collective experience and the usage trends we have observed. We will provide detailed code samples, design and development approaches, and a step-by-step guide on how to set up and run these examples, along with access to a GitHub repository. We will also dive deep into the use case of how AWS NLP solutions can help achieve operational efficiency in healthcare with an automated claims adjunction use case.

This section comprises the following chapters:

4
Automating Document Processing Workflows

In the previous chapter, we were introduced to **Amazon Comprehend** and **Amazon Comprehend Medical**, and we covered how to use these services to derive insights from text. We also spent some time understanding how Natural Language Processing algorithms work, the different types of insights you can uncover, and we also ran code samples trying out the Amazon Comprehend APIs.

In this chapter, we will walk through our first real-world use case of automating a document management workflow that many organizations struggle with today. We put together this solution based on our collective experience and the usage trends we have observed in our careers. Fasten your seat belts and get ready to experience architecting an end-to-end AI solution one building block at a time and watch it taking shape in front of you. We expect to be hands-on throughout the course of this chapter, but we have all the code samples we need to get going.

We will dive deep into how you can automate document processing with **Amazon Textract** and then we will cover how you can set up compliance and control in the documents using **Amazon Comprehend**. Lastly, we will talk about architecture best practices while designing **real-time document processing** workflows versus **batch processing.** We will provide detailed code samples, designs, and development approaches, and a step-by-step guide on how to set up and run these examples along with access to GitHub repositories.

In this chapter, we will cover the following topics:

- Automating document processing workflows
- Setting up compliance and control
- Processing real-time document workflows versus batch document workflows

Technical requirements

For this chapter, you will need access to an AWS account. Please make sure to follow the instructions specified in the *Technical requirements* section in *Chapter 2, Introducing Amazon Textract*, to create your AWS account, and log in to the AWS Management Console before trying the steps in this chapter.

The Python code and sample datasets for a walk-through of this chapter's code are provided at the following link: `https://github.com/PacktPublishing/ Natural-Language-Processing-with-AWS-AI-Services/tree/main/ Chapter%2004`. Please use the instructions in the following sections along with the code in the repository to build the solution.

Check out the following video to see the Code in Action at `https://bit. ly/3GlcCet`.

Automating document processing workflows

We have discussed in the previous chapter how Amazon Textract can help us digitize scanned documents such as PDF and images by extracting text from any document. We also covered how Amazon Comprehend can help us extract insights from these documents, including entities, **Personal Identifiable Information** (**PII**), and sentiments.

Now, these services can be used together in an architecture to automate the document processing workflows for most organizations, be it a financial organization or healthcare, which we will cover in *Chapter 12, AI and NLP in Healthcare*.

Let's start with a fictitious bank, *LiveRight Pvt Ltd.*, whose customers are applying for home loans. We all know this loan origination process involves more than 400 documents to be submitted and reviewed by the bank before approval is forthcoming for your home loan. Automating this process will make it easier for banks as well as customers to get loans. The challenge with automating these workflows is that there are more than 1,000 templates for the loan origination process and going with any **Optical Character Recognition (OCR)** system will require managing these templates. Moreover, these OCR template-based approaches are not scalable and break with format changes. That's why we have Amazon Textract to extract text from any documents, enabling these documents to be automated and processed in hours rather than months or weeks.

You have extracted the data from these forms or semi-structured documents. You will now want to set up compliance and control on the data extracted from these documents; for example, making sure that if the data is PII, you can mask it for further processing. You will also want to extract the entities if you want to focus on the loan approval process, for example, the loan amount or the details of the requester. This is where Amazon Comprehend can help. In fact, you can perform custom classification of the documents submitted and the custom entities based on your requirements with Amazon Comprehend; for example, documents extracted by Textract and sent to Amazon Comprehend for custom classification to classify whether the document submitted is a driving license or W2 form.

The following is the architecture of how you can use Amazon Textract and Amazon Comprehend together to automate your existing document flow:

Figure 4.1 – Automating document processing workflows

In this architecture, you have documents coming in, and these documents may be financial documents, legal documents, mortgage applications, and so on. You send these documents to Amazon Textract to extract text from these documents. Once you have extracted text from these documents, you can send this text to Amazon Comprehend to extract insights. These insights can classify these documents based on document type, it can identify PII from these documents, or it can be **named entity recognition (NER)** using custom entity recognition. We cover custom entities in *Chapter 14, Auditing Named Entity Recognition Workflows*, and document classification in *Chapter 15, Classifying Documents and Setting up Human in the Loop for Active Learning*.

In this section, we covered how you can easily and quickly set up an automated document processing workflow with Amazon Textract and Amazon Comprehend by using these services together. In the next section, we will talk about how you can use these services together to set up compliance and control for LiveRight Pvt Ltd., especially by means of masking or redacting the PII data in their forms.

Setting up compliance and control

In this section, we will talk about how LiveRight Pvt Ltd. can set up compliance and control as well as automate their loan origination process using Amazon Textract and Amazon Comprehend. We will walk you through the following architecture using code samples in a Jupyter notebook:

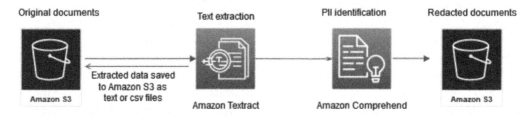

Figure 4.2 – Setting up compliance and control

We will walk you through this architecture using a single document and sample code. However, this architecture can be automated to process a large number of documents using the **step function** and **lambda functions** in a serverless manner. In this architecture, we will show you the following:

1. How you can upload a sample document and extract the text using **Amazon Textract** and save the extracted data as .txt or .csv files back to an **Amazon S3 bucket**.

2. Then, we will show you how you can use **Amazon Comprehend's** real-time or sync API to detect PII.

3. We will then cover how you can use the Amazon Comprehend PII detection job to mask and redact the PII in the extracted text/CSV file in **Amazon S3**.

4. How you can find the redacted document text in Amazon S3 as an output of the Comprehend PII detection job.

So, let's get started with setting up the notebook.

Setting up to solve the use case

already done.

If you have not done so in the previous chapters, you will first have to create an Amazon SageMaker Jupyter notebook and set up **Identity and Access Management (IAM)** permissions for that notebook role to access the AWS services we will use in this notebook. After that, you will need to clone the GitHub repository (https://github.com/PacktPublishing/Natural-Language-Processing-with-AWS-AI-Services). Please perform the following steps to complete these tasks before we can execute the cells from our notebook:

1. Follow the instructions documented in the *Create an Amazon SageMaker Jupyter notebook instance* section within the *Setting up your AWS environment* section in *Chapter 2, Introducing Amazon Textract*, to create your Jupyter notebook instance.

> **IAM Role Permission while Creating Amazon SageMaker Jupyter Notebooks**
>
> Accept the default option for the IAM role at notebook creation time to allow access to any S3 bucket.

2. Once you have created the notebook instance and its status is **InService**, click on **Open Jupyter** in the **Actions** menu heading for the notebook instance.

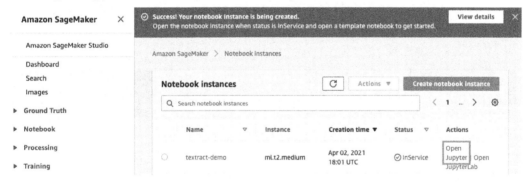

Figure 4.3 – Opening the Jupyter notebook

This will take you to the home folder of your notebook instance.

3. Click on **New** and then select **Terminal**, as shown in the following screenshot:

Figure 4.4 – Opening Terminal in a Jupyter notebook

4. In the terminal window, first, type cd SageMaker and then type git clone
    https://github.com/PacktPublishing/Natural-Language-
    Processing-with-AWS-AI-Services, as shown in the following screenshot:

Figure 4.5 – git clone command

5. Now, exit the terminal window, go back to the home folder, and you will see a
    folder called Chapter 04. Click the folder and you should see a notebook called
    Chapter 4 Compliance and control.ipynb.

6. Open this notebook by clicking it.

Next, we will cover the additional IAM prerequisites.

Additional IAM prerequisites

To train the Comprehend custom entity recognizer and to set up real-time endpoints, we have to enable additional policies and update the trust relationships for our SageMaker notebook role. To do this, attach `AmazonS3FullAccess`, `TextractFullAccess`, and `ComprehendFullAccess` policies to your Amazon SageMaker Notebook IAM Role. To execute this step, please refer to *Changing IAM permissions and trust relationships for the Amazon SageMaker notebook execution role* in the *Setting up your AWS environment* section in *Chapter 2, Introducing Amazon Textract.*

Now that we have the necessary IAM roles and notebook set up in the Amazon SageMaker notebook instance, let's jump to the code walk-through.

Automating documents for control and compliance

In this section, we will give a code walk-through of the architecture we discussed for automating documents using Amazon Textract and setting compliance and control with PII masking using Amazon Comprehend in *Figure 14.2* using this notebook:

1. Execute the cell under *Step 1 – Setup and install libraries* in the Jupyter notebook you just set up at the following link, `https://github.com/ PacktPublishing/Natural-Language-Processing-with- AWS-AI-Services/blob/main/Chapter%2004/Chapter%204%20 Compliance%20and%20control.ipynb`, to ensure that you have the libraries needed for the notebook. Note that in this cell, you are getting the Amazon SageMaker execution role for the notebook along with the SageMaker session. You are setting up boto3 libraries to call Amazon Textract, Amazon Comprehend, and Amazon S3 APIs. You are also using the SageMaker session to access the default SageMaker S3 bucket where you will be storing the data for this lab using a prefix or folder.

2. Now, we will start with the sample bank statement. Execute the cells under *Step 2, Extracting text from a sample document* in the Jupyter notebook, to display the sample document to extract text and redact the PII:

```
documentName = "bankstatement.png"
display(Image(filename=documentName))
```

You will get the following response:

Statement Ending 09/21/2018

Page 1 of 4

RETURN SERVICE REQUESTED

John Doe
123 Main Street
Baltimore, MD 21224

Managing Your Accounts

🏛	Primary Branch	Canton
👤	Phone Number	443-573-4800
📱	Online Banking	HowardBank.com
☎	Telephone Banking	1-877-527-2703
✉	Mailing Address	3301 Boston Street Baltimore, MD 21224

Summary of Accounts

Account Type	Account Number	Ending Balance
HOWARD RELATIONSHIP CHECKING	XXXXXXXX4101	$5,684.22

HOWARD RELATIONSHIP CHECKING-XXXXXXXX4101

Primary Checking

Account Summary

Date	Description	Amount
09/01/2018	Beginning Balance	$18,805.47
	3 Credit(s) This Period	$4,293.20
	20 Debit(s) This Period	$17,414.45
09/21/2018	Ending Balance	$5,684.22

Account Activity

Post Date	Description	Debits	Credits	Balance
09/01/2018	Beginning Balance			$18,805.47
09/04/2018	Signature POS Debit 09/02 MD BALTIMORE GIANT FOOD INC SEQ# 071582	$57.48		$18,747.99
09/04/2018	Nationstar dba Mr Cooper XXXXXX6179	$1,989.60		$16,758.39
09/05/2018	HMS WARRANTY 80 0247 3680 5829389	$42.99		$16,715.40
09/05/2018	SAMS CLUB MC ONLINE PMT CKF426104254POS	$4,671.42		$12,043.98
09/05/2018	DISCOVER BANK ETRANSFER	$8,212.00		$3,831.98
09/06/2018	BLTMORE GAS ELEC ONLINE PMT	$160.75		$3,671.23
09/06/2018	AMAZON	$170.00		$3,501.23
09/06/2018	DEVONSHIRE II CO CONS CP BC5198	$195.00		$3,306.23
09/07/2018	DEPOSIT		$653.25	$3,959.48
09/07/2018	TARGET ONLINE PMT	$88.59		$3,870.89
09/10/2018	ATM Withdrawal 09/07 MD BALTIMORE 10101 PHILDELPHIA RD SEQ# 008838	$180.00		$3,690.89
09/10/2018	Signature POS Debit 09/08 MD BALTIMORE GIANT FOOD I	$70.11		$3,620.78
09/10/2018	L A FITNESS	$12.98		$3,607.80
09/11/2018	AT&T MOBILITY ONLINE PMT	$116.22		$3,491.58
09/14/2018	DEPOSIT		$606.62	$4,098.20
09/14/2018	DIRECT DEP		$3,033.33	$7,131.53
09/14/2018	Signature POS Debit 09/13 MD BALTIMORE GIANT	$19.86		$7,111.67
09/17/2018	ATM Withdrawal 09/15 WV INWOOD MARTINSBURG-INWOOD	$400.00		$6,711.67
09/17/2018	Signature POS Debit 09/16 MD BALTIMORE GIANT	$14.06		$6,697.61

Member **FDIC**

Figure 4.6 – Sample bank statement

3. Now we will invoke Amazon Textract's Detect Document Text Sync API, https://boto3.amazonaws.com/v1/documentation/api/latest/reference/services/textract.html#Textract.Client.detect_document_text, which extracts only text from documents in near-real time to extract data from the sample bank statement using the following code:

```
client = boto3.client(service_name='textract',
            region_name= 'us-east-1',
            endpoint_url='https://textract.us-east-1.
amazonaws.com')
with open(documentName, 'rb') as file:
        img_test = file.read()
        bytes_test = bytearray(img_test)
        print('Image loaded', documentName)
response = client.detect_document_text(Document={'Bytes':
bytes_test})
print(response)
```

    You get a JSON response from Amazon Textract using the Detect Document Text Sync API.

4. Now we will extract text from this JSON response using the Amazon Textract parser library we installed in *Step 1*. Run the following code to parse the Textract JSON response to text:

```
doc = Document(response)
page_string = ''
for page in doc.pages:
        for line in page.lines:
                page_string += str(line.text)
print(page_string)
```

    Now that we have the extracted text from the Textract JSON response, let's move on to the next step.

5. In this step, we will save the extracted text from the bank statement to a text/CSV file and upload it to Amazon S3 for processing with the Amazon Comprehend batch job. Run the notebook cell *Step 3, Save the extracted text to a text/CSV file and upload it to an Amazon S3 bucket*, to save the data in a text file and then upload it to Amazon S3.

6. Now that we have extracted the text from bank statements, converted it into a text file, and uploaded it to Amazon S3, in this step, we will detect PII from the text using Amazon Comprehend Detect PII Sync APIs. Run the notebook cell *Step 4, Check for PII using the Amazon Comprehend Detect PII Sync API*, to call the Comprehend APIs by passing the extracted text from Amazon Textract:

a) First, initialize the boto3 handle for Amazon Comprehend:

```
`comprehend = boto3.client('comprehend')
```

b) Then, call Amazon Comprehend and pass it the aggregated text from our sample bank statement image to Comprehend detect PII entities: https://boto3. amazonaws.com/v1/documentation/api/latest/reference/ services/comprehend.html#Comprehend.Client.detect_pii_ entities:

```
piilist=comprehend.detect_pii_entities(Text = page_
string, LanguageCode='en')
redacted_box_color='red'
dpi = 72
pii_detection_threshold = 0.00
print ('Finding PII text...')
not_redacted=0
redacted=0
for pii in piilist['Entities']:
    print(pii['Type'])
    if pii['Score'] > pii_detection_threshold:
                print ("detected as type
'"+pii['Type']+"' and will be redacted.")
                redacted+=1

    else:
        print (" was detected as type '"+pii['Type']+"',
but did not meet the confidence score threshold and will
not be redacted.")
        not_redacted+=1
print ("Found", redacted, "text boxes to redact.")
print (not_redacted, "additional text boxes were
detected, but did not meet the confidence score
threshold.")s3_entity_key = prefix + "/train/entitylist.
csv"
```

You will get a response with identifying PII from the text, which will be redacted in the next step using the Amazon Comprehend PII analysis job.

```
Finding PII text...
DATE_TIME
detected as type 'DATE_TIME' and will be redacted.
NAME
detected as type 'NAME' and will be redacted.
PHONE
detected as type 'PHONE' and will be redacted.
ADDRESS
detected as type 'ADDRESS' and will be redacted.
PHONE
detected as type 'PHONE' and will be redacted.
ADDRESS
detected as type 'ADDRESS' and will be redacted.
DATE_TIME
detected as type 'DATE_TIME' and will be redacted.
DATE_TIME
detected as type 'DATE_TIME' and will be redacted.
DATE_TIME
detected as type 'DATE_TIME' and will be redacted.
DATE_TIME
detected as type 'DATE_TIME' and will be redacted.
DATE_TIME
detected as type 'DATE TIME' and will be redacted.
```

Figure 4.7 – PII detection using Amazon Comprehend in a bank statement

We will mask/redact these 15 PII entities we found in the sample bank statement.

7. Next, we will call the `StartPiiEntitiesDetectionJob` API to start an asynchronous PII entity detection job for a collection of documents. For this example, we are just using one document sample. You can redact a large number of documents using this job. Run the notebook cell *Step 5, Mask PII using the Amazon Comprehend PII Analysis Job*, to set up and start the PII redaction analysis job with Amazon Comprehend:

    a) Then job requires the S3 location of documents to be redacted and the S3 location of where you want the redacted output. Run the following cell to specify the location of the S3 text file we want to be redacted:

```
import uuid
InputS3URI= "s3://"+bucket+ "/pii-detection-redaction/
pii_data.txt"
print(InputS3URI)
OutputS3URI="s3://"+bucket+"/pii-detection-redaction"
print(OutputS3URI)
```

b) Now we will call `comprehend.start_pii_entities_detection_job` by setting parameters for redaction and passing the input S3 location where data is stored by running the following notebook cell:

```
response = comprehend.start_pii_entities_detection_job(
    InputDataConfig={
        'S3Uri': InputS3URI,
        'InputFormat': 'ONE_DOC_PER_FILE'
    },
    OutputDataConfig={
        'S3Uri': OutputS3URI

    },
    Mode='ONLY_REDACTION',
    RedactionConfig={
        'PiiEntityTypes': [
            'ALL',
        ],
        'MaskMode': 'MASK',
        'MaskCharacter': '*'
    },
    DataAccessRoleArn = role,
    JobName=job_name,
    LanguageCode='en',
)
```

> **Note**
> Using this API or batch job, you have the choice to specify the mode, redaction config, and language.

Here are the parameters that can be modified as shown in the following code block:

```
Mode='ONLY_REDACTION'|'ONLY_OFFSETS',
    RedactionConfig={
        'PiiEntityTypes': [
            'BANK_ACCOUNT_NUMBER'|'BANK_
ROUTING'|'CREDIT_DEBIT_NUMBER'|'CREDIT_DEBIT_CVV'|
'CREDIT_DEBIT_EXPIRY'|'PIN'|'EMAIL'|'ADDRESS'|'NAME'|
'PHONE'|'SSN'|'DATE_TIME'|'PASSPORT_NUMBER'|'DRIVER_
```

```
ID'|'URL'|'AGE'|'USERNAME'|'PASSWORD'|'AWS_ACCESS_KEY'
|'AWS_SECRET_KEY'|'IP_ADDRESS'|'MAC_ADDRESS'|'ALL',
        ],
        'MaskMode': 'MASK'|'REPLACE_WITH_PII_ENTITY_
TYPE',
        'MaskCharacter': 'string'
```

Refer to the API documentation for more details: https://docs.aws.amazon.com/comprehend/latest/dg/API_StartPiiEntitiesDetectionJob.html.

c) The job will take roughly 6-7 minutes. The following code is to check the status of the job. The cell execution will be completed once the job is complete:

```
from time import sleep
job = comprehend.describe_pii_entities_detection_
job(JobId=events_job_id)
print(job)
waited = 0
timeout_minutes = 10
while job['PiiEntitiesDetectionJobProperties']
['JobStatus'] != 'COMPLETED':
    sleep(60)
    waited += 60
    assert waited//60 < timeout_minutes, "Job timed out
after %d seconds." % waited
    job = comprehend.describe_pii_entities_detection_
job(JobId=events_job_id)
```

You will get a JSON response, and this job will take 5-6 minutes. You can go and grab a coffee until the notebook cell is running and you have a response.

8. Once the job is successful, we will now show you the extracted, redacted document output in this step. Run the notebook cell *Step 6*, *View the redacted/masked output in the Amazon S3 bucket*, to extract the output from the Amazon S3 bucket:

```
filename="pii_data.txt"
s3_client = boto3.client(service_name='s3')
output_data_s3_file =
job['PiiEntitiesDetectionJobProperties']
['OutputDataConfig']['S3Uri'] + filename + '.out'
print(output_data_s3_file)
```

```
output_data_s3_filepath=output_data_s3_file.split("//")
[1].split("/")[1]+"/"+output_data_s3_file.split("//")
[1].split("/")[2]+"/"+output_data_s3_file.split("//")[1].
split("/")[3]+"/"+output_data_s3_file.split("//")[1].
split("/")[4]
```

```
print(output_data_s3_filepath)
```

```
f = BytesIO()
```

```
s3_client.download_fileobj(bucket, output_data_s3_
filepath, f)
```

```
f.seek(0)
```

```
print(f.getvalue())
```

You will get the following redacted bank statement:

s3://sagemaker-us-east-1-███████/pii-detection-redaction/186389221476-PII-03c308e8e9743f188cd16b88d898cd5e/outpu
t/pii_data.txt.out
pii-detection-redaction/███████PII-03c308e8e9743f188cd16b88d898cd5e/output/pii_data.txt.out
b'HOWARDBANKStatement Ending ************* 1 of 4RETURN SERVICE REQUESTEDManaging Your AccountsIIIIPrimary Branch **
******** DoePhone Number ************** **** StreetBaltimore, MD 21224Online Banking HowardBank.com5Telephone*******
*******Bankinga3301 ****** StreetMailing AddressBaltimore, MD 21224Summary of AccountsAccount TypeAccount NumberEndin
g BalanceHOWARD RELATIONSHIP CHECKINGXXXXXXXX4101$5,684.22HOWARD RELATIONSHIPPrimary CheckingAccount SummaryDateDescr
iptionAmount09*************** Balance$18,805.473 Credit(s) This Period$4,293.2020 Debit(s) This Period$17,414.4509*
************* Balance$5,684.22Account ActivityPost DateDescriptionDebitsCreditsBalance09**************** Balance$18,
805.4709**************** POS Debit ***** MD BALTIMORE GIANT FOOD$57.48$18,747.99INC SEQ# 07158209****2018Nationstar
dba Mr Cooper XXXXXX6179$1,989.60$16,758.3909****2018HMS WARRANTY 8002473680 5829389$42.99$16,715.4009/**/2018SAMS CL
UB MC ONLINE PMT CKF426104254POS$4,671.42$12,043.9809***/2018DISCOVER BANK ETRANSFER$8,212.00$3,831.9809****2018BLTMO
RE GAS ELEC ONLINE PMT$160.75$3,671.2309/**/2018AMAZON$170.00$3,501.2309/**/2018DEVONSHIRE ** CO CONS CP BC5198$195.0
0$3,306.2309****2018DEPOSIT$653.25$3,959.4809****2018TARGET ONLINE PMT$88.59$3,870.8909****2018ATM Withdrawal ***** M
D BALTIMORE 10101$180.00$3,690.89PHILDELPHIA RD SEQ# 00883809****2018Signature POS Debit ***** MD BALTIMORE GIANT FOO
D$70.11$3,620.78I09/***2018A FITNESS$12.98$3,607.8009****2018AT&T MOBILITY ONLINE PMT$116.22$3,491.5809/14/2018DEPOSI
T$606.62$4,098.2009/14/2018DIRECT DEP$3,033.33$7,131.5309/14/2018Signature POS Debit ***** MD BALTIMORE GIANT$19.8
6$7,111.6709/17/2018ATM Withdrawal ***** WV INWOOD$400.00$6,711.67MARTINSBURG-INWOOD09**************** POS Debit ***
** MD BALTIMORE GIANT$14.06$6,697.61\n\n'

Figure 4.8 – Redacted bank statement using the Amazon Comprehend PII Redaction job

In the output, you can see that the Amazon Comprehend PII job has masked the PII data, such as an address, name, SSN, and bank account number identified using the Amazon Comprehend Detect PII entity.

In this section, we walked you through an end-to-end conceptual architecture for automating documents for compliance and control. In the next section, we will talk about best practices for real-time document processing workflows versus batch processing workflows.

Processing real-time document workflows versus batch document workflows

In this section, we will talk about some best practices while architecting solutions using Amazon Textract for real-time workflows versus batch processing document workflows.

Let's compare the Textract real-time APIs against the batch APIs we discussed in *Chapter 2, Introducing Amazon Textract*, with the help of the following table:

	Sync processing	Batch document processing
Textract APIs	Detect document text, analyze document text (forms and tables) Invoice parser – Analyze Expense API	Start document text, get document text, Refer to Chapter 2, Introducing Amazon Textract, for details.
Supported document types (we keep updating this based on customer feedback)	Currently images only	Both images and PDF supported
Page count	Single page per API call	Multi-page as well as single-page support
Handwriting support	Supports handwritten text	Supports handwritten text
Language support	Supports multiple languages	Supports multiple languages
Compliance	HIPAA, SOC, ISO, and PCI	HIPAA, SOC, ISO, and PCI

Figure 4.9 – Textract sync APIs versus batch APIs

> **Note**
>
> The pricing of Textract is based on which of the three different APIs you are going to use out of Analyze Document (forms, table), Detect Text (text extraction), and Analyze Expense (invoices and receipts). You will not be charged irrespective of whether you use the sync or async (batch) implementation of these, so, feel free to design your architecture based on your need for real-time processing versus batch processing as pricing is based on the number of documents processed with one of the three APIs, irrespective of batch or real-time mode. Check prices here: `https://aws.amazon.com/textract/pricing/`.

For example, LiveRight pvt Ltd. can use the batch or real-time implementation of the detect text API to detect text from their bank statements to process millions of documents.

We covered architecture in *Figure 14.2*. This architecture implemented the Amazon Textract Detect Text Sync API in the code walk-through. Now, let's see how we can automate the architecture through Lambda functions for scale to process multiple documents:

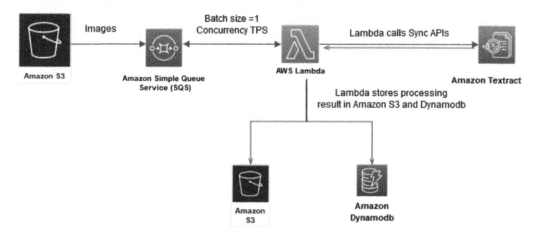

Figure 4.10 – Synchronous document processing workflow

In the preceding architecture, we walked you through how you can process scanned images using the proposed synchronous document processing workflow using the sync APIs of Amazon Textract. Here are the steps for this architecture:

- Documents uploaded to Amazon S3 will send a message to an Amazon SQS queue to analyze a document. Amazon SQS is a serverless managed queuing service that polls the documents into the queue.

- A Lambda function is invoked synchronously with an event that contains a queue message.

- The Lambda function then calls Amazon Textract sync APIs and stores the Textract output or response in either Amazon S3 or response metadata in the Amazon DynamoDB table. Amazon DynamoDB is a NoSQL database managed by AWS that is like a key/value store.

You control the throughput of your pipeline by controlling the batch size and Lambda concurrency.

Now we will walk you through the following architecture best practices for scaling multi-page scanned documents, which can be PDF or images using batch APIs of Amazon Textract:

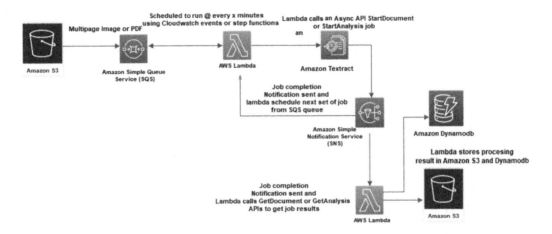

Figure 4.11 – Batch document processing workflow

In the preceding diagram, we have an architecture to walk through how batch processing workflow works with Amazon Textract batch jobs:

- Multipage PDFs and images are uploaded in Amazon S3. These documents are sent to the **Amazon Simple Queue Service (SQS)** queue.

- A job scheduler Lambda function runs at a certain frequency, for example, every 5 minutes, and polls for messages in the SQS queue.

- For each message in the queue, it submits an Amazon Textract job to process the document and continues submitting these jobs until it reaches the maximum limit of concurrent jobs in your AWS account.

- As Amazon Textract finishes processing a document, it sends a completion notification to an **Amazon Simple Notification Service (SNS)** topic.

- SNS then triggers the job scheduler Lambda function to start the next set of Amazon Textract jobs.

- SNS also sends a message to an SQS queue, which is then processed by a Lambda function to get results from Amazon Textract. The results are then stored in a relevant dataset, for example, DynamoDB or Amazon S3.

This GitHub link, `https://github.com/aws-samples/amazon-textract-serverless-large-scale-document-processing`, has code samples to implement both the suggested architecture and it also has some additional components to backfill in case the documents already exist in the Amazon S3 bucket. Please feel free to set up and use this if you have large documents to experiment with.

You can also use the following GitHub solution, `https://github.com/aws-samples/amazon-textract-textractor`, to implement large-scale document processing with Amazon Comprehend insights.

In this section, we covered architecture best practices for using real-time processing or batch processing with Amazon Textract. We also presented some already-existing GitHub implementations for large-scale document processing with Amazon Textract. Now, let's summarize what we have covered in this chapter.

Summary

In this chapter, we covered how you can use Amazon Textract to automate your existing documents. We introduced a fictional bank use case with the help of *LiveRight Pvt Ltd*. We showed you how using an architecture can help banks automate their loan origination process and set up compliance and control with Amazon Comprehend. We also covered code samples using a sample bank statement, and how you can extract data from the scanned bank statement and save it into a `CSV.text` file in Amazon S3 for further analysis. Then, we showed you how you can use Amazon Comprehend to detect PII using a sync API and how you can redact that sample bank data text/CSV in Amazon S3 using an Amazon Comprehend batch PII redaction job.

We then covered some architecture patterns for using real-time processing document workflows versus batch processing workflows. We also provided some GitHub implementations that can be used to process large-scale documents.

In this chapter, you learned the differences between when to use and how to use real-time APIs versus batch APIs for document automation. You also learned how you can set up PII redaction with Amazon Comprehend PII jobs.

In the next chapter, we will look at a different use case, but one that's equally popular among enterprises looking to leverage NLP to maximize their business value by building smart search indexes. We will cover how you can use Amazon Textract and Amazon Comprehend along with Amazon Elasticsearch and Amazon Kendra to create a quick NLP-based search. We will introduce the use case, discuss how to design the architecture, establish the prerequisites, and walk through in detail the various steps required to build the solution.

Further reading

- *Building a serverless document scanner using Amazon Textract and AWS Amplify*, by Moheeb Zara (`https://aws.amazon.com/blogs/compute/building-a-serverless-document-scanner-using-amazon-textract-and-aws-amplify/`)

- *Automatically extract text and structured data from documents with Amazon Textract*, by Kashif Imran and Martin Schade (`https://aws.amazon.com/blogs/machine-learning/automatically-extract-text-and-structured-data-from-documents-with-amazon-textract/`)

5
Creating NLP Search

In the previous chapters, you were introduced to Amazon Textract for extracting text from documents, and Amazon Comprehend to extract insights with no prior **Machine Learning (ML)** experience as a prerequisite. In the last chapter, we showed you how you can combine these features together to solve a real-world use case for document automation by giving an example of loan processing.

In this chapter, we will use the Amazon Textract and Amazon Comprehend services to show you how you can quickly set up an intelligent search solution with the integration of powerful elements, such as **Amazon Elasticsearch**, which is a managed service to set up search and log analytics, and **Amazon Kendra**, which is an intelligent managed search solution powered by ML for natural language search.

We will cover the following topics in this chapter:

- Going over search use cases and choices for search solutions
- Building a search solution for scanned images using Amazon Elasticsearch
- Setting up an enterprise search solution using Amazon Kendra

Technical requirements

For this chapter, you will need access to an AWS account. Before getting started we recommend that you create an AWS account by going through these steps here:

1. Open `https://portal.aws.amazon.com/billing/signup`.

2. Please go through and execute the steps provided on the web page to sign up.

3. Log in to your AWS account when prompted in the sections.

The Python code and sample datasets for the Amazon Textract examples are provided on the book's GitHub repo at `https://github.com/PacktPublishing/Natural-Language-Processing-with-AWS-AI-Services/tree/main/Chapter%2005`.

Check out the following video to see the Code in Action at `https://bit.ly/3nygP5S`.

Creating NLP-powered smart search indexes

Every organization has lots of documents in the form of paper and in their archives too. The challenge is that these documents lie mostly in separate silos and not all in one place. So, for these organizations to make a business decision based on the hidden information in their siloed documents is extremely challenging. Some approaches these organizations take to make their documents searchable is putting the documents in a data lake. However, extracting meaningful information from these documents is another challenge as it would require a lot of NLP expertise, ML skills, and infrastructure to set that up. Even if you were able to extract insights from these documents, another challenge will then be setting up a scalable search solution.

In this section, we will address these challenges by using the AWS AI services we introduced in previous chapters and then talk about how they can be used to set up a centralized document store.

Once all the documents are in a centralized storage service such as Amazon S3, which is a scalable and durable object store similar to Dropbox, we can use *Amazon Textract* as covered in *Chapter 2, Introducing Amazon Textract,* to extract text from these documents, and use *Amazon Comprehend* as covered in *Chapter 3, Introducing Amazon Comprehend,* to extract NLP-based insights such as entities, keywords, sentiments, and more. Moreover, we can then quickly index the insights and the text and send it to Amazon Elasticsearch or Amazon Kendra to set up a smart search solution.

The following diagram shows the architecture we will cover in this section:

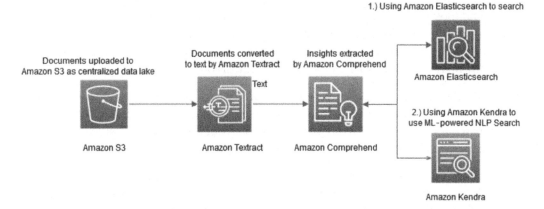

Figure 5.1 – Creating an NLP-powered search index

In *Figure 5.1*, you can see the two options we have to build a search index. The options are as follows:

1. Using Amazon Elasticsearch to build a search on top of your document processing pipeline with Amazon Textract and Amazon Comprehend

2. Using Amazon Kendra to build a serverless intelligent search on top of your existing document processing pipeline with Amazon Textract and Amazon Comprehend

If you are looking for a natural language-based search solution powered by ML where you can ask human-like questions rather than searching for keywords, you can choose Amazon Kendra for the search, as Amazon Kendra is an AWS AI service powered by ML. Amazon Kendra offers natural language search functionality and will provide you with NLP-based answers, meaning human-like contextual answers. For example, imagine you are setting up the search function on your IT support documents in Salesforce. Using Amazon Kendra you can ask direct questions such as *"where is the IT desk located?"* and Amazon Kendra will give you an exact response, such as "*the sixth floor*," whereas in Amazon Elasticsearch you can only perform keyword-based search.

Moreover, you can also integrate Amazon Kendra into Amazon Lex, which is a service to create chatbots. You can deploy a smart search chatbot on your website powered by Amazon Lex and Amazon Kendra. Also, Amazon Kendra comes with a lot of connectors to discover and index your data for search, including Amazon S3, OneDrive, Google Drive, Salesforce, relational databases such as RDS, and many more supported by third-party vendors.

You can set up a search on many different interesting use cases, for example, for financial analysts searching for financial events, as they have to scroll through tons of SEC filing reports and look for meaningful financial entities such as mergers and acquisitions. Using the proposed pipeline along with Amazon Comprehend Events can easily reduce the time and noise while scrolling through these documents and update their financial models in case of any financial events such as mergers or acquisitions.

For healthcare companies, they can use the set of services and options offered by Amazon Comprehend Medical to create a smart search for healthcare data, where a doctor can log in and search for relevant keywords or information from the centralized patient data in Amazon HealthLake. We will cover more on this use case in this chapter.

We all know finding jobs is extremely difficult. It's harder even for talent acquisition companies hunting for good candidates to search for relevant skills across thousands of resumes. You can use the proposed solution to set up a resume processing pipeline where you can upload the resumes of various candidates in Amazon S3 and search for relevant skills based on the jobs you are looking for.

In this section, we covered two options with which to set up smart search indexes. In the next section, we will show you how you can set up this architecture to create an NLP-powered search application where **Human Resources** (**HR**) admin users can quickly upload candidates' scanned resumes and other folks can log in and search for relevant skill sets based on open job positions.

Building a search solution for scanned images using Amazon Elasticsearch

In the previous chapters, we spoke about how you can use Amazon Lambda functions to create a serverless application. In this section, we will walk you through the following architecture to set up a scanned image-based search solution by calling the Amazon Textract and Amazon Comprehend APIs using an Amazon Lambda function. We are going to use Amazon Elasticsearch for this use case. However, you can also replace Amazon Elasticsearch with Amazon Kendra to create an ML-based search solution where you can use natural language to ask questions while searching.

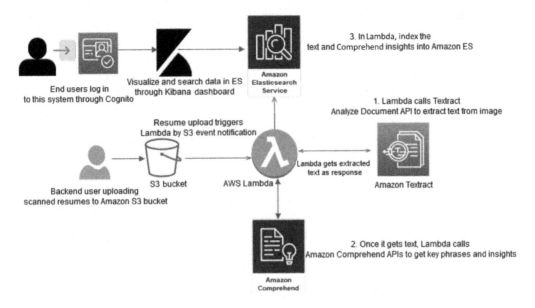

Figure 5.2 – Building NLP search using Amazon Elasticsearch

The AWS service used in the previous architecture is **Amazon Cognito** to set up the login for your backend users.

Amazon S3 is used for centralized storage. Amazon Lambda functions are used as serverless event triggers when the scanned resumes are uploaded to Amazon S3, and then we use both Amazon Textract and Amazon Comprehend to extract text and insights such as key phrases and entities. Then we index everything into Amazon Elasticsearch. Your end users can log in through Cognito, and will access Amazon Elasticsearch through a Kibana dashboard that comes integrated with Amazon Elasticsearch for visualization.

Prerequisites

We will use an AWS CloudFormation template to spin up the resources needed for this chapter. CloudFormation templates are scripts written in YAML or JSON format to spin up resources or **Infrastructure as Code (IaC)**. AWS CloudFormation templates write IaC and set all the necessary permissions for you:

1. Click `https://forindexing.s3.eu-west-1.amazonaws.com/template-export-textract.yml` to download and deploy an AWS CloudFormation template.

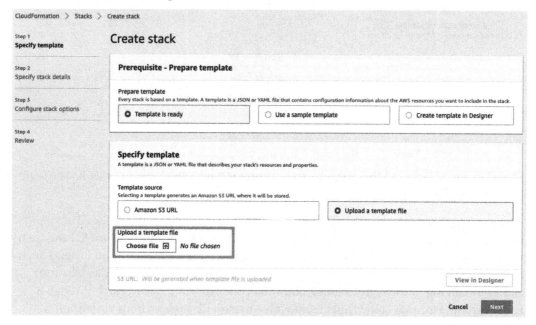

Figure 5.3 – CloudFormation template stack

2. Scroll down to **Parameters**, enter your email address in the relevant field, and enter `documentsearchapp` for **DOMAINNAME** as shown in the following screenshot:

Parameters

Parameters are defined in your template and allow you to input custom values when you create or update a stack.

CognitoAdminEmail
E-mail address of the Cognito admin name

[REDACTED]

DOMAINNAME
Name for the Amazon ES domain that this template will create. Domain names must start with a lowercase letter and must be between 3 and 28 characters. Valid characters are a-z (lowercase only), 0-9.

documentsearchapp

Figure 5.4 – Enter parameters

3. Scroll down and check all three acknowledgments under **Capabilities and transforms**, then click **Create stack**.

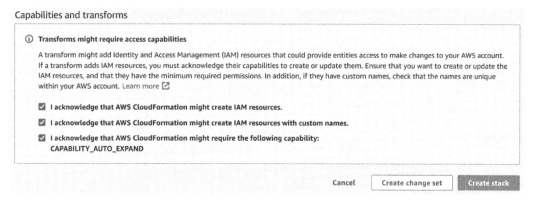

Figure 5.5 – The Capabilities and transforms section

4. You will see your stack creation in progress. Wait till it's completed as shown in the following screenshot – you can refresh to see the changing status. It might take 20 minutes to deploy this stack so go grab a quick coffee:

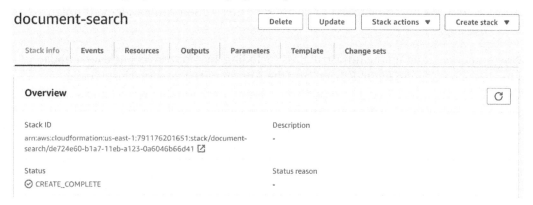

Figure 5.6 – CloudFormation resources creation complete

> **Note:**
>
> You will get an email with the login details to Cognito while your stack is being created. Make sure you check the same email you provided while creating this stack. An admin can add multiple users' email addresses through the Amazon Cognito console once it's deployed. Those emails can be sent to end users for logging in to the system once the resumes' data has been uploaded to Amazon S3.

5.   Go to the **Outputs** tab, and scroll down to the **Outputs** section.

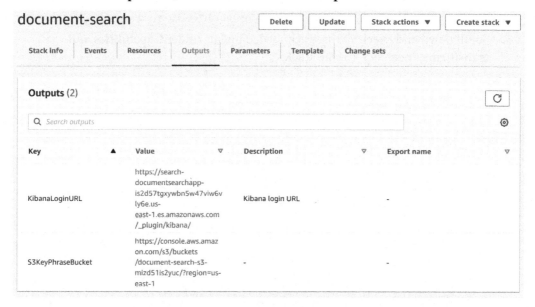

Figure 5.7 – CloudFormation outputs

6.   Copy the values for **S3KeyPhraseBucket** and **KibanaLoginURL** from the **Value** section. We are going to use these links for this section while walking through this app.

Now you have set up up the infrastructure, including an Amazon S3 bucket, Lambda functions, the Cognito login, Kibana, and the Amazon Elasticsearch cluster using CloudFormation. You have the output from CloudFormation for your S3 bucket and Kibana dashboard login URLs. In the next section, we will walk you through how you can upload scanned images to interact with this application as an admin user.

Uploading documents to Amazon S3

We'll start with the following steps for uploading documents to Amazon S3:

1. Click on the S3 link copied from the CloudFormation template output in the previous section. Then download the sample resume at `https://github.com/PacktPublishing/Natural-Language-Processing-with-AWS-AI-Services/blob/main/Chapter%2005/resume_sample.PNG`, and upload it in S3 by clicking on the **Upload** button followed by **Add files**.

Figure 5.8 – Scanned image in Amazon S3

2. This upload triggers an Amazon S3 event notification to the AWS Lambda function. To check that, go to the **Properties** tab and then scroll down to **Event notifications** as shown in the following screenshot:

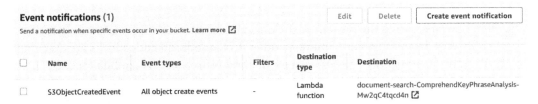

Figure 5.9 – S3 event notifications to notify the AWS Lambda function

3. Click on the Lambda function link shown under **Destination**. We will inspect this Lambda function in the next section.

We have uploaded the sample scanned resume to Amazon S3, and also showed you where you can find the S3 event notifications that trigger a Lambda function. In the next section, let's explore what is happening in the Lambda function.

Inspecting the AWS Lambda function

In this section, we will inspect the code blocks of AWS Lambda and the API calls made to Amazon Textract and Amazon Comprehend along with Amazon Elasticsearch.

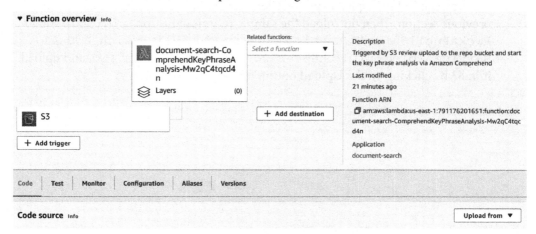

Figure 5.10 – AWS Lambda function

The deployment code is too large for this function to show up in this AWS Lambda console. You can access the code through through the following GitHub repo instead, at `https://github.com/PacktPublishing/Natural-Language-Processing-with-AWS-AI-Services/blob/main/Chapter%2005/lambda/index.py`:

1. First, we are getting the files through Amazon S3 events as shown in the following code block from the main Lambda handler. In Lambda, all code blocks are executed from this main handler. The `handler` method is invoked by Lambda for each function invocation and acts as an entry point. The code outside the handler contains functions that can be called from the main handler and some global variables:

    ```
    def handler(event, context):
    bucket = event['Records'][0]['s3']['bucket']['name']
    key = unquote_plus(event['Records'][0]['s3']
    ['object']['key'])
    ```

2. The following code downloads the file from Amazon S3 to process it with Textract and Comprehend:

    ```
            s3.Bucket(bucket).download_
    file(Key=key,Filename='/tmp/{}')
            with open('/tmp/{}', 'rb') as document:
    ```

```
        imageBytes = bytearray(document.read())
    print("Object downloaded")
```

3. After getting the objects or scanned resumes from S3 events and reading through a Lambda function, we will call the Amazon Textract AnalyzeDocument API, a real-time API to extract the text, using the following code:

```
response = textract.analyze_document(Document={'Bytes':
imageBytes},FeatureTypes=["TABLES", "FORMS"])
document = Document(response)
```

4. We will parse the response to extract the lines of text to be sent to Amazon Comprehend:

```
blocks=response['Blocks']
        for block in blocks:
            if block['BlockType'] == 'LINE':
                text += block['Text']+"\n"
        print(text)
```

5. Once we have extracted text, we will call the Comprehend Keyphrase API by putting it in a list variable to be indexed later:

> **Note:**
>
> Comprehend sync APIs allow up to 5,000 characters as input so make sure your text is not more than 5,000 characters long.

```
keyphrase_response = comprehend.detect_key_
phrases(Text=text, LanguageCode='en')
KeyPhraseList=keyphrase_response.get("KeyPhrases")
  for s in KeyPhraseList:
                            textvalues.append(s.
get("Text")
```

6. Now we will extract entities using the Comprehend DetectEntities API and save it in a map data structure variable to be indexed later:

```
detect_entity= comprehend.detect_entities(Text=text,
LanguageCode='en')
EntityList=detect_entity.get("Entities")
for s in EntityList:
```

```
                                              textvalues_
entity.update([(s.get("Type").strip('\t\n\r'),s.
get("Text").strip('\t\n\r'))]
```

7. Now we will create an Amazon S3 URL to be indexed:

```
s3url='https://s3.console.aws.amazon.com/s3/
object/'+bucket+'/'+key+'?region='+region
```

8. We have the text, keyphrases, and entities, as well as the S3 link of the uploaded document. Now we will index it all and upload it in Elasticsearch:

```
searchdata={'s3link':s3url,'KeyPhrases':textvalues,
'Entity':textvalues_entity,'text':text, 'table':table,
'forms':forms}
```
```
print(searchdata)
```
```
print("connecting to ES")
```
```
es=connectES()
```
```
es.index(index="document", doc_type="_doc",
body=searchdata)
```

> **Note:**
> In case the resumes have tables or forms, we have prepared to index them as well. Moreover, this solution can also be used for **invoice search.**

In this section, we walked you through how you can extract text and insights from the documents uploaded to Amazon S3. We also indexed the data into Amazon Elasticsearch. In the next section, we will walk you through how you can log in to Kibana using your admin login email setup while creating CloudFormation templates and visualize the data in the Kibana dashboard.

Searching for and discovering data in the Kibana console

In this section, we will cover how you can sign up to Kibana through Amazon Cognito by using the email you entered as the admin while deploying the resources through AWS CloudFormation. Then we will walk you through how you can set up your index in Kibana. We will cover how you can discover and search the data in the Kibana dashboard based on entity, keyword, and table filters from Amazon Comprehend. Lastly, you can download the searched resume link from Amazon S3.

We will cover walkthroughs including signing up to the Kibana console, making the index discoverable for the search functionality, and searching for insights in Kibana.

Signing up to the Kibana console

In these steps, we will walk you through how you can log in to Kibana using the CloudFormation-generated output link:

1. Click on the Kibana login link you got from the CloudFormation output as shown in the following screenshot:

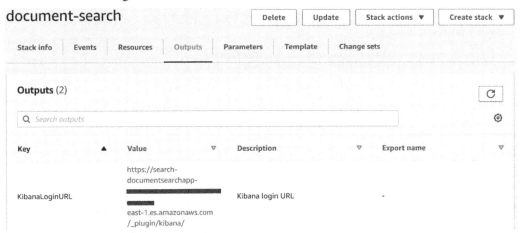

Figure 5.11 – CloudFormation output – Kibana URL

2. This link will redirect you to this console:

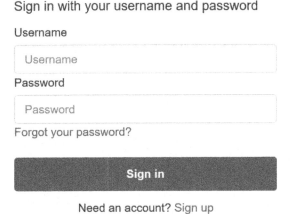

Figure 5.12 – Kibana sign-in dialog

> **Note:**
> You can sign up additional end users using the **Sign up** button shown in the previous screenshot.

3. You should have got an email with a username and temporary password – enter those details in the preceding dialog, and click on **Sign in**.

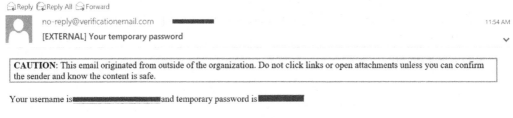

Figure 5.13 – Verification and password login email

4. It will ask you to change your password the first time you sign in. After changing your password, you will be redirected to the Kibana console.

We have covered how to sign up for Kibana. In the next section, we will walk you through setting up the index in Kibana.

Making the index discoverable for the search functionality

In this section, we will walk you through setting up an index in Kibana for searching:

1. Click on **Discover** when you reach the Kibana console and we will walk you through setting up your index in Kibana.

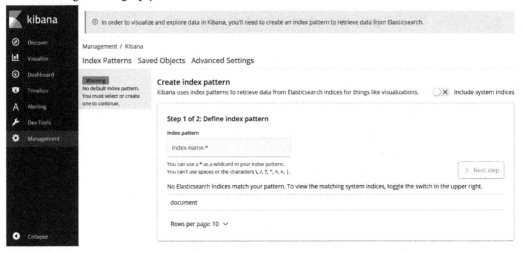

Figure 5.14 – Kibana Create index pattern page

2.   Enter document in the **Index pattern** field, as shown in the following screenshot, then click **Next step**:

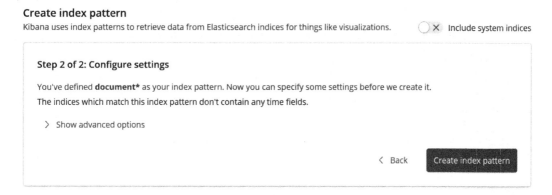

Create index pattern

Kibana uses index patterns to retrieve data from Elasticsearch indices for things like visualizations.   ○ ✕ Include system indices

Step 1 of 2: Define index pattern

Index pattern

document*

You can use a * as a wildcard in your index pattern.
You can't use spaces or the characters \, /, ?, ", <, >, |.

> Next step

✓ **Success!** Your index pattern matches **1 index**.

document

Rows per page: 10 ∨

Figure 5.15 – Define index pattern

3.   Click on **Create index pattern**. This will make your Elasticsearch index discoverable.

Create index pattern

Kibana uses index patterns to retrieve data from Elasticsearch indices for things like visualizations.   ○ ✕ Include system indices

Step 2 of 2: Configure settings

You've defined **document*** as your index pattern. Now you can specify some settings before we create it.
The indices which match this index pattern don't contain any time fields.

> Show advanced options

< Back   Create index pattern

Figure 5.16 – Create index pattern

We have created an index. Now we will start searching for insights.

Searching for insights in Kibana

In this section, we will walk you through searching for insights in Kibana:

1.   Click on **Discover** and on the left-hand side you will find entities and key phrases that can be added to your search filters under **Available Fields**.

Figure 5.17 – Kibana's Discover dashboard (a)

Let's look at another output shown in the following screenshot:

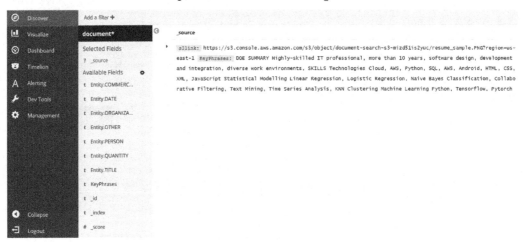

Figure 5.18 – Kibana's Discover dashboard (b)

2. **Entity search**: Let's search for a candidate by date and title by adding the available fields of **Entity.TITLE** and **Entity.dATE** for a quick search. You can click on **Add a filter** and these filters will get added as seen in the following screenshot. You can see that it found someone with the big data analytics title in July 2017:

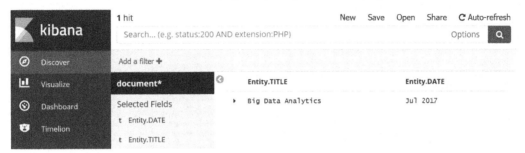

Figure 5.19 – Adding an entity filter to selected fields

3. **Keyword search using the keyphrases and table**: Add the **KeyPhrases** and **table filters** from **available fields** and you will get a table summary of all the skills you are looking for, along with keyphrases about the candidate.

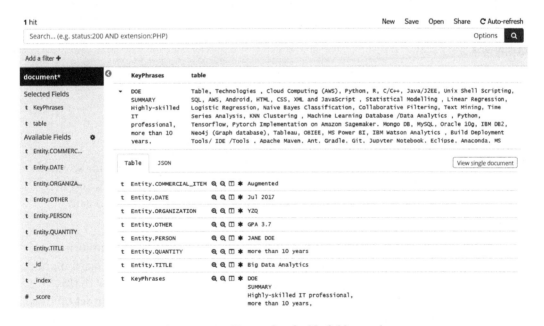

Figure 5.20 – Keyword and table fields search

4. **Doing a generic keyword search**: Now I am looking for someone with both Amazon SageMaker and MySQL skills. Let's enter `Amazon Sagemaker and MySQL` in the search field and see whether we have a candidate resume matching our needs. We are able to find a candidate resume with both these skills as highlighted in the following screenshot:

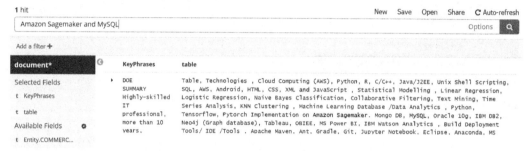

Figure 5.21 – Keyword search with AND condition

5. **Downloading the resume of the candidate matched**: We can download the resume of the matched candidate by adding an S3 link on **selected fields** as follows:

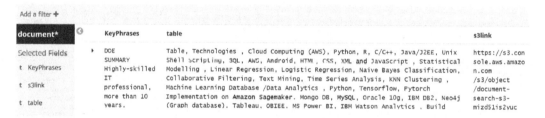

Figure 5.22 – S3 link to download the resume

In this section, we gave you an architecture overview of the search solution for scanned images where an admin user uploads the scanned documents in Amazon S3, and then showed how to sign up for the Kibana dashboard and search for keywords to gain meaningful insights from the scanned documents.

We walked you through the steps to set up the architecture using AWS CloudFormation template one-click deploy, and you can check the *Further reading* section to learn more about how to create these templates. We also showed how you can interact with this application by uploading some sample documents. We guided you on how to set up the Kibana dashboard and provide some sample queries to gain insights from the keywords and entities as filters.

In the next section, we will explore a Kendra-powered search solution. Let's get started exploring Amazon Kendra and what you can uncover by using it to power Textract and Comprehend in your document processing workflows.

Setting up an enterprise search solution using Amazon Kendra

In this section, we will cover how you can quickly create an end-to-end serverless document search application using Amazon Kendra.

In this section, we will cover the steps to get started.

Git cloning the notebook

We will walk through the steps to git clone the notebook and show code samples to set up the kendra based search architecture using simple boto3 APIs.

1. In the SageMaker Jupyter notebook you set up in the previous chapters, Git clone `https://github.com/PacktPublishing/Natural-Language-Processing-with-AWS-AI-Services/`.

2. Go to `Chapter 05/Ch05-Kendra Search.ipynb` and start running the notebook.

> **Note:**
> Please add Kendra IAM access to the SageMaker notebook IAM role so that you can call Kendra APIs through this notebook. In previous chapters, you already added IAM access to Amazon Comprehend and Textract APIs from the SageMaker notebook.

Creating an Amazon S3 bucket

We will show you how you can create a Amazon S3 bucket. We will use this bucket as a Kendra datasource and also to store extracted data from Amazon Textract.

1. Create an Amazon S3 bucket by going to the Amazon S3 console at `https://s3.console.aws.amazon.com/s3/home?region=us-east-1`.

2. Click on the **Create bucket** button and enter any bucket name as shown in the following screenshot:

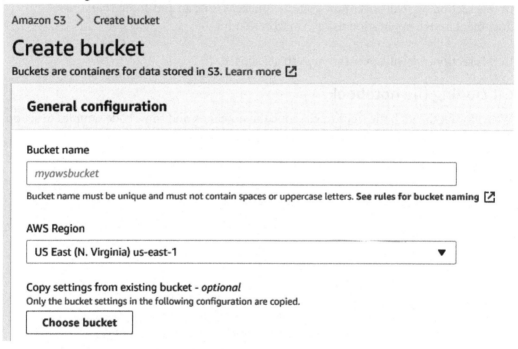

Figure 5.23 – Create an Amazon S3 bucket

3. Scroll down and click on **Create bucket**.

4. Copy the created bucket name, open `Chapter 05/Ch05-Kendra Search.ipynb`, and paste it in the following cell in place of `'<your s3 bucket name>'` to get started:

```
# Define IAM role
role = get_execution_role()
print("RoleArn: {}".format(role))
sess = sagemaker.Session()
s3BucketName = '<your s3 bucket name>'
prefix = 'chapter5'
```

We have the notebook ready and the Amazon S3 bucket created for this section's solution. Let's see a quick architecture walkthrough in the next section to understand the key components and then we will walk you through the code in the notebook you have set up.

Walking through the solution

Setting up an enterprise-level search can be hard. That's why we have Amazon Kendra, which can crawl data from various data connectors to create a quick and easy search solution. In the following architecture, we will walk you through how you can set up a document search when you have your PDF documents in Amazon S3. We will extract the data using Amazon Textract from these PDF documents and send it to Amazon Comprehend to extract some key entities such as **ORGANIZATION, TITLE, DATE**, and so on. These entities will be used as filters while we sync the documents directly into Amazon Kendra for search.

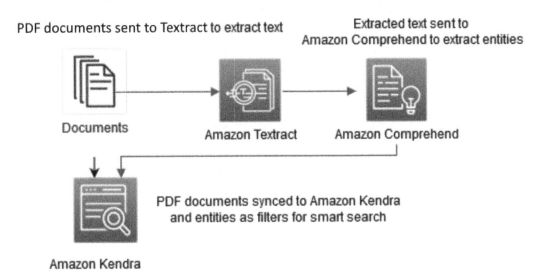

Figure 5.24 – Architecture for the Amazon Kendra-powered search with Textract and Comprehend

So, we gave you a high-level implementation architecture in the previous diagram. In the next section, we will walk you through how you can build this out with few lines of code and using the Python Boto3 APIs.

Code walkthrough

In this section, we will walk you through how you can quickly set up the proposed architecture:

1. We will refer to this notebook: `https://github.com/PacktPublishing/Natural-Language-Processing-with-AWS-AI-Services/blob/main/Chapter%2005/Ch05-Kendra%20Search.ipynb`. The following code presents the Boto3 client setup for Comprehend, Kendra, and Textract APIs

   ```
   comprehend = boto3.client('comprehend')
   textract= boto3.client('textract')
   kendra= boto3.client('kendra')
   ```

2. Now we will upload the PDF document at `https://github.com/PacktPublishing/Natural-Language-Processing-with-AWS-AI-Services/blob/main/Chapter%2005/resume_Sample.pdf` from this repo to Amazon S3.

   > **Note:**
   >
   > You can upload as many documents for search as you wish. For this demonstration, we are providing just one sample. Please feel free to play around by uploading your documents to Amazon S3 and generating metadata files before you start syncing your documents to Amazon Kendra.

   For extracting text from the PDF uploaded to Amazon S3, we will use the same code as we used for the asynchronous processing covered in *Chapter 2, Introducing Amazon Textract*.

3. The following code shows text extraction from Amazon Textract:

   ```
   text=""
   for resultPage in response:
       for item in resultPage["Blocks"]:
           if item["BlockType"] == "LINE":
               #print ('\033[94m' + item["Text"] +
   '\033[0m')
               text += item['Text']+"\n"
   print(text)
   ```

The sample results shown in the following screenshot contain the text from the PDF:

```
Phone: (555) 4444 I Email: abc@email.com
JANE DOE
SUMMARY
Highly-skilled IT professional bringing more than 10 years in software design, development and integration
across diverse work environments.
SKILLS
Technologies
Cloud Computing (AWS), Python, R, C/C++, Java/J2EE, Unix Shell Scripting, SQL, AWS,
Android, HTML, CSS, XML and JavaScript
Statistical Modelling
Linear Regression, Logistic Regression, Naive Bayes Classification, Collaborative
Filtering, Text Mining, Time Series Analysis, KNN Clustering
Machine Learning
Python, Tensorflow, Pytorch Implementation on Amazon Sagemaker.
```

Figure 5.25 – Extracted text response from Amazon Textract for the resume data

4. Now we will send this text to Amazon Comprehend for entity extraction by running the following code:

```
entities= comprehend.detect_entities(Text=text,
LanguageCode='en')
```

5. Now we will create an Amazon Kendra index. Go to the Kendra console at `https://console.aws.amazon.com/kendra/home?region=us-east-1#indexes` and click the **Create index** button. Specify `Search` for **Index name**, then scroll down and click on **Create a new role (Recommended)**, shown highlighted in the following screenshot:

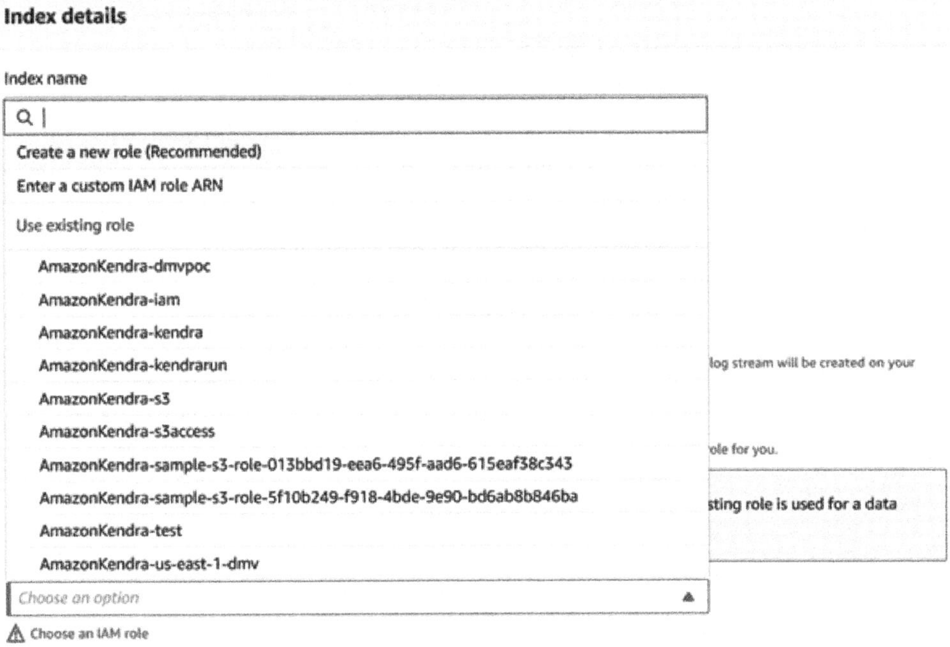
Index details
Index name
Create a new role (Recommended)
Enter a custom IAM role ARN
Use existing role
AmazonKendra-dmvpoc
AmazonKendra-iam
AmazonKendra-kendra
AmazonKendra-kendrarun
AmazonKendra-s3
AmazonKendra-s3access
AmazonKendra-sample-s3-role-013bbd19-eea6-495f-aad6-615eaf38c343
AmazonKendra-sample-s3-role-5f10b249-f918-4bde-9e90-bd6ab8b846ba
AmazonKendra-test
AmazonKendra-us-east-1-dmv
Choose an option
Choose an IAM role
log stream will be created on your
ole for you.
sting role is used for a data

Figure 5.26 – Create a new role for the Kendra index

6. Enter `AmazonKendra-us-east-1-kendra` as the role name and click on **Next**. Your role name will be prefixed with `AmazonKendra-us-east-1-`.

7. For **Configure user access control**, Use **tokens for access control**? select **No** and click **Next**.

8. For **Specify provisioning**, choose **Developer Edition** and click on **Create**. Alternatively, you can run the following notebook cell after creating an IAM role to create the index programmatically:

> **Note:**
> If you created the index using the console, please skip the programmatic creation and avoid running the following notebook cell to create the index.

```python
response = kendra.create_index(
    Name='Search',
    Edition='DEVELOPER_EDITION',
    RoleArn='<enter IAM role by creating IAM role in IAM
console')
print(response)
```

> **Note:**
> Index creation can take up to 30 minutes.

9. After creating the index, we need to get the index ID to run through this notebook. Once the index is created, click on **Index** and go to **Index Settings** to copy the index ID.

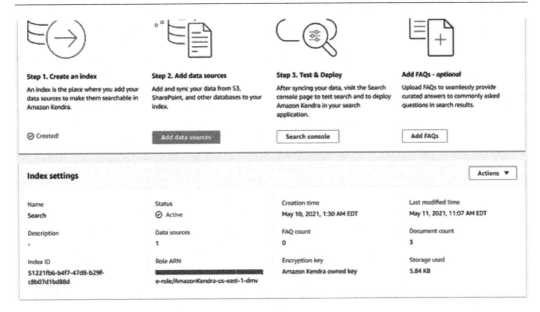

Figure 5.27 – Copying the Kendra index ID from the Kendra console

Alternatively, if you created the index programmatically using the *CreateIndex API*, its response will contain an index ID of 36 digits that you need to copy and paste to run the next piece of code to update the search filters based on the Comprehend entities.

10. Copy and paste the Kendra index ID over the placeholder in the following cell, then run the cell to update the index we created with filters for search. Refer to the notebook for the complete code to add all the filters:

```
response = kendra.update_index(
    Id="<paste Index Id from Create Index response>",
    DocumentMetadataConfigurationUpdates=[
        {
            'Name':'ORGANIZATION',
            'Type':'STRING_LIST_VALUE',
            'Search': {
                'Facetable': True,
                'Searchable': True,
                'Displayable': True
            }
        }}
```

11. Now we will define the list of categories recognized by Comprehend:

```
categories = ["ORGANIZATION", "PERSON", "DATE",
"COMMERCIAL_ITEM", "OTHER", "TITLE", "QUANTITY"]
```

12. Now we will iterate over the entities and generate a metadata file to populate the filters based on the entities from Amazon Comprehend:

```
for e in entities["Entities"]:
    if (e["Text"].isprintable()) and (not "\"" in
e["Text"]) and (not e["Text"].upper() in category_
text[e["Type"]]):
            #Append the text to entity data to be
used for a Kendra custom attribute
            entity_data[e["Type"]].add(e["Text"])
            #Keep track of text in upper case so that
we don't treat the same text written in different cases
differently
            category_text[e["Type"]].
append(e["Text"].upper())
            #Keep track of the frequency of the text
so that we can take the text with highest frequency of
occurrance
            text_frequency[e["Type"]][e["Text"].
upper()] = 1
    elif (e["Text"].upper() in category_text[e["Type"]]):
            #Keep track of the frequency of the text
so that we can take the text with highest frequency of
occurrance
            text_frequency[e["Type"]][e["Text"].
upper()] += 1
print(entity_data)
```

13. You will get a response back detailing the Comprehend entity types and values detected in the text from the PDF document.

```
{'ORGANIZATION': {'Amazon NLP AI Services', 'IBM', 'Amazon Athena', 'YZQ Organization', 'Amazon', 'ABC Company', 'Jup
yter', 'Amazon Quicksight', 'XYZ College', 'AWS', 'Coursera'}, 'PERSON': {'JANE DOE'}, 'DATE': {'Aug 2016', 'August 2
017', 'May 2011', 'Jul 2017'}, 'COMMERCIAL_ITEM': {'Notebook', 'Augmented', 'Code Star'}, 'OTHER': {'GPA 3.7', 'abc@e
mail.com', 'Data', '(555) 4444 I'}, 'TITLE': {'Glue', 'Lakeformation', 'Mongo DB', 'Outlook', 'R', 'IDE_', 'Java/J2EE
', 'Database', 'Lambda', 'PowerPoint', 'Tools', 'Oracle 10g', 'Neo4j', 'OBIEE', 'Watson Analytics', 'Naïve', 'AI/ML S
tack', 'Ant', 'KNN Clustering', 'HTML', 'Git', 'MS Power BI', 'Python', 'Anaconda', 'Word', 'Analytics', 'Big Data An
alytics', 'Tensorflow', 'MySQL', 'Excel', 'JIRA', 'Android', 'CSS', 'Coursera', 'XML', 'JavaScript', 'Unix Shell Scri
pting', 'C/C++', 'Pytorch', 'Access', 'Big Data', 'Sagemaker', 'Apache Maven', 'Tableau', 'DB2', 'Eclipse', 'SQL', 'G
radle'}, 'QUANTITY': {'more than 10 years'}}
```

Figure 5.28 – Comprehend's extracted entities

14. Populate the Kendra metadata list from the previous entities for Amazon Kendra attributes filter:

```
elimit = 10
for et in categories:
```

15. Take the `elimit` number of recognized text strings that have the highest frequency of occurrence:

```
    el = [pair[0] for pair in sorted(text_frequency[et].
items(), key=lambda item: item[1], reverse=True)]
[0:elimit]
    metadata[et] = [d for d in entity_data[et] if
d.upper() in el]
metadata["_source_uri"] = documentName
attributes["Attributes"] = metadata
```

16. The last step is to save this file with the `metadata.json`. Make sure the filename is the original PDF document filename followed by `metadata.json` in the Amazon S3 bucket where your PDF document is uploaded:

```
s3 = boto3.client('s3')
prefix= 'meta/'
with open("metadata.json", "rb") as f:
    s3.upload_file( "metadata.json", s3BucketName,'%s/%s'
% ("meta","resume_Sample.pdf.metadata.json"))
```

We gave you a code walkthrough on how to upload a PDF document and extract data from it using Amazon Textract and then use Amazon Comprehend to extract entities. We then created a metadata file using the filters or entities extracted by Comprehend and uploaded it into Amazon S3. In the next section, we will walk you through how you can set up Amazon Kendra sync with the S3 document you uploaded, and how you can create a `meta` folder and place your metadata files there so that Amazon Kendra picks them up as metadata filters during the Kendra sync.

Searching in Amazon Kendra with enriched filters from Comprehend

In this section, we will walk you through how you can sync the documents to the index you have created, along with the filters in the metadata file:

1. Set the Kendra data source as the Amazon S3 bucket to which you uploaded your documents. Navigate to **Amazon Kendra | Indexes | <Name of the Index> | Data sources | Add data source | Amazon S3**, as shown in the following screenshot:

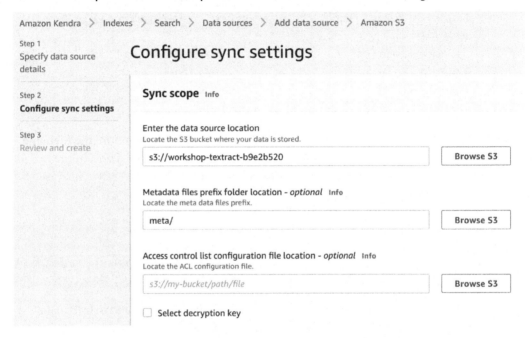

Figure 5.29 – Configuring Amazon Kendra sync

2. Enter s3://<your bucket name> in the **Enter the data source location** field, and under **Metadata files prefix folder location - optional**, enter meta/ as shown in the previous screenshot.

3. In the **IAM role** section, choose **Create a new role** and enter AmazonKendra-s3 in the **Role name** field.

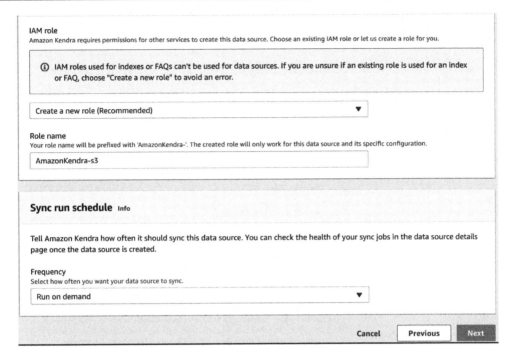

Figure 5.30 – The run-on-demand schedule for Kendra

4. Then set the frequency for the sync run schedule to be **Run on demand** and click **Next**.

5. Click on **Review + Create**.

6. After your data source has been created, click on **Sync now**.

Once the sync is successful, all your documents in Amazon S3 will be synced and the Kendra filters will be populated with the metadata attributes extracted by Amazon Comprehend.

In the next section, we will walk you through how you can navigate to the Amazon Kendra console to search.

Searching in Amazon Kendra

Amazon Kendra comes with a built-in search UI that can be used for testing the search functionality.

You can also deploy this UI in a React app after testing. The page at `https://docs.aws.amazon.com/kendra/latest/dg/deploying.html` has the deployment UI code available, which can be integrated with any serverless application using API Gateway and Lambda.

You can also use the `Kendra.query()` API to retrieve results from the index you created in Kendra.

In this section, we will walk you through using the built-in Kendra search console:

1. Navigate to **Amazon Kendra | Indexes | Search | Search console** and you will find a Kendra-powered built-in search UI as shown in the following screenshot. Enter `person with cloud skills` in the search field:

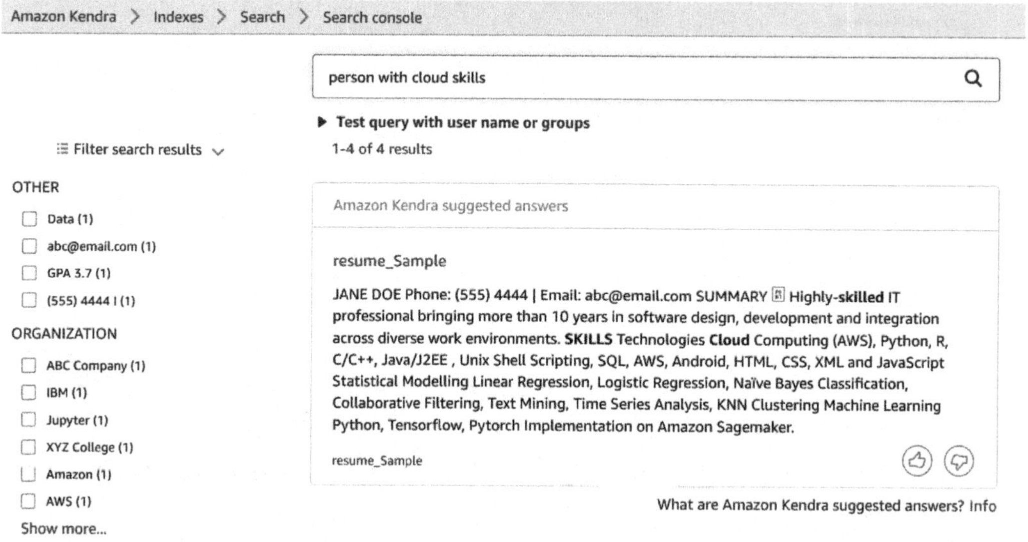

Figure 5.31 – Kendra query results

Amazon Kendra is able to give you a contextual answer containing Jane Doe, whose resume we indexed.

It also provides you with filters based on Comprehend entities on the left-hand side to quickly sort individuals based on entities such as **ORGANIZATION, TITLE, DATE**, and their word count frequencies.

You can also create *Comprehend custom entities,* as we covered in *Chapter 4, Automated Document Processing Workflows,* to enrich your metadata filters based on your business needs.

2. Next, type the `person with 10 years of experience` query into the Kendra Search console.

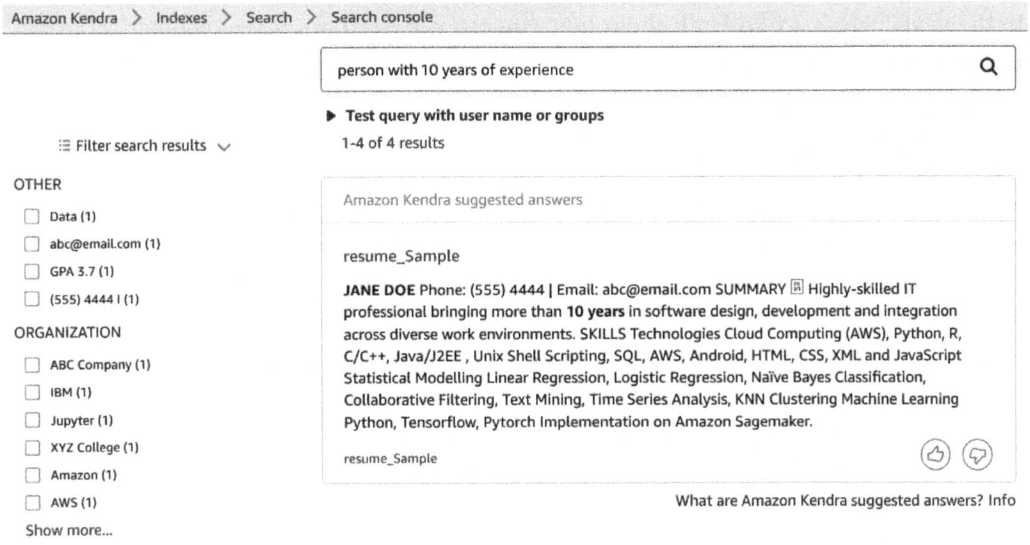

Figure 5.32 – Kendra query results with filters on the left from Comprehend's metadata enrichment

Amazon Kendra is able to provide you with the exact contextual answer. You can also boost the response in Kendra based on relevance and provide feedback using the thumbs-up and thumbs-down buttons to improve your Kendra model.

> **Note:**
> Amazon Kendra supports the use of PDF, Word, JSON, TXT, PPT, and HTML documents for the search functionality. Feel free to add more documents through this pipeline for better search results and accuracy.

Summary

In this chapter, we covered two options to set up an intelligent search solution for your document-processing workflow. The first option involved setting up an NLP-based search quickly using Amazon Textract, Amazon Comprehend, and Amazon Elasticsearch using a Lambda function in a CloudFormation template for your scanned resume analysis, and can be used with anything scanned, such as images, invoices, or receipts. For the second option, we covered how you can set up an enterprise-level serverless scalable search solution with Amazon Kendra for your PDF documents. We also walked you through how you can enrich the Amazon Kendra search with additional attributes or metadata generated from Amazon Comprehend named entities.

In the next chapter, we will talk about how you can use AI to improve customer service in your contact center.

Further reading

- *Building an NLP-powered search index with Amazon Textract and Amazon Comprehend* by Mona Mona and Saurabh Shrivastava (`https://aws.amazon.com/blogs/machine-learning/building-an-nlp-powered-search-index-with-amazon-textract-and-amazon-comprehend/`)

- *Build an intelligent search solution with automated content enrichment* by Abhinav Jawadekar and Udi Hershkovich (`https://aws.amazon.com/blogs/machine-learning/build-an-intelligent-search-solution-with-automated-content-enrichment/`)

6
Using NLP to Improve Customer Service Efficiency

So far, we have seen a couple of interesting real-world NLP use cases with intelligent document processing solutions for loan applications in *Chapter 4, Automating Document Processing Workflows*, and built smart search indexes in *Chapter 5, Creating NLP Search*. NLP-based indexing for content search is becoming very popular because it bridges the gap between traditional keyword-based searches, which can be frustrating unless you know exactly what keyword to use, and natural language, to quickly search for what you are interested in. We also saw how we can use Amazon Textract and Amazon Comprehend with services such as Amazon Elasticsearch (`https://aws.amazon.com/elasticsearch-service/`), a service that's fully managed by AWS and provides search and analytics capabilities offered by the open source Elasticsearch, but without the need for infrastructure heavy lifting, installation, or maintenance associated with setting up an Elasticsearch cluster, and Amazon Kendra (`https://aws.amazon.com/kendra/`), a fully managed enterprise search engine powered by ML that provides NLP-based search capabilities, to create an end-to-end smart search solution. In this chapter, we will address a ubiquitous use case that has been around for decades, if not centuries, and yet remains highly important for any business; that is, customer service improvement.

Businesses cannot thrive without customers, and customer satisfaction is a key metric that has a direct correlation to the profitability of an organization. While the touchpoints that organizations have with customers during the sales cycle are important, what is even more important is the effectiveness of their customer service process. Organizations need to respond quickly to customer feedback, understand the emotional undercurrent of a customer conversation, and resolve their issues in the shortest possible time. Happy customers are loyal customers and, of course, this means that the customer churn will be low, which will help keep costs low and improve profitability.

To see improving customer service in action, we will build an AI solution that uses the AWS NLP service known as Amazon Comprehend to analyze historical customer service records to derive key topics using Amazon Comprehend Topic Modeling, train a custom classification model that will predict routing topics for call routing using Amazon Comprehend Custom Classification, and use Amazon Comprehend Detect Sentiments to understand the emotional sentiment of the customer feedback. We will be hands-on throughout this chapter, but we have all the code samples we need to get going.

In this chapter, we will cover the following topics:

- Introducing the customer service use case
- Building an NLP solution to improve customer service

Technical requirements

For this chapter, you will need access to an AWS account. Please make sure that you follow the instructions specified in the *Technical requirements* section of *Chapter 2, Introducing Amazon Textract*, to create your AWS account. You will also need to log into the AWS Management Console before trying the steps in the *Building an NLP solution to improve customer service* section.

The Python code and sample datasets for our solution can be found at `https://github.com/PacktPublishing/Natural-Language-Processing-with-AWS-AI-Services/tree/main/Chapter%2006`. Please use the instructions in the following sections, along with the code in this repository, to build the solution.

Check out the following video to see the Code in Action at `https://bit.ly/2ZpWveN`.

Introducing the customer service use case

So, how can NLP help us improve customer service? To illustrate our example, let's go back to our fictitious banking corporation, **LiveRight Holdings private limited**. **LiveRight** has contact centers in many states of the US, and they receive more than 100,000 calls every day from customers with queries and issues on various topics, such as credit, accounts, debt, and more. While they have a competent team of agents who are highly experienced in handling customer requests, their first-tier triage teams often struggle with interpreting the nature of the customer's request within the first minute of conversation, which is an important SLA for them. This is required to determine which agents to route the request to. They have a team of specialized agents based on product type and experience levels. Junior agents handle customers who are happy with the products, while the challenge of dealing with irate customers is often the task of more experienced agents.

LiveRight's senior management is unhappy with the first-tier team's performance as they are constantly failing to meet the 1-minute SLA. This is further exacerbated by the fact that in the last 3 months, the first-tier team has been incorrectly routing unhappy customers to junior agents, resulting in an increased customer churn. Therefore, senior management wants to automate the first-tier triage process, which will enable their teams to address these issues. **LiveRight** has hired you to design a solution architecture that can automatically determine the routing option and the sentiment of the customer conversation. As the enterprise architect for the project, you have decided to use Amazon Comprehend to leverage its pre-trained ML model for sentiment detection, Comprehend's built-in Topic Modeling feature to determine common themes in a training dataset to determine routing option labels, and the Custom Classifier feature of Amazon Comprehend to incrementally create your own classifier for customer request routing, without the need to build complex NLP algorithms. The components of the solution we will build are shown in the following diagram:

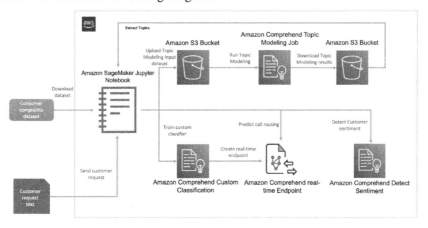

Figure 6.1 – NLP solution build for customer service

We will be walking through this solution using an Amazon SageMaker Jupyter notebook, which will allow us to review the code and results as we execute it step by step. For code samples on how to build this solution as a real-time workflow using AWS Lambda (a serverless, event-driven compute service for running code), please refer to the *Further reading* section:

1. As a first step, we will preprocess our input dataset, which contains consumer complaints available in this book's GitHub repository, load this into an S3 bucket, and run an Amazon Comprehend Topic Modeling job to determine routing option labels.

2. We will then create the training dataset with the routing option labels that have been assigned to the consumer complaints from our input dataset, and then upload this into an S3 bucket.

3. We will use Amazon Comprehend Custom Classification to train a classifier model using the training dataset we created previously.

4. Finally, we will create an Amazon Comprehend real-time endpoint to deploy the trained model and show you how to predict the routing option. We will then show you how to use the Amazon Comprehend Detect Sentiment API to determine the sentiment of the customer conversation in real time.

In this section, we introduced the customer service problem we are trying to solve with our NLP solution, reviewed the challenges faced by **LiveRight**, and looked at an overview of the solution we will build. In the next section, we will walk through the build of the solution step by step.

Building an NLP solution to improve customer service

In the previous section, we introduced the contact center use case for customer service, covered the architecture of the solution we will be building, and briefly walked through the solution components and workflow steps. In this section, we will start executing the tasks to build our solution. But first, there are some prerequisites that we must take care of.

Setting up to solve the use case

If you have not done so already in the previous chapters, you will have to create an Amazon SageMaker Jupyter notebook, and then set up **Identity and Access Management (IAM)** permissions for that notebook role to access the AWS services we will use in this notebook. After that, you will need to clone this book's GitHub repository (https://github.com/PacktPublishing/Natural-Language-Processing-with-AWS-AI-Services), create an Amazon S3 (https://aws.amazon.com/s3/) bucket, go to the Chapter 06 folder, open the chapter6-nlp-in-customer-service-github.ipynb notebook, and provide the bucket name in the notebook to start execution.

> **Note**
>
> Please ensure you have completed the tasks mentioned in the *Technical requirements* section.

If you have already completed the following steps in one of the previous chapters, please go to the *Preprocessing the customer service history data* section:

1. Please refer to the Amazon SageMaker documentation to create a notebook instance: https://docs.aws.amazon.com/sagemaker/latest/dg/gs-setup-working-env.html. To follow these steps, please sign into **AWS Management Console** and type in and select **Amazon SageMaker** from the search window. Then, navigate to the **Amazon SageMaker** console.

2. Select **Notebook instances** and create a Notebook instance by specifying an instance type, storage, and an IAM role.

> **IAM role permissions while creating Amazon SageMaker Jupyter notebooks**
>
> Accept the default for the IAM role at notebook creation time to allow access to any S3 bucket. Select **ComprehendFullAccess** as a permission policy by clicking on the IAM role and navigating to the Identity and Access Management console for the role being created. You can always go back to the IAM role for your notebook instances and attach other permissions policies as required.

3. Once you've created the notebook instance and its status is **InService**, click on **Open Jupyter** in the **Actions** menu heading for the notebook instance:

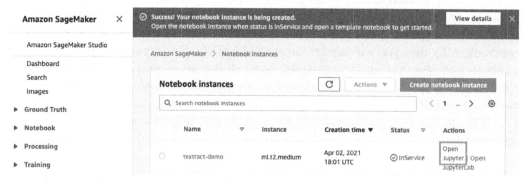

Figure 6.2 – Opening the Jupyter notebook

This will take you to the home folder of your notebook instance.

4. Click on **New** and select **Terminal**, as shown in the following screenshot:

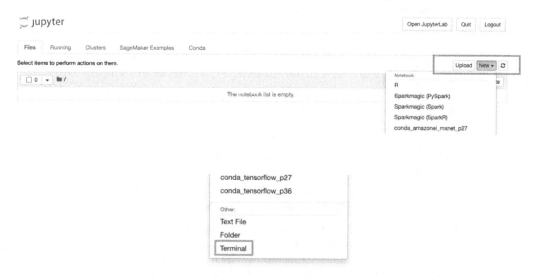

Figure 6.3 – Opening a Terminal in a Jupyter notebook

5. In the Terminal window, type `cd SageMaker` and then `git clone https://github.com/PacktPublishing/Natural-Language-Processing-with-AWS-AI-Services`, as shown in the following screenshot:

Jupyter

```
sh-4.2$ pwd
/home/ec2-user
sh-4.2$ cd SageMaker/
sh-4.2$ git clone https://github.com/PacktPublishing/Natural-Language-Processing-with-AWS-AI-Services
```

Figure 6.4 – git clone command

6. Now, exit the Terminal window and go back to the home folder. You will see a folder called `Natural-Language-Processing-with-AWS-AI-Services`. Click it; you will see a folder called `Chapter 06`. Click this folder; you should see a notebook called `chapter6-nlp-in-customer-service-github`.

7. Open this notebook by clicking it.

8. Follow the steps in this notebook that correspond to the next few subheadings in this section by executing one cell at a time. Please read the descriptions provided above each notebook cell.

Now that we have set up our notebook and cloned the repository, let's add the permissions policies we need to successfully run our code sample.

Additional IAM prerequisites

To train the Comprehend custom entity recognizer and set up real-time endpoints, we have to enable additional policies and also update the Trust Relationships for our SageMaker notebook role. Please complete the following steps to do this:

1. Please attach the `ComprehendFullAccess` policies to your Amazon SageMaker Notebook IAM role. To execute this step, please refer to the *Changing IAM permissions and Trust relationships for the Amazon SageMaker notebook execution role* subsection in the *Setting up your AWS environment* section of *Chapter 2, Introducing Amazon Textract*.

2. Your SageMaker Execution Role should have access to S3 already. If not, add the following JSON statement as an inline policy. For instructions, please refer to the *Changing IAM permissions and Trust relationships for the Amazon SageMaker notebook execution role* subsection in the *Setting up your AWS environment* section of *Chapter 2, Introducing Amazon Textract*:

```
{ "Version": "2012-10-17", "Statement": [ {
    "Action": [
        "s3:GetObject",
        "s3:ListBucket",
        "s3:PutObject"
```

```
    ],
    "Resource": ["*"],
    "Effect": "Allow"
        }
    ]
}
```

3. Finally, update the Trust relationships for your SageMaker Notebook execution role.
    For instructions, please refer to the *Changing IAM permissions and Trust relationships*
    for the Amazon SageMaker notebook execution role subsection in the *Setting up your*
    AWS environment section of *Chapter 2, Introducing Amazon Textract*:

```
{ "Version": "2012-10-17", "Statement": [
  { "Effect": "Allow",
    "Principal":
      { "Service":
        [ "sagemaker.amazonaws.com",
          "s3.amazonaws.com",
          "comprehend.amazonaws.com" ]
      },
      "Action": "sts:AssumeRole" }
  ]
}
```

Now that we have set up our Notebook and set up an IAM role to run the walkthrough
notebook, in the next section, we will start processing the data for topic modeling.

Preprocessing the customer service history data

Let's begin by downloading and reviewing the customer service records we will use for this chapter. We will use the Consumer Complaints data for the State of Ohio from the Consumer Financial Protection Bureau for our solution: `https://www.consumerfinance.gov/data-research/consumer-complaints/search/?dataNormalization=None&dateRange=1y&date_received_max=2021-05-17&date_received_min=2020-05-17&searchField=all&state=OH&tab=Map`. You can try other datasets from this site, or your own unique customer service data. For your convenience, the complaints data is included as a CSV file in the GitHub repository: `https://github.com/PacktPublishing/Natural-Language-Processing-with-AWS-AI-Services/blob/main/Chapter%2006/topic-modeling/initial/complaints_data_initial.csv`. This should be available to you when you clone the repository. You can click on the CSV file by going to the folder it is present in inside the notebook to review its contents. Alternatively, you can view it using the code provided in the `chapter6-nlp-in-customer-service-github.ipynb` notebook.

Open the notebook and perform the following steps:

1. Execute the cells under **Prerequisites** to ensure we have the libraries we need for the notebook. Note that in this cell, you are getting the Amazon SageMaker Execution Role for the notebook. Please ensure that you create an Amazon S3 bucket (`https://docs.aws.amazon.com/AmazonS3/latest/userguide/create-bucket-overview.html`) and provide the bucket name in the line. Type in a prefix of your choice or accept what is already provided in the notebook:

    ```
    bucket = '<bucket-name>'
    prefix = 'chapter6'
    ```

2. Execute the cells under **Preprocess the Text data**.

    First, we will load the CSV file containing the consumer complaints data (this is already provided to you in this book's GitHub repository at (`https://github.com/PacktPublishing/Natural-Language-Processing-with-AWS-AI-Services/blob/main/Chapter%2006/topic-modeling/initial/complaints_data_initial.csv`) into a pandas DataFrame object for easy manipulation:

    ```
    raw_df = pd.read_csv('topic-modeling/initial/complaints_data_initial.csv')
    raw_df.shape
    ```

When we execute the preceding cell, we will see that the notebook returns a shape of (11485, 18), which means there are 11,485 rows and 18 columns. We are only interested in the **Consumer complaint narrative** field, so we will drop the rest of the fields from the dataset. After we execute this cell, the shape should change to (5152, 1):

```
raw_df = raw_df.dropna(subset=['Consumer complaint
narrative'])
raw_df = pd.DataFrame(raw_df['Consumer complaint
narrative'].copy())
raw_df.shape
```

Now, let's convert this back into an updated CSV file:

```
raw_df.to_csv('topic-modeling/raw/complaints_data_subset.
csv', header=False, index=False)
```

Execute the cells in the notebook to clean up the textual content in our CSV file, including restructuring the text into individual sentences so that each consumer complaint is a separate line. For the source of this code block and a very good discussion on how to use the Python regex function with sentences, please refer to https://stackoverflow.com/questions/4576077/how-can-i-split-a-text-into-sentences. Continue executing the cells to remove unnecessary spaces or punctuation, create a new CSV file with these changes, and upload it to an S3 bucket. We will also create a new pandas DataFrame object with the formatted content so that we can use it in the subsequent steps. Please execute all the remaining cells in the notebook from *Preprocess the Text data*:

```
# Write the formatted sentences into a CSV file
import csv
fnfull = "topic-modeling/input/complaints_data_formatted.
csv"
with open(fnfull, "w", encoding='utf-8') as ff:
    csv_writer = csv.writer(ff, delimiter=',', quotechar
= '"')
    for infile in all_files:
        for num, sentence in enumerate(infile):
            csv_writer.writerow([sentence])
# Let's store the formatted CSV into a Pandas DataFrame
# as we will use this to create the training dataset for
our custom classifier
columns = ['Text']
```

```
form_df = pd.read_csv('topic-modeling/input/complaints_
data_formatted.csv', header=None, names = columns)
```

```
form_df.shape
```

```
# Upload the CSV file to the input prefix in S3 to be
used in the topic modeling job
```

```
s3 = boto3.client('s3')
```

```
s3.upload_file('topic-modeling/input/complaints_data_
formatted.csv', bucket, prefix+'/topic_modeling/input/
topic_input.csv')
```

3. Next, we will run an Amazon Comprehend Topic Modeling job on this formatted
    CSV file to extract a set of topics that can be applied to our list of consumer
    complaints. These topics represent and help us identify the subject area or the theme
    for the related text, as well as represent the common set of words with the same
    contextual reference throughout the document. For more details, please refer to
    Amazon Comprehend Topic Modeling at https://docs.aws.amazon.com/
    comprehend/latest/dg/topic-modeling.html.

    To get started, go to the AWS Console (please refer to the *Technical requirements*
    section if you don't have access to the AWS Console) and type Amazon
    Comprehend in the services search window at the top of the console. Then, navigate
    to the Amazon Comprehend Console.

    Click the **Launch Amazon Comprehend** button.

    Click on **Analysis jobs** in the left pane and click on **Create job** on the right, as
    shown in the following screenshot:

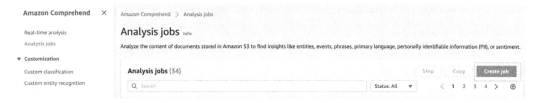

Figure 6.5 – Creating an analysis job

Type in a name for your analysis job and select **Topic modeling** as the analysis type from the built-in jobs list. Provide the location of the CSV file in your S3 bucket in the **Input data** section, with **Data source** set to **My documents** and **Number of topics** set to 8, as shown in the following screenshot:

Job settings

Name

chapter6-topic-modeling-1

The name can have up to 256 characters. Valid characters: A-Z, a-z, 0-9, space, and % + . / : = @ _ - (hyphen)

Analysis type Info

Topic modeling   ▼

🅞 Job encryption Info

Input data Info

Data source

🅞 **My documents**
     We recommend providing at least 1,000 documents containing at least 100 words each.

◯ **Example documents**
     Example documents are available only in English

S3 location
Paste the URL of an input data file in S3, or select a bucket or folder location in S3.

s3://nlp-book-samples/chapter6/topic_modeling/input/topic_input.csv | Browse S3

Input format - *optional* Info

Choose input format   ▼

Number of topics Info

8

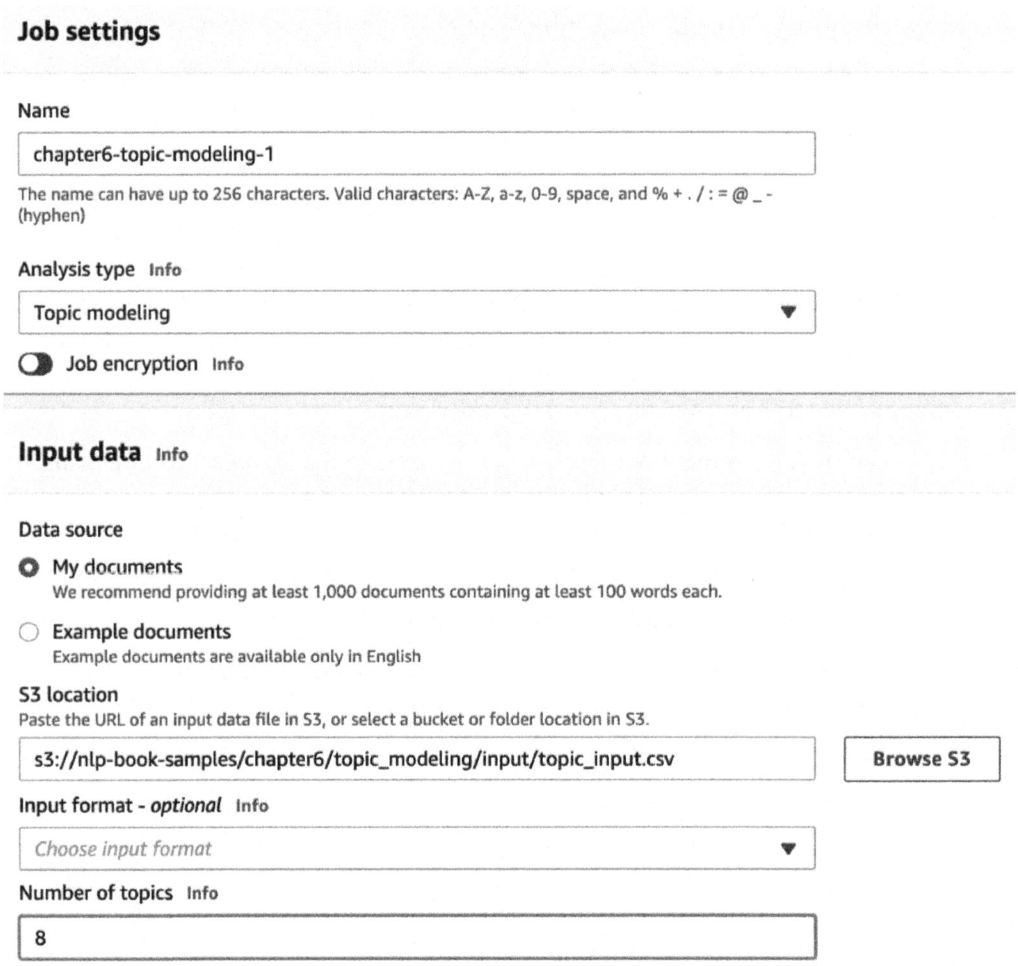

Figure 6.6 – Creating topic modeling job inputs – part1

Provide the details for the rest of the fields and click on **Create job**, as shown in the following screenshot:

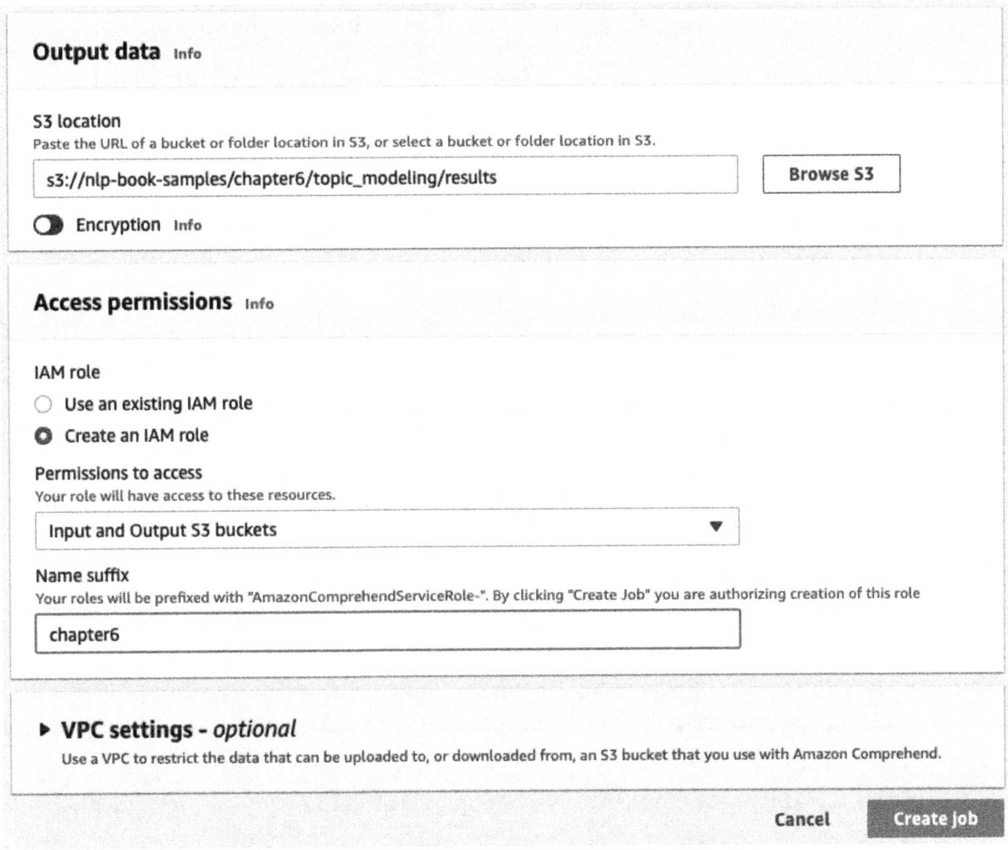

Output data Info

S3 location
Paste the URL of a bucket or folder location in S3, or select a bucket or folder location in S3.

s3://nlp-book-samples/chapter6/topic_modeling/results

Browse S3

🔘 Encryption Info

Access permissions Info

IAM role
○ Use an existing IAM role
◉ Create an IAM role

Permissions to access
Your role will have access to these resources.

Input and Output S3 buckets ▼

Name suffix
Your roles will be prefixed with "AmazonComprehendServiceRole-". By clicking "Create Job" you are authorizing creation of this role

chapter6

▶ **VPC settings - *optional***
Use a VPC to restrict the data that can be uploaded to, or downloaded from, an S3 bucket that you use with Amazon Comprehend.

Cancel   Create job

Figure 6.7 – Creating topic modeling job inputs – part 2

You should see a job submitted status after the IAM role propagation is completed, as shown in the following screenshot. The job should take about 30 minutes to complete, which gives you time to have a quick snack or a coffee/tea. Now, click on the job's name, copy the S3 link provided in the **Output data location** field, and go back to your notebook. We will continue the steps in the notebook:

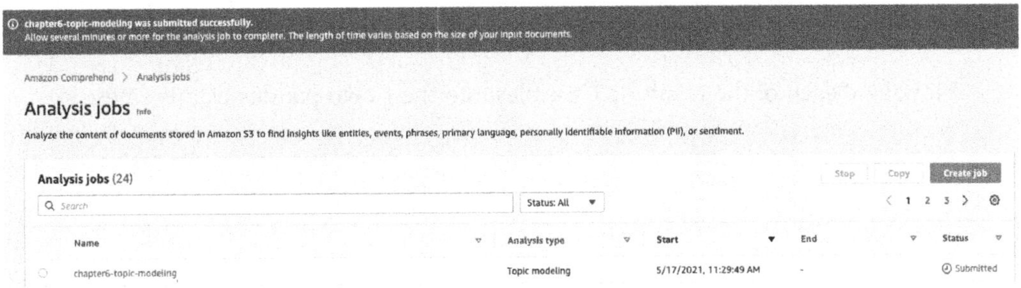

ⓘ chapter6-topic-modeling was submitted successfully.
Allow several minutes or more for the analysis job to complete. The length of time varies based on the size of your input documents.

Amazon Comprehend > Analysis jobs

Analysis jobs Info

Analyze the content of documents stored in Amazon S3 to find insights like entities, events, phrases, primary language, personally identifiable information (PII), or sentiment.

Analysis jobs (24)   Stop Copy Create job

Q Search		Status: All ▼			‹ 1 2 3 › ⚙
Name	▽	Analysis type	▽	Start ▼	End ▽	Status ▽
○ chapter6-topic-modeling		Topic modeling		5/17/2021, 11:29:49 AM	-	⊘ Submitted

Figure 6.8 – Topic modeling job submitted

4. We will now execute the cells in the Process Topic Modeling Results section.

To download the results of the Topic Modeling job, we need the **Output data location** S3 URI that you copied in the previous step. In the first cell in this section of the notebook, replace the contents of the tpprefix variable – specifically **<name-of-your-output-data-s3-prefix>** – with the results prefix from the S3 URI, as shown in the following code block. This is the string after the results prefix and before the output prefix in your S3 URI:

```
# Output data location S3 URI

https://s3.console.aws.amazon.com/s3/object/<bucket>/
chapter6/topic_modeling/results/123456789-TOPICS-long-
hash-code/output/output.tar.gz?region=us-east-1

tpprefix = prefix+'/topic_modeling/results/<name-of-your-
comprehend-topic-modeling-job>/output/output.tar.gz'
```

The revised code should look as follows. When executed, it will download the output.tar.gz file locally and extract it:

```
# Let's first download the results of the topic modeling
job.

# Please copy the output data location from your topic
modeling job for this step and use it below

directory = "results"

parent_dir = os.getcwd()+'/topic-modeling'

# Path

path = os.path.join(parent_dir, directory)

os.makedirs(path, exist_ok = True)

print("Directory '%s' created successfully" %directory)

tpprefix = prefix+'/topic_modeling/results/123456789-
TOPICS-long-hash-code/output/output.tar.gz'

s3.download_file(bucket, tpprefix, 'topic-modeling/
results/output.tar.gz')

!tar -xzvf topic-modeling/results/output.tar.gz
```

Now, load each of the resulting CSV files into their own pandas DataFrames:

```
tt_df = pd.read_csv('topic-terms.csv')

dt_df = pd.read_csv('doc-topics.csv')
```

The topic terms DataFrame contains the topic number, what term corresponds to the topic, and how much weight this term contributes to the topic. Execute the code shown in the following code block to review the contents of the topic terms DataFrame:

```
for i,x in tt_df.iterrows():

    print(str(x['topic'])+":"+x['term']+":"+str(x['weight']))
```

We may have multiple topics in the same line, but for this solution, we are not interested in these duplicates, so we will drop them:

```
dt_df = dt_df.drop_duplicates(subset=['docname'])
```

Now, let's filter the topics so that we select the topic with the maximum weight distribution for text it refers to:

```
ttdf_max = tt_df.groupby(['topic'], sort=False)
['weight'].max()
```

Load these into their own DataFrame and display them:

```
newtt_df = pd.DataFrame()
for x in ttdf_max:
    newtt_df = newtt_df.append(tt_df.query('weight ==
@x'))
newtt_df = newtt_df.reset_index(drop=True)
newtt_df
```

Having reviewed the consumer complaints input text data, the masked characters that are displayed mainly correspond to debt-related complaints from customers, so we will replace the masked terms with **debt** and replace the word **Husband** with **family**. These terms will become the training labels for our Amazon Comprehend Custom Classification model, which we will then use to automate request routing in the next section. Please execute the following code in the notebook:

```
form_df.assign(Label='')
for i, r in dt_df.iterrows():
    line = int(r['docname'].split(':')[1])
    top = r['topic']
    tdf = newtt_df.query('topic == @top')
    term = tdf['term'].values[0]
    if term == 'xxxx':
        term = 'debt'
```

```
    if term == 'husband':
        term = 'family'
    form_df.at[line, 'Label'] = term
```

Create the `custom-classification` and `train` folders, which we need in the notebook to execute the next step, as shown in the following code block:

```
directory = "custom-classification"
parent_dir = os.getcwd()

path = os.path.join(parent_dir, directory)
os.makedirs(path, exist_ok = True)
print("Directory '%s' created successfully" %directory)

directory = "train"
parent_dir = os.getcwd()+'/custom-classification'

path = os.path.join(parent_dir, directory)
os.makedirs(path, exist_ok = True)
print("Directory '%s' created successfully" %directory)
```

Now, let's rearrange the columns so that we have the label as the first column. We will convert this into a CSV file and upload it into our S3 bucket. This CSV file will be the training dataset for our Amazon Comprehend Custom Classification model:

```
form_df = form_df[['Label','Text']]
form_df.to_csv('custom-classification/train/train.csv',
header=None, index=False)
s3.upload_file('custom-classification/train/train.csv',
bucket, prefix+'/custom_classification/train/train.csv')
```

5. Now, we will go back to the Amazon Comprehend AWS Console to train our Custom Classification model, which can predict a label for a given text. These labels are the topics we modeled in the previous section. With Amazon Comprehend Custom, you can train models that are unique to your business incrementally on top of the pre-trained, highly powerful Comprehend models. So, these custom models leverage what the default Comprehend model already knows, thereby training quickly, They are also more accurate than if you were to build a custom classification model from the ground up. You can run this training process without any ML skills with just a few clicks in the Amazon Comprehend console. For more details, please refer to `https://docs.aws.amazon.com/comprehend/latest/dg/how-document-classification.html`.

    To get started, go to the AWS Console (please refer to the *Technical requirements* section at the beginning of this chapter if you don't have access to the AWS Console) and type Amazon Comprehend in the services search window at the top of the console. Then, navigate to the Amazon Comprehend Console.

    Click the **Launch Amazon Comprehend** button.

    Click on **Custom classification** under the **Customization** title in the left pane.

    Click on **Train classifier**, as shown in the following screenshot:

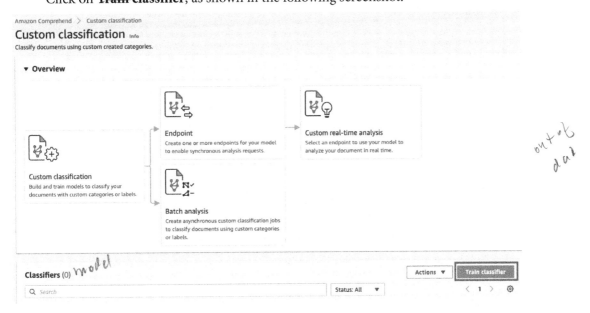

Figure 6.9 – Train classifier button

Enter a name for your classifier, leave the language as English, and set **Classifier mode** to **Multi-class**. (For our solution, we predict one label per document. If you need to predict multiple labels per document, you can use the **Multi-label** mode.) Select **CSV file** under **Training data format**, as shown in the following screenshot:

Train classifier Info

Classifier settings

Name

chapter6-cust-class-1

The name can have up to 63 characters, and it must be unique. Valid characters: A-Z, a-z, 0-9, and - (hyphen)

Language

English ▼

⬤ Classifier encryption Info

Training data Info

Classifier mode

⦿ Using Multi-class mode	◯ Using Multi-label mode
The training data file must have one class and one document on each line. It must have at least 10 documents for each class.	The training data file must have one or more classes and one document on each line. It must have at least 10 documents for each class.
Example	Example

COMEDY	document text 1
COMEDY	document text 2
DRAMA	document text 3

COMEDY	document text 1
DRAMA	document text 2
COMEDY I DRAMA	document text 3

Training data format

To train your custom model, you must provide training data. This data must be formatted as either a CSV file or as one or more augmented manifest files.

⦿ CSV file Info

A two-column CSV file that contains classes in one column and training data in the other. The required format depends on the classifier mode.

Figure 6.10 – Custom classifier inputs – part 1

Provide our training dataset's **S3 location**; that is, the one we created in the previous section. For **IAM role**, if you created an **AmazonComprehendServiceRole** in the previous chapters, use that, or select **Create an IAM role** and choose **Any S3 Bucket** from the list. Click the **Train classifier** button, as shown in the following screenshot:

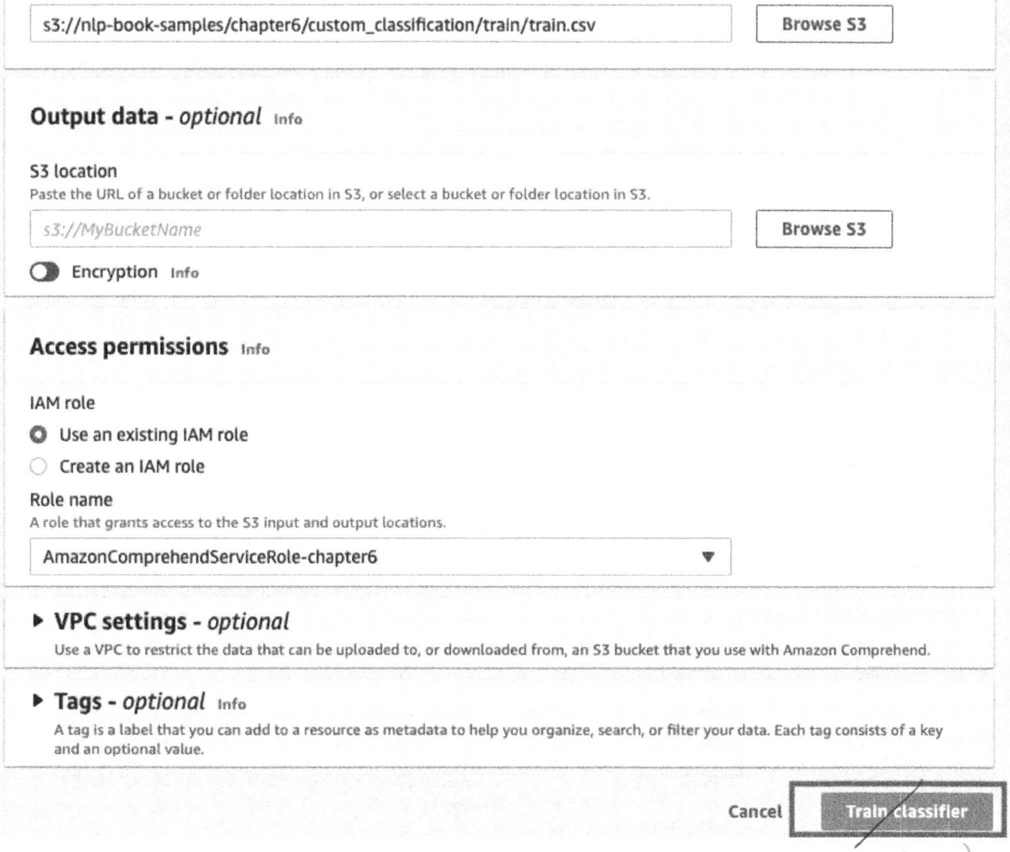

Figure 6.11 – Custom classifier inputs – part 2

The training job will be submitted. Shortly after, the training job's status will change to **Training**, as shown in the following screenshot:

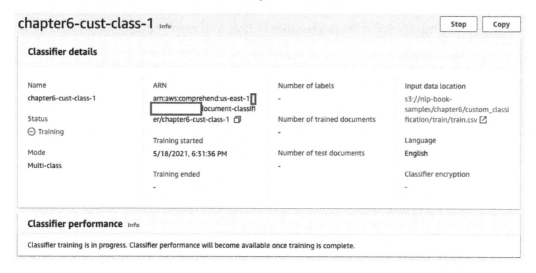

Figure 6.12 – Custom classifier training

Training will take approximately 1 hour to complete. The status will change to **Trained** when the job completes, as shown in the following screenshot:

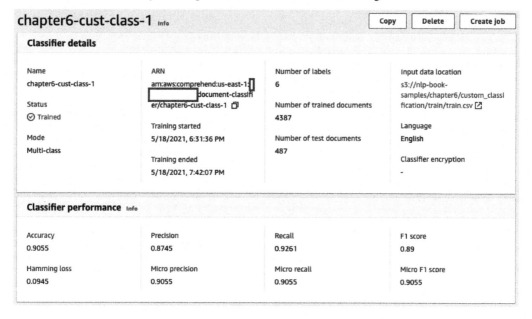

Figure 6.13 – Custom classifier training complete

6. Now that we have finished training our classifier, we will create a real-time endpoint to deploy the model. We will use this endpoint in our solution to run predictions for routing requests.

    Click on the name of your classifier in the Amazon Comprehend console. Then, scroll down to the **Endpoints** section and click **Create endpoint**, as shown in the following screenshot:

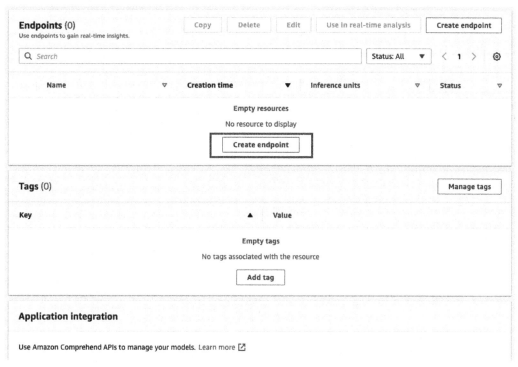

Figure 6.14 – Creating a Comprehend endpoint

Type in a name for your endpoint, provide an inference unit value of 1, and click on **Create endpoint**, as shown in the following screenshot. Inference units determine the price and capacity of the provisioned endpoint. An inference unit provides a prediction throughput of 100 characters every second. For more details, please refer to Amazon Comprehend's pricing guide at `https://aws.amazon.com/comprehend/pricing/`:

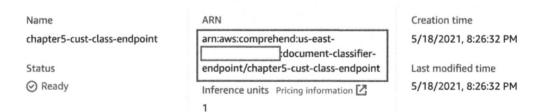

Figure 6.15 – Creating Comprehend endpoint inputs

Once the endpoint has been created, please make a note of the endpoint's ARN by clicking on the name of the endpoint, as shown in the following screenshot. This will be required for running inference in the notebook:

Endpoint details

Name	ARN	Creation time
chapter5-cust-class-endpoint	arn:aws:comprehend:us-east-____:document-classifier-endpoint/chapter5-cust-class-endpoint	5/18/2021, 8:26:32 PM
Status		Last modified time
⊘ Ready	Inference units Pricing information 🔗	5/18/2021, 8:26:32 PM
	1	

Figure 6.16 – Comprehend endpoint ARN

7. As a next step, we will navigate back to our notebook and execute the steps in the *Automate Request Routing* section.

Provide the endpoint ARN you took note of in the previous step in the notebook cell:

```
endpoint_arn = '<comprehend-custom-classifier-endpoint-
arn>'
```

Now, let's execute the next cell, which shows us how to run the real-time analysis with our endpoint. For input, we will use a sample text message that's been assigned to the `test_text` variable, as shown in the following code:

```
test_text = 'because of your inability to accept my
payments on time I now have a really bad credit score,
you need to fix this now'
comprehend = boto3.client('comprehend')
response = comprehend.classify_document(Text=test_text,
EndpointArn=endpoint_arn)
print(response)
```

Our custom classifier returns a response, as shown in the following code block:

```
{'Classes': [{'Name': 'account', 'Score':
0.9856781363487244}, {'Name': 'credit', 'Score':
0.013113172724843025}, {'Name': 'debt', 'Score':
0.0005924980505369604}], 'ResponseMetadata':
{'RequestId': 'c26c226c-3878-447e-95f5-60b4d91bb536',
'HTTPStatusCode': 200, 'HTTPHeaders': {'x-amzn-
requestid': 'c26c226c-3878-447e-95f5-60b4d91bb536',
'content-type': 'application/x-amz-json-1.1', 'content-
length': '151', 'date': 'Wed, 19 May 2021 17:35:38 GMT'},
'RetryAttempts': 0}}
```

Run the code given in the following code block to select the `Name` property with the highest confidence score from the response. This will be the department or the option that the customer request will be routed to in the contact center:

```
cls_df = pd.DataFrame(response['Classes'])
max_score = cls_df['Score'].max()
routing_type = cls_df.query('Score == @max_score')
['Name'].values[0]
print("This request should be routed to: " + routing_
type)
```

This code will return the following response:

```
This request should be routed to: account
```

8. As a next step, we will execute the steps in the *Automate Feedback Analysis* section.

To analyze the sentiment of the customer conversation, we will use the **Amazon Comprehend Detect Sentiment API**. This is a built-in feature in Amazon Comprehend and does not require us to train any models. We can directly call the API with input. It will return the sentiment of the text, as follows:

```
sent_response = comprehend.detect_sentiment(
    Text=test_text,
    LanguageCode='en'
)
print("The customer's feedback sentiment is: " + sent_
response['Sentiment'])
The customer's feedback sentiment is: NEGATIVE
```

That concludes the solution build for this chapter. Please refer to the *Further reading* section for examples that are similar to this use case. In the case of **LiveRight**, you can integrate this build into the existing contact center workflow and scale the solution using **Amazon Transcribe**, **AWS StepFunctions**, and **AWS Lambda**. An example of how to do this is shown in the following diagram:

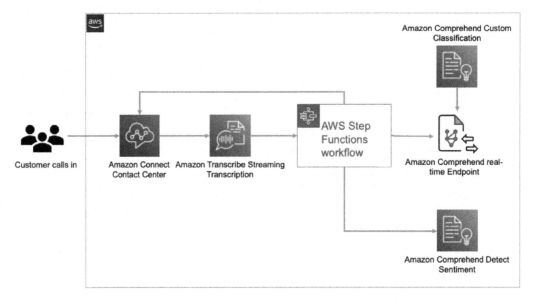

Figure 6.17 – NLP in customer service with a real-time transcription

Amazon Transcribe provides real-time streaming transcription capabilities to convert a customer call from speech into text. Please refer to https://aws.amazon.com/transcribe/ for more details. An AWS Step Functions (https://aws.amazon.com/step-functions/) workflow that enables orchestration of a complete process flow with AWS Lambda (a fully managed serverless compute service that can run code without the need to provision servers (https://aws.amazon.com/lambda/)) and multiple AWS services can be set up to be triggered on receipt of a transcription of a specified length. The Step Functions workflow will call an AWS Lambda function to detect the routing option for the customer request, and the call can be automatically routed to that option, or/and the customer request/feedback sentiment can be analyzed by calling the Detect Sentiment API, as we saw in the *Automate feedback analysis* section. The outcome is that while the call is in progress, the contact center agent will have an automated response with a predicted routing option and sentiment, which, in turn, helps resolve the customer's request quickly and efficiently.

Summary

In this chapter, we learned how to build an NLP solution to accelerate customer service efficiencies using Amazon Comprehend's Topic Modeling feature, Detect Sentiment feature, and by training our own custom classifier to predict routing options using Comprehend Custom Classification before hosting it using Comprehend real-time endpoints. We also saw how we can leverage the flexibility of powerful and accurate NLP models without the need for any ML skills. For your enterprise needs, Amazon Comprehend scales seamlessly to process millions of documents, provides usage-based pricing, supports batch inference, and with autoscaling support for real-time endpoints, you can manage your inference request volumes and control your inference costs effectively.

For our solution, we started by introducing the customer service use case, the inherent challenges with the way things are set up currently, and the need to perform automated routing and sentiment detection to control the high customer churn caused by current inefficient processes. We then designed an architecture to use Amazon Comprehend to identify common themes or topics, create a training dataset, train a custom classifier to predict routing options, and to run sentiment analysis on the customer request. We assumed that you were the solution architect that had been assigned to this project, and we provided an overview of the solution components, along with a diagram of the architecture in *Figure 6.1*.

We then went through the prerequisites for the solution build, set up an Amazon SageMaker notebook instance, cloned our GitHub repository, and started executing the code in the notebook based on the instructions provided in this chapter.

In the next chapter, we will look at a slightly related use case on using NLP to run the voice of the customer analytics process. We will introduce the use case, discuss how to design the architecture, establish the prerequisites, and walk through the various steps required to build the solution.

Further reading

- *Announcing the launch of Amazon Comprehend custom entity recognition real-time endpoints*, by Mona Mona and Prem Ranga (`https://aws.amazon.com/blogs/machine-learning/announcing-the-launch-of-amazon-comprehend-custom-entity-recognition-real-time-endpoints/`).

- *Active learning workflow for Amazon Comprehend custom classification models – Part 2*, by Shanthan Kesharaju, Joyson Neville Lewis, and Mona Mona (`https://aws.amazon.com/blogs/machine-learning/active-learning-workflow-for-amazon-comprehend-custom-classification-part-2/`).

7

Understanding the Voice of Your Customer Analytics

In the previous chapters, to see improving customer service in action, we built an AI solution that uses the **AWS NLP** service **Amazon Comprehend** to first analyze historical customer service records to derive key topics using Amazon Comprehend Topic Modeling and train a custom classification model that will predict routing topics for call routing using **Amazon Comprehend Custom Classification**. Finally, we used **Amazon Comprehend detect sentiment** to understand the emotional aspect of the customer feedback.

In this chapter, we are going to focus more on the emotional aspect of the customer feedback, which could be an Instagrammer, Yelp reviewer, or your aunt posting comments about your business on Facebook, and so on and so forth.

Twenty years back, it was extremely tough to find out as soon as possible what people felt about your products and get meaningful feedback to improve them. With globalization and the invention of social media, nowadays, everyone has social media apps and people express their emotions more freely than ever before. We all love tweeting about Twitter posts and expressing our opinions in happy, sad, angry, and neutral modes. If you are a very popular person such as a movie star or a business getting millions of such comments, the challenges become going through large volumes of tweets posted by your fans and then quickly finding out whether your movie did well or it was a flop. In the case of a business, a company, or a start-up, people quickly know by reading comments whether your customer service and product support are good or not.

Social media analytics is a really popular and challenging use case. In this chapter, we will focus on text analytics use cases. We will talk about some of the very common use cases where the power of NLP will be combined with analytics to analyze unstructured data from chats, social media comments, emails, or PDFs. We will show you how you can quickly set up powerful analytics for social media reviews.

We will navigate through the following sections:

- Challenges of setting up a text analytics solution
- Setting up a Yelp review text analytics workflow

Technical requirements

For this chapter, you will need access to an AWS account. Before getting started, we recommend that you create an AWS account, and if you have not created one, please refer to the previous chapter for sign-up details. You can skip signup if you already have an existing AWS account and are following instructions from past chapters for creating the AWS account. The Python code and sample datasets for Amazon Textract examples are at the repository link here: `https://github.com/PacktPublishing/ Natural-Language-Processing-with-AWS-AI-Services/tree/main/ Chapter%2007`.

We will walk you through the setup steps on how you can set up the preceding code repository on a Jupyter notebook with the correct IAM permissions in the *Setting up to solve the use case* section.

Check out the following video to see the Code in Action at `https://bit. ly/3mfioWX`.

Challenges of setting up a text analytics solution

One of the challenges most organizations face is getting business insights from unstructured data.

This data can be in various formats, such as chats, PDF documents, emails, tweets, and so on. Since this data does not have a structure, it's really challenging for the traditional data analytics tool to perform analytics on it. This is where Amazon Textract and Amazon Comprehend can help.

Amazon Textract can make this unstructured data structured by extracting text and then Amazon Comprehend can extract insights. Once we have the data in text, you can perform serverless **Extract, Transform, Load (ETL)** by using **Amazon Glue** and convert it into a structured format. Moreover, you can use **Amazon Athena** to perform serverless ad hoc SQL analytics on the unstructured text you just extracted and transformed using Glue ETL. Amazon Glue can also crawl your unstructured data or text extracted from Amazon Textract in Amazon S3 and store it in a Hive metadata store.

Lastly, you can also analyze and visualize this data using **Amazon QuickSight** to gain business insight.

Amazon QuickSight helps you create quick visualizations and dashboards to be shared with your business or integrated into an application for your end users. For example, you are using Instagram for business and want to analyze the comments posted on your product pictures and create a real-time dashboard to know whether people are posting positive or negative comments about them. You can use the components mentioned to create a real-time social media analytics dashboard.

We all love eating out in a restaurant. The challenge is picking the best restaurant based just on reviews.

We are going to show you how you can analyze Yelp reviews by using the succeeding architecture:

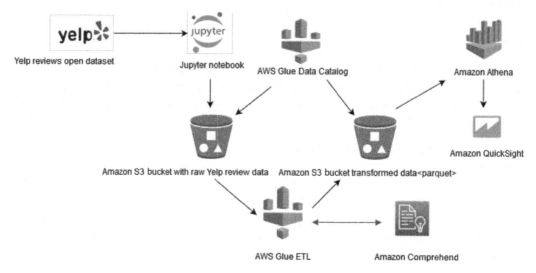

Figure 7.1 – Social media analytics serverless architecture

The architecture in *Figure 7.1* walks you through how you take raw data and transform it to provide new insights, optimize datasets in your data lake, and visualize the serverless results. We will start by doing the following:

1. Getting the Yelp review dataset and uploading it to an Amazon S3 bucket using the Jupyter notebook.

2. Registering the raw data in the AWS Glue Data Catalog by crawling it.

3. Performing AWS Glue ETL on this raw data cataloged in the AWS Glue Data Catalog. Once registered in the AWS Glue Data Catalog, after crawling the Yelp reviews data in AWS S3, this ETL will transform the raw data into Parquet format and enrich it with Amazon Comprehend insights.

4. Now we can crawl and catalog this data again in the AWS Glue Data Catalog. Cataloging adds the tables and metadata for Amazon Athena for ad hoc SQL analytics.

5. Lastly, you can quickly create visualizations on this transformed Parquet data crawled in Amazon Athena using Amazon QuickSight. Amazon QuickSight integrates directly with Amazon Athena as well as Amazon S3 as a data source for visualization.

You can also convert this solution into a real-time streaming solution by using Amazon Kinesis Data Firehose, which will call these Yelp reviews and Twitter APIs, and directly store near real-time streaming data in Amazon S3, and from there you can use AWS Glue ETL and cataloging with Amazon Comprehend to transform and enrich with NLP. Then this transformed data can be directly visualized in QuickSight and Athena. Moreover, you can use AWS Lambda functions and step functions to set up a completely serverless architecture and automate these steps.

In this section, we covered the challenges of setting up a text analytics workflow with unstructured data and proposed architecture. In the next section, we will walk you through how you can build this out for a Yelp reviews dataset or any social media analytics dataset using a few lines of code through a Jupyter notebook.

Setting up a Yelp review text analytics workflow

In this section, we will walk you through how you can build this out for a Yelp reviews dataset or any social media analytics dataset by following the steps using a Jupyter notebook and Python APIs:

- Setting up to solve the use case
- Walking through the solution using a Jupyter notebook

The setup steps will involve the steps to configure **Identity and Access Management (IAM)** roles and the walkthrough notebook will walk you through the architecture. So, let's get started.

Setting up to solve the use case

If you have not done so in the previous chapters, you will first have to create an Amazon SageMaker Jupyter notebook and set up **IAM** permissions for that notebook role to access the AWS services we will use in this notebook. After that, you will need to clone the GitHub repository (`https://github.com/PacktPublishing/Natural-Language-Processing-with-AWS-AI-Services`), go to the `Chapter 07` folder, and open the `chapter07 social media text analytics.ipynb` notebook:

1. You can refer to the Amazon SageMaker documentation to create a notebook instance: `https://docs.aws.amazon.com/sagemaker/latest/dg/gs-setup-working-env.html`. To follow these steps, please sign in to the **AWS Management Console**, type `Amazon SageMaker` in the search window, select it, and navigate to the **Amazon SageMaker** console.

2. Select **Notebook instances** and create a notebook instance by specifying an instance type, storage, and an IAM role.

3. When creating a SageMaker notebook for this setup, you will need IAM access to the services that follow:

    A. AWS Glue to run ETL jobs and crawl the data

    B. AWS Athena to call Athena APIs through the notebook

    C. AWS Comprehend to perform sentiment analysis

    D. AWS QuickSight for visualization

    E. AWS S3 access

    Make sure your IAM for the notebook has the following roles:

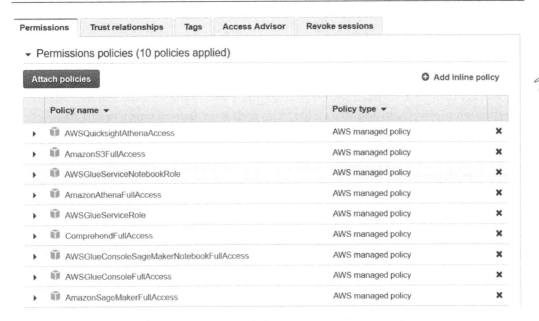

Figure 7.2 – Important IAM roles to run the notebook

You can modify an existing notebook role you are using to add these permissions. In *Figure 7.2* is the SageMaker IAM role that you used to create your notebook instance. You can navigate to that role and click **Attach policies** to make sure you have the necessary roles for your notebook to execute the service APIs we are going to use.

Follow through the steps in this notebook that correspond to the next few subheadings in this section, by executing one cell at a time. Please do read the descriptions provided in each notebook cell.

Additional IAM pre-requisites for invoking AWS Glue from this notebook

In the previous section, we walked you through how to set up the notebook and important IAM roles to run this notebook. In this section, we assume that you are already in the notebook and we have added instructions in the notebook on how you can get the execution role of the notebook and enable it to invoke AWS Glue jobs from this notebook.

Go to the notebook and follow the *Finding out the current execution role of the notebook* section by running the following code:

```
import sagemaker
from sagemaker import get_execution_role
sess = sagemaker.Session()
```

```
role = get_execution_role()
role_name = role[role.rfind('/') + 1:]
print(role_name)
```

You will get the role associated with this notebook. Now, in the next section, we will walk you through how you can add AWS Glue as an additional trusted entity to this role.

Adding AWS Glue and Amazon Comprehend as an additional trusted entity to this role

This step is needed if you want to pass the execution role of this notebook while calling Glue APIs as well, without creating an additional role. If you have not used AWS Glue before, then this step is mandatory. If you have used AWS Glue previously, then you should have an already existing role that can be used to invoke Glue APIs. In that case, you can pass that role while calling Glue (later in this notebook) and skip this next step:

1. On the IAM dashboard, click on **Roles** on the left-side navigation and search for the **role**. Once the role appears, click on **Role** to go to its **Summary** page.

2. Click on the **Trust relationships** tab on the **Summary** page to add AWS Glue as an additional trusted entity.

3. Click on **Edit trust relationship** and replace the JSON with this JSON:

```
{
    "Version": "2012-10-17",
    "Statement": [
        {
            "Effect": "Allow",
            "Principal": {
                "Service": [
                    "sagemaker.amazonaws.com",
                    "glue.amazonaws.com"
                ]
            },
            "Action": "sts:AssumeRole"
        }
    ]
}
```

4. Once this is complete, click on **Update Trust Policy** and you are done.

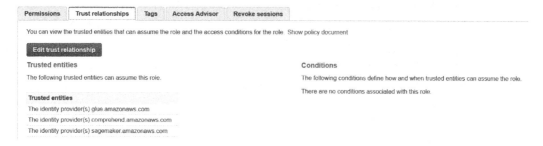

Figure 7.3 – Setting up trust with Glue in an IAM role

In this section, we covered how you can set up the Jupyter notebook and the necessary IAM permissions to run the Jupyter notebook. In the next section, we will walk you through the solution by the notebook setup you did.

Walking through the solution using Jupyter Notebook

In this section, we will walk you through how you can build this out for a Yelp review dataset or any social media analytics dataset by following the given steps using a Jupyter notebook and Python APIs:

1. Download the review dataset from Yelp Reviews NLP Fast.ai, which we have already done for you in the notebook.

2. Register the raw dataset as a table with the AWS Glue Data Catalog.

3. Run PySpark (AWS Glue job) to convert the dataset into Parquet and get the review sentiment with Amazon Comprehend.

4. Store the transformed results in a newly curated dataset.

5. Run a serverless query for the optimized dataset with Amazon Athena.

6. Provide visual insights of the results with Amazon QuickSight or Bokeh AWS Glue Data Catalog.

7. Go to this notebook and run the following steps in the code block to set up the libraries:

```
import boto3
import botocore
import json
import time
import os
```

```
import project_path
from lib import workshop
glue = boto3.client('glue')
s3 = boto3.resource('s3')
s3_client = boto3.client('s3')
session = boto3.session.Session()
region = session.region_name
account_id = boto3.client('sts').get_caller_identity().
get('Account')
database_name = 'yelp' # AWS Glue Data Catalog Database
Name
raw_table_name = 'raw_reviews' # AWS Glue Data Catalog
raw table name
parquet_table_name = 'parq_reviews' # AWS Glue Data
Catalog parquet table name
open_data_bucket = 'fast-ai-nlp'
```

8. We have imported the necessary libraries for notebook setup and defined the database name and table names for the AWS Glue Data Catalog. In the next step, we will download the Yelp reviews dataset by running the following code:

```
try:
    s3.Bucket(open_data_bucket).download_file('yelp_
review_full_csv.tgz', 'yelp_review_full_csv.tgz')
except botocore.exceptions.ClientError as e:
    if e.response['Error']['Code'] == "404":
        print("The object does not exist.")
    else:
        raise
```

9. Now, we will run the following code to untar or unzip this review dataset:

```
!tar -xvzf yelp_review_full_csv.tgz
```

10. There are two CSV files in the tarball. One is called train.csv, the other is test.csv. For those interested, the readme.txt file describes the dataset in more detail.

11. We will use Python pandas to read the CSV files and view the dataset. You will notice the data contains two unnamed columns for the rating and review. The rating is between 1 and 5 and the review is a free-form text field:

```
import pandas as pd

pd.set_option('display.max_colwidth', -1)

df = pd.read_csv('yelp_review_full_csv/train.csv',
header=None)

df.head(5)
```

12. You get the following output:

	0	1
0	5	dr. goldberg offers everything i look for in a general practitioner. he's nice and easy to talk to without being patronizing; he's always on time in seeing his patients; he's affiliated with a top-notch hospital (nyu) which my parents have explained to me is very important in case something happens and you need surgery; and you can get referrals to see specialists without having to see him first. really, what more do you need? i'm sitting here trying to think of any complaints i have about him, but i'm really drawing a blank.
1	2	Unfortunately, the frustration of being Dr. Goldberg's patient is a repeat of the experience I've had with so many other doctors in NYC -- good doctor, terrible staff. It seems that his staff simply never answers the phone. It usually takes 2 hours of repeated calling to get an answer. Who has time for that or wants to deal with it? I have run into this problem with many other doctors and I just don't get it. You have office workers, you have patients with medical needs, why isn't anyone answering the phone? It's incomprehensible and not work the aggravation. It's with regret that I feel that I have to give Dr. Goldberg 2 stars.
2	4	Been going to Dr. Goldberg for over 10 years. I think I was one of his 1st patients when he started at MHMG. He's been great over the years and is really all about the big picture. It is because of him, not my now former gyn Dr. Markoff, that I found out I have fibroids. He explores all options with you and is very patient and understanding. He doesn't judge and asks all the right questions. Very thorough and wants to be kept in the loop on every aspect of your medical health and your life.
3	4	Got a letter in the mail last week that said Dr. Goldberg is moving to Arizona to take a new position there in June. He will be missed very much. \n\nI think finding a new doctor in NYC that you actually like might almost be as awful as trying to find a date!
4	1	I don't know what Dr. Goldberg was like before moving to Arizona, but let me tell you, STAY AWAY from this doctor and this office. I was going to Dr. Johnson before he left and Goldberg took over when Johnson left. He is not a caring doctor. He is only interested in the co-pay and having you come in for medication refills every month. He will not give refills and could less about patients's financial situations. Trying to get your 90 days mail away pharmacy prescriptions through this guy is a joke. And to make matters even worse, his office staff is incompetent. 90% of the time when you call the office, they'll put you through to a voice mail, that NO ONE ever answers or returns your call. Both my adult children and husband have decided to leave this practice after experiencing such frustration. The entire office has an attitude like they are doing you a favor. Give me a break! Stay away from this doc and the practice. You deserve better and they will not be there when you really need them. I have never felt compelled to write a bad review about anyone until I met this pathetic excuse for a doctor who is all about the money.

Figure 7.4 – Raw Yelp review data

13. Now, we will upload the file created previously to S3 to be used later by executing the following notebook code:

```
file_name = 'train.csv'

session.resource('s3').Bucket(bucket).Object(os.path.
join('yelp', 'raw', file_name)).upload_file('yelp_review_
full_csv/'+file_name)
```

We downloaded the Yelp dataset and stored it in a raw S3 bucket. In the next section, we will create the AWS Glue Data Catalog database.

Creating the AWS Glue Catalog database

In this section, we will walk you through how you can define a table and add it to the Glue Data Catalog database. Glue crawlers automatically crawl your data from Amazon S3 or from any on-premises database as it supports multiple data stores. You can also bring your own Hive metadata store and get started with crawlers. Once you have created a crawler, you can perform Glue ETL jobs as these jobs use these Data Catalog tables as source data and target data. Moreover, the Glue ETL job will read and write to the data stores that are specified in the source and target Data Catalog tables in Glue crawlers. There is a central Glue Data Catalog for each AWS account:

1. We are going to use the `glue.create_database` API (`https://boto3.amazonaws.com/v1/documentation/api/latest/reference/services/glue.html#Glue.Client.create_database`) to create a Glue database:

    ```
    workshop.create_db(glue, account_id, database_name,
    'Database for Yelp Reviews')
    ```

2. Now we will create the raw table in Glue (`https://docs.aws.amazon.com/glue/latest/dg/tables-described.html`). There is more than one way to create a table in Glue:

    A. *Using an AWS Glue crawler*: We have classifiers that automatically determine the schema of the dataset while crawling using a built-in classifier. You can also use a custom classifier if your data schema has a complicated nested JSON structure.

    B. *Creating a table manually or using the APIs*: You create a table manually in the console or by using an API. You specify the schema to be classified when you define the table.

    > **Note:**
    >
    > For more information about creating a table using the AWS Glue console, see *Working with Tables on the AWS Glue Console*: `https://docs.aws.amazon.com/glue/latest/dg/console-tables.html`.

3. We are using the `glue.create_table` API to create tables:

```
location = 's3://{0}/yelp/raw'.format(bucket)
response = glue.create_table(
    CatalogId=account_id,
    DatabaseName=database_name,
    TableInput={
        'Name': raw_table_name,
        'Description': 'Raw Yelp reviews dataset',
        'StorageDescriptor': {
            'Columns': [
                {
                    'Name': 'rating',
                    'Type': 'tinyint',
                    'Comment': 'Rating of from the Yelp
review'
                },
                {
                    'Name': 'review',
                    'Type': 'string',
                    'Comment': 'Review text of from the
Yelp review'
                }
            ],
            'Location': location,
            'InputFormat': 'org.apache.hadoop.mapred.
TextInputFormat',
            'OutputFormat': 'org.apache.hadoop.hive.
ql.io.HiveIgnoreKeyTextOutputFormat',
            'SerdeInfo': {
                'SerializationLibrary': 'org.apache.
hadoop.hive.serde2.OpenCSVSerde',
                'Parameters': {
                    'escapeChar': '\\',
                    'separatorChar': ',',
                    'serialization.format': '1'
                }
            },
```

```
        },
        'TableType': 'EXTERNAL_TABLE',
        'Parameters': {
            'classification': 'csv'
        }
    }
)
```

The preceding code will create tables in the AWS Glue Data Catalog.

4. Now we will visualize this data using the Amazon Athena `pyAthena` API. To see the raw Yelp reviews, we will be installing this Python library for querying the data in the Glue Data Catalog with Athena:

```
!pip install PyAthena
```

5. The following code will help us visualize the database and tables in Glue for the raw dataset:

```
from pyathena import connect
from pyathena.pandas.util import as_pandas
cursor = connect(region_name=region, s3_staging_
dir='s3://'+bucket+'/yelp/temp').cursor()
cursor.execute('select * from ' + database_name + '.' +
raw_table_name + ' limit 10')
df = as_pandas(cursor)
df.head(5)
```

6. You will see the following table in the output:

	rating	review
0	4	I love that NY NY's food court isn't set up li...
1	3	I had the brisket & pastrami. most ny type del...
2	4	best meat to bread ratio i've experienced. ...
3	5	OMG! Greenberg's serves up some of the most d...
4	3	The System: nn1 Star: Almost impossible to get...

Figure 7.5 – Athena output for the raw dataset in Glue Data Catalog

So, we covered how you can create a Glue Data Catalog and crawl the raw Yelp data we downloaded in Amazon S3. Then we showed you how you can visualize this data in Amazon Athena using `pyAthena` libraries. In the next section, we will walk you through how you can transform this data.

Transforming raw data to provide insights and visualization

Now we will walk you through how you can transform the raw data using PySpark in an AWS Glue job to call Amazon Comprehend APIs to get sentiment analysis on the review, convert the data into Parquet, and partition by sentiment. This will allow us to optimize analytics queries when viewing data by sentiment and return just the values we need, leveraging the columnar format of Parquet.

We covered Comprehend's detect sentiment real-time API in *Chapter 3*, *Introducing Amazon Comprehend*. In this job, we will use the real-time batch detect sentiment APIs.

We will create a PySpark job to add a primary key and run a batch of reviews through Amazon Comprehend to get a sentiment analysis of the reviews. The job will limit the number of rows it converts, but this code could be modified to run the entire dataset:

1. In order to run your code in AWS Glue, we will upload the code and dependencies directly to S3 and pass those locations while invoking the Glue job. We will write the ETL job using Jupyter Notebook's cell magic `%%writefile`. We are using the AWS Glue script next to transform or perform ETL on the Yelp reviews dataset by using Glue transform and adding a sentiment column to the DataFrame by analyzing sentiment using Amazon Comprehend:

```
%%writefile yelp_etl.py
import os
import sys
import boto3
from awsglue.transforms import *
from awsglue.utils import getResolvedOptions
from pyspark.context import SparkContext
from awsglue.context import GlueContext
from awsglue.job import Job
from awsglue.dynamicframe import DynamicFrame
import pyspark.sql.functions as F
from pyspark.sql import Row, Window, SparkSession
from pyspark.sql.types import *
from pyspark.conf import SparkConf
```

```
from pyspark.context import SparkContext
from pyspark.sql.functions import *
args = getResolvedOptions(sys.argv, ['JOB_NAME', 'S3_
OUTPUT_BUCKET', 'S3_OUTPUT_KEY_PREFIX', 'DATABASE_NAME',
'TABLE_NAME', 'REGION'])
sc = SparkContext()
glueContext = GlueContext(sc)
spark = glueContext.spark_session
job = Job(glueContext)
job.init(args['JOB_NAME'], args)
```

2. We have imported the necessary APIs and now we will convert the Glue
    DynamicFrame to a Spark DataFrame to read the data from our Glue Data Catalog.
    We will select the review and rating columns from the database and the table we
    created in the Glue Data Catalog:

```
yelp = glueContext.create_dynamic_frame.from_
catalog(database=args['DATABASE_NAME'], table_
name=args['TABLE_NAME'], transformation_ctx =
"datasource0")
yelpDF = yelp.toDF().select('rating', 'review')
```

We are defining some limits such as how many characters are to be sent for batch
detect sentiment – MAX_SENTENCE_LENGTH_IN_CHARS – what the batch size of
reviews sent for getting sentiment should be – COMPREHEND_BATCH_SIZE – and
how many batches are to be sent:

```
MIN_SENTENCE_LENGTH_IN_CHARS = 10
MAX_SENTENCE_LENGTH_IN_CHARS = 4500
COMPREHEND_BATCH_SIZE = 5
NUMBER_OF_BATCHES = 10
ROW_LIMIT = 1000 #Number of reviews we will process for
this workshop
```

3. Each task handles 5*10 records and we are calling the Comprehend batch detect
    sentiment API to get the sentiment and add that sentiment after the transformation
    with AWS Glue. Creating a function where we are passing the text list and calling
    the batch detect sentiment API was covered in *Chapter 3, Introducing Amazon
    Comprehend*:

```
ComprehendRow = Row("review", "rating", "sentiment")
def getBatchComprehend(input_list):
```

```
    arr = []
    bodies = [i[0] for i in input_list]
    client = boto3.client('comprehend',region_
name=args['REGION'])
    def callApi(text_list):
        response = client.batch_detect_sentiment(TextList
= text_list, LanguageCode = 'en')
        return response


    for i in range(NUMBER_OF_BATCHES):
        text_list = bodies[COMPREHEND_BATCH_SIZE * i :
COMPREHEND_BATCH_SIZE * (i+1)]
        #response = client.batch_detect_
sentiment(TextList = text_list, LanguageCode = 'en')
        response = callApi(text_list)
        for r in response['ResultList']:
            idx = COMPREHEND_BATCH_SIZE * i + r['Index']
            arr.append(ComprehendRow(input_list[idx][0],
input_list[idx][1], r['Sentiment']))


    return arr
```

4. The following code will grab a sample set of records with a review size under the
    Comprehend limits:

```
yelpDF = yelpDF \
  .withColumn('review_len', F.length('review')) \
  .filter(F.col('review_len') > MIN_SENTENCE_LENGTH_IN_
CHARS) \
  .filter(F.col('review_len') < MAX_SENTENCE_LENGTH_IN_
CHARS) \
  .limit(ROW_LIMIT)
record_count = yelpDF.count()
print('record count=' + str(record_count))
yelpDF = yelpDF.repartition(record_count/(NUMBER_OF_
BATCHES*COMPREHEND_BATCH_SIZE))
```

5.   We are using the Glue DataFrame to concatenate the submission ID and body tuples into arrays of a similar size and transforming the results:

```
group_rdd = yelpDF.rdd.map(lambda l: (l.review.
encode("utf-8"), l.rating)).glom()


transformed = group_rdd \
  .map(lambda l: getBatchComprehend(l)) \
  .flatMap(lambda x: x) \
  .toDF()
print("transformed count=" + str(transformed.count()))
```

We are converting the transformed DataFrame with sentiments into Parquet format and saving it in our transformed Amazon S3 bucket:

```
transformedsink = DynamicFrame.fromDF(transformed,
glueContext, "joined")
parquet_output_path = 's3://' + os.path.join(args['S3_
OUTPUT_BUCKET'], args['S3_OUTPUT_KEY_PREFIX'])
print(parquet_output_path)
datasink5 = glueContext.write_dynamic_frame.from_
options(frame = transformedsink, connection_type =
"s3", connection_options = {"path": parquet_output_path,
"partitionKeys": ["sentiment"]}, format="parquet",
transformation_ctx="datasink5")


job.commit()
```

6.   The key point in this code is how easy it is to get access to the AWS Glue Data Catalog leveraging the Glue libraries:

```
glueContext.create_dynamic_frame.from_catalog- Read table
metadata from the Glue Data Catalog using Glue libs to
load tables into the job.
yelpDF = yelp.toDF() - Easy conversion from Glue
DynamicFrame to Spark DataFrame and vice-versa
joinedsink= DynamicFrame.fromDF(joinedDF, glueContext,
"joined").
```

7. Write S3 using `glueContext.write_dynamic_frame.from_options` with the following options:

- Partition the data based on columns – `connection_options = {"path":` `parquet_output_path, "partitionKeys": ["sentiment"]}`.

    Convert data to a columnar format – `format="parquet"`.

8. We will be uploading the `github_etl.py` script to S3 now so that Glue can use it to run the PySpark job. You can replace it with your own script if needed. If your code has multiple files, you need to zip those files and upload them to S3 instead of uploading a single file like is being done here:

```
script_location = sess.upload_data(path='yelp_etl.py',
bucket=bucket, key_prefix='yelp/codes')
```
```
s3_output_key_prefix = 'yelp/parquet/'
```

9. Next, we'll be creating a Glue client via Boto3 so that we can invoke the `create_job` API of Glue. The `create_job` API will create a job definition that can be used to execute your jobs in Glue. The job definition created here is mutable. While creating the job, we are also passing the code location as well as the dependencies' locations to Glue. The `AllocatedCapacity` parameter controls the hardware resources that Glue will use to execute this job. It is measured in units of **DPU**. For more information on **DPU**, please see `https://docs.aws.amazon.com/` `glue/latest/dg/add-job.html`:

```
from time import gmtime, strftime
import time
timestamp_prefix = strftime("%Y-%m-%d-%H-%M-%S",
gmtime())
job_name = 'yelp-etl-' + timestamp_prefix
response = glue.create_job(
    Name=job_name,
    Description='PySpark job to extract Yelp review
sentiment analysis',
    Role=role, # you can pass your existing AWS Glue role
here if you have used Glue before
    ExecutionProperty={
        'MaxConcurrentRuns': 1
    },
    Command={
        'Name': 'glueetl',
```

```
                'ScriptLocation': script_location
        },
        DefaultArguments={
            '--job-language': 'python',
            '--job-bookmark-option': 'job-bookmark-disable'
        },
        AllocatedCapacity=5,
        Timeout=60,
    )
glue_job_name = response['Name']
print(glue_job_name)
```

10. The aforementioned job will be executed now by calling the `start_job_run` API. This API creates an immutable run/execution corresponding to the job definition created previously. We will require the `job_run_id` value for the particular job execution to check the status. We'll pass the data and model locations as part of the job execution parameters:

```
job_run_id = glue.start_job_run(JobName=job_name,
                                Arguments = {
                                '--S3_OUTPUT_
BUCKET': bucket,
                                '--S3_OUTPUT_KEY_
PREFIX': s3_output_key_prefix,
                                '--DATABASE_
NAME': database_name,
                                '--TABLE_NAME':
raw_table_name,
                                '--REGION':
region
                                }) ['JobRunId']
print(job_run_id)
```

> **Note:**
> This job will take approximately 2 minutes to run.

11. Now we will check the job status to see whether it is SUCCEEDED, FAILED, or STOPPED. Once the job has succeeded, we have the transformed data in S3 in Parquet format, which we will use to query with Athena and visualize with QuickSight. If the job fails, you can go to the AWS Glue console, click on the **Jobs** tab on the left, and from the page, click on this particular job and you will be able to find the CloudWatch Logs link (the link under **Logs**) for these jobs, which can help you to see what exactly went wrong in the job execution:

```
job_run_status = glue.get_job_run(JobName=job_
name,RunId=job_run_id)['JobRun']['JobRunState']
while job_run_status not in ('FAILED', 'SUCCEEDED',
'STOPPED'):
    job_run_status = glue.get_job_run(JobName=job_
name,RunId=job_run_id)['JobRun']['JobRunState']
    print (job_run_status)
    time.sleep(60)
print(job_run_status)
```

In the next section, we will walk you through how to use a Glue crawler to discover the transformed data.

Using a Glue crawler to discover the transformed data

Most AWS Glue users use a crawler to populate the AWS Glue Data Catalog with tables as a primary method. To do this, what you have to do is add a crawler within your Data Catalog to traverse your data stores. The output of the crawler consists of one or more metadata tables that are defined in your Data Catalog. **ETL** jobs that you define in AWS Glue use these metadata tables as sources and targets:

- A crawler can crawl both file-based and table-based data stores. Crawlers can crawl the data from various types of data stores, such as Amazon S3, RDS, Redshift, DynamoDB, or on-premises databases:

```
parq_crawler_name = 'YelpCuratedCrawler'
parq_crawler_path = 's3://{0}/yelp/parquet/'.
format(bucket)
            response = glue.create_crawler(
    Name=parq_crawler_name,
    Role=role,
    DatabaseName=database_name,
    Description='Crawler for the Parquet Yelp Reviews
```

```
with Sentiment',
    Targets={
        'S3Targets': [
            {
                'Path': parq_crawler_path
            }
        ]
    },
    SchemaChangePolicy={
        'UpdateBehavior': 'UPDATE_IN_DATABASE',
        'DeleteBehavior': 'DEPRECATE_IN_DATABASE'
    },
    TablePrefix='reviews_'
)
```

- **Start the Glue Crawler**: You can use the Glue crawler to populate the AWS Glue Data Catalog with tables. The crawler will automatically crawl your data source, which can be an on-premises database or raw CSV files in Amazon S3, and create a metadata table in the Glue Data Catalog, as well as inferring the schema. Glue ETL jobs use these metadata tables in the Glue Data Catalog as sources and targets. You can also bring your existing Hive data catalog to run Glue ETL:

```
response = glue.start_crawler(
    Name=parq_crawler_name
)
print ("Parquet Crawler: https://{0}.console.aws.amazon.
com/glue/home?region={0}#crawler:name={1}".format(region,
parq_crawler_name))
```

- Go to the link in the output to visualize your crawler in Amazon Athena:

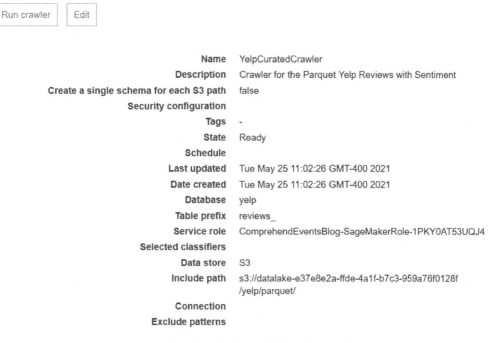

Figure 7.6 – Yelp curated crawler

- **Checking the Glue crawler status**: We will now monitor the crawler status, waiting for it to get back into the READY state, meaning the crawler completed its crawl. You can also look at the CloudWatch logs for the crawler for more details:

```
crawler_status = glue.get_crawler(Name=parq_crawler_name)
['Crawler']['State']
while crawler_status not in ('READY'):
    crawler_status = glue.get_crawler(Name=parq_crawler_
name)['Crawler']['State']
    print(crawler_status)
    time.sleep(30)
```

Once you get an output of READY, move on to the next step. In this section, we showed you how you can crawl the transformed Parquet data for Yelp reviews, which has sentiment scores from Amazon Comprehend in the AWS Glue Data Catalog. In the next section, we will cover how you can visualize this data to gain meaningful insights into the voice of customer analytics.

Viewing the transformed results

We will again use the PyAthena library to run queries against the newly created dataset with sentiment results and in the Parquet format. In the interest of time, we will be using the Bokeh AWS Glue Data Catalog within the notebook to visualize the results instead of Amazon QuickSight:

- QuickSight is able to use the same Athena queries to visualize the results as well as numerous built-in connectors to many data sources:

```
cursor.execute('select rating, review, sentiment from
yelp.reviews_parquet')
                df = as_pandas(cursor)
df.head(10)
```

- Here's the output of querying the Glue Data Catalog via Amazon Athena to get the rating, review, and sentiment from the Yelp reviews table:

Out[34]:

	rating	review	sentiment
0	2	Meet up with some friends Sat night to have so...	POSITIVE
1	5	these guys are great! not only did the tech se...	POSITIVE
2	5	I've been going to this place for 29 years. Th...	POSITIVE
3	4	Super duper friendly staff!!! The people playi...	POSITIVE
4	5	5 stars, this place is as good as it gets! I d...	POSITIVE
5	4	Very nice place to eat! Friendly device, great...	POSITIVE
6	4	I was pleasantly surprised by the amazing food...	POSITIVE
7	3	Timing is what it's all about people!! \nThe ...	POSITIVE
8	4	The food is good. I took it to go. When I got...	POSITIVE
9	4	Have the chicken avocado burrito. It was great.	POSITIVE

Figure 7.7 – Athena query to select rating and sentiment from the Yelp transformed table in the Glue Data Catalog

- **Group the data in the DataFrame by sentiment**: Using the pandas DataFrame functionality, we will do `groupby` locally. Alternatively, we could have used the built-in SQL and aggregate functions in Athena to achieve the same result:

```
group = df.groupby(('sentiment'))
group.describe()
```

Next, you will find the output of the `groupby` sentiment query:

`Out[35]:`

sentiment	rating				review			freq
	count	unique	top	freq	count	unique	top	
MIXED	220	5	3	81	220	220	A neighbor recommended Franks all about time a...	1
NEGATIVE	333	5	1	211	333	333	Back in the day before there were $14 gourmet ...	1
NEUTRAL	12	3	1	6	12	12	I would try to help a real non-profit that is ...	1
POSITIVE	435	5	5	176	435	435	This place is a little fat Mexican girl's drea...	1

Figure 7.8 – Output of the groupby sentiment query

We can see from the preceding output that we have more positive reviews than negative ones for the Yelp reviews dataset.

- The Bokeh framework has a number of built-in visualizations. We will use Bokeh to visualize reviews by sentiment and rating in subsequent code.

- *Visualize by rating*: We will now compare what the Comprehend API came up with compared to the user rating in the dataset. We are changing `groupby` in the DataFrame to change the dataset:

```
group = df.groupby(('rating'))
group.describe()
```

You will find the output of the query result grouped by rating in the following screenshot:

`Out[37]:`

rating	review				sentiment			
	count	unique	top	freq	count	unique	top	freq
1	256	256	I called Central Towing last night because I h...	1	256	4	NEGATIVE	211
2	178	178	10pm on a Friday night. Wanted a hassle free ...	1	178	3	NEGATIVE	97
3	191	191	Alright store and what you would normally expe...	1	191	4	POSITIVE	87
4	190	190	Food was delicious, has a store too.	1	190	3	POSITIVE	146
5	185	185	I stopped at this waffle house it was really g...	1	185	4	POSITIVE	176

Figure 7.9 – Output of the query result grouped by rating

- Now, we will show you how you can plot this in Bokeh:

```
source = ColumnDataSource(group)
",".join(source.column_names)
rating_cmap = factor_cmap('rating', palette=Spectral5,
```

```
factors=sorted(df.rating.unique()))
p = figure(plot_height=350, x_range=group)
p.vbar(x='rating', top='review_count', width=1, line_
color="white",
        fill_color=rating_cmap, source=source)
p.xgrid.grid_line_color = None
p.xaxis.axis_label = "Rating"
p.yaxis.axis_label = "Count"
p.y_range.start = 0
```

You will find the bar graph showing the count of users with their ratings.

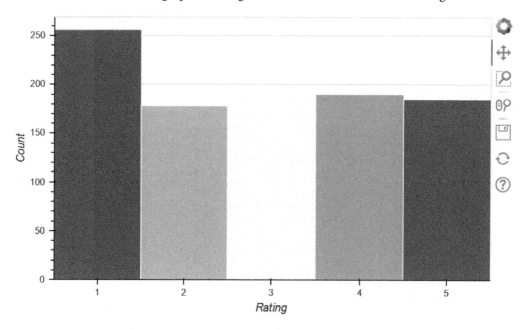

Figure 7.10 – User rating by count

We can see that the most popular rating given is 1 and the least popular is 2. We covered in this section how you can use simple queries in Amazon Athena and visualization tools such as Bokeh to perform quick visualization and SQL analytics on the Yelp reviews dataset enriched with the sentiment from Amazon Comprehend. We got some cool insights, such as most of the reviews are positive, and also the most popular rating given by users is 1. You can further drill down and get very specific insights into particular comments by using simple SQL. This helps drive business outcomes very quickly. In the next section, we will walk you through how you can easily create a QuickSight dashboard to gain some cool insights for your business users.

Amazon QuickSight visualization

In this section, we will walk you through how you can set up or get started with Amazon QuickSight and visualize the tables in Athena, which was transformed with sentiments using AWS Glue and Comprehend:

1. You can follow along with the `Getting Started` guide for QuickSight at `https://docs.aws.amazon.com/quicksight/latest/user/getting-started.html` to set up your account and then follow the code block to navigate to the QuickSight console:

    ```
    print('https://{0}.quicksight.aws.amazon.com/sn/start?#'.
    format(region))
    ```

2. **Manage S3 Access in QuickSight**: We need to do this mandatory step to make sure we do not get an access denied exception while accessing Amazon Athena with Amazon QuickSight.

3. Go to **Manage QuickSight | Security and permission | Add or remove | In S3.** Click on **details** | select the bucket you want to query | **update.**

QuickSight access to AWS services

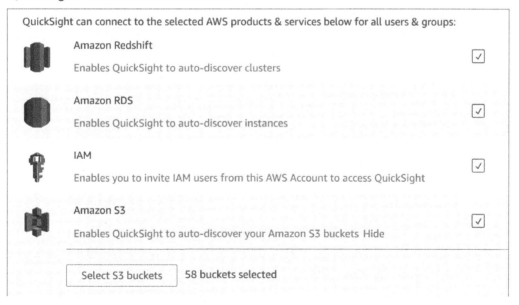

QuickSight can connect to the selected AWS products & services below for all users & groups:

| | Amazon Redshift | |
| | Enables QuickSight to auto-discover clusters | ☑ |

| | Amazon RDS | |
| | Enables QuickSight to auto-discover instances | ☑ |

| | IAM | |
| | Enables you to invite IAM users from this AWS Account to access QuickSight | ☑ |

| | Amazon S3 | |
| | Enables QuickSight to auto-discover your Amazon S3 buckets Hide | ☑ |

| Select S3 buckets | 58 buckets selected |

Figure 7.11 – Manage QuickSight access for the S3 data lake

4. Click on the **Create Dataset** option and you will see the following options:

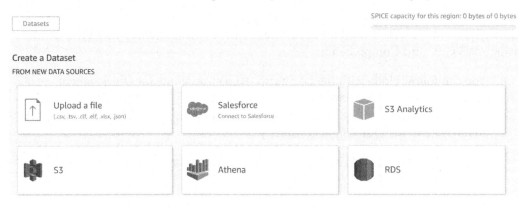

Figure 7.12 – Amazon QuickSight setup with the Create a Dataset option

5. Choose **Athena** from the preceding options. Click the **New data set** button and select **Athena data source**. Name the data source and choose the Yelp **Glue database** and **reviews_parquet** table. Finish the creation by clicking the **Create data source** button. QuickSight supports a number of data connectors.

6. In the **Data source name** textbox, enter the name `yelp_reviews` and click **Create data source**. Also, click on **validated**.

Figure 7.13 – Creating an Athena data source in QuickSight

7. Next, you will be selecting the **Yelp** database we created in the Glue Data Catalog and the **reviews_parquet** table.

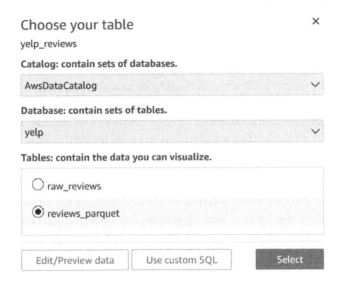

Figure 7.14 – Select the table to visualize in QuickSight

8. Click on **Save and Visualize**.

In this section, we covered how you can create a QuickSight dashboard to analyze Yelp reviews. In the next section, we will talk about deleting the resources you created during this exercise to avoid incurring charges.

Cleaning up

In this section, we will walk you through code samples in the notebook to clean up AWS resources created while going through the Yelp sentiment analysis solution to avoid incurring a cost.

Run the cleanup steps to delete the resources you have created for this notebook by running the following code:

```
response = glue.delete_crawler(Name=parq_crawler_name)
response = glue.delete_job(JobName=glue_job_name)
response = glue.delete_database(
    CatalogId = account_id,
    Name = database_name
)
workshop.delete_bucket_completely(bucket)
```

We deleted the Glue crawlers, Glue ETL jobs, and the database we created using the notebook here. Let's move on to the next section to wrap it up.

Summary

In this chapter, we covered how you can set up a text analytics solution with your existing social media analytics workflow. We gave a specific example of using the Yelp reviews dataset and using serverless ETL with NLP using Amazon Comprehend to set up a quick visual dashboard using Amazon QuickSight. We also covered ad hoc SQL analytics using Amazon Athena to understand the voice or sentiment of the majority of your users using some easy SQL queries. This solution can be implemented with any social media integration, such as Twitter, Reddit, and Facebook, in batch or real-time mode.

In the case of a real-time setup, you would integrate Kinesis Data Firehose to have near real-time streaming tweets or social media feeds in this proposed workflow or architecture. Check out the *Further reading* section for a really cool **AI-driven social media dashboard** to implement this architecture at scale.

Another approach you can take in terms of document automation is to have Amazon Textract extract data from your PDFs in the case of RFPs or agreements, and this pipeline can be used to gather sentiment quickly paragraph-wise after performing Glue ETL on the extracted text.

In the next chapter, we will talk about how you can use AI to automate media workflows to reduce costs and monetize content.

Further reading

- *How to scale sentiment analysis using Amazon Comprehend, AWS Glue and Amazon Athena* by Roy Hasson (`https://aws.amazon.com/blogs/machine-learning/how-to-scale-sentiment-analysis-using-amazon-comprehend-aws-glue-and-amazon-athena/`)

- *AI-Driven Social Media Dashboard* (`https://aws.amazon.com/solutions/implementations/ai-driven-social-media-dashboard/`)

- *Harmonize, Query, and Visualize Data from Various Providers using AWS Glue, Amazon Athena, and Amazon QuickSight* by Ben Snively (`https://aws.amazon.com/blogs/big-data/harmonize-query-and-visualize-data-from-various-providers-using-aws-glue-amazon-athena-and-amazon-quicksight/`)

8
Leveraging NLP to Monetize Your Media Content

As we have seen in this book so far, AI, and specifically NLP, has a wide range of uses in areas hitherto considered traditional IT spurred on by the rapid proliferation of data and the democratization of **machine learning** (**ML**) with cloud computing. In the previous chapter, we saw a cool example of how you can bring color to social media reviews and other forms of textual data by running voice of the customer analytics with sentiment detection. We saw how you can use AWS Glue to crawl raw data from Amazon S3, use Amazon Athena to interactively query this data, transform the raw data using PySpark (`http://spark.apache.org/docs/latest/api/python/index.html`) in an AWS Glue job to call Amazon Comprehend APIs (which provide ready-made intelligence with pre-trained NLP models) to get sentiment analysis on the review, convert the data into Parquet, and partition it (`https://docs.aws.amazon.com/athena/latest/ug/partitions.html`) by sentiment to optimize analytics queries. In this chapter, we will change gears and look at a use case that has gained tremendous popularity in recent times due to the increased adoption of streaming media content, specifically how to monetize content.

The gap between online advertising and print media advertising is ever widening. According to this article, `https://www.marketingcharts.com/advertising-trends-114887`, quoting a PwC outlook report on global entertainment and media (`https://www.pwc.com/outlook`), online advertising spend was estimated to be approximately $58 billion higher than TV advertising, and $100 billion higher than magazine and newspaper advertising in 2020 even with the COVID-19 pandemic considered.

This, of course, is also driven by the increased usage of smart consumer devices and the explosion of the internet age consumer trends. Google Ads is one of the most popular ad-serving platforms today, accounting for 80% of Alphabet's (the public holding company that owns Google) revenues, raking in $147 billion in 2020 according to this article: `https://www.cnbc.com/2021/05/18/how-does-google-make-money-advertising-business-breakdown-.html`. You read that right: online advertisements are indeed a big deal. So, when you are next thinking of posting that cool travel video or your recipe for an awesome chili con carne, you could actually be making money out of your content. You may ask, this is all great but how does NLP help in this case? Read on to find out!

The answer, as you probably already guessed, is context-based ad serving. Suppose you have an intelligent solution that could listen to the audio/text in your content, understand what is being discussed, identify topics that represent the context of the content, look up ads related to the topic, and stitch these ads back into your content seamlessly without having to train any ML models: wouldn't that be swell? Yes, that's exactly what we will be building now.

We will navigate through the following sections:

- Introducing the content monetization use case
- Building the NLP solution for content monetization

Technical requirements

For this chapter, you will need access to an AWS account. Please make sure to follow the instructions specified in the *Technical requirements* section in *Chapter 2, Introducing Amazon Textract*, to create your AWS account, and log in to the AWS Management Console before trying the steps in the *Building the NLP solution for content monetization* section.

The Python code and sample datasets for our solution can be found here: `https://github.com/PacktPublishing/Natural-Language-Processing-with-AWS-AI-Services/tree/main/Chapter%2008`. Please use the instructions in the following sections along with the code in the repository to build the solution.

Check out the following video to see the Code in Action at `https://bit.ly/317mcSh`.

Introducing the content monetization use case

We know NLP can help enhance the customer service experience and understand better what our customers are telling us. We will now use NLP to determine the context of our media content and stitch ads into the content relevant to that context. To illustrate our example, let's go back to our fictitious banking corporation called **LiveRight Holdings Private Limited**. LiveRight's management has decided they now need to expand to more geographies as they are seeing a lot of demand for their model of no-frills banking that cuts their operational costs and transfers the savings back to their customers. They have decided to hire you as their marketing technology architect, putting you in charge of all their content creation, but challenge you to devise a way for the content to pay for itself due to their low-cost policies. You come up with the idea of creating fun educational videos that show the latest trends in the intersection of banking and technology. There is a lot of demand for such videos since they are free to watch, you can intersperse them with ads to get monetary returns, and they serve to raise awareness of the bank in the process.

You have thought through the solution design and decide to use the following:

- **AWS Elemental MediaConvert** (`https://aws.amazon.com/mediaconvert/`), a managed video transcoding service that can convert and enhance your video content to multiple versions for broadcasting

- **Amazon Transcribe** (`https://aws.amazon.com/transcribe/`) to get a transcript of the video content

- **Amazon Comprehend** (`https://aws.amazon.com/comprehend/`) to leverage its pre-trained ML model for topic modeling to determine common themes in the textual content of the video that will, in turn, drive the ad selection process

- **AWS Elemental MediaTailor** (`https://aws.amazon.com/mediatailor/`), a managed service that can take as input media content, assemble this into an online channel delivery, and stitch ads onto the video content

The components of the solution we will build are as shown in the following figure:

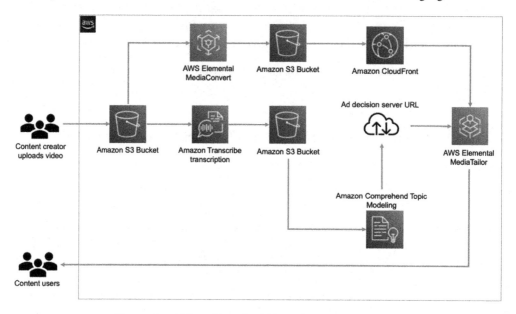

Figure 8.1 – NLP solution build for content monetization

We will be walking through this solution using the AWS Management Console (https://aws.amazon.com/console/) and an Amazon SageMaker Jupyter notebook (https://docs.aws.amazon.com/sagemaker/latest/dg/nbi.html), which will allow us to review the code and results as we execute it step by step. If you do not have access to the AWS Management Console, please follow the detailed instructions in the *Technical requirements* section in *Chapter 2, Introducing Amazon Textract,* of this book.

As a first step, we will look at the sample video file provided in the GitHub repository (https://github.com/PacktPublishing/Natural-Language-Processing-with-AWS-AI-Services/blob/main/Chapter%2008/media-content/bank-demo-prem-ranga.mp4). The sample video is from a demonstration of AWS AI services for document processing. For a full version of this video, please refer to https://www.youtube.com/watch?v=vBtxjXjr_HA. We will upload this sample video to an S3 bucket:

1. After the video is loaded to the S3 bucket, we will use AWS Elemental MediaConvert to create the broadcast versions of our sample video content.

2. In parallel, we will open our Amazon SageMaker Jupyter notebook to run the code to create an Amazon Transcribe transcription job to convert the audio track from our sample video to text.

3. We will use Amazon Comprehend Topic Modeling to detect the topics from this text.

4. We will then use the sample URL from the **Google Ad Decision** server (`https://support.google.com/admanager/table/9749596`), a **Video Ad Serving Template** (**VAST**) tag URL that is generated by an ad server containing placeholders for the following.

   a) Durations in the video content to play the ads

   b) A content source ID referred by the tag `'cmsid'` and a video content ID referred by the tag `'vid'`, which we will populate to stitch in the ads specific to the topic we detected from the transcribed text in the previous step

5. We will then create an Amazon CloudFront distribution for the output video files from the AWS Elemental MediaConvert job.

6. Finally, we will use **AWS Elemental MediaTailor** to create a new configuration for broadcast-grade streaming content, which will take our MediaConvert output files available via the CloudFront distribution and the ad decision server URL we modified in the previous step to create a new video file with the ads inserted.

In this section, we introduced the content monetization requirement we are trying to build with our NLP solution, reviewed the challenges faced by LiveRight, and looked at an overview of the solution we will build. In the next section, we will walk through the building of a solution step by step.

Building the NLP solution for content monetization

In the previous section, we introduced a requirement for content monetization, covered the architecture of the solution we will be building, and briefly walked through the solution components and workflow steps. In this section, we will start executing the tasks to build our solution. But first, there are prerequisites we will have to take care of.

Setting up to solve the use case

If you have not done so in the previous chapters, you will as a prerequisite have to create an Amazon SageMaker Jupyter notebook instance and set up **Identity and Access Management (IAM)** permissions for that notebook role to access the AWS services we will use in this notebook. After that, you will need to clone the GitHub repository (`https://github.com/PacktPublishing/Natural-Language-Processing-with-AWS-AI-Services`), create an Amazon S3 (`https://aws.amazon.com/s3/`) bucket, and provide the bucket name in the notebook to start execution. Please follow the next steps to complete these tasks before we can execute the cells from our notebook:

> **Note**
>
> Please ensure you have completed the tasks mentioned in the *Technical requirements* section. If you have already created an Amazon SageMaker notebook instance and cloned the GitHub repository for the book in a previous chapter, you can skip some of these steps. Please go directly to the step where you open the notebook folder corresponding to this chapter.

1. If not already done, follow the instructions documented in the *Creating an Amazon SageMaker Jupyter notebook instance* section in the *Setting up your AWS environment* section in *Chapter 2, Introducing Amazon Textract,* to create your Jupyter notebook instance.

> **IAM role permissions while creating Amazon SageMaker Jupyter notebooks**
>
> Accept the default option for the IAM role at notebook creation time to allow access to any S3 bucket.

2. Once you create the notebook instance and its status is **InService**, click on **Open Jupyter** in the **Actions** menu for the notebook instance.

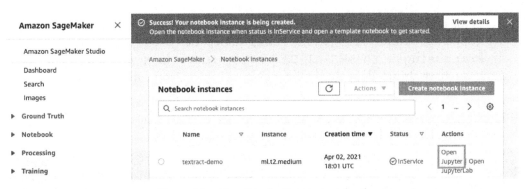

Figure 8.2 – Opening the Jupyter notebook

This will take you to the home folder of your notebook instance.

3. Click on **New** as shown in the following figure and select **Terminal**:

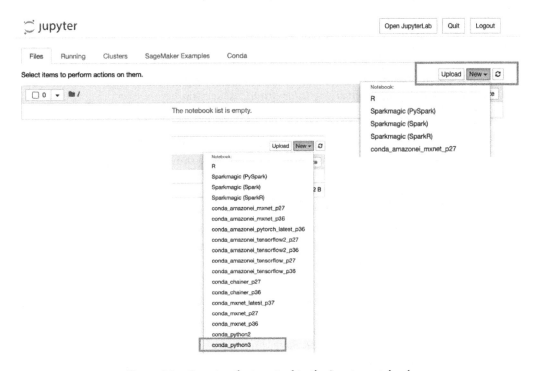

Figure 8.3 – Opening the terminal in the Jupyter notebook

4. In the terminal window, first type `cd SageMaker` and then type `git clone https://github.com/PacktPublishing/Natural-Language-Processing-with-AWS-AI-Services`, as shown in the following screenshot. If you have already done this in the previous chapters, you don't have to clone the repository again.

⟳ Jupyter

```
sh-4.2$ pwd
/home/ec2-user
sh-4.2$ cd SageMaker/
sh-4.2$ git clone https://github.com/PacktPublishing/Natural-Language-Processing-with-AWS-AI-Services
```

Figure 8.4 – The git clone command

5. Now, exit the terminal window and go back to the home folder and you will see a folder called `Chapter 08`. Click the folder and you should see a notebook called `contextual-ad-marking-for-content-monetization-with-nlp-github.ipynb`.

6. Open this notebook by clicking it.

7. Leave the notebook open for now. We will first execute the steps in the *Uploading the sample video and converting it for broadcast* section before executing the steps in the notebook.

Now that we have set up our notebook and cloned the repository, let's now add the permissions policies we need to successfully run our code sample.

Additional IAM prerequisites

To run the notebook, we have to enable additional policies and also update the trust relationships for our SageMaker notebook role. Please complete the following steps to do this:

1. If not already done, please attach `ComprehendFullAccess` and `AmazonTranscribeFullAccess` policies to your Amazon SageMaker notebook IAM role. To execute this step, please refer to the *Changing IAM permissions and trust relationships for the Amazon SageMaker notebook execution role* in the *Setting up your AWS environment* section in *Chapter 2, Introducing Amazon Textract*.

2. Your SageMaker execution role should have access to S3 already. If not, add the following JSON statement as an inline policy. For instructions, please refer to the *Changing IAM permissions and trust relationships for the Amazon SageMaker notebook execution role* section in the *Setting up your AWS environment* section in *Chapter 2, Introducing Amazon Textract*:

```
{ "Version": "2012-10-17", "Statement": [ {
    "Action": [
        "s3:GetObject",
        "s3:ListBucket",
        "s3:PutObject"
    ],
    "Resource": ["*"],
    "Effect": "Allow"
        }
    ]
}
```

3. Finally, update the trust relationships. For instructions, please refer to the *Changing IAM permissions and trust relationships for the Amazon SageMaker notebook execution role* section in the *Setting up your AWS environment* section in *Chapter 2, Introducing Amazon Textract*:

```
{ "Version": "2012-10-17", "Statement": [
  { "Effect": "Allow",
    "Principal":
      { "Service":
        [ "sagemaker.amazonaws.com",
          "s3.amazonaws.com",
"transcribe.amazonaws.com",
          "comprehend.amazonaws.com" ]
      },
        "Action": "sts:AssumeRole" }
    ]
}
```

Now that we have set up our notebook and set up the IAM role to run the walk-through notebook, in the next section, we will start with creating broadcast versions of our sample video.

Uploading the sample video and converting it for broadcast

In this section we will create two S3 buckets and get the sample video uploaded for processing. Please execute the following steps:

1. Navigate to our GitHub url - `https://github.com/PacktPublishing/Natural-Language-Processing-with-AWS-AI-Services/blob/main/Chapter%2008/media-content/bank-demo-prem-ranga.mp4` and click on the **Download** button at the right middle of the page to download the video file to your computer.

2. Now create two Amazon S3 buckets, one for our media input and the other for media output. Follow the instructions detailed in the *Creating an Amazon S3 bucket, a folder, and uploading objects* section in the *Setting up your AWS environment* section in *Chapter 2, Introducing Amazon Textract,* of this book. Ensure that the block public access is on for both the buckets.

3. In the Amazon S3 media input bucket, create a folder or prefix called `chapter8`. Within this folder, create a folder called `rawvideo`. Follow the instructions detailed in the *Creating an Amazon S3 bucket, a folder, and uploading objects* section in the *Setting up your AWS environment* section in *Chapter 2, Introducing Amazon Textract*, of this book.

4. Now upload the `bank-demo-prem-ranga.mp4` file into the `rawvideo` folder. So, within the S3 bucket, the video file should be present in the path `chapter8/rawvideo/bank-demo-prem-ranga.mp4`.

5. Now, we will pivot to creating the broadcast version of the video using AWS Elemental MediaConvert. In the AWS Management Console, in the search bar at the top, type `Media`, select **AWS Elemental MediaConvert**, and in the console, click on **Get started**.

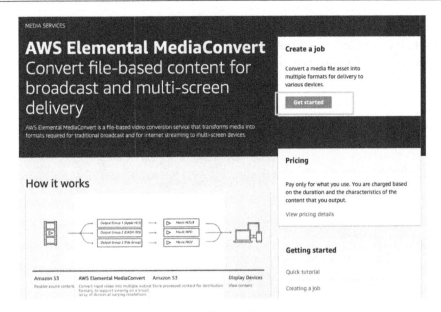

Figure 8.5 – AWS Elemental MediaConvert

6. In the **Create job** UI, under **Input 1**, for **Input file URL**, please provide the full S3 path of where you uploaded the sample video file in *Step 4*. This should be `s3://<media-input-bucket>/chapter8/rawvideo/bank-demo-prem-ranga.mp4`.

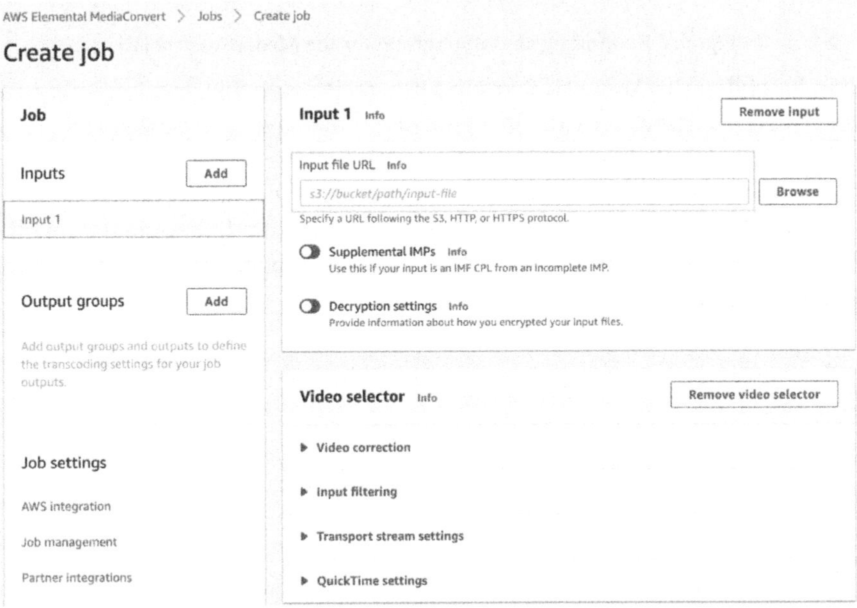

Figure 8.6 – Providing a job input file URL

7. Now, click the **Add** button in **Output groups** in the left panel of the screen, select **Apple HLS** as the option in **Add output group**, and click **Select**. Output groups determine the types of content artifacts produced and on what devices they can be played.

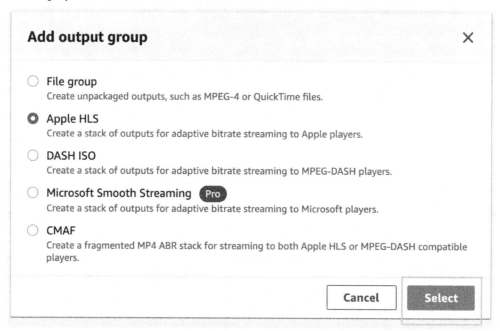

Figure 8.7 – Adding an output group for the MediaConvert job

8. Now, let's fill in the Apple HLS group settings. Provide the custom group name as HLS. In **Destination**, provide the name of the media output bucket you created in *Step 3* along with a prefix in the format s3://<media-output-bucket>/ bankdemo. The AWS Elemental MediaConvert service will process the sample video file into Apple HLS content files for broadcasting. In **Segment control**, choose **Segmented files**. Choose 10 for **Segment length (sec)** and 3 for **Minimum segment length (sec)**.

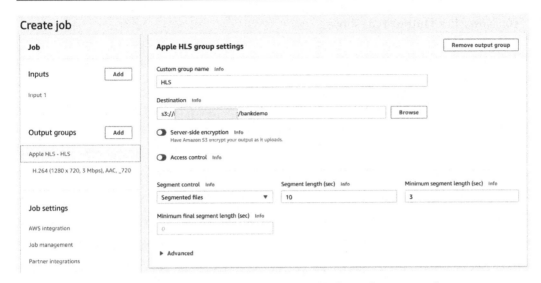

Figure 8.8 – Adding output group settings for the MediaConvert job

9.   Scroll down to **Outputs** and type _720 for **Name modifier** for **Output 1**. Do *not* click on **Create** yet.

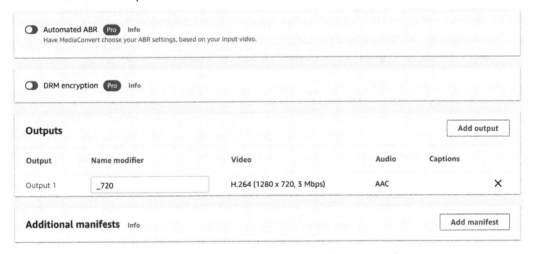

Figure 8.9 – Adding outputs for the MediaConvert job

10. Now, click **Output 1**, as shown:

Figure 8.10 – Clicking Output 1

11. As shown in the following screenshot, type dt for **Segment modifier** in **Output settings**. In the **Resolution (w x h)** fields, type 1280 and 720. Type 3000000 for **Bitrate (bits/s)**. Leave the rest of the fields as the default.

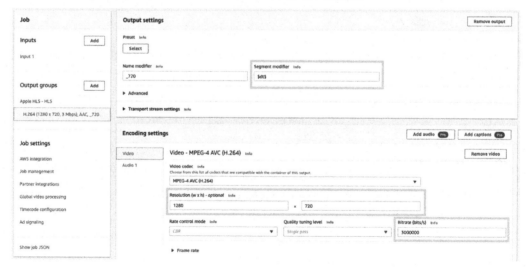

Figure 8.11 – Modifying the output and encoding settings

12. On the left panel, under **Job settings**, click **AWS integration**. On the right, under **Service access**, for **Service role control**, select **Create a new service role, full permissions**. Accept the default name populated in **New role name**. Scroll down and click on **Create**.

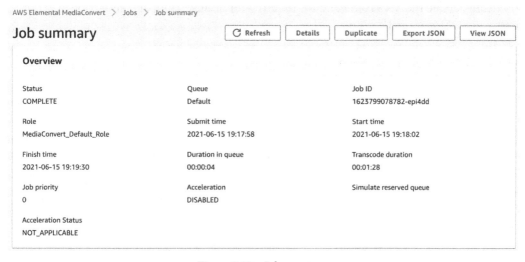

Figure 8.12 – Adding service access for the MediaConvert job

13. The job should complete in a couple of minutes. Click on the **Job ID** to review the summary view of the job, as shown in the following screenshot:

AWS Elemental MediaConvert > Jobs > Job summary

Job summary

| Refresh | Details | Duplicate | Export JSON | View JSON |

Overview

Status	Queue	Job ID
COMPLETE	Default	1623799078782-epi4dd

Role	Submit time	Start time
MediaConvert_Default_Role	2021-06-15 19:17:58	2021-06-15 19:18:02

Finish time	Duration in queue	Transcode duration
2021-06-15 19:19:30	00:00:04	00:01:28

Job priority	Acceleration	Simulate reserved queue
0	DISABLED	

Acceleration Status
NOT_APPLICABLE

Figure 8.13 – Job summary

14. Once the status shows **COMPLETE**, type S3 in the search bar at the top of the screen and go to the S3 console. Under **Buckets**, type the name of the media output bucket you created in *Step 3* previously and click on the bucket name. You should see a number of files here all starting with the name bankdemo, as shown in the following screenshot:

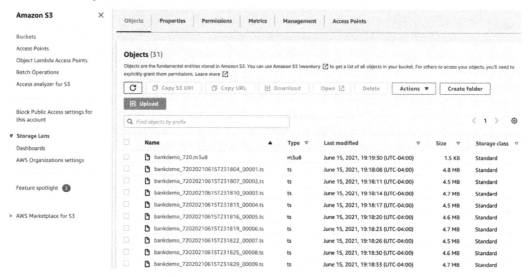

Figure 8.14 – AWS Elemental MediaConvert Apple HLS output files

We have now successfully completed the steps required to convert our sample video file into broadcast-enabled output files, which is required for us to insert ads into the video. In the next section, we will run a transcription of the audio content from our video, run topic modeling, create the **VAST** ad tag URL required for ad insertion, and show how we can perform content monetization.

Running transcription, finding topics, and creating a VAST ad tag URL

Open the notebook you cloned from the GitHub repository (`https://github.com/PacktPublishing/Natural-Language-Processing-with-AWS-AI-Services/blob/main/Chapter%2008/contextual-ad-marking-for-content-monetization-with-nlp-github.ipynb`) in the *Setting up to solve the use case* section and execute the cells step by step, as follows:

> **Note**
>
> Please ensure you have executed the steps in the *Technical requirements, Setting up to solve the use case,* and *Uploading the sample video and converting it for broadcast* sections before you execute the cells in the notebook.

1. Execute the first three cells under the **Transcribe** section to ensure we have the libraries we need for the notebook. Note that in the first cell you are importing libraries, in the second cell you are creating folders needed for Topic Modeling, and in the third cell you are specifying the S3 bucket and prefix. You should have already created two S3 buckets prior to running this notebook, as mentioned in the *Uploading the sample video and converting it for broadcast* section. Please provide the media input bucket name in the line, type a prefix of your choice, or you can accept what is already provided in the notebook. In this cell, we also define the Python SDK handle for Amazon S3 using Boto3, an AWS SDK for Python development (`https://boto3.amazonaws.com/v1/documentation/api/latest/index.html`):

    ```
    bucket = '<your-s3-bucket>'
    prefix = 'chapter8'
    s3=boto3.client('s3')
    ```

2. Execute the next cell to define a method for running an Amazon Transcribe transcription job to convert the audio content of our sample video file to text. Note that we are setting MediaFormat as mp4. We will be using the original sample video file from the GitHub repository (`https://github.com/PacktPublishing/Natural-Language-Processing-with-AWS-AI-Services/blob/main/Chapter%2008/media-content/bank-demo-prem-ranga.mp4`) as the input for the transcription job:

    ```
    import time
    import boto3
    def transcribe_file(job_name, file_uri, transcribe_
    ```

```
client):
    transcribe_client.start_transcription_job(
        TranscriptionJobName=job_name,
        Media={'MediaFileUri': file_uri},
        MediaFormat='mp4',
        LanguageCode='en-US'
    )
```

3. Provide a job name (a text string) for the transcription so we are able to identify this job down the line. Get the Boto3 handle for the Amazon Transcribe service, pass the S3 location of our sample video file we loaded in the media input S3 bucket, and call the `transcribe_file` method to run the transcription job:

```
job_name = 'media-monetization-transcribe'
transcribe_client = boto3.client('transcribe')
file_uri = 's3://'+bucket+'/'+prefix+'/'+'rawvideo/bank-
demo-prem-ranga.mp4'
transcribe_file(job_name, file_uri, transcribe_client)
```

4. Now, navigate to the AWS Management Console in a new tab, type Amazon Transcribe in the search bar at the top, and open the Amazon Transcribe console. Click on **Transcription jobs** in the left pane. You should see your transcription job with the job name you specified earlier. When the job completes, the status should change to **Complete**.

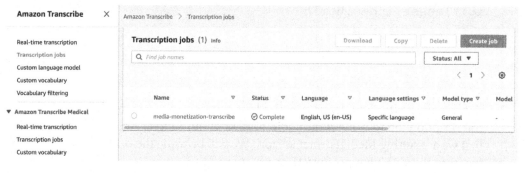

Figure 8.15 – Amazon Transcribe transcription job

5. Now come back to the notebook and execute the next cell to get the S3 location of the transcription results:

```
job = transcribe_client.get_transcription_
job(TranscriptionJobName=job_name)

job_status = job['TranscriptionJob']
['TranscriptionJobStatus']

if job_status in ['COMPLETED', 'FAILED']:
    print(f"Job {job_name} is {job_status}.")

    if job_status == 'COMPLETED':
        print(f"Download the transcript from\n"
              f"\t{job['TranscriptionJob']['Transcript']
['TranscriptFileUri']}")
```

6. We will now execute the code cells in the **Comprehend Topic Modeling** section step by step. As a first step, we will retrieve the transcription output (transcript. csv) to convert the paragraph of text into individual lines (transcript_ formatted.csv) to send as input to the Amazon Comprehend Topic Modeling job. Execute the code in the notebook cell as shown in the following code block:

```
raw_df = pd.read_json(job['TranscriptionJob']
['Transcript']['TranscriptFileUri'])

raw_df = pd.DataFrame(raw_df.at['transcripts','results'].
copy())

raw_df.to_csv('topic-modeling/raw/transcript.csv',
header=False, index=False)

import csv

folderpath = r"topic-modeling/raw" # make sure to put the
'r' in front and provide the folder where your files are

filepaths = [os.path.join(folderpath, name) for name in
os.listdir(folderpath) if not name.startswith('.')] # do
not select hidden directories

fnfull = "topic-modeling/job-input/transcript_formatted.
csv"

for path in filepaths:
    print(path)
    with open(path, 'r') as f:
        content = f.read() # Read the whole file
        lines = content.split('.') # a list of all
sentences
```

```
        with open(fnfull, "w", encoding='utf-8') as ff:
            csv_writer = csv.writer(ff, delimiter=',',
quotechar = '"')
            for num,line in enumerate(lines): # for each
sentence
                csv_writer.writerow([line])
f.close()
s3.upload_file('topic-modeling/job-input/transcript_
formatted.csv', bucket, prefix+'/topic-modeling/
job-input/tm-input.csv')
```

7.   We will run an Amazon Comprehend Topic Modeling job on this formatted CSV file to extract a set of topics that are applicable for our transcript. These topics represent and help us identify what the subject area or the theme for the related text is and represent the common set of words with the same contextual reference throughout the transcript. For more details, please refer to *Amazon Comprehend Topic Modeling*: https://docs.aws.amazon.com/comprehend/latest/dg/topic-modeling.html.

8.   To get started, go to the AWS Management Console (please refer to *Technical requirements* in *Chapter 2, Introducing Amazon Textract,* of this book if you don't have access to the AWS Management Console), type Amazon Comprehend in the **services** search bar at the top of the console, and navigate to the Amazon Comprehend console:

Click the **Launch Amazon Comprehend** button.

Click on **Analysis jobs** in the left pane and click on **Create job** on the right, as follows:

Figure 8.16 – Creating an analysis job

Type a name for your analysis job and set the analysis type as **Topic modeling** from the built-in jobs list:

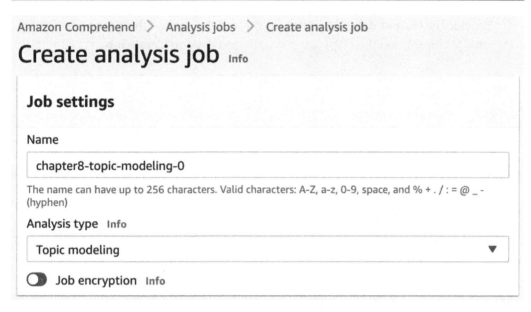

Figure 8.17 – Creating Topic Modeling job inputs 1

Provide the location of the CSV file (the `transcript_formatted.csv` file that we uploaded to S3 in preceding steps) in your *S3 bucket* in the **Input Data** section with the data source as **My documents** and the number of topics as 2, as shown:

Input data Info

Data source

⦿ **My documents**
   We recommend providing at least 1,000 documents containing at least 100 words each.

◯ **Example documents**
   Example documents are available only in English

S3 location
Paste the URL of an input data file in S3, or select a bucket or folder location in S3.

| s3:// ▭ /chapter8/topic-modeling/job-input/tm-input.csv | Browse S3 |

Input format - *optional* Info

| One document per line ▼ |

Number of topics Info

| 2 |

Maximum of 100

Figure 8.18 – Creating Topic Modeling job inputs 2

Provide the **Output data** S3 location, as shown (you can use the same S3 bucket you used for input), and then type a name suffix and click on **Create job**.

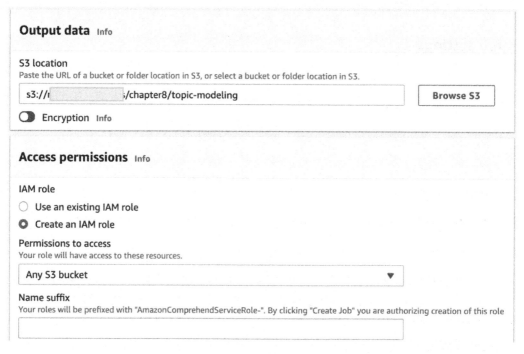

Figure 8.19 – Creating Topic Modeling job inputs 3

You should see a **job submitted** status after the IAM role propagation is completed. After 30 minutes, the job status should change to **Completed**. Now click on the job name and copy the S3 link provided in the **Output data location** field and go back to your notebook. We will continue the steps in the notebook.

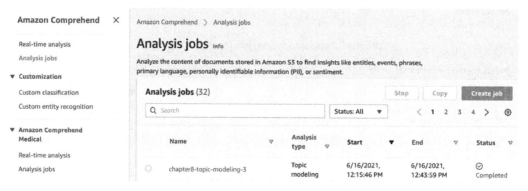

Figure 8.20 – Topic Modeling job completed

9. We will now execute the cells in the **Process Topic Modeling Results** section:

a.) To download the results of the Topic Modeling job, we need the output data location S3 URI that we copied in the previous step. In the first cell in this section of the notebook, replace the contents of the `tpprefix` variable, specifically `<path-to-job-output-tar>`, with the string highlighted in bold from the S3 URI you copied shown in the following code block.

> **Note**
>
> The output data location S3 URI you copied in the preceding step is `s3://<your-s3-bucket>/chapter8/topic-modeling/`**`<aws-account-nr>-TOPICS-<long-hash-nr>/`**`output/output.tar.gz`

b.) The revised code should look as follows and when executed will download the `output.tar.gz` file locally and extract it:

```
directory = "results"
parent_dir = os.getcwd()+'/topic-modeling'
path = os.path.join(parent_dir, directory)
os.makedirs(path, exist_ok = True)
print("Directory '%s' created successfully" %directory)
tpprefix = prefix+'/'+' topic-modeling/<aws-account-nr>-
TOPICS-<long-hash-nr>/output/output.tar.gz'
s3.download_file(bucket, tpprefix, 'topic-modeling/
results/output.tar.gz')
!tar -xzvf topic-modeling/results/output.tar.gz
```

c.) Now, load each of the resulting CSV files to their own pandas DataFrames:

```
tt_df = pd.read_csv('topic-terms.csv')
dt_df = pd.read_csv('doc-topics.csv')
```

d.) The `topic terms` DataFrame contains the topic number, what term corresponds to the topic, and the weightage this term contributes to the topic. Execute the code shown in the following code block to review the contents of the `topic terms` DataFrame:

```
for i,x in tt_df.iterrows():

print(str(x['topic'])+":"+x['term']+":"+str(x['weight']))
```

e.) We may have multiple topics on the same line, but for this solution, we are not interested in these duplicates, so we will drop them:

```
dt_df = dt_df.drop_duplicates(subset=['docname'])
```

f.) Let's now filter the topics such that we select the topic with the maximum weight distribution for the text it refers to:

```
ttdf_max = tt_df.groupby(['topic'], sort=False)
['weight'].max()
```

g.) Load these into their own DataFrame and display it:

```
newtt_df = pd.DataFrame()
for x in ttdf_max:
    newtt_df = newtt_df.append(tt_df.query('weight ==
@x'))
newtt_df = newtt_df.reset_index(drop=True)
newtt_df
```

h.) We will select the content topic term as it has the highest weight and assign this to a variable for use in the subsequent steps:

```
adtopic = newtt_df.at[1,'term']
```

10. We will now use the topic to look up ad content and create a VAST ad tag URL that will be used as an input to insert ads into the broadcast video files we created using AWS Elemental MediaConvert. The authors have provided two sample CSV files containing content metadata for looking up ads. ad-index.csv (https://github.com/PacktPublishing/Natural-Language-Processing-with-AWS-AI-Services/blob/main/Chapter%2008/media-content/ad-index.csv) contains a list of topics as keys and sample cmsid and vid values. cmsid indicates the content management source ID in Google Ad Server, which is what we are using as the ad decision server for our example, and vid indicates the video content ID in Google Ad Server. adserver.csv (https://github.com/PacktPublishing/Natural-Language-Processing-with-AWS-AI-Services/blob/main/Chapter%2008/media-content/adserver.csv) contains the sample Google ad decision server URL that we need to modify in this step. For this example, we'll use the topic we discovered from our Topic Modeling job as the key to fetch cmsid and vid.

We will then substitute these in the VAST ad marker URL before creating the AWS Elemental MediaTailor configuration. Execute the code cells as shown in the following code block:

```
adindex_df = pd.read_csv('media-content/ad-index.csv',
header=None, index_col=0)
```

```
adindex_df
```

a.) Please note this is from the sample `ad-index.csv` file that the authors created for this demo. When you use this solution for your use case, you will need to create a Google Ads account to get the `cmsid` and `vid` values. For more details, please see this link: `https://support.google.com/admanager/topic/1184139?hl=en&ref_topic=7506089`.

b.) Run the code in the following snippet to select the `cmsid` and `vid` values based on our topic:

```
advalue = adindex_df.loc[adtopic]
```

```
advalue
```

c.) We get the following response:

```
1               cmsid=176
```

```
2       vid=short_tencue
```

d.) Now we will create the ad server URL to use with AWS Elemental MediaTailor. Let's first copy the placeholder URL available in our GitHub repo (`https://github.com/PacktPublishing/Natural-Language-Processing-with-AWS-AI-Services/blob/main/Chapter%2008/media-content/adserver.csv`), which has pre-roll, mid-roll, and post-roll segments filled in:

```
ad_rawurl = pd.read_csv('media-content/adserver.csv',
header=None).at[0,0].split('&')
```

```
ad_rawurl
```

e.) We get the following response:

```
['https://pubads.g.doubleclick.net/gampad/
ads?sz=640x480',
 'iu=/124319096/external/ad_rule_samples',
 'ciu_szs=300x250',
 'ad_rule=1',
 'impl=s',
 'gdfp_req=1',
```

```
'env=vp',
'output=vmap',
'unviewed_position_start=1',
'cust_params=deployment%3Ddevsite%26sample_
ar%3Dpremidpost',
'cmsid=',
'vid=',
'correlator=[avail.random]']
```

f.) We will now replace the `cmsid` and `vid` values highlighted in the preceding response with the values corresponding to our topic and reformat the URL:

```
ad_formattedurl = ''
for x in ad_rawurl:
    if 'cmsid' in x:
        x = advalue[1]
    if 'vid' in x:
        x = advalue[2]
    ad_formattedurl += x + '&'

ad_formattedurl = ad_formattedurl.rstrip('&')
ad_formattedurl
```

g.) We get the following response. Copy the contents of the following URL:

```
'https://pubads.g.doubleclick.net/gampad/
ads?sz=640x480&iu=/124319096/external/ad_rule_
samples&ciu_szs=300x250&ad_rule=1&impl=s&gdfp_
req=1&env=vp&output=vmap&unviewed_position_
start=1&cust_params=deployment%3Ddevsite%26sample_
ar%3Dpremidpost&cmsid=176&vid=short_
tencue&correlator=[avail.random]'
```

Alright, that brings us to the end of this section. We successfully transcribed our sample video file using Amazon Transcribe, ran an Amazon Comprehend Topic Modeling job on the transcript, selected a topic, and stitched together an ad server VAST tag URL with the ad content ID corresponding to the topic. In the next section, we will use AWS Elemental MediaTailor to create new video output with the ad segments inserted, and we will test it by playing the video.

Inserting ads and testing our video

Before we can proceed forward, we need to create an Amazon CloudFront (`https://aws.amazon.com/cloudfront/`) content delivery distribution for the video output files we transcoded with AWS Elemental MediaConvert in the *Uploading the sample video and converting it for broadcast* section.

Amazon CloudFront is a managed content delivery network that can be used for site hosting, APIs, and image, media, and video file delivery, with live or on-demand streaming formats, configured for global distribution or based on the selected price class. Please follow the next steps to set up the CloudFront distribution for your transcoded video files:

1. In the AWS Management Console, type `CloudFront` in the search bar at the top, and then select **Amazon CloudFront** and click **Create Distribution**.

Figure 8.21 – Amazon CloudFront Create Distribution

2. On the next page, click **Get Started** to proceed to the **Create Distribution** page. Please note there are multiple sections to be filled. In the **Origin Settings** part of the page, click the list box for **Origin Domain Name** and select the media output bucket that contains the video output files from the AWS Elemental MediaConvert job. Select **Yes** for **Restrict Bucket Access**, and select **Create a New Identity** for **Origin Access Identity**. Select **Yes, Update Bucket Policy** for **Grant Read Permissions on Bucket**.

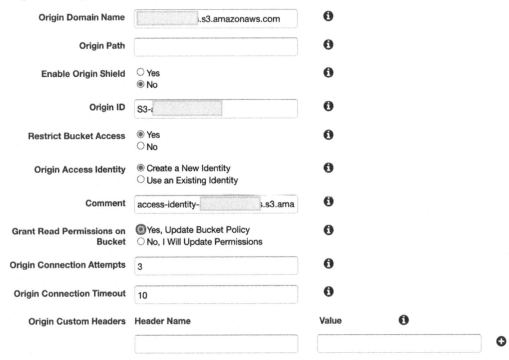

Figure 8.22 – Origin Settings for Create Distribution in Amazon CloudFront

3. Scroll down to the **Default Cache Behavior Settings** area and change **Viewer Protocol Policy** to **Redirect HTTP to HTTPS**. For **Cache Policy**, click the list box and select **Managed-Elemental-MediaPackage**.

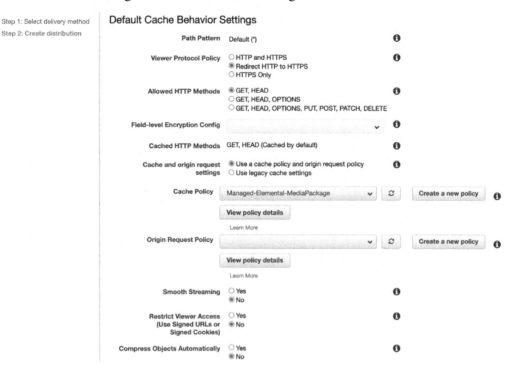

Figure 8.23 – Default Cache Behavior Settings

4. Scroll down to the **Distribution Settings** area and select the price class based on where you are located. Leave the rest of the settings as they are, scroll down, and click **Create Distribution**.

Distribution Settings

Price Class	Use Only U.S., Canada and Europe ⌄ ⓘ
Amazon WAF Web ACL	None ⌄ ⓘ
Alternate Domain Names (CNAMEs)	ⓘ
SSL Certificate	◉ Default CloudFront Certificate (*.cloudfront.net)

Choose this option if you want your users to use HTTPS or HTTP to access your content with the CloudFront domain https://d111111abcdef8.cloudfront.net/logo.jpg).
Important: If you choose this option, CloudFront requires that browsers or devices support TLSv1 or later to access

○ Custom SSL Certificate (example.com):

Choose this option if you want your users to access your content by using an alternate domain name, such as
You can use a certificate stored in Amazon Certificate Manager (ACM) in the US East
(N. Virginia) Region, or you can use a certificate stored in IAM.

ⓘ

Request or Import a Certificate with ACM

Learn more about using custom SSL/TLS certificates with CloudFront.
Learn more about using ACM.

Supported HTTP Versions	◉ HTTP/2, HTTP/1.1, HTTP/1.0 ○ HTTP/1.1, HTTP/1.0 ⓘ
Default Root Object	ⓘ
Standard Logging	○ On ◉ Off ⓘ
S3 Bucket for Logs	ⓘ
Log Prefix	ⓘ

Figure 8.24 – Distribution Settings

5. Once the distribution is created, the status will change to **Deployed** and the state will change to **Enabled**. Copy the value of the domain name from the distribution.

Figure 8.25 – Distribution is enabled

6. We will now use this distribution as a content source to create new video output with the ads inserted. In the AWS Management Console, type `MediaTailor` in the services search bar, and select it to go to the AWS Elemental MediaTailor console. Click **Create configuration** to get started.

Figure 8.26 – AWS Elemental MediaTailor

7. On the **Create configuration** page, under **Required settings**, provide an ad campaign name. In the **Content source** field, paste the Amazon CloudFront distribution domain name that you copied in the preceding steps. Finally, in the **Ad decision server** field, type the modified VAST ad tag URL you created in the last step of the *Running transcription, finding topics, and creating a VAST ad tag URL* section. Scroll down and click **Create configuration**.

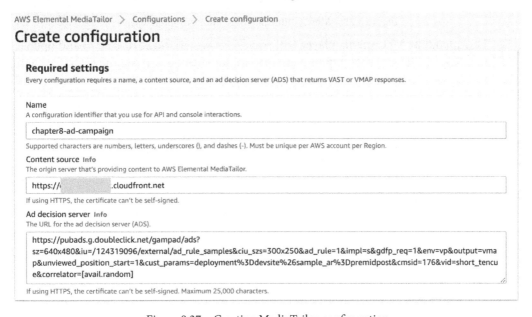

Figure 8.27 – Creating MediaTailor configuration

8. The created configuration is displayed as shown in the following screenshot. Copy the HLS playback prefix as we need it in the next step.

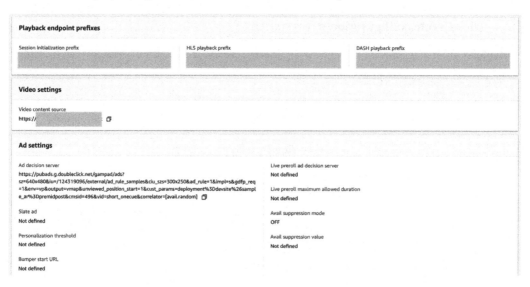

Figure 8.28 – MediaTailor playback endpoint prefixes

9. Download the VLC media player (https://www.videolan.org/) and open it. Click on **File** and then **Open Network**. In the **URL** field, paste the HLS playback prefix you copied in the previous step, and at the end of the string, after the forward slash, type bankdemo.m3u8. This is the manifest file for the MediaTailor video output with the ads inserted. The full URL should look as follows (this is an example representative URL): https://<generated-hash-nr>.mediatailor. us-east-1.amazonaws.com/v1/master/<generated-hash-nr>/<chapter8-ad-campaign>/bankdemo.m3u8.

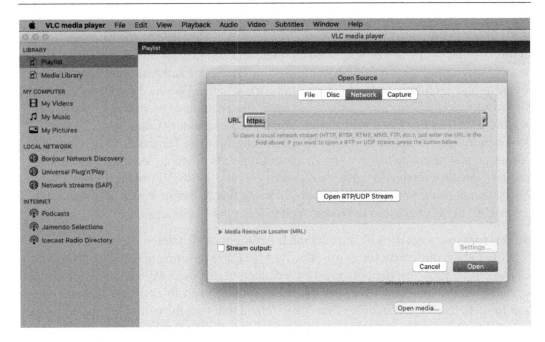

Figure 8.29 – Testing the video output using the VLC media player

10. Click **Open**. The video will start playing momentarily. Please note it takes a couple of minutes for the ad insertion to reflect in the video. You should see a 10-second pre-roll, a 10-second mid-roll, and post-roll ad space in the video. Since we used the sample ad server URL, we don't see actual ads here, but once you register with an ad decision server, you can get the actual ad content included by following the steps in this solution.

And that concludes the solution build for this chapter. Please refer to the *Further reading* section for more details on media content monetization with AWS AI and media services.

Summary

In this chapter, we learned how to build an intelligent solution for media content monetization using the AWS AI services Amazon Transcribe and Amazon Comprehend, the Amazon CloudFront content delivery network, and the AWS media services Elemental MediaConvert and Elemental MediaTailor by taking a sample MP4 video file. We covered all this by first transcoding it into Apple HLS output files using MediaConvert, then creating atranscription from the MP4 file using Amazon Transcribe, analyzing the transcript, and detecting topics using Amazon Comprehend Topic Modeling, creating a VAST ad decision server URL. We also covered creating a distribution for the transcoded video content using Amazon CloudFront and using this distribution and the ad decision server URL to insert ads into the transcoded video using MediaTailor.

For our solution, we started by introducing the content monetization use case for LiveRight, the requirement for a cost-effective expansion resulting in using content to pay for content creation. We then designed an architecture that used AWS AI services, media services, and the content delivery network to assemble an end-to-end walk-through of how to monetize content in video files. We assumed that you, the reader, are the architect assigned to this project, and we reviewed an overview of the solution components along with an architectural illustration in *Figure 8.1*.

We then went through the prerequisites for the solution build, set up an Amazon SageMaker notebook instance, cloned our GitHub repository, and started executing the steps using the AWS Management Console and the code in the notebook based on instructions from this chapter.

In the next chapter, we will look at an important use case, metadata extraction, using named entity recognition. We will, as before, introduce the use case, discuss how to design the architecture, establish the prerequisites, and walk through in detail the various steps required to build the solution.

Further reading

- Monetizing your media workflows (`https://aws.amazon.com/media/resources/monetization/`)

- *Announcing AWS Media Intelligence Solutions* by Vasi Philozelligence-solutions/)

9
Extracting Metadata from Financial Documents

In the previous chapter, we learned how to build an intelligent solution for media content monetization using AWS AI services. We did this by talking about how our fictitious company **LiveRight Holdings private limited** requires a cost-effective expansion for content monetization. We designed an architecture using AWS AI services, media services, and the content delivery network for an end-to-end walkthrough of how to monetize content in video files.

In this chapter, we will look at how AWS AI services can help us extract metadata for financial filing reports for **LiveRight Holdings**. This will allow their financial analysts to look into important information and make better decisions concerning financial events such as mergers, acquisitions, and IPOs.

We will talk about what metadata is and why it is important to extract metadata. Then, we will cover how to use Amazon Comprehend entity extraction and how Amazon Comprehend events can be used to extract metadata from documents.

In this chapter, we will be covering the following topics:

- Extracting metadata from financial documents
- Setting up the use case

Technical requirements

For this chapter, you will need access to an AWS account. Please make sure that you follow the instructions specified in the *Technical requirements* section of *Chapter 2, Introducing Amazon Textract*, to create your AWS account, and log into the AWS Management Console before trying the steps in the *Extracting metadata from financial documents* section.

The Python code and sample datasets for our solution can be found at `https://github.com/PacktPublishing/Natural-Language-Processing-with-AWS-AI-Services/tree/main/Chapter%2009`. Please use the instructions in the following sections, along with the code in the aforementioned repository, to build the solution.

Check out the following video to see the Code in Action at `https://bit.ly/3jBxp3E`.

Extracting metadata from financial documents

In this section, we will talk about a use case where **LiveRight Holdings private limited** is attempting to acquire AwakenLife Pvt Ltd. They are going to do a press release soon and financial analysts are curious to identify the important metadata such as the acquisition date, amount, organization, and so forth so that they can act according to the market. LiveRight analyzed the Amazon Whole Foods merger to determine what it can learn and how metadata extraction will be useful for its due diligence. We will use the Amazon Whole Foods merger sample dataset to understand how you can perform metadata extraction using the preceding architecture:

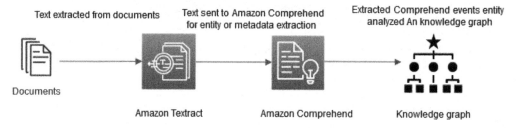

Figure 9.1 – Metadata extraction architecture

In this architecture, we will start with large financial documents for extracting metadata. We will show you how you can use Amazon Textract batch processing jobs to extract data from this large document and save this extracted data as a text file. Then, we will show you how to extract entities from this text file using Comprehend Events and visualize the relationships between the entity using a knowledge graph. Alternatively, you can use Amazon Neptune, which is a graph database that's used to visualize these relations.

In the next section, we'll look at this architecture by using Jupyter Notebook code.

Setting up the use case

In this section, we will cover how to get started and walk you through the architecture shown in the preceding diagram.

We have broken down the solution code walkthrough into the following sections:

- Setting up the notebook code and S3 bucket creation
- Uploading sample documents and extracting text using Textract
- Metadata extraction using Comprehend
- Starting Comprehend Events job with the SDK
- Collecting the Comprehend Events job results from S3
- Analyzing the output of Comprehend Events

Setting up the notebook code and S3 Bucket creation

Follow these steps to set up the notebook:

1. In the SageMaker Jupyter notebook you set up in the previous chapters, Git clone `https://github.com/PacktPublishing/Natural-Language-Processing-with-AWS-AI-Services/`.

2. Then, go to `/Chapter 09/chapter 09 metadata extraction.ipynb` and start running the notebook.

3. Now that we have set up the notebook, we'll create an Amazon S3 bucket. Follow the steps provided in *Chapter 2, Introducing Amazon Textract*, to create an Amazon S3 bucket.

4. Copy the created bucket, open your sample code from *Chapter 9, Extracting Metadata from Financial Documents* (Chapter 09/chapter 09 metadata extraction.ipynb), and paste it into the following notebook cell to get started:

```
bucket = '<your s3 bucket name>'
```

> **Note**
>
> We assume that your notebook has IAM access for Amazon Comprehend full access, Amazon S3 full access, and Amazon Textract full access. If you do not have access, you will get an access denied exception.

If you get an access denied exception while running any of the steps in this notebook, please go to *Chapter 2, Introducing Amazon Textract*, and set up the relevant IAM roles.

In the next section, we will walk you through the code so that you understand how the architecture works.

Uploading sample documents and extracting text using Textract

In this section, we will walk you through how you can quickly set up the proposed architecture shown in *Figure 9.1*. We have already created an Amazon S3 bucket where your output and sample documents will be stored. We also pasted that S3 bucket's name in the notebook cell. If you haven't done this yet, please complete the preceding steps.

We will refer to the following notebook: https://github.com/PacktPublishing/Natural-Language-Processing-with-AWS-AI-Services/blob/main/Chapter%2009/chapter%2009%20metadata%20extraction.ipynb. Let's get started:

1. First, we must download the sample PDF financial press release document from Amazon S3.

    Now, we must upload it using the upload_file S3 command via the sample_financial_news_doc.pdf boto3 API to an S3 bucket for processing. The same bucket will be used to return service output:

```
filename = "sample_financial_news_doc.pdf"
s3_client.upload_file(filename, bucket, filename)
```

> **Note**
>
> This PDF file consists of a press release statement of the Whole Foods and Amazon merger in 2017 and consists of 156 pages.

2. Now, we will run Amazon Textract to convert this PDF into a text file; Amazon Comprehend accepts a text input file with UTF 8 encoding for metadata extraction as input. You can run the notebook code to start an asynchronous processing job to extract text from documents. We explained how the asynchronous Textract batch processing code works in detail in *Chapter 2, Introducing Amazon Textract*. If you want to deep dive, please refer to that chapter. Run the following cell to get the job results:

```
jobId = startJob(bucket, filename)
print("Started job with id: {}".format(jobId))
if(isJobComplete(jobId)):
    response = getJobResults(jobId)
```

At this point, you will get a Job ID. Wait until the job's status changes from in progress to complete:

```
Started job with id: 5e1770681a137478b04edd3016151865a257a1d8a369f9b35e74157d830ef3e1
Job status: IN_PROGRESS
Job status: IN_PROGRESS
Job status: IN_PROGRESS
```

Figure 9.2 – Textract job status

3. Now, we will convert the extracted data from Amazon Textract into a UTF 8 text file for Amazon Comprehend by running the following notebook cell:

```
text_filename = 'sample_finance_data.txt'
doc = Document(response)
with open(text_filename, 'w', encoding='utf-8') as f:
    for page in doc.pages:
        page_string = ''
        for line in page.lines:
            #print((line.text))
            page_string += str(line.text)
        #print(page_string)
        f.writelines(page_string + "\n")
```

The financial press release document text will be extracted from the press release documents:

```
Amazon (NASDAQ:AMZN) and Whole Foods Market, Inc. (NASDAQ:WFM) today announced that they
have entered into a definitive merger agreement under which Amazon will acquire Whole Foods
Market
for $42 per share in an all-cash transaction valued at approximately $13.7 billion, includi
ng Whole Foods
Market's net debt. "Millions of people love Whole Foods Market because they offer the best
natural
and organic foods, and they make it fun to eat healthy," said Jeff Bezos, Amazon founder an
d CEO.
"Whole Foods Market has been satisfying, delighting and nourishing customers for nearly fou
r decades -
they're doing an amazing job and we want that to continue." "This partnership presents an o
pportunity
to maximize value for Whole Foods Market's shareholders, while at the same time extending o
ur
mission and bringing the highest quality, experience, convenience and innovation to our cus
```

Figure 9.3 – Text extracted from the press release document using Amazon Textract

In this section, we covered how to extract text data from a press release document (a 2017 press release about Amazon's acquisition of Whole Foods), which consists of 156 pages, into text format using Amazon Textract. In the next section, we will talk about how to extract metadata from this document using Comprehend entity detection sync APIs and Comprehend events async jobs.

Metadata extraction using Comprehend

In this section, we will use the aforementioned text file to extract metadata using the Amazon Comprehend Events API.

Comprehend Events API

Amazon Comprehend Events is a very specific API that can help you analyze financial events such as mergers, acquisitions, IPO dates, press releases, bankruptcy, and more. It extracts important financial entities such as IPO dates, the merger parties' names, and so on from these events and establishes relationships so that financial analysts can act in real time on their financial models and make accurate predictions and quick decisions.

Amazon Comprehend Events can help you analyze asynchronous jobs. To do this, you must ensure you do the following first:

- Set up an Amazon Comprehend Events job through the AWS Console.
- Set up an Amazon Comprehend Events job through the notebook (https://github.com/PacktPublishing/Natural-Language-Processing-with-AWS-AI-Services/blob/main/Chapter%2009/chapter%20 09%20metadata%20extraction.ipynb) using boto3 Python APIs.

> **Note**
> You can choose one of the aforementioned approaches to analyze your press release documents using Amazon Comprehend events.

Let's start by setting up an Amazon Comprehend Events job using the Amazon Comprehend consol:

1. Open the Amazon Comprehend console by going to `https://console.aws.amazon.com/comprehend/v2/home?region=us-east-1#home`.

2. Go to **Analysis Jobs** -> **Create Analysis Job**.

3. In **Job Settings**, enter **Name: Test-events**. You will see that we can choose from various types of analysis, such as **Sentiment**, **PII**, **Entity**, and **Topic modeling**. Choose **Events**. For **Language** choose **English**, while for **Target Event Types**, choose all the available options, as shown in the following screenshot:

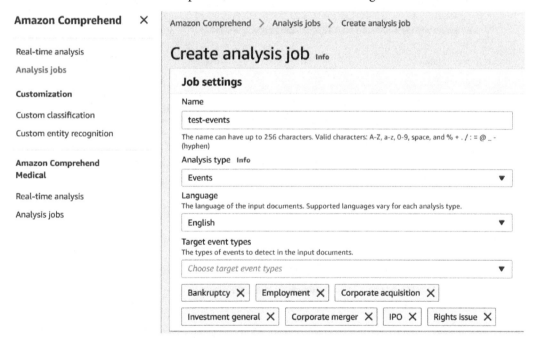

Figure 9.4 – Creating a Comprehend events analysis job

4. For **Input data**, select **My documents** and provide the **S3 location** information of your input text file; for example, `s3://<your bucket>/ sample_finance_data.txt`. Choose one document per line for **Input format**.

> **Note**
>
> We are using one document per line as the input format instead of one document per file. This is because the total file size of this press release document is 655 KB and the limit for one document per file is 10 KB. One document per line format can have 5,000 lines in a single document; the press release document we are using for this demo contains 156 lines.

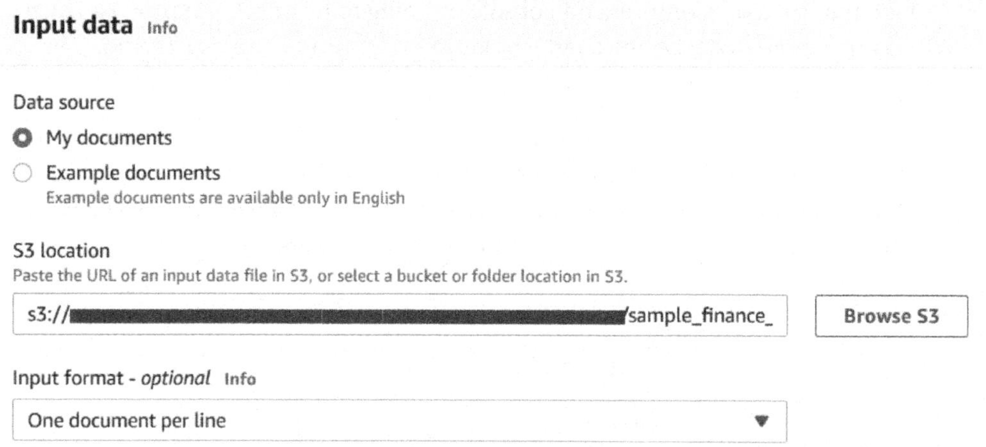

Input data Info

Data source

◉ My documents

◯ Example documents
Example documents are available only in English

S3 location
Paste the URL of an input data file in S3, or select a bucket or folder location in S3.

| s3:// ██████████████████████████████/sample_finance_ | Browse S3 |

Input format - *optional* Info

| One document per line ▼ |

Figure 9.5 – Choosing Input data for the analysis job

5. For **Output Data**, under **S3 location**, enter the location where you want your output to be saved. It will be the same bucket you created in the previous step; that is, s3://<your-bucket>:

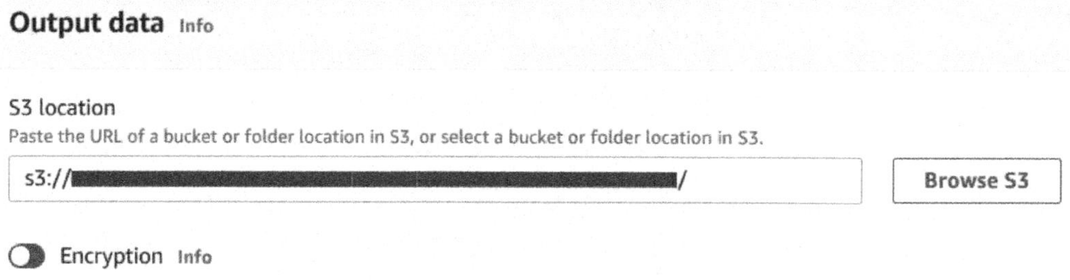

Output data Info

S3 location
Paste the URL of a bucket or folder location in S3, or select a bucket or folder location in S3.

| s3:// ██████████████████████████████/ | Browse S3 |

◖ Encryption Info

Figure 9.6 – Choosing an output S3 location for the analysis job

6. For **Access permissions**, choose **Create an IAM Role**. For **Name suffix**, write
    `events-role`:

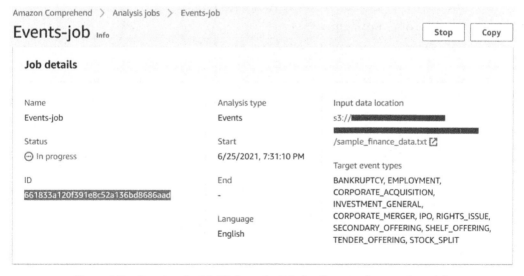

Figure 9.7 – Setting up access permissions by creating an IAM role

7. Click on the **Create Job** button to trigger an events job. Grab a coffee/tea as this job
    will take 15 minutes to complete.

8. Once your job is complete, go to **Events-job**, copy the job ID, as highlighted in
    the following screenshot, and move back to the **Collect Results from S3** notebook
    section so that you can use this as the Events `Job ID`:

Amazon Comprehend > Analysis jobs > Events-job

Events-job Info   Stop   Copy

Job details

Name	Analysis type	Input data location
Events-job	Events	s3:// ▮▮▮▮▮▮▮▮▮▮▮▮▮▮
		▮▮▮▮▮▮▮▮▮▮▮▮▮▮▮▮▮▮
Status	Start	/sample_finance_data.txt ⧉
☺ In progress	6/25/2021, 7:31:10 PM	
		Target event types
ID	End	BANKRUPTCY, EMPLOYMENT,
661833a120f391e8c52a136bd8686aad	-	CORPORATE_ACQUISITION,
		INVESTMENT_GENERAL,
	Language	CORPORATE_MERGER, IPO, RIGHTS_ISSUE,
	English	SECONDARY_OFFERING, SHELF_OFFERING,
		TENDER_OFFERING, STOCK_SPLIT

Figure 9.8 – Copying the job ID from the Job details page after creating a job

> **Note**
>
> If you are creating events using the Amazon Comprehend console, skip the *Start an asynchronous job with the SDK* section in the notebook and move on to the *Collect the results from S3* section.

In this section, we covered how to create a Comprehend Events job using the **AWS Console** for a large financial press release document. Skip the next section if you have already set up using the console.

Starting Comprehend Events jobs with the SDK

In this section, we will switch back to our notebook to start an asynchronous job with the SDK. Let's get started:

1. Create an IAM role by going to the IAM console at `https://console.aws.amazon.com/iam/home?region=us-east-1#/home`. Ensure that you create an IAM role with access to Comprehend and have specified S3. Paste the following into the cell:

    ```
    job_data_access_role = 'arn:aws:iam::<your account
    number>:role/service-role/AmazonComprehendServiceRole-
    test-events-role'
    ```

2. Run the following cell to set up other Events job parameters, such as event types and input data format:

    ```
    input_data_format = 'ONE_DOC_PER_LINE'
    job_uuid = uuid.uuid1()
    job_name = f"events-job-{job_uuid}"
    event_types = ["BANKRUPTCY", "EMPLOYMENT", "CORPORATE_
    ACQUISITION",
                    "INVESTMENT_GENERAL", "CORPORATE_MERGER",
    "IPO",
                    "RIGHTS_ISSUE", "SECONDARY_OFFERING",
    "SHELF_OFFERING",
                    "TENDER_OFFERING", "STOCK_SPLIT"]
    ```

3. Run the following cell to trigger the Events analysis job. This job is calling the Python boto 3 starts event detection job API. Go to `https://boto3.amazonaws.com/v1/documentation/api/latest/reference/services/comprehend.html#Comprehend.Client.start_events_detection_job` to learn more:

```
response = comprehend_client.start_events_detection_job(
    InputDataConfig={'S3Uri': input_data_s3_path,
                     'InputFormat': input_data_format},
    OutputDataConfig={'S3Uri': output_data_s3_path},
    DataAccessRoleArn=job_data_access_role,
    JobName=job_name,
    LanguageCode='en',
    TargetEventTypes=event_types
)
events_job_id = response['JobId']
```

In this section, we covered how to trigger Comprehend Events analysis jobs using the SDK. At this point, we have a job ID that we will use in the next section to collect the output and analyze the metadata.

Collecting the results from S3

In this section, we will analyze the output results of this job in Amazon S3. Let's get started:

1. If you used the Amazon Comprehend console previously, you must have copied the Job ID at the end of that section. Please paste it in the following cell by uncommenting it. Then, run the cell:

```
events_job_id ="<Job ID>"
```

2. If you used the Amazon Comprehend SDK to trigger Events analysis jobs, continue with the following cell to track the job's status:

```
job = comprehend_client.describe_events_detection_job(JobId=events_job_id)
waited = 0
timeout_minutes = 30
while job['EventsDetectionJobProperties']['JobStatus'] != 'COMPLETED':
    sleep(60)
```

```
    waited += 60
        assert waited//60 < timeout_minutes, "Job timed out
after %d seconds." % waited
        job = comprehend_client.describe_events_detection_
job(JobId=events_job_id)
```

3. Once the job is completed, you can get the output from Amazon S3 by running the
    following cell:

```
output_data_s3_file = job['EventsDetectionJobProperties']
['OutputDataConfig']['S3Uri'] + text_filename + '.out'
results = []
with smart_open.open(output_data_s3_file) as fi:
        results.extend([json.loads(line) for line in
fi.readlines() if line])
```

In this section, we covered how to track a Comprehend Events job's completion using
SDKs and collect the output from Amazon S3. Now that we have collected the results, we
will analyze the results and metadata that have been extracted.

Analyzing the output of Comprehend Events

In this section, we will show you different ways you can analyze the output of
Comprehend Events. This output can be used by financial analysts to predict market
trends or look up key information in large datasets. But first, let's understand the
Comprehend Events system's output (https://docs.aws.amazon.com/
comprehend/latest/dg/how-events.html):

-   The system returns JSON output for each submitted document. The structure of the
    response is shown here:

```
result = results[0]
result
```

In the response, you get entities, as well as entities grouped as mentions,
arguments, and triggers, along with the confidence score. We will see these
terms being used throughout the notebook:

```
      'Type': 'EMPLOYMENT'}],
    'Type': 'EMPLOYMENT'},
  {'Arguments': [{'EntityIndex': 2, 'Role': 'INVESTEE', 'Score': 0.999677},
    {'EntityIndex': 11, 'Role': 'DATE', 'Score': 0.977672}],
   'Triggers': [{'BeginOffset': 2795,
     'EndOffset': 2806,
     'GroupScore': 1.0,
     'Score': 0.660339,
     'Text': 'transaction',
     'Type': 'CORPORATE_ACQUISITION'},
    {'BeginOffset': 2960,
     'EndOffset': 2971,
     'GroupScore': 0.999965,
     'Score': 0.678594,
     'Text': 'transaction',
     'Type': 'CORPORATE_ACQUISITION'}],
   'Type': 'CORPORATE_ACQUISITION'}],
 'File': 'sample_finance_data.txt',
 'Line': 0}
```

Figure 9.9 – Comprehend events JSON output

- Events are groups of triggers. The API's output includes the text, character offset, and type of each trigger, along with the confidence score. The confidence of event group membership is provided by GroupScore. Run the following notebook cell to take a look at these:

```
result['Events'][1]['Triggers']
```

The following is the output of the preceding code:

```
Out[34]:  [{'BeginOffset': 160,
            'EndOffset': 167,
            'GroupScore': 1.0,
            'Score': 0.999959,
            'Text': 'acquire',
            'Type': 'CORPORATE_ACQUISITION'},
           {'BeginOffset': 210,
            'EndOffset': 213,
            'GroupScore': 0.999974,
            'Score': 0.828479,
            'Text': 'all',
            'Type': 'CORPORATE_ACQUISITION'},
           {'BeginOffset': 219,
            'EndOffset': 230,
            'GroupScore': 0.501301,
            'Score': 0.98162,
            'Text': 'transaction',
            'Type': 'CORPORATE_ACQUISITION'},
```

Figure 9.10 – Comprehend events triggers

acquire and transaction are related to the CORPORATE_ACQUISTION type event.

- Arguments are linked to entities by `EntityIndex`, along with the classification confidence of the role assignment. It talks about how the entity is related to the event. Run the following code to understand this:

```
result['Events'][1]['Arguments']
```

The output of `arguments` will look as follows:

```
Out[35]:  [{'EntityIndex': 5, 'Role': 'AMOUNT', 'Score': 0.998241},
          {'EntityIndex': 4, 'Role': 'DATE', 'Score': 0.994679},
          {'EntityIndex': 2, 'Role': 'INVESTEE', 'Score': 0.999588},
          {'EntityIndex': 0, 'Role': 'INVESTOR', 'Score': 0.999565},
          {'EntityIndex': 3, 'Role': 'INVESTEE', 'Score': 0.975579},
          {'EntityIndex': 8, 'Role': 'DATE', 'Score': 0.994265}]
```

Figure 9.11 – Comprehend events arguments

`Investee`, `Amount`, and `Date` are roles with entity indexes and confidence scores.

- Entities are groups of `Mentions` that consist of `text`, character `offset`, and `type` of each mention, along with their confidence scores. The confidence of the entity group's membership is provided by `Group Scores`. Let's run the following cell to understand this:

```
result['Entities'][5]['Mentions']
```

The following output shows what the `Mention` entity looks like:

```
Out[36]:  [{'BeginOffset': 190,
            'EndOffset': 193,
            'GroupScore': 1.0,
            'Score': 0.998241,
            'Text': '$42',
            'Type': 'MONETARY_VALUE'},
           {'BeginOffset': 255,
            'EndOffset': 268,
            'GroupScore': 0.871696,
            'Score': 0.999512,
            'Text': '$13.7 billion',
            'Type': 'MONETARY_VALUE'}]
```

Figure 9.12 – Comprehend events mentions

`entityIndex` 5 refers to the `Type` `Monetary_Value` in the output.

Now that we know what `entity`, `arguments`, and `mentions` are, let's visualize the relationships between them.

Visualizing events and entities

In the remainder of the notebook, we'll provided several tabulations and visualizations to help you understand what the API is returning. First, we'll look at spans, both triggers and entity mentions. One of the most essential visualization tasks for sequence labeling tasks is highlighting tagged text in documents. For demonstration purposes, we'll do this with **displaCy**, which is a built-in dependency visualizer that lets you check your model's predictions in your browser (https://explosion.ai/demos/displacy):

1. Run the following code to convert entity into displaCy format. Convert the output of Events into displaCy format:

    ```
    entities = [
        {'start': m['BeginOffset'], 'end': m['EndOffset'],
    'label': m['Type']}
        for e in result['Entities']
        for m in e['Mentions']
    ]
    ```

2. Use the following code to map triggers:

    ```
    triggers = [
        {'start': t['BeginOffset'], 'end': t['EndOffset'],
    'label': t['Type']}
        for e in result['Events']
        for t in e['Triggers']
    ]
    ```

3. Run the following code so that spans is sorted so that displaCy can process it correctly:

    ```
    spans = sorted(entities + triggers, key=lambda x:
    x['start'])
    tags = [s['label'] for s in spans]
    output = [{"text": raw_texts[0], "ents": spans, "title":
    None, "settings": {}}]
    ```

4. Now, we will render all entities participating in the event by running the following notebook code:

    ```
    displacy.render(output, style="ent", options={"colors":
    color_map}, manual=True)
    ```

The following is the output of running the preceding code:

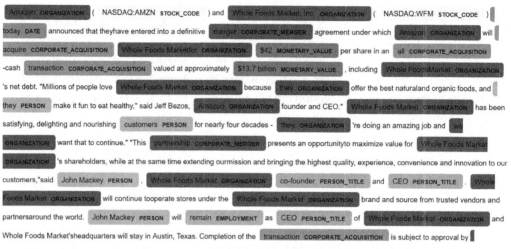

Figure 9.13 – Comprehend events and entities

We have color-coded the events based on the relationships that were found. Just by looking at the highlighted entities and relationships that are the same color, we can see that John Mackey is the co-founder and CEO and that he will remain employed.

Rendering tabular data

Many financial users use `Events` to create structured data from unstructured text. In this section, we'll demonstrate how to do this with pandas.

First, we must flatten the hierarchical JSON data into a pandas DataFrame by doing the following:

1. Create the `entities` DataFrame. The entity indices must be explicitly created:

```
entities_df = pd.DataFrame([
    {"EntityIndex": i, **m}
    for i, e in enumerate(result['Entities'])
    for m in e['Mentions']
])
```

2. Create the `events` DataFrame. The `Event` indices must be explicitly created:

```
events_df = pd.DataFrame([
    {"EventIndex": i, **a, **t}
    for i, e in enumerate(result['Events'])
```

```
        for a in e['Arguments']
        for t in e['Triggers']
])
```

3. The following code will join the two tables into one flat data structure:

```
events_df = events_df.merge(entities_df,
on="EntityIndex", suffixes=('Event', 'Entity'))
```

The following is the output of `EntityIndex` as a tabular structure:

Out[49]:

	EventIndex	EntityIndex	Role	ScoreEvent	BeginOffsetEvent	EndOffsetEvent	GroupScoreEvent	TextEvent	TypeEvent	Begin
0	0	4	DATE	0.999686	119	125	1.000000	merger	CORPORATE_MERGER	
1	0	4	DATE	0.999686	119	125	1.000000	merger	CORPORATE_MERGER	
2	0	4	DATE	0.999914	654	665	0.999946	partnership	CORPORATE_MERGER	
3	0	4	DATE	0.999914	654	665	0.999946	partnership	CORPORATE_MERGER	
4	1	4	DATE	0.999959	160	167	1.000000	acquire	CORPORATE_ACQUISITION	
...	...	...	...	...	...	...	...	...	...	
675	4	9	EMPLOYEE	0.999974	2677	2683	1.000000	remain	EMPLOYMENT	
676	4	9	EMPLOYEE	0.999974	2677	2683	1.000000	remain	EMPLOYMENT	
677	4	10	EMPLOYEE_TITLE	0.999974	2677	2683	1.000000	remain	EMPLOYMENT	
678	5	11	DATE	0.660339	2795	2806	1.000000	transaction	CORPORATE_ACQUISITION	
679	5	11	DATE	0.678594	2960	2971	0.999965	transaction	CORPORATE_ACQUISITION	

680 rows × 15 columns

Figure 9.14 – Comprehend events entity as a DataFrame

We can see that its easy to analyze and extract important events and metadata respective to those events such as Date and time as a python pandas dataframe. Once your data is in dataframe this can be easily saved into downstream applications such as a database or a graph database for furthur analysis.

Tabular representation of analytics

We're primarily interested in the *event structure*, so let's make that more transparent by creating a new table with `Roles` as a column header, grouped by event:

- The following code will do this for us:

```
def format_compact_events(x):
    This code will take the most commonly occurring
EventType and the set of triggers.
    d = {"EventType": Counter(x['TypeEvent']).most_
common()[0][0],
```

```
    "Triggers": set(x['TextEvent'])}
```

This code will loop for each argument Role, collect the set of mentions in the group.

```
    for role in x['Role']:
```

```
        d.update({role: set((x[x['Role']==role]
['TextEntity']))})
```

```
    return d
```

- The following code will group data by `EventIndex` and format:

```
event_analysis_df = pd.DataFrame(
```

```
    events_df.groupby("EventIndex").apply(format_compact_
events).tolist()
```

```
).fillna('')
```

```
event_analysis_df
```

The following screenshot shows the output of the DataFrame representing the tabular format of Comprehend Events:

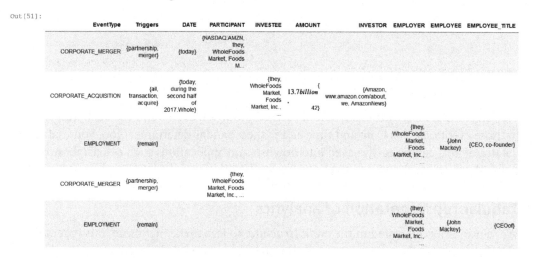

Figure 9.15 – Comprehend events tabular representation

In the preceding output, we have a tabular representation of the event type, date, investee, investor, employer, employee, and title, all of which can easily be used by financial analysts to look into the necessary metadata.

Graphing event semantics

The most striking representation of the output of Comprehend Events can be found in a semantic graph, which is a network of the entities and events that have been referenced in a document(s). The code we will cover shortly (please open the pyvis link for this) uses two open source libraries: Networkx and pyvis. Networkx is a Python package that's used to create, manipulate, and study the structure, dynamics, and functions of complex networks (https://networkx.org/), while pyvis (https://pyvis.readthedocs.io/en/latest/) is a library that allows you to quickly generate visual networks to render events system output. The vertices represent entity mentions and triggers, while the edges are the argument roles held by the entities concerning the triggers in the graph.

Formatting data

The system output must be conformed to the node (that is, the vertex) and edge list format required by Networkx. This requires iterating over triggers, entities, and argument structural relations. Note that we can use the GroupScore and Score keys on various objects to prune nodes and edges where the model has less confidence. We can also use various strategies to pick a "canonical" mention from each mention group to appear in the graph; here, we have chosen the mention with the longest string-wise extent. Run the following code to format it:

- Entities are associated with events by group, not individual mentions for simplicity. The following method assumes that the canonical mention is the longest one:

```
def get_canonical_mention(mentions):
    extents = enumerate([m['Text'] form in mentions])
    longest_name = sorted(extents, key=lambda x:
len(x[1]))
    return [mentions[longest_name[-1][0]]]
```

- Set a global confidence threshold:

```
thr = 0.5
```

- In the following code, we are representing nodes as (id, type, tag, score, mention_type) tuples:

```
trigger_nodes = [
    ("tr%d" % i, t['Type'], t['Text'], t['Score'],
"trigger")
```

```
for i, e in enumerate(result['Events'])
    for t in e['Triggers'][:1]
        if t['GroupScore'] > thr
]
entity_nodes = [
    ("en%d" % i, m['Type'], m['Text'], m['Score'],
"entity")
    for i, e in enumerate(result['Entities'])
    for m in get_canonical_mention(e['Mentions'])
        if m['GroupScore'] > thr
]
```

- In the following code, we are representing edges as (`trigger_id`, `node_id`, `role`, `score`) tuples:

```
argument_edges = [
    ("tr%d" % i, "en%d" % a['EntityIndex'], a['Role'],
a['Score'])
    for i, e in enumerate(result['Events'])
    for a in e['Arguments']
        if a['Score'] > thr
```

- To create a compact graph, once the nodes and edges have been defined, we can create and visualize the graph by using the following code block:

```
G = nx.Graph()
```

- Iterate over the `triggers` and entity `mentions`, as follows:

```
for mention_id, tag, extent, score, mtype in trigger_
nodes + entity_nodes:
    label = extent if mtype.startswith("entity") else tag
    G.add_node(mention_id, label=label, size=score*10,
color=color_map[tag], tag=tag, group=mtype)
```

- The following code iterates over the argument role assignments:

```
for event_id, entity_id, role, score in argument_edges:
    G.add_edges_from(
        [(event_id, entity_id)],
        label=role,
```

```
          weight=score*100,
          color="grey"
    )
```

- The following code drops `mentions` that don't participate in events:

```
G.remove_nodes_from(list(nx.isolates(G)))
nt = Network("600px", "800px", notebook=True, heading="")
nt.from_nx(G)
nt.show("compact_nx.html")
```

The following is the output in graph format:

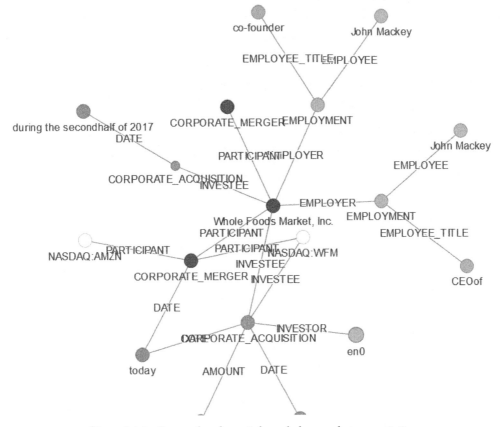

Figure 9.16 – Comprehend events knowledge graph representation

In the preceding output, if we traverse this graph, we can see the relationships between the entity, known as Whole Foods, which is a participant in the corporate merger, and its employer. This is John Macey, whose title is CEO.

A more complete graph

The preceding graph is compact and only relays essential event type and argument role information. We can use a slightly more complicated set of functions to graph all of the information returned by the API.

This convenient function in `events_graph.py`. It plots a complete graph of the document, showing all `events`, `triggers`, and `entities`, as well as their groups:

```
import events_graph as evg
```

```
evg.plot(result, node_types=['event', 'trigger', 'entity_
group', 'entity'], thr=0.5)
```

The following is the output in graph format:

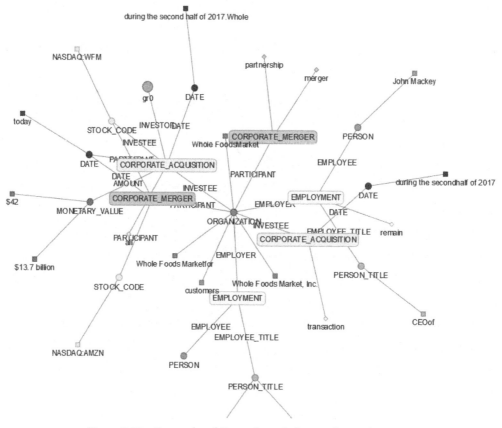

Figure 9.17 – Comprehend Events knowledge graph visualization

> **Note**
> You can use **Amazon Neptune** for large-scale knowledge graph analysis with Amazon Comprehend Events.

Here, we have extracted the metadata and analyzed it in a tabular manner and showed how we can present it in a graph. You can use Amazon Neptune for large-scale knowledge graph analysis with Amazon Comprehend Events, as we covered in *Figure 9.1*.

To deep dive into how you can do this using Amazon Neptune, please refer to the *Further reading* section for the relevant blog, which will walk you through how you can build a knowledge graph in Amazon Neptune using Amazon Comprehend Events.

> **Note**
> Entities extracted with Comprehend Events are going to be different than Comprehend detect entity API as events are specific to the financial event's entity and relationship extraction.

You can also extract metadata from Amazon Comprehend for Word or PDF documents using either a detect entity, a custom entity, or even Comprehend Events in the case of financial documents and enrich the document labeling process using **SageMaker Ground Truth**. SageMaker Ground Truth is a service that is primarily used for labeling data.

Summary

In this chapter, we learned why metadata extraction is really important before looking at the use case for **LiveRight**, our fictitious bank, which had acquisitions that made a press release statement. Financial analysts wanted to quickly evaluate the events and entities concerning this press release and wanted to make market predictions. We looked at an architecture to help you accomplish this. In the architecture shown in *Figure 1.1*, we spoke about how you can use AWS AI services such as Amazon Textract to extract text from the sample press release documents. Then, we saved all the text with utf-8 encoding in the Amazon S3 bucket for Amazon Comprehend entity or metadata extractions jobs.

We used an Amazon Comprehend Events job to extract entities and relationships between the entity. We have provided a *walkthrough video* link of the *Comprehend Events feature* in the *Further reading* section if you wish to learn more. We also provided two ways to configure Comprehend Events job; that is, use either the AWS console or AWS Python boto3 APIs. Finally, we talked about how you can visualize this relationship between extracted metadata using either a graph API such as `displayCy`, `Networkx`, or `pyvis,` or using Amazon Neptune's graph database. We also suggested that this metadata can be further used as an input to data labeling using **Amazon SageMaker Ground Truth**.

In the next chapter, we will talk about how you can perform content monetization for your cool websites.

Further reading

To learn more about the topics that were covered in this chapter, take a look at the following resources:

- *Building a knowledge graph in Amazon Neptune using Amazon Comprehend Events*, by Brian O'Keefe, Graham Horwood, and Navtanay Sinha (`https://aws. amazon.com/blogs/database/building-a-knowledge-graph-in- amazon-neptune-using-amazon-comprehend-events/`).

- *Announcing the launch of Amazon Comprehend Events*, by Graham Horwood, Sameer Karnik, and Ben Snively (`https://aws.amazon.com/blogs/ machine-learning/announcing-the-launch-of-amazon- comprehend-events/`).

- *Fintech Snacks 2 – Extracting Market-Moving Events with Amazon Comprehend Events*, by Mona Mona and Evan Peck (`https://www.youtube.com/ watch?v=QvmVT_8y7-Y`).

10
Reducing Localization Costs with Machine Translation

About a decade and a half ago (before the internet was what it is today), one of the authors went on a sightseeing trip to Switzerland. It was an impulsive, last-minute decision and was carried out with not a lot of planning. The travel itself was uneventful, and the author was aware that German is an acceptable language in Switzerland, and so busied himself with the English to German *Rosetta tone* during the trip. Based on advice from friends who had been to Switzerland before, a rough itinerary was put together that included visits to Zurich, Interlaken, Bern, and so on. With his very naïve German and, more importantly, due to the excellent English spoken by the Swiss, the author relaxed and even started enjoying his trip – until, of course, he went to Geneva, where everyone spoke only French. His attempt to converse in English was met with indifference, and the only French words the author knew were "oui" (meaning "yes") and "au revoir" (meaning "goodbye")! The author ended up having to use sign language, pointing to menu items in restaurants, asking about places to visit by showing a tourist guidebook, and so on to get through his next few days. If only the author had access to the advanced ML-based translation solutions that are so common today – Geneva would have been a breeze.

In his book *The World Is Flat* published in 2005 (almost the same time this author was on his way to Geneva), *Thomas L. Friedman* detailed the implications of globalization in the context of how technological advancements, including personal computers and the internet, have led to collapsing economical distinctions and boundaries, so much so that it has leveled the global arena. When enterprises go global, one of the most common tasks they encounter is the need to translate the language of their websites into the local language of the country or state they choose to operate in. This is called localization. Traditionally, organizations hired a team of translators who painstakingly translated the content of their websites, page by page, taking care to retain the correct context of what was being expressed. This was manually fed into multiple pages to stand up their websites. This was both time-consuming and cost-prohibitive but since it was a necessary task, organizations had no choice. Today, with the advent of ML-based translation capabilities such as Amazon Translate, localization can be performed at a fraction of the cost compared to before.

In the previous chapter, we saw how to harness the power of NLP with AWS AI services to extract metadata for financial filing reports for **LiveRight** so that their financial analysts can look into important information and make better decisions with respect to financial events such as mergers, acquisitions, and IPOs. In this chapter, we will see how NLP and AWS AI services help to automate website localization using **Amazon Translate** (`https://aws.amazon.com/translate/`), a ML-based translation service that supports 71 languages. You do not need to perform any ML training to use Amazon Translate as it is pre-trained and supports invocations through a simple API call. For use cases that are unique to your business, you can use advanced features of Amazon Translate such as **Named Entity Translation Customization** (`https://docs.aws.amazon.com/translate/latest/dg/how-custom-terminology.html`), **Active Custom Translation** (`https://docs.aws.amazon.com/translate/latest/dg/customizing-translations-parallel-data.html`), and so on.

To learn how to build a cost-effective localization solution, we will cover the following topics:

- Introducing the localization use case
- Building a multi-language web page using machine translation

Technical requirements

For this chapter, you will need access to an AWS account. Please make sure that you follow the instructions specified in the *Technical requirements* section of *Chapter 2, Introducing Amazon Textract*, to create your AWS account. Make sure that you log into the AWS Management Console before trying the steps in the *Building a multi-language web page using machine translation* section.

The Python code and sample datasets for our solution can be found at the link here: `https://github.com/PacktPublishing/Natural-Language-Processing-with-AWS-AI-Services/tree/main/Chapter%2010`. Please use the instructions in the following sections along with the code in the repository to build the solution.

Check out the following video to see the Code in Action at `https://bit.ly/3meYsn0`.

Introducing the localization use case

In the past few chapters, we looked at a variety of ways NLP can help us understand our customers better. We learned how we can build applications to detect sentiments, monetize content, detect unique entities, and understand context, references, and other analytics processes that help organizations gain important insights about their business. In this chapter, we will learn how to automate the process of translating website content into multiple languages. To illustrate this example, we'll assume that our fictitious banking corporation, **LiveRight Holdings Private Limited**, has decided to expand internationally to delight potential customers in Germany, Spain, and the cities Mumbai and Chennai in India. The launch date for these four pilot regions is coming up fast; that is, in the next 3 weeks. The expansions operations lead has escalated his concerns to senior management, stating that the IT teams may not be ready with the websites in the corresponding local languages of German, Spanish, Hindi, and Tamil on time for the launch. You get a frantic call from the director of IT, your boss, and she has asked you, the application architect, to design and build the websites within the next 2 weeks so that they can use the last week for acceptance testing.

You know that a manual approach is out of the question as it's going to be impossible to hire translators, complete the work, and build up the websites within 2 weeks. After some quick research, you decide to use **Amazon Translate**, an ML-based translation service, to automate the translation process for the websites. You check the Amazon Translate pricing page (`https://aws.amazon.com/translate/pricing/`) and realize that you can translate a million characters for as low as $15 and that, more importantly, for the first 12 months, you can take advantage of the **AWS Free Tier** (`https://aws.amazon.com/free/`), which allows you to translate 2 million characters per month, free of charge. For the pilot sites, you perform a character count and see that it's around 500K characters. In the meantime, your director reaches out to ask you to create a quick demonstratable prototype of the **About Us** page (`https://github.com/PacktPublishing/Natural-Language-Processing-with-AWS-AI-Services/blob/main/Chapter%2010/input/aboutLRH.html`) in the four target languages of German, Spanish, Hindi, and Tamil.

We will be walking through this solution using the AWS Management Console and an Amazon SageMaker Jupyter notebook. Please refer to the *Signing up for an AWS account* section of the *Setting up your AWS environment* section of *Chapter 2, Introducing Amazon Textract*, for detailed instructions on how to sign up for an AWS account and sign into the **AWS Management Console**.

First, we will create an **Amazon SageMaker** Jupyter notebook instance (if you haven't done so already in the previous chapters), clone the repository into our notebook instance, open the Jupyter notebook for our solution walkthrough (`https://github.com/PacktPublishing/Natural-Language-Processing-with-AWS-AI-Services/blob/main/Chapter%2010/Reducing-localization-costs-with-machine-translation-github.ipynb`), and execute the steps in the notebook. Detailed instructions will be provided in the *Building a multi-language web page using machine translation* section. Let's take a look:

1. In the notebook, we will view the English version of the **About Us** page.

2. Then, we will review the HTML code of the **About Us** page to determine what tag components need translating.

3. Next, we will install an HTML parser library for Python (`https://www.crummy.com/software/BeautifulSoup/bs4/doc/`) and extract the text content of the tags we are interested in from our HTML page into a list.

4. We will use the **boto3 AWS Python SDK** for **Amazon Translate** to get a handle on and invoke the translation function. We will do this in a loop to get the translated content in German, Spanish, Hindi, and Tamil.

5. Then, we will take the original HTML (in English) and update it with content for the corresponding tags for each of the four languages to create four separate HTML pages.

6. Finally, we will display the HTML pages to review the translations.

Once you've done this, you can upload the HTML to an **Amazon S3** bucket and set up an **Amazon CloudFront** distribution to provision your website globally in minutes. For more details on how to do this, please refer to this link: `https://docs.aws.amazon.com/AmazonS3/latest/userguide/website-hosting-cloudfront-walkthrough.html`. In this section, we introduced the localization requirements for **LiveRight**, the people who are looking to expand internationally, and who need local language-specific web pages for their launch in these markets. In the next section, we will learn how to build the solution.

Building a multi-language web page using machine translation

In the previous section, we introduced a requirement for web page localization, covered the design aspects for the solution we will be building, and briefly walked through the solution components and workflow steps. In this section, we will start executing the tasks to build our solution. But first, there are some prerequisites we will have to take care of.

Setting up to solve the use case

If you have not done so in the previous chapters, as a prerequisite, you will have to create an Amazon SageMaker Jupyter notebook instance and set up **Identity and Access Management (IAM)** permissions for that notebook role to access the AWS services we will use in this notebook. After that, you will need to clone the GitHub repository (`https://github.com/PacktPublishing/Natural-Language-Processing-with-AWS-AI-Services`) and create an Amazon S3 (`https://aws.amazon.com/s3/`) bucket. Finally, you must go to the `Chapter 10` folder and open the `Reducing-localization-costs-with-machine-translation-github.ipynb` notebook to start the execution process.

> **Note**
> Please ensure you have completed the tasks mentioned in the *Technical requirements* section.

Follow the instructions documented in the *Creating an Amazon SageMaker Jupyter Notebook instance* section of the *Setting up your AWS environment* section of *Chapter 2, Introducing Amazon Textract*, to create your Jupyter Notebook instance. Let's get started:

> **Important – IAM role permissions while creating Amazon SageMaker Jupyter notebooks**
>
> Accept the default for the IAM role at notebook creation time to allow access to any S3 bucket.

1. Once you've created the notebook instance and set its status to **InService**, please attach the `TranslateFullAccess` policy to your Amazon SageMaker notebook IAM role. To execute this step, please refer to the *Changing IAM permissions and trust relationships for the Amazon SageMaker notebook execution role* section of the *Setting up your AWS environment* section of *Chapter 2, Introducing Amazon Textract*.

2. Now, go back to your notebook instance and click on **Open Jupyter** from the **Actions** menu:

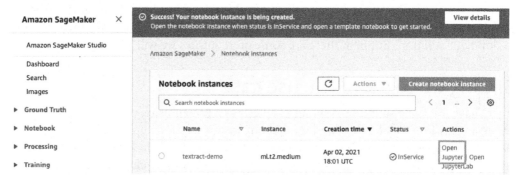

Figure 10.1 – Opening the Jupyter notebook

This will take you to the home folder of your notebook instance.

3. Click on **New** and select **Terminal**, as shown in the following screenshot:

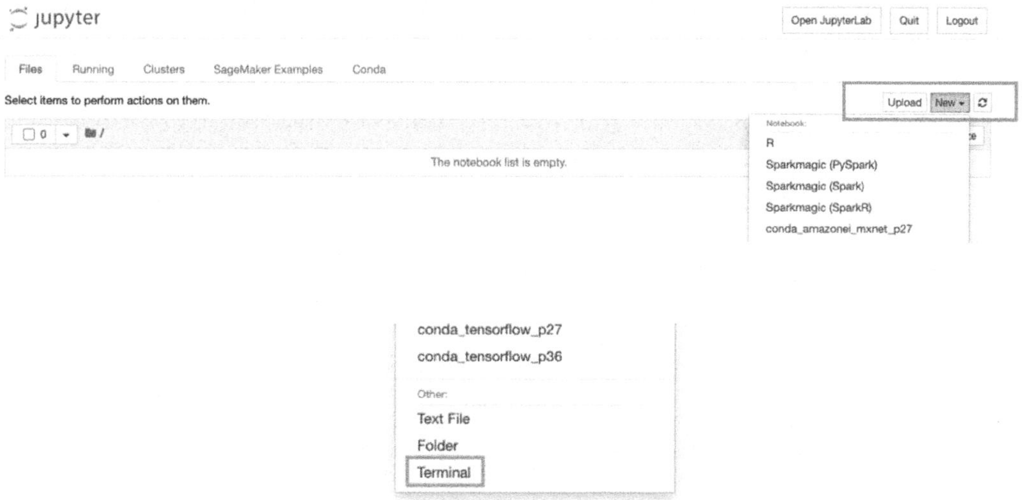

Figure 10.2 – Opening a terminal in Jupyter notebook

4. In the terminal window, type `cd SageMaker` and then `git clone https://github.com/PacktPublishing/Natural-Language-Processing-with-AWS-AI-Services`, as shown in the following screenshot. If you have already done this in the previous chapters for this notebook instance, you don't have to clone the repository again:

```
sh-4.2$ pwd
/home/ec2-user
sh-4.2$ cd SageMaker/
sh-4.2$ git clone https://github.com/PacktPublishing/Natural-Language-Processing-with-AWS-AI-Services
```

Figure 10.3 – The git clone command

5. Now, exit the terminal window and go back to the home folder – you will see a folder called `Natural-Language-Processing-with-AWS-AI-Services`. Upon clicking this folder, you will see `chapter-10-localization-with-machine-translation`. Click this folder and then open the `Reducing-localization-costs-with-machine-translation-github.ipynb` notebook.

Now that we have created our notebook instance and cloned our repository, we can start running our notebook code.

Running the notebook

Open the notebook you cloned from this book's GitHub repository (`https://github.com/PacktPublishing/Natural-Language-Processing-with-AWS-AI-Services/blob/main/Chapter%2010/Reducing-localization-costs-with-machine-translation-github.ipynb`), as we discussed in the *Setting up to solve the use case* section, and execute the cells step by step, as follows:

> **Note**
>
> Please ensure you have executed the steps in the *Technical requirements* and *Setting up to solve the use case* sections before you execute the cells in the notebook.

1. Execute the first cell in the notebook, under the *Input HTML Web Page* section, to render the HTML for the English version of our web page:

```
from IPython.display import IFrame
IFrame(src='./input/aboutLRH.html', width=800,
height=400)
```

2. You will see that the page has a few headings and then a paragraph talking about **Family Bank**, a subsidiary of **LiveRight Holdings**:

Figure 10.4 – English version of the web page

3. Execute the following cell to review the HTML code for our web page:

```
!pygmentize './input/aboutLRH.html'
```

4. We will see the following output for the web page. The areas highlighted in the following output are the tags we are interested in translating for our target web pages. In this code block, we can define the title of the web page and some default JavaScript imports:

```
<!DOCTYPE html>
<html>
    <head>
        <title>Live Well with LiveRight</title>
        <meta name="viewport" charset="UTF-8"
content="width=device-width, initial-scale=1.0">
        <script src="https://ajax.googleapis.com/ajax/
libs/jquery/3.4.0/jquery.min.js"></script>
        <script src="https://cdnjs.cloudflare.com/ajax/
libs/popper.js/1.12.9/umd/popper.min.js"></script>
        <script src="https://maxcdn.bootstrapcdn.com/
bootstrap/4.0.0/js/bootstrap.min.js"></script>
        <script src="https://sdk.amazonaws.com/js/
aws-sdk-2.408.0.min.js"></script>
        <script src="https://cdnjs.cloudflare.com/ajax/
libs/Chart.js/2.4.0/Chart.min.js"></script>
    </head>
```

5. Now, we will define the body of the page with the h1, h2, and h3 headings, as shown in the following code block:

```
    <body>
        <h1>Family Bank Holdings</h1>
        <h3>Date: <span id="date"></span></h3>
        <div id="home">
            <div id="hometext">
        <h2>Who we are and what we do</h2>
```

6. Next, we will define the actual body of the text as an h4 heading to highlight it, as shown in the following code block:

```
        <h4><p>A wholly owned subsidiary of LiveRight,
we are the nation's largest bank for SMB owners and
cooperative societies, with more than 4500 branches
spread across the nation, servicing more than 5 million
customers and continuing to grow.
            We offer a number of lending products to
our customers including checking and savings accounts,
lending, credit cards, deposits, insurance, IRA and more.
Started in 1787 as a family owned business providing low
interest loans for farmers struggling with poor harvests,
LiveRight helped these farmers design long distance water
channels from lakes in neighboring districts
            to their lands. The initial success helped
these farmers invest their wealth in LiveRight and later
led to our cooperative range of products that allowed
farmers to own a part of LiveRight.
            In 1850 we moved our HeadQuarters to New
York city to help build the economy of our nation by
providing low interest lending products to small to
medium business owners looking to start or expand their
business.
            From 2 branches then to 4500 branches
today, the trust of our customers helped us grow to
become the nation's largest SMB bank. </p>
        </h4>
    </div>
    </div>
```

7. Now, we will start the JavaScript section in the HTML to get the current date to be displayed, as shown in the following code block:

```
        <script>
        // get date
            var today = new Date();
            var dd = String(today.getDate()).padStart(2,
'0');
            var mm = String(today.getMonth() +
1).padStart(2, '0'); //January is 0!
            var yyyy = today.getFullYear();
            today = mm + '/' + dd + '/' + yyyy;
```

```
                document.getElementById('date').innerHTML =
today; //update the date
        </script>
    </body>
    <style>
```

8. Finally, we will declare the CSS styles (https://www.w3.org/Style/CSS/Overview.en.html) that we need for each of the sections. First, here is the style for the body of the web page:

```
body {
        overflow: hidden;
        position: absolute;
        width: 100%;
        height: 100%;
        background: #404040;
        top: 0;
        margin: 0;
        padding: 0;
        -webkit-font-smoothing: antialiased;
}
```

9. The following is the style for the background and the background text widgets, which are called home and hometext:

```
#home {
        width: 100%;
        height: 80%;
        bottom: 0;
        background-color: #ff8c00;
        color: #fff;
        margin: 0px;
        padding: 0;
    }
#hometext {
        top: 20%;
        margin: 10px;
        padding: 0;
    }
```

10. Finally, we will define the styles for each of the headings and paragraphs in our web page:

```
h1 {
        text-align: center;
        color: #fff;
        font-family: 'Lato', sans-serif;
}
h2 {
        text-align: center;
        color: #fff;
        font-family: 'Lato', sans-serif;
}
h3 {
        text-align: center;
        color: #fff;
        font-family: 'Lato', sans-serif;
}
h4 {
        font-family: 'Lato', sans-serif;
}
p {
        font-family: 'Lato', sans-serif;
}

</style>
</html>
```

11. Now, we will execute the cells in the *Prepare for Translation* section. Execute the first cell to install the HTML parser we need for our solution, called `Beautiful Soup` (`https://www.crummy.com/software/BeautifulSoup/bs4/doc/`):

```
!pip install beautifulsoup4
```

12. Next, run the following cell to load our English HTML page code into a variable so that we can parse it using `Beautiful Soup`:

```
html_doc = ''
input_htm = './input/aboutLRH.html'
with open(input_htm) as f:
    content = f.readlines()
for i in content:
    html_doc += i+' '
```

13. Now, parse the HTML page:

```
from bs4 import BeautifulSoup
soup = BeautifulSoup(html_doc, 'html.parser')
```

14. Let's define the list of HTML tags we are interested in and load the text content for those HTML tags into a dictionary:

```
tags = ['title','h1','h2','p']
x_dict = {}
for tag in tags:
    x_dict[tag] = getattr(getattr(soup, tag),'string')
x_dict
```

15. We will get the following response:

```
{'title': 'Live Well with LiveRight',
 'h1': 'Family Bank Holdings',
 'h2': 'Who we are and what we do',
 'p': "A wholly owned subsidiary of LiveRight, we are
the nation's largest bank for SMB owners and cooperative
societies, with more than 4500 branches spread across
the nation, servicing more than 5 million customers and
continuing to grow.\n          We offer a number of
lending products to our customers including checking
and savings accounts, lending, credit cards, deposits,
insurance, IRA and more. Started in 1787 as a family
owned business providing low interest loans for farmers
struggling with poor harvests, LiveRight helped these
farmers design long distance water channels from lakes
in neighboring districts\n              to their lands.
The initial success helped these farmers invest their
wealth in LiveRight and later led to our cooperative
range of products that allowed farmers to own a part
of LiveRight.\n              In 1850 we moved our
HeadQuarters to New York city to help build the economy
of our nation by providing low interest lending products
to small to medium business owners looking to start or
expand their business.\n              From 2 branches
then to 4500 branches today, the trust of our customers
helped us grow to become the nation's largest SMB bank.
"}
```

16. Now, we will execute the cells in the *Translate to target languages* section. In the first cell, we will import the boto3 library (https://boto3.amazonaws.com/v1/documentation/api/latest/index.html), the Python SDK for AWS services, create a handle for Amazon Translate, and then translate our web page into our target languages:

```
import boto3
translate = boto3.client(service_name='translate',
region_name='us-east-1', use_ssl=True)
out_text = {}
languages = ['de','es','ta','hi']
```

```
for target_lang in languages:
    out_dict = {}
    for key in x_dict:
        result = translate.translate_text(Text=x_
dict[key],
            SourceLanguageCode="en",
TargetLanguageCode=target_lang)
        out_dict[key] = result.get('TranslatedText')
    out_text[target_lang] = out_dict
```

17. Now, let's execute the cells in the *Build webpages for translated text* section. This section is split into four subsections – one for each target language. Execute the cells under *German Webpage*. The code assigns the HTML parser's output to a new variable, updates the HTML tag values with translated content from the preceding step, and then writes the complete HTML to an output HTML file for the language. For simplicity, the code from the four separate cells under this subsection is grouped like so:

```
web_de = soup
web_de.title.string = out_text['de']['title']
web_de.h1.string = out_text['de']['h1']
web_de.h2.string = out_text['de']['h2']
web_de.p.string = out_text['de']['p']
de_html = web_de.prettify()
with open('./output/aboutLRH_DE.html','w') as de_w:
    de_w.write(de_html)
IFrame(src='./output/aboutLRH_DE.html', width=800,
height=500)
```

18. We will get the following output:

Beteiligungen für Familienbanken

Date: 06/29/2021

Wer wir sind und was wir machen

Als hundertprozentige Tochtergesellschaft von Liveright sind wir die größte Bank des Landes für SMB-Eigentümer und Genossenschaftsgesellschaften mit mehr als 4500 Filialen im ganzen Land, betreuen mehr als 5 Millionen Kunden und wachsen weiter. Wir bieten unseren Kunden eine Reihe von Kreditprodukten an, darunter Scheck- und Sparkonten, Kredite, Kreditkarten, Einlagen, Versicherungen, IRA und mehr. LiveRight wurde 1787 als Familienunternehmen gegründet, das Zinsdarlehen für Landwirte, die mit schlechten Ernten zu kämpfen hatten, und half diesen Landwirten, Fernwasserkanäle von Seen in benachbarten Bezirken zu entwerfen in ihr Land. Der anfängliche Erfolg half diesen Landwirten, ihr Vermögen in Liveright zu investieren, und führte später zu unserer kooperativen Produktpalette, die es den Landwirten ermöglichte, einen Teil von LiverRight zu besitzen. Im Jahr 1850 verlegten wir unseren Hauptsitz nach New York City, um zum Aufbau der Wirtschaft unseres Landes beizutragen, indem wir kleinen bis mittleren Unternehmern, die ihr Geschäft beginnen oder ausbauen möchten, Produkte mit niedrigen Zinsen zur Verfügung stellen. Von 2 Filialen bis hin zu 4500 Filialen heute hat uns das Vertrauen unserer Kunden geholfen, zur größten KMB-Bank des Landes zu werden.

Figure 10.5 – The translated German web page

19. Execute the cells under *Spanish Webpage*. The code assigns the HTML parser's output to a new variable, updates the HTML tag values with translated content from the preceding step, and then writes the complete HTML to an output HTML file for the language. For simplicity, the code from the four separate cells under this subsection is grouped, like so:

```
web_es = soup
web_es.title.string = out_text['es']['title']
web_es.h1.string = out_text['es']['h1']
web_es.h2.string = out_text['es']['h2']
web_es.p.string = out_text['es']['p']
es_html = web_es.prettify()
with open('./output/aboutLRH_ES.html','w') as es_w:
    es_w.write(es_html)
IFrame(src='./output/aboutLRH_ES.html', width=800,
height=500)
```

20. We will get the following output:

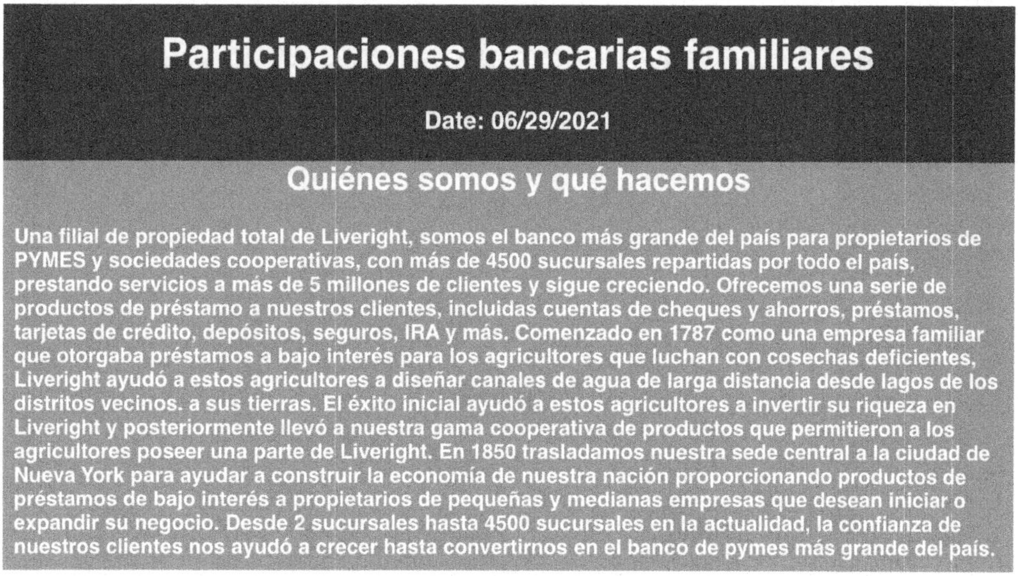

Participaciones bancarias familiares

Date: 06/29/2021

Quiénes somos y qué hacemos

Una filial de propiedad total de Liveright, somos el banco más grande del país para propietarios de PYMES y sociedades cooperativas, con más de 4500 sucursales repartidas por todo el país, prestando servicios a más de 5 millones de clientes y sigue creciendo. Ofrecemos una serie de productos de préstamo a nuestros clientes, incluidas cuentas de cheques y ahorros, préstamos, tarjetas de crédito, depósitos, seguros, IRA y más. Comenzado en 1787 como una empresa familiar que otorgaba préstamos a bajo interés para los agricultores que luchan con cosechas deficientes, Liveright ayudó a estos agricultores a diseñar canales de agua de larga distancia desde lagos de los distritos vecinos. a sus tierras. El éxito inicial ayudó a estos agricultores a invertir su riqueza en Liveright y posteriormente llevó a nuestra gama cooperativa de productos que permitieron a los agricultores poseer una parte de Liveright. En 1850 trasladamos nuestra sede central a la ciudad de Nueva York para ayudar a construir la economía de nuestra nación proporcionando productos de préstamos de bajo interés a propietarios de pequeñas y medianas empresas que desean iniciar o expandir su negocio. Desde 2 sucursales hasta 4500 sucursales en la actualidad, la confianza de nuestros clientes nos ayudó a crecer hasta convertirnos en el banco de pymes más grande del país.

Figure 10.6 – The translated Spanish web page

21. Execute the cells under *Hindi Webpage*. The code assigns the HTML parser's output to a new variable, updates the HTML tag values with translated content from the preceding step, and then writes the complete HTML to an output HTML file for the language. For simplicity, the code from the four separate cells under this subsection is grouped, like so:

```
web_hi = soup
web_hi.title.string = out_text['hi']['title']
web_hi.h1.string = out_text['hi']['h1']
web_hi.h2.string = out_text['hi']['h2']
web_hi.p.string = out_text['hi']['p']
hi_html = web_hi.prettify()
with open('./output/aboutLRH_HI.html','w') as hi_w:
    hi_w.write(hi_html)
IFrame(src='./output/aboutLRH_HI.html', width=800,
height=500)
```

22. We will get the following output:

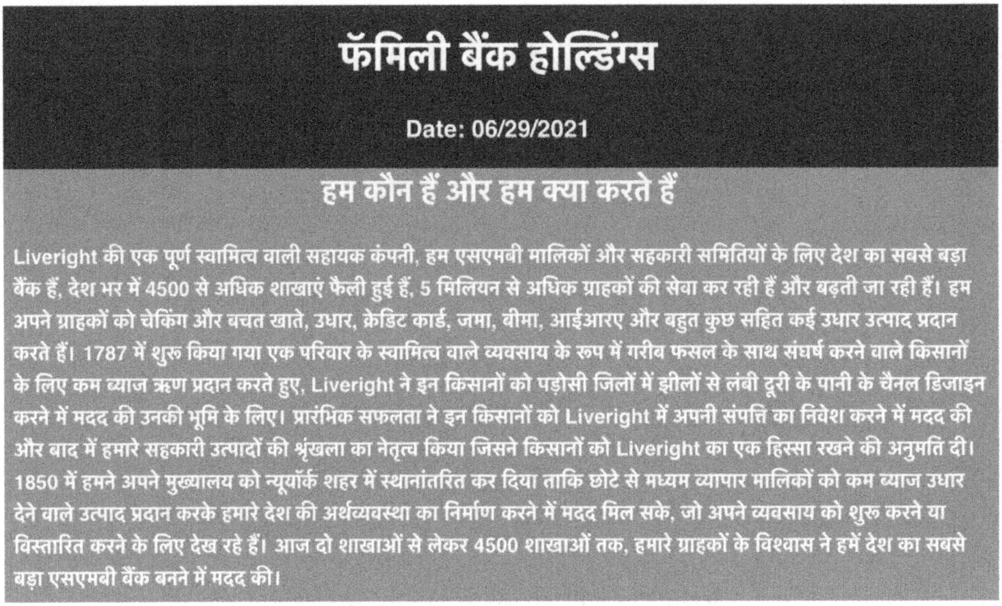

फॅमिली बैंक होल्डिंग्स

Date: 06/29/2021

हम कौन हैं और हम क्या करते हैं

Liveright की एक पूर्ण स्वामित्व वाली सहायक कंपनी, हम एसएमबी मालिकों और सहकारी समितियों के लिए देश का सबसे बड़ा बैंक हैं, देश भर में 4500 से अधिक शाखाएं फैली हुई हैं, 5 मिलियन से अधिक ग्राहकों की सेवा कर रही हैं और बढ़ती जा रही हैं। हम अपने ग्राहकों को चेकिंग और बचत खाते, उधार, क्रेडिट कार्ड, जमा, बीमा, आईआरए और बहुत कुछ सहित कई उधार उत्पाद प्रदान करते हैं। 1787 में शुरू किया गया एक परिवार के स्वामित्व वाले व्यवसाय के रूप में गरीब फसल के साथ संघर्ष करने वाले किसानों के लिए कम ब्याज ऋण प्रदान करते हुए, Liveright ने इन किसानों को पड़ोसी जिलों में झीलों से लंबी दूरी के पानी के चैनल डिजाइन करने में मदद की उनकी भूमि के लिए। प्रारंभिक सफलता ने इन किसानों को Liveright में अपनी संपत्ति का निवेश करने में मदद की और बाद में हमारे सहकारी उत्पादों की श्रृंखला का नेतृत्व किया जिसने किसानों को Liveright का एक हिस्सा रखने की अनुमति दी। 1850 में हमने अपने मुख्यालय को न्यूयॉर्क शहर में स्थानांतरित कर दिया ताकि छोटे से मध्यम व्यापार मालिकों को कम ब्याज उधार देने वाले उत्पाद प्रदान करके हमारे देश की अर्थव्यवस्था का निर्माण करने में मदद मिल सके, जो अपने व्यवसाय को शुरू करने या विस्तारित करने के लिए देख रहे हैं। आज दो शाखाओं से लेकर 4500 शाखाओं तक, हमारे ग्राहकों के विश्वास ने हमें देश का सबसे बड़ा एसएमबी बैंक बनने में मदद की।

Figure 10.7 – The translated Hindi web page

23. Execute the cells under *Tamil Webpage*. The code assigns the HTML parser's output to a new variable, updates the HTML tag values with translated content from the preceding step, and then writes the complete HTML to an output HTML file for the language. For simplicity, the code from the four separate cells under this subsection is grouped, like so:

```
web_ta = soup
web_ta.title.string = out_text['ta']['title']
web_ta.h1.string = out_text['ta']['h1']
web_ta.h2.string = out_text['ta']['h2']
web_ta.p.string = out_text['ta']['p']
ta_html = web_ta.prettify()
with open('./output/aboutLRH_TA.html','w') as ta_w:
    ta_w.write(ta_html)
IFrame(src='./output/aboutLRH_TA.html', width=800,
height=500)
```

24. We will get the following output:

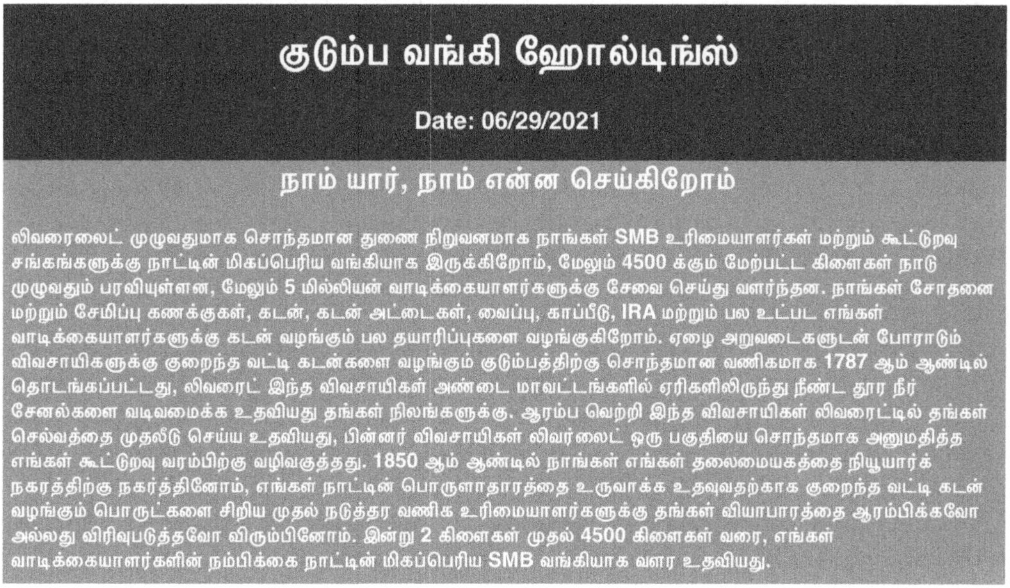

Figure 10.8 – The translated Tamil web page

25. In some instances, you may see that custom brand names or product terms specific to your organization may not be translated into the required context in your target language. In these cases, use **Amazon Translate Custom Terminology** to ensure Amazon Translate can identify the context for these unique words. For more details, you can refer to the following documentation: `https://docs.aws.amazon.com/translate/latest/dg/how-custom-terminology.html`.

And that concludes the solution build for this chapter. As we mentioned previously, you can upload your web pages to an Amazon S3 bucket (`https://boto3.amazonaws.com/v1/documentation/api/latest/guide/s3-uploading-files.html`) and use Amazon CloudFront (`https://docs.aws.amazon.com/AmazonS3/latest/userguide/website-hosting-cloudfront-walkthrough.html`) to distribute your website globally in minutes. Further with support for translating 2 million characters per month for the first 12 months free of charge, and only $15 for every 1 million characters after that, your translation costs are significantly minimized. For additional ideas on how you can use Amazon Translate for your needs, please refer to the *Further reading* section.

Summary

In this chapter, we learned how to build content localization for web pages quickly and in a highly cost-efficient way with Amazon Translate, an ML-based translation service that provides powerful machine translation models behind an API endpoint for ease of access. First, we reviewed a use case for our fictitious corporation, called **LiveRight Holdings**, which was looking to expand internationally and needed to launch its website in four different languages in 3 weeks. LiveRight did not have the time or funding to hire experienced translators to perform the website conversion manually. The director of IT at LiveRight hired you to devise a solution that's quick and cost-effective.

For this, you designed a solution using Amazon Translate that used a Python HTML parser to extract the relevant tag content from the English version of the HTML page, translate it into German, Spanish, Hindi, and Tamil, and then create new HTML pages with the translated content included. To execute the solution, we created an Amazon SageMaker Jupyter notebook instance, assigned the IAM permissions for Amazon Translate to the notebook instance, cloned the GitHub repository for this chapter, and then walked through the solution by executing the code blocks one cell at a time. Finally, we displayed the HTML pages containing the translated content in the notebook for reviewing purposes.

In the next chapter, we will look at an interesting use case, as well as an important application of NLP: building conversational interfaces using chatbots to work with a document's contents and provide this as a self-help tool for consumers. We will use **LiveRight Holdings** again to illustrate this use case, while specifically addressing the needs of the mortgage department officers who conduct homebuyer research for design product offerings. As we did in this chapter, we will introduce the use case, discuss how to design the architecture, establish the prerequisites, and walk through the various steps required to build the solution.

Further reading

To learn more about the topics that were covered in this chapter, take a look at the following resources:

- *Translating your website or application automatically with Amazon Translate in your CI/CD pipeline,* by Carlos Afonso (`https://aws.amazon.com/blogs/machine-learning/translating-your-website-or-application-automatically-with-amazon-translate-in-your-ci-cd-pipeline/`)

- *Customizing your machine translation using Amazon Translate Active Custom Translation,* by Watson Srivathsan and Xingyao Wang (`https://aws.amazon.com/blogs/machine-learning/customizing-your-machine-translation-using-amazon-translate-active-custom-translation/`)

- *Translate Text Between Languages in the Cloud* (`https://aws.amazon.com/getting-started/hands-on/translate-text-between-languages-cloud/`)

- *Translate video captions and subtitles using Amazon Translate,* by Siva Rajamani and Raju Penmatcha (`https://aws.amazon.com/blogs/machine-learning/translate-video-captions-and-subtitles-using-amazon-translate/`)

- *The World Is Flat* (`https://www.amazon.com/World-Flat-History-Twenty-first-Century/dp/0374292884`)

11
Using Chatbots for Querying Documents

Imagine if you could have a two-way conversation with the text data in your documents. Let's suppose you subscribe to a number of journals that send you research articles on technology trends. These articles may cover multiple industries and technologies, but you are interested in insights about a specific industry and technology. Traditionally, you would have a team of people combing through these documents to interpret, understand, and recommend the direction you need to take. What if you could get all the data and answers you need just by flipping open your phone and talking to a chatbot that gives you the answers from your document corpus? Wouldn't that be awesome? That's the power of combining **natural language processing** (**NLP**) technology with chatbots. You can literally talk to your documents, and get a response too.

In the previous chapter, we discussed how businesses were relying on technology to help them expand internationally, but traditional manual translation to localize customer-facing websites was both time- and cost-prohibitive. We then built a solution that utilized the potential of **machine learning** (**ML**) based translation capabilities with **Amazon Translate** to tackle website localization challenges efficiently.

In this chapter, as before, we will go back to our favorite banking corporation, *LiveRight Holdings*, and help them solve a unique use case with NLP and chatbots. But before we get to the challenge and the solution, let's discuss the philosophy behind combining a conversational interface (aka the chatbot) with a text-based search for documents (more on this soon). Remember how we said the patterns that NLP can help uncover in seemingly unrelated documents is like the treasure in Ali Baba's cave (*Chapter 1, NLP in the Business Context and Introduction to AWS AI Services* – we know, it feels like eons ago)? What if you had your own personal genie (as in the story of Aladdin) that could give you the insights you needed based on your questions? When we combine NLP and chatbots, it is like asking the genie to dole out treasures from Ali Baba's cave, on-demand, at your convenience. If you recollect, we did cover how to create smart search indexing with NLP before, but the solution we will discuss in this chapter takes it one step further to make searching even more user-friendly. To learn how to build a chatbot for querying documents, we will navigate through the following sections:

- Introducing the chatbot use case
- Creating an **Amazon Kendra** index with **Amazon S3** as a data source
- Building an **Amazon Lex** chatbot
- Deploying the solution with **AWS CloudFormation**

Technical requirements

For this chapter, you will need access to an **AWS Account**. Please make sure to follow the instructions specified in the *Technical requirements* section in *Chapter 2, Introducing Amazon Textract*, to create your AWS Account, and log in to the **AWS Management Console**. If you need to understand how to upload objects to Amazon S3 buckets, please refer to the *Creating an Amazon S3 bucket, a folder, and uploading objects* section. Please complete these tasks before trying the steps in *Building a chatbot for querying documents*.

For this chapter, we will be performing all of our tasks using the AWS Management Console. The GitHub repository provides the input documents and the FAQ list we need for our solution, available here: `https://github.com/PacktPublishing/Natural-Language-Processing-with-AWS-AI-Services/tree/main/Chapter%2011`.

Please use the instructions in the following sections to build the solution.

Introducing the chatbot use case

Let's now discuss how using a chatbot with NLP can benefit businesses. Using an example is always helpful, so let's go back to our fictitious banking corporation **LiveRight Holdings Private Limited**. The **Mortgage Product Research (MPR)** department for LiveRight's mortgages business is an important entity within the organization, as their recommendations directly influence what mortgage products, features, and choices are offered to LiveRight's customers. This has a direct impact on LiveRight's revenues and profitability, as mortgage products are responsible for more than 40% of LiveRight's annual revenues. The MPR team receives hundreds of research documents incrementally on a monthly basis, both from mass subscription-based industry analysts and specialized independent researchers. Typically, the documents provide insights, trend reports, and detailed perspectives on what buyers look for in a home, the role of real estate agents, how home prices impact the sellers, and so on. These documents go to an Amazon S3 bucket that already has thousands of documents and is growing.

A "day in the life of" scenario for the MPR team is to read these copious documents, analyze their content, identify areas, trends, and metrics of interest and categorize these facts, and eventually, these are collected, assessed together by the team as a whole in a day-long group meeting activity, compared with statistics from the past months, and finally, the recommendations are written down to be sent to executives, as well as fed into ML models for determining mortgage product features. Documents are received either at the end of the previous month or at the beginning of the month, and the team takes the whole month to read, analyze, categorize, discuss, and make recommendations. LiveRight's senior management has long suspected this, rightly, to be a very time-consuming and cost-prohibitive process, and as an organization that prides itself in being economical, wanted to automate the process to save time and reduce costs. Having seen how using NLP with AWS AI services has helped them in some of their other use cases, they reach out to you, the ML Enterprise Architect, to help them re-design this process and build an efficient solution. Additionally, senior management wanted to harness the potential of the very talented researchers in the MPR for new innovations rather than wasting their time on menial and repetitive tasks.

You find this request from LiveRight both challenging and exciting, as it's a use case that's tailor-made for NLP and AI. You immediately decide that the best way to help the MPR team discuss and decide on their recommendations would be an **intelligent AI assistant** that participates in their meetings – listening to their questions and answering them for them. After some analysis, you decide to go with Amazon Lex (`https://aws.amazon.com/lex/`), a fully managed AI service powered by ML models to build intelligent chatbots that can interact in both voice and text with continuous learning capabilities, and Amazon Kendra (`https://aws.amazon.com/kendra/`), a fully managed ML-powered enterprise search service that uses NLP to create intelligent indexes for your documents, accepts your queries in natural language, and returns responses which match the context accurately. You check the Amazon Lex pricing (`https://aws.amazon.com/lex/pricing/`) and realize that, for 8,000 speech requests and 2,000 text request interactions with the chatbot in the US East (N. Virginia) region, it will cost you only $33.50 a month. You check the Amazon Kendra pricing (`https://aws.amazon.com/kendra/pricing/`) and see that the Developer Edition supports 10,000 documents and 4,000 queries per day, at a price of $1.125 per hour or $810 per month. You decide to use the Developer Edition for the pilot phase and move to the Enterprise Edition after user acceptance.

> **Note**
> These prices are correct at the time of writing. Please check the links for an up-to-date figure.

You are now ready to build the solution. As mentioned before, we will be walking through this solution entirely using the AWS Management Console (`https://aws.amazon.com/console/`). If you do not have access to the AWS Management Console, please follow the detailed instructions in the *Technical requirements* section in *Chapter 2, Introducing Amazon Textract* of this book.

First, let's complete the pre-requisites before we move on to the solution build:

1. Download the sample home buyer research documents from our GitHub repository. From your local computer, open an internet browser (preferably **Google Chrome** *version 9.1* and above) and go to `https://github.com/PacktPublishing/Natural-Language-Processing-with-AWS-AI-Services/tree/main/Chapter%2011`.

2. Download each of the four documents present by clicking the document name, one document at a time.

3. On the document page, click the **Download** button on the right to download the document to your computer.

4. Upload these downloaded documents to an Amazon S3 bucket, as per the instructions provided in the *Creating an Amazon S3 bucket, a folder, and uploading objects* section in *Chapter 2, Introducing Amazon Textract,* of this book. When creating the Amazon S3 folder in the bucket, please use the following folder/prefix paths – `chapter11/kendra-faq/faqs.csv`, `chapter11/kendra/2019-NAR-HBS.pdf`, `chapter11/kendra/2020-generational-trends-report-03-05-2020.pdf`, `chapter11/kendra/ Zillow-home-buyers-report.pdf`.

5. Now, you are ready to start building the solution.

In this section, we introduced the need for chatbots with NLP and the business benefits associated with this solution. In the next section, we will walk through the building of the solution step-by-step.

Creating an Amazon Kendra index with Amazon S3 as a data source

In this section, we will first create an Amazon Kendra index and add the S3 bucket to which we uploaded our sample research documents in the previous section, as an Amazon S3 data source.

Note

Before you continue, please ensure you have executed the steps in the *Technical requirements* section and the pre-requisites mentioned in the *Introducing the chatbot use case* section.

Please execute the following steps to create your Amazon Kendra index:

1. If not already done, log in to your **AWS Management Console** as per the instructions in the *Technical requirements* section in *Chapter 2, Introducing Amazon Textract*.

2. Type kendra in the **Services** search bar in the top center of the page and select **Amazon Kendra** from the list. When the **Amazon Kendra** console opens up, click **Create an Index**, as shown here:

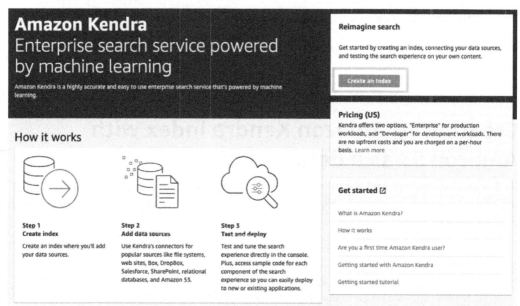

Figure 11.1 – Creating an Amazon Kendra index

3. In the **Specify index details** page, type a name for your index, add an optional description, select **Create a new role (Recommended)** from the **IAM role** list box, and type a **Role name**, as shown in the following screenshot. Then, click **Next** to continue:

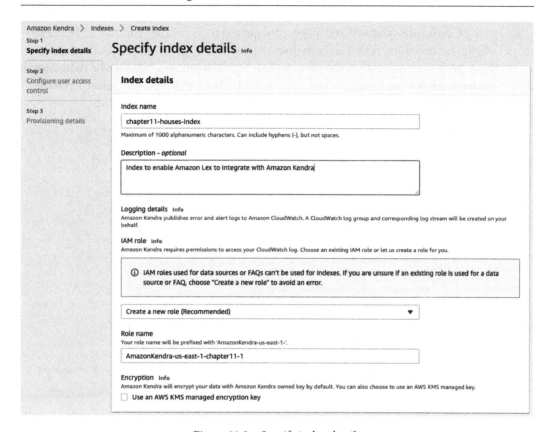

Figure 11.2 – Specify index details

4. Leave the default selections in the **Configure user access control** page and click **Next** to continue.

5. Leave the default selection to point to **Developer edition** in the **Specify provisioning** page and click **Create**. Amazon Kendra will start the index creation job. It may take about 15 to 30 minutes, so feel free to grab some snacks and coffee/tea in the meantime.

6. When the index has been successfully created, click the **Add data sources** button to proceed.

7. In the **Add a data source connector to your Amazon Kendra index** page, scroll down and click **Add connector** in the **Amazon S3** card under **Select data source connector type**.

8. In the **Specify data source details** page, type the **Data source name** and click **Next**.

9. In the **Configure sync settings** page, provide the name of the Amazon S3 bucket to which you uploaded your research documents as part of the pre-requisite steps in the *Introducing the chatbot use case* section. Scroll down and expand the **Additional configuration – optional** section, and in the **Include patterns** tab, select **Prefix** in the **Type** list box, type chapter11/kendra, and click the **Add** button:

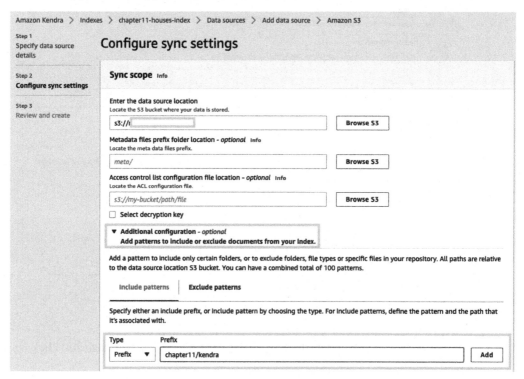

Figure 11.3 – Configure sync settings

10. Now, scroll down a little in the page to the **IAM role** info and select **Create a new role (Recommended)** in the **IAM role** list box and type a **Role name** of your choice. In the **Sync Run Schedule** info, select **Run on demand** for **Frequency**. Click **Next** to continue.

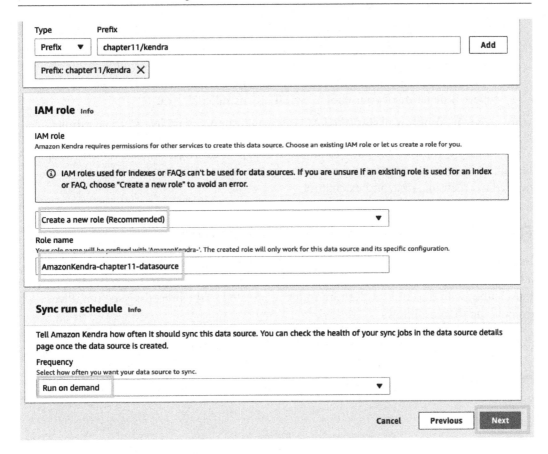

Figure 11.4 – Data source sync settings IAM role and run schedule

11. Review your inputs and click **Add data source**. Amazon Kendra will first propagate the IAM role and then create the data source.

12. After the data source has been created, click the **Sync now** button to index our documents for searching.

13. The sync will take about 30 minutes (time for your next break). After it completes, you can review the **Sync run history**.

14. Now, we will add a few FAQs to the index to enable adding more context to the search. Select the **FAQs** option from the left pane under the **Data management** heading for your index and click **Add FAQ**.

15. Type a **FAQ name** of your choice. Select **.csv file – Basic** in the **FAQ file format** list box. Scroll down to S3 and type the S3 bucket and prefix location of where you uploaded the `faqs.csv` file in the pre-requisite steps of the *Introducing the chatbot use case* section. In the **IAM role**, select **Create a new role (Recommended)** and type a **Role name** of your choice. Scroll down and click **Add**.

16. Amazon Kendra will start the FAQ job which should complete in a few minutes.

We have now completed the steps required to set up an intelligent search for our sample research documents using Amazon Kendra. In the next section, we will build the steps needed to create an Amazon Lex chatbot.

Building an Amazon Lex chatbot

In this section, we will execute the steps needed to build an Amazon Lex chatbot and use a built-in *intent* (which is a task performed by the bot based on a user request) to integrate our chatbot with the Amazon Kendra index we created in the preceding section. Please execute the steps as follows:

1. In the AWS Management Console, type `lex` in the **Services** search bar at the top center of the page and select **Amazon Lex** from the list to go to the Amazon Lex console. On the left pane of the Amazon Lex console, click the **Switch to the new Lex V2 console** link, as shown in the next screenshot:

Figure 11.5 – Switch to the new Lex V2 console

2. On the Lex V2 console page, click **Create bot** on the right, as shown here:

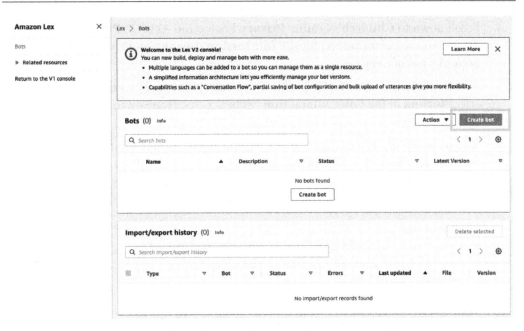

Figure 11.6 – Create bot

3. In the **Configure bot settings** page, select **Create** for the **Creation method**. Under
    Bot configuration, type HomeBuyerResearch for the **Bot name**. In the **IAM
    permissions** section, select **Create a role with basic Amazon Lex permissions** for
    the **Runtime role**.

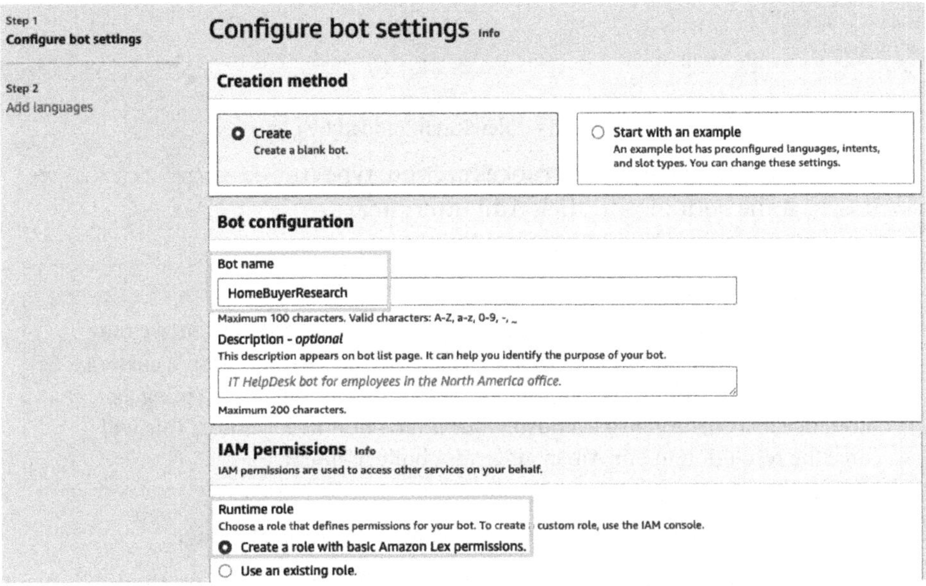

Figure 11.7 – Configure bot settings

4. Scroll down to **Children's Online Privacy Protection Act (COPPA)** and select **No**. Type 5 and select **minute(s)** for the **Idle session timeout**, and click **Next** on the bottom right of the page.

5. In the **Add language to bot** page, leave the **Select language** as **English (US)**, and select **Joanna** in the **Voice interaction** list box. Click **Done** on the bottom right of the page.

6. When the bot is created, Amazon Lex will automatically add an intent called `NewIntent` to start the bot building process.

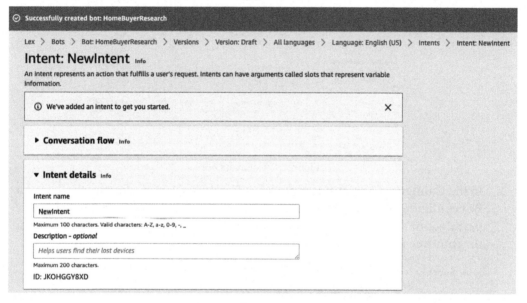

Figure 11.8 – "NewIntent" added by Lex

7. Scroll down to the **Sample utterances** section, type `utterance for new intent` at the bottom, and click **Add utterance**.

> **Note**
> Amazon Lex requires one custom intent by default. For our solution, we only need the Kendra built-in intent. So, we will make the `NewIntent` a custom intent (that's mandatory for building the bot) unresolvable by providing an utterance that will not be used during our interaction with the bot. This will force the resolution to our Amazon Kendra built-in intent.

8. Scroll down and click **Save Intent** at the bottom right of the page.

9. Now, let's go back to the intents list. Click **Back to intents list** on the top left pane under the **Amazon Lex** heading.

10. In the **Intents** page, click **Add intent** on the right, and select **Use built-in intent**, as shown in the following screenshot:

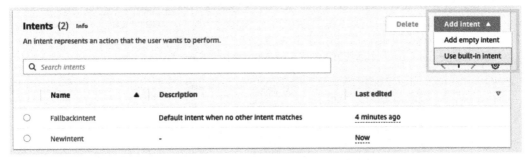

Figure 11.9 – Add built-in intent

11. In the **Use built-in intent** popup, type kendra in the list box, and select **AMAZON.KendraSearchIntent**.

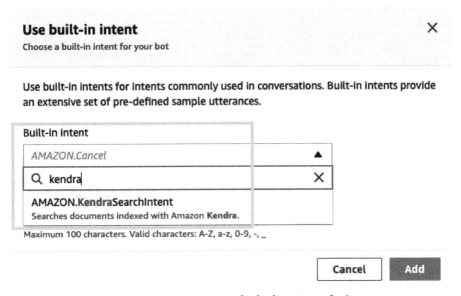

Figure 11.10 – Amazon Kendra built-in intent for Lex

12. In the **Intent name** field that appears, type ResearchBuyers, and in the **Amazon Kendra index** field that appears, select the index name you created in the preceding section (which is chapter11-houses-index if you used the same name mentioned in the book), and click **Add**.

13. Scroll down to the **Closing responses** section and type Here is what I found for your query:((x-amz-lex:kendra-search-response-answer-1)) in the **Message** field, and click on **Save Intent**. After the intent is saved, click on **More response options**.

14. In the **Closing responses editor** window that appears, click on **Add**, select **Add text message group**, and in the **Message group** card that appears, type `I found a FAQ question for you: ((x-amz-lex:kendra-search-response-question_answer-question-1))` and the answer is `((x-amz-lex:kendra-search-response-question_answer-answer-1))` in the **Message** field, and click **Update responses**. Click **Save Intent** once again.

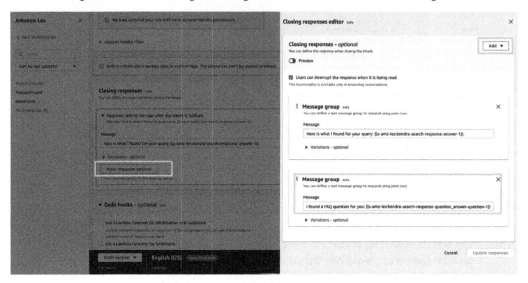

Figure 11.11 – Adding text message group

15. Now, scroll to the top of the page and click **Language: English (US)** from the blue navigation links at the top of the page.

16. Scroll down and click **Build** at the bottom right of the page. This should take about a couple of minutes, but not more.

17. When the bot has been completely built, click the **Test** button next to the **Build** button at the bottom of the page.

18. The **Test Draft version** popup appears at the right of the page. Type `Who is a first-time buyer?` in the input widget at the bottom and press **Enter**.

19. The bot responds with an answer from the documents we added to our Amazon Kendra index:

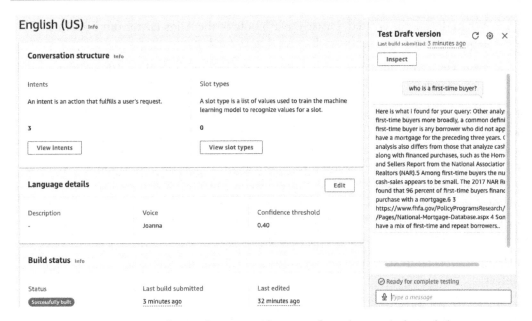

Figure 11.12 – Bot responding to the query with content from the sample research documents

20. Now, scroll to the top of the page and click **Versions** on the blue navigation links.

21. On the **Versions** page, click the **Create version** button on the right.

22. Scroll down to the bottom of the page and click the **Create** button.

23. The new version is successfully created for our bot. Make a note of the version number created, as we will need this in the next few steps.

24. Now, in the left pane under the **Deployment** heading, click on **Aliases**,

25. Click on **Create Alias** at the right of the page. In the **Create alias** page, type an **Alias name** of your choice, or type `hbr-web-ui`. Scroll down and choose the bot version you created in the preceding step by clicking **Choose an existing version** under **Associate with a version**, and click the **Create** button at the bottom right of the page.

> **Note**
> If you are creating a version for the first time, please select the **Version 1** that will be displayed for you

26. When the alias is created, please make a note of the **Alias ID** for our bot. This is required in the next section when we deploy the bot.

27. Also, click your bot's name using the blue navigation links at the top of the page and make a note of your **Bot ID** – we will also need this for deployment.

And that is a wrap for building our Amazon Lex chatbot. In the next section, we will use AWS CloudFormation (`https://aws.amazon.com/cloudformation/`), a managed service that provides the ability to write infrastructure-provisioning tasks as **JSON** or **YAML** template code, and thus automate the deployment of resources we need for building solutions in AWS. The Amazon Lex blog post, *Deploy a Web UI for Your Chatbot*, by Oliver Atoa and Bob Strahan, provides an AWS CloudFormation template example for integrating an Amazon Lex chatbot into a website: `https://aws.amazon.com/blogs/machine-learning/deploy-a-web-ui-for-your-chatbot/`.

We will use this template to create a website in which we will embed our chatbot as a widget.

Deploying the solution with AWS CloudFormation

In the preceding two sections, we saw a step-by-step account of how to create an index and associate documents from an Amazon S3 bucket as a data source using Amazon Kendra, and how to build an Amazon Lex chatbot and integrate that with our Amazon Kendra index using a built-in intent. This completes the majority of our solution build. In this section, we will use an AWS CloudFormation template sample from the accompanying repository for the blog post we mentioned in the previous section: `https://github.com/aws-samples/aws-lex-web-ui/tree/master/templates`.

Let's get started:

1. Click `https://github.com/aws-samples/aws-lex-web-ui/tree/master/templates` and scroll down to the **Launch** section on the web page and click the first **Launch Stack** button for the **CodeBuild mode**.

Launch

To launch a stack using the CodeBuild Mode (faster and easier), click this button:

Click the following button to launch a stack using the Pipeline Mode:

CloudFormation Resources

The CloudFormation stack can create resources in your AWS account including:

-   Amazon Lex bot. You can optionally pass the bot name of an existing one to avoid creating a new one.
-   Cognito Identity Pool used to pass temporary AWS credentials to the web app. You can optionally pass the ID of an existing Cognito Identity Pool to avoid creating a new one.
-   CodeBuild project to configure and deploy to S3 when using the CodeBuild Deployment Mode. If using the Pipeline Deployment Mode, a CodeBuild project is created to bootstrap a CodeCommit repository whit the application source.
-   S3 buckets to host the web application and to store build artifacts.
-   Lambda functions used as CloudFormation Custom Resources to facilitate custom provisioning logic
-   CloudWatch Logs groups automatically created to log the output of the Lambda functions
-   Associated IAM roles for the stack resources

If using the Pipeline Deployment Mode, the stack also creates the following resources:

-   CodeCommit repository loaded with the source code in this project. This is only created when using the pipeline deployment mode
-   A continuous delivery pipeline using CodePipeline and CodeBuild. The pipeline automatically builds and deploys changes to the app committed to the CodeCommit repo

Figure 11.13 – Launching AWS CloudFormation stack

2. This action will open the AWS CloudFormation service in your AWS Management Console and take you to the **Create Stack** page. Click **Next**.

3. Type a name of your choice for the **Stack name** and the **CodeBuildName**. Or you can use the examples provided.

4. Scroll down to the section named **Lex V2 Bot Configuration Parameters**. Type or paste the **Bot ID** that you copied from the preceding section in the **LexV2BotId** field. Type or paste the **Alias ID** you copied from the preceding section in the **LexV2BotAliasId** field. Leave the **LexV2BotLocaleId** field as en_US.

BootstrapBucket
S3 bucket containing pre-staged nested templates and source artifacts

> aws-bigdata-blog

BootstrapPrefix
S3 prefix where the templates and source are stored under

> artifacts/aws-lex-web-ui/artifacts

Lex V1 Bot Configuration Parameters

BotName
Name of an existing Lex Bot to be used by the web ui. NOTE: You must also enter your published bot alias in the BotAlias field below.

>

BotAlias
WARNING: For production deployments, use your bot's published alias here. The $LATEST alias should only be used for manual testing. Amazon Lex limits the number of runtime requests that you can make to the $LATEST version of the bot.

> $LATEST

Lex V2 Bot Configuration Parameters

LexV2BotId
Bot ID (not bot name) of an existing Lex V2 Bot to be used by the web ui. NOTE: You must also enter your Bot alias ID in the LexV2BotAliasId field below.

> F66TWFSDTY

LexV2BotAliasId
Use your Lex V2 bot's alias id (not alias name) here

> QJSXLKSAPV

LexV2BotLocaleId
Specify your bot's supported locale ids. By default this list contains only en_US. Other Lex V2 supported values are de_DE, en_AU, en_GB, es_419, es_ES, es_US, fr_CA, fr_FR, it_IT, ja_JP. A comma separated list of values can be supplied with the first value in the list being the default value. The remaining items can be selected in the Lex Web UI menu. See "https://docs.aws.amazon.com/lexv2/latest/dg/lex2.0.pdf" for details on supported languages and locales.

> en_US

Figure 11.14 – Creating stack, Lex V2 Bot Configuration Parameters

5. Scroll down to **Bot Behavior Parameters** and change the **ForceCognitoLogin** to `true`. This will force the users to sign up to **Amazon Cognito** (https://aws. amazon.com/cognito/), a fully managed user authentication and authorization service for web and mobile applications. Once they have signed up, they can use their credentials to log in to the website to access the chatbot.

6. Scroll down a little and provide a name for the **CognitoIdentityPoolName**.

7. Scroll down to the **Web Application Parameters** section and type `You can ask me questions on home buyers. For example - what is important for home buyers?` in the **WebAppConfBotInitialText** field. The chatbot will display this message when it is launched. Type `Say 'what is important for home buyers' to get started` in the **WebAppConfBotInitialSpeech** field. The bot will voice prompt the user with this message when the microphone icon is clicked.

8. Scroll down a little to the **WebAppConfToolbarTitle** field and type `ResearchHomeBuyers`. Then, click **Next**.

9. On this page, leave the defaults as they are and click **Next** at the bottom of the page.

10. Scroll down to the **Capabilities** section and select both the checkboxes to acknowledge the creation of IAM resources and that it may need the capability to auto expand. Click **Create Stack**.

11. It may take about 15 minutes to create all the resources we need for the solution. For details on the resources that will be created, please refer to the following: `https://github.com/aws-samples/aws-lex-web-ui/blob/master/templates/README.md#cloudformation-resources`.

12. When the status of the CloudFormation stack changes to `Create_Complete`, the resources we need have been provisioned. Before we bring up our website, we need to make a change to our parent website to ensure it is sending the right utterance to our chatbot. Click the **Outputs** tab of your CloudFormation stack to bring up the list of resources that were provisioned. Copy the value for the key called **WebAppBucket**. This is the name of the Amazon S3 bucket created to host your website:

WebAppBucket   chapter11-lex-web-ui-〈

Figure 11.15 – S3 bucket hosting our website

13. Now, go to your **Services** search bar at the top center of your page, type `S3`, and click **Amazon S3** from the list. In the Amazon S3 console, under **Buckets**, type the value you copied in the previous step. This should bring up the S3 bucket. Click the bucket name to display its object list, and click `parent.html` from the list.

14. In the **Object overview** page for `parent.html`, click the **Download** button in the top-right corner. This will download `parent.html` to your computer:

Figure 11.16 – Downloading parent.html

15. Open `parent.html` in your favorite text editor and change the value of the panel-heading tag to `Send "what is important for buyers" utterance to iframe`, as shown in the following screenshot. To bring this entry up, search for `Buy Flowers`.

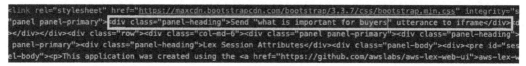

Figure 11.17 – Changing the panel-heading tag in parent.html

16. Continue to search for Buy Flowers and change the parameter for the sendUtterance function to 'what is important for buyers?', as shown in the following screenshot:

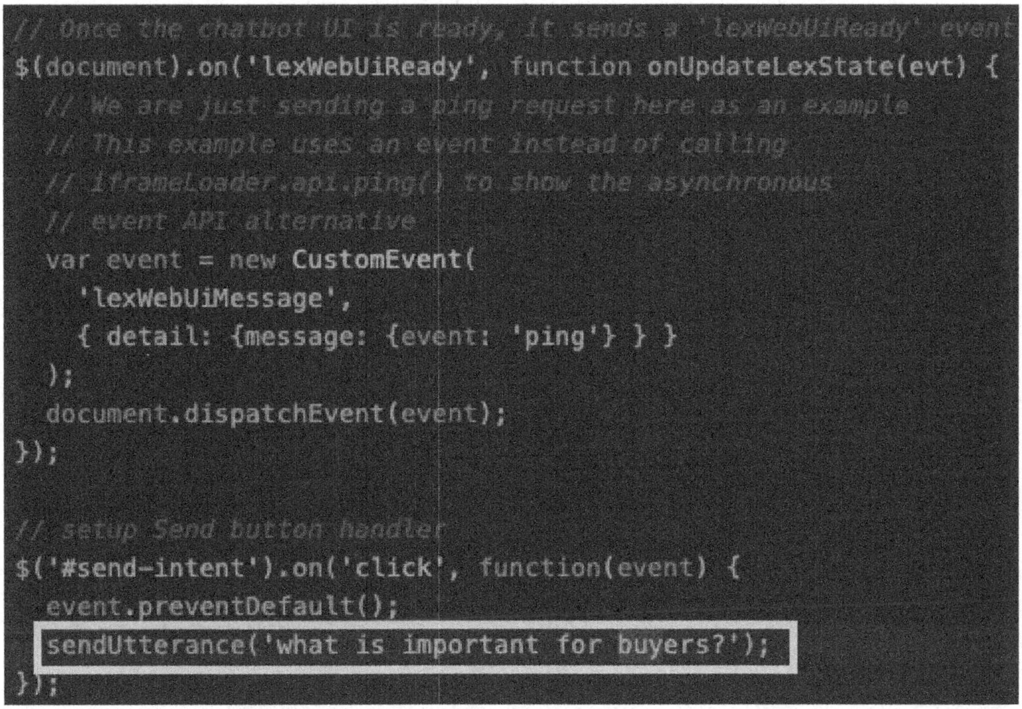

```javascript
// Once the chatbot UI is ready, it sends a 'lexWebUiReady' event
$(document).on('lexWebUiReady', function onUpdateLexState(evt) {
  // We are just sending a ping request here as an example
  // This example uses an event instead of calling
  // iframeLoader.api.ping() to show the asynchronous
  // event API alternative
  var event = new CustomEvent(
    'lexWebUiMessage',
    { detail: {message: {event: 'ping'} } }
  );
  document.dispatchEvent(event);
});

// setup Send button handler
$('#send-intent').on('click', function(event) {
  event.preventDefault();
  sendUtterance('what is important for buyers?');
});
```

Figure 11.18 – Changing the send utterance function input

17. Now, go back to your Amazon S3 console, open the **WebAppBucket** that you downloaded the parent.html from, click **Upload**, and click on **Add files**.

18. Select the modified parent.html from your local computer, scroll down, and click **Upload**.

19. One of the resources that were provisioned by the CloudFormation stack was a CloudFront distribution. **Amazon CloudFront** (`https://aws.amazon.com/cloudfront/`) is a fully managed content delivery network that enables the delivery of websites, applications, data, and media globally in minutes in a highly secure manner. Since we modified one of the web application HTML files in the previous steps, we need to invalidate the cache of our CloudFront distribution so that the changes are reflected in our website. In the **Services** search bar, type `CloudFront`, and click **CloudFront** in the list to go to the Amazon CloudFront console:

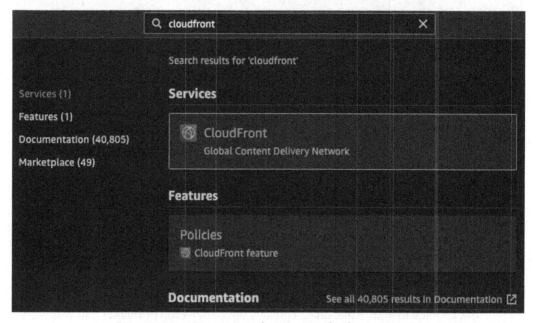

Figure 11.19 – Navigating to the Amazon CloudFront console

20. In the **CloudFront distributions** page, check the **Origin** field. You should see an entry here that matches the name of the **WebAppBucket** value you copied from the **Outputs** tab of your CloudFormation stack. Click the **ID** for this entry.

21. In the details page for your CloudFront distribution, click the **Invalidations** tab to open it. Then, click the **Create Invalidation** button.

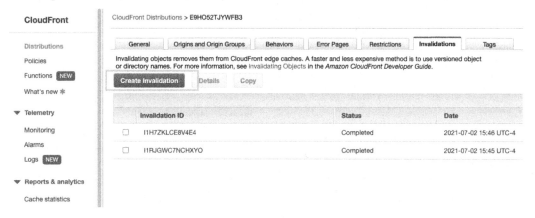

Figure 11.20 – Creating invalidation for your CloudFront distribution

22. In the **Create Invalidation** popup that appears, type a forward slash symbol (/) in the **Object Paths** field and click **Invalidate**, as shown in the following screenshot. This should take about 5 minutes or so:

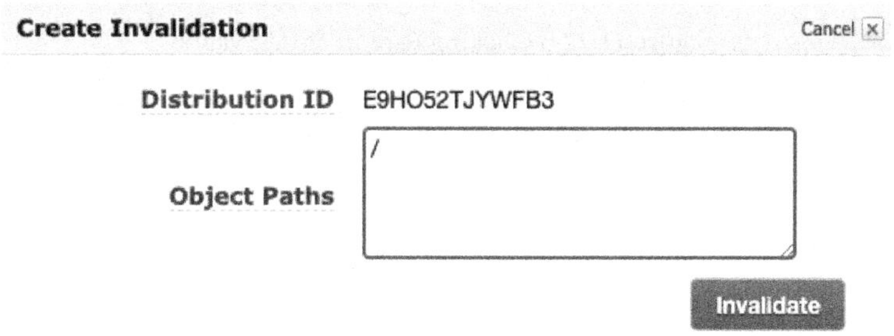

Create Invalidation   Cancel ⊠

Distribution ID   E9HO52TJYWFB3

Object Paths   /

                                                                      Invalidate

Figure 11.21 – Invalidating CloudFront distribution

23. Once the invalidation is completed, go back to the **Outputs** tab of your stack in the **Amazon CloudFormation** console and click the **ParentPageUrl** value:

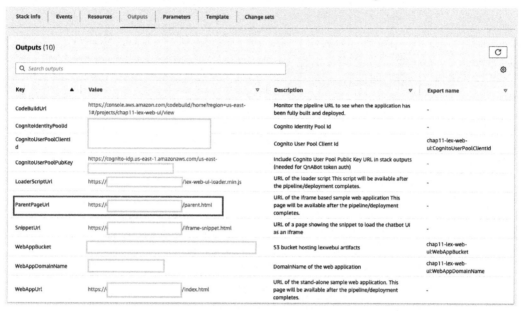

Figure 11.22 – Clicking ParentPageUrl value

24. This will launch the website you provisioned, along with your chatbot. But before you can use your chatbot, Amazon Cognito will force you to sign into your website, as shown. If this is the first time you are accessing the website, click on the **Sign up** button and follow the instructions to sign up:

Figure 11.23 – Signing up or signing in to your website

25. You will receive a verification code in your email after you complete the sign-up process. Enter the verification code to be signed in:

We have sent a code by email to r***@a***.com.
Enter it below to confirm your account.

Verification Code

Confirm Account

Didn't receive a code?   Resend it

Figure 11.24 – Entering the verification code

26. Now that you have signed in, your website along with your chatbot as a widget will be displayed. Click the **Send** button to send the first utterance to the bot. You can type subsequent questions:

Figure 11.25 – Text interaction with your Amazon Lex chatbot widget embedded in parent website

27. Click the microphone button in the chat widget to talk to your bot. The bot will respond back in the voice, as shown in the next screenshot. Accept the notification from your browser to allow it to use the microphone to proceed.

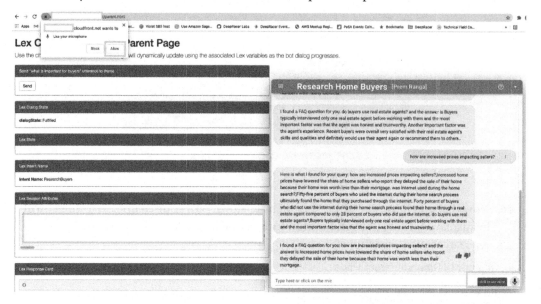

Figure 11.26 – Voice interaction with your chatbot

And that concludes the solution build for this chapter. Feel free to try out the solution and leave us your feedback. You can customize what we built in this chapter for your own needs very easily. For additional ideas on how you can use Amazon Kendra and Amazon Lex for your needs, please refer to the *Further reading* section.

Summary

In this chapter, we built a solution using Amazon Kendra to automate searching for and deriving insights from document corpuses without having to manually read through the documents, understand the context, interpret the meaning, identify content across documents relevant to a common topic, and so on. We also saw how to set up an intelligent AI-based chat assistant using Amazon Lex that implicitly integrated with the Amazon Kendra intelligent search feature to provide a seamless chat and voice interface for (literally) "talking" to the document. Finally, we used a best practices approach with AWS CloudFormation to deploy our chatbot to a parent website as an embedded widget and distributed it using the Amazon CloudFront content delivery network.

Interestingly, NLP has diverse uses in the field of medicine, as we will see in the next chapter, where we will review how NLP and AI technologies have helped transform modern-day medical claims processing. We will start by discussing how to automatically extract data from medical intake forms, how to understand the clinical data using **Amazon Comprehend Medical** (`https://aws.amazon.com/comprehend/medical/`), and how to set up a serverless real-time pipeline for the adjudication of medical claims. As before, we will introduce the use case, discuss how to design the architecture, establish the pre-requisites, and walk through in detail the various steps required to build the solution.

Further reading

- *Enhancing enterprise search with Amazon Kendra* by Leonardo Gomez: `https://aws.amazon.com/blogs/machine-learning/enhancing-enterprise-search-with-amazon-kendra/`

- *How Citibot's chatbot search engine uses AI to find more answers* by Francisco Zamora, Bratton Riley, and Nicholas Burden: `https://aws.amazon.com/blogs/machine-learning/how-citibots-chatbot-search-engine-uses-ai-to-find-more-answers/`

- *Building an omnichannel Q and A chatbot with Amazon Connect, Amazon Lex, Amazon Kendra, and the open-source QnABot project* by Bob Strahan and Michael Widell: `https://aws.amazon.com/blogs/machine-learning/building-a-multi-channel-qa-chatbot-with-amazon-connect-amazon-lex-amazon-kendra-and-the-open-source-qnabot-project/?nc1=b_rp`

12
AI and NLP in Healthcare

In the previous chapter, we covered how AWS AI services can be used to set up a chatbot with your document workflows using **Amazon Lex** and **Amazon Kendra**. In this chapter, we will talk about how **Amazon Textract** and **Amazon Comprehend Medical** can help digitize medical claims in healthcare. We will talk about the healthcare industry's claims processing system and why it's important to automate medical claims. Then, we will walk you through how you can use Amazon Textract to digitize these claims in paper form and use postprocessing to validate them. Then, we will show you how you can extract NLP insights from these claims, such as whether the person was diabetic or not, using Amazon Comprehend Medical APIs.

For invalid claims, we will show you how to easily set up notifications to notify the person submitting the claims to resubmit it with the right data, such as ZIP code or claim ID. Lastly, we will show you some architecture patterns that help automate everything using AWS Lambda functions. By doing so, you will spin up an end-to-end serverless solution that will reduce time to market for the claims processing workflow. This happens because you do not have to set up and manage servers or scale to process millions of such claims.

We will cover the following topics in this chapter:

- Introducing the automated claims processing use case
- Understanding how to extract and validate data from medical intake forms
- Understanding clinical data with Amazon Comprehend Medical
- Understanding invalid medical form processing with notifications
- Understanding how to create a serverless pipeline for medical claims

Technical requirements

For this chapter, you will need access to an AWS account:

- Please make sure that you follow the instructions specified in the *Technical requirements* section of *Chapter 2*, *Introducing Amazon Textract*, to create your AWS account.
- Log into the AWS Management Console before trying the steps in the *Improving the accuracy of document processing workflows* section.

The Python code and sample datasets for our solution can be found at `https://github.com/PacktPublishing/Natural-Language-Processing-with-AWS-AI-Services/tree/main/Chapter%2012`. Please use the instructions in the following sections, along with the code in the preceding repository, to build the solution.

Check out the following video to see the Code in Action at `https://bit.ly/3GrClSK`.

Introducing the automated claims processing use case

In the healthcare industry, there were approximately 6.1 billion medical claims submitted in 2018 according to the *2018 CAHQ index report* (`https://www.caqh.org/sites/default/files/explorations/index/report/2018-index-report.pdf`), and this number is expected to continue rising in the upcoming years.

Healthcare payer companies are constantly looking for efficient and cost-effective ways to process such volumes of claims in a scalable manner. With the current manual process of claim processing, it takes too much time to process these claims. So, healthcare companies are looking at AI and ML approaches to automating and digitizing these claims. Once they can digitize these, it becomes really easy to drive insights such as improving the population's overall health. Moreover, analyzing these claim documents might help you identify behaviors that can help prevent a medical condition from being developed. Also, healthcare payers are looking for a solution that is also compliant, such as *HIPAA-compliant*. For those of you outside the US, HIPAA is a healthcare-specific compliance law for the healthcare industry in the US.

So, we now understand why automating claims is so important. Now, we will talk about how we can help you automate this pipeline using AWS AI services such as Amazon Textract to digitize the claim process. You can do this by extracting text from these scanned claim documents and verifying them using NLP, along with Amazon Comprehend Medical, to get some patient health insights from these claims.

In this use case, our fictitious company, *LiveRight Holdings Private Limited*, is working with a healthcare insurance provider known as *AwakenLife* to process the claims that have been submitted by their insurance holders. These claims are mostly scanned images and most of their time and effort is spent on processing these claims since some of them are invalid. This leads to a loss to the organization. Since LiveRight has already been using Amazon Textract to automate, digitize, and further innovate their document processing workflows in the preceding chapters, they have recommended using *AwakenLife* so that they can use some of these AWS AI services to improve and automate their overall claims process. In this chapter, we will set up a simple AI-based workflow to validate the claims for AwakenLife, which can further reduce their overall processing time.

This solution is highly cost-effective and scalable as these services are serverless and scale to process documents based on your need. In this chapter, we will walk you through the following architecture:

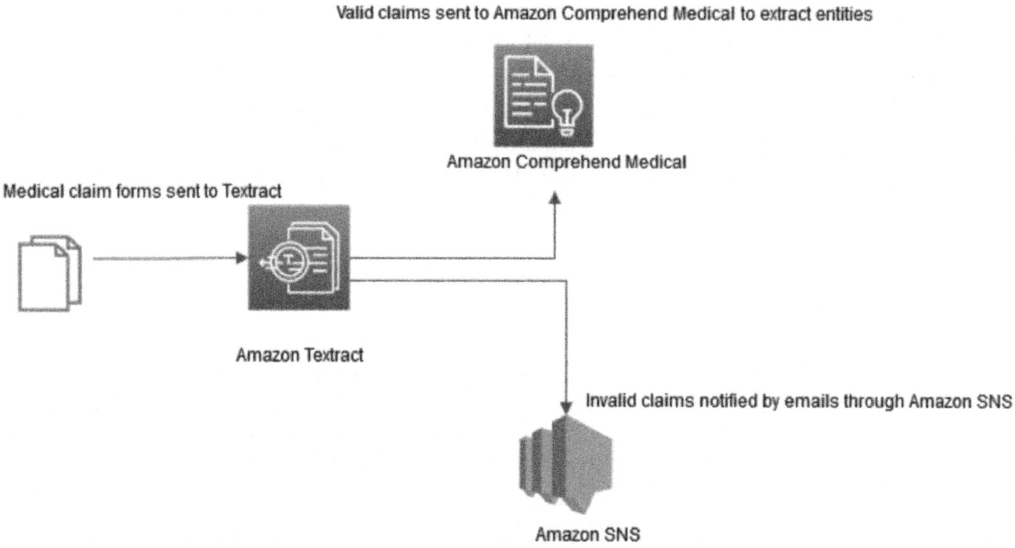

Figure 12.1 – Medical claim processing architecture for the notebook

In the preceding diagram, we can see the following:

- You have your medical intake forms, which can be in image or PDF format, that are sent to Amazon Textract for digitization or text extraction.

- Amazon Textract extracts text from these highly unstructured medical intake documents.

- You must *postprocess* Amazon Textract's response to validate the claims. For this blog, we are using a ZIP code and claim ID to make sure the claims are valid. You can customize these validation rules based on your business case.

- Once the ZIP code and claim ID have been validated, valid data is sent to Amazon Comprehend Medical to gain insights and entities such as patient procedure.

- If the ZIP code and claim ID are not valid, an email is sent to the stakeholder, notifying them that it's an invalid claim.

We will walk through the previous architecture using a Jupyter notebook. Once we've done this, we will cover an architecture on how to make this implementation automated using event-based lambda functions.

In the next section, we will talk about how you can use Amazon Textract to extract data from medical intake forms.

Understanding how to extract and validate data from medical intake forms

In this section, we will show you how to use Amazon Textract to extract key-value pairs or form data from a medical intake form. Then, using simple logic, you will verify whether the extracted values are valid or invalid.

If you have not done so in the previous chapters, you will have to create an Amazon SageMaker Jupyter notebook and set up **Identity and Access Management (IAM)** permissions for that notebook role. By doing so, you will be able to access the AWS services we will use in this notebook. After that, you will need to clone this book's GitHub repository (`https://github.com/PacktPublishing/Natural-Language-Processing-with-AWS-AI-Services`), go to the `Chapter 12` folder, and open the `ch 12 automating claims processing.ipynb` notebook.

> **Note:**
> Make sure that the IAM role in the notebook has **AmazonSNSFullAccess**, **AmazonComprehendMedicalFullAccess**, and **AmazonTextractFullAccess**.

Now, using this notebook, we will learn how to extract data using Textract APIs and validate them using some postprocessing logic via a sample medical intake form:

1. We will use the following sample medical intake form to get started. Run the following code block to load the sample medical form, which is a valid medical form for claims:

    ```
    documentName = "validmedicalform.png"
    display(Image(filename=documentName))
    ```

You will see that the following medical intake form has been loaded:

MEDICARE ☑	MEDICAID ☐		
NAME Test1 Name1		BIRTH DATE 7-20-1975	
ADDRESS 1 Test1 St			
CITY Testcity1	STATE MA	Single ☐ Married ☑ Other ☐	
ZIP CODE 01742	TELEPHONE 712-674-3619		
ID NUMBER a-184054-222			
INSURANCE PLAN NAME myplan1			
PROCEDURE Blood glucose/reagent strips			
EMPLOYER MyEmployer			
READ BACK OF FORM BEFORE COMPLETING & SIGNING THIS FORM. PATIENT'S OR AUTHORIZED PERSON'S SIGNATURE I authorize the release of any medical or other information necessary to process this claim. I also request payment of government benefits either to myself or to the party who accepts assignment below. SIGNED Test1 Name1		DATE 07-25-2019	
SYMPTOM DATE 06-03-2019			
DIAGONOSIS Diabetic			
RESERVED FOR LOCAL USE			

Figure 12.2 – Sample valid medical intake form

Now, we will extract the medical intake form's data by calling the Amazon Textract Analyze Document API with the Form feature enabled. This is a sync API and we covered it in detail in *Chapter 2, Introducing Amazon Textract*. We have created a function that takes any document image as input and returns a Textract response. We will talk about how this function can be automated using a lambda function in the last section of this chapter, *Understanding how to create a serverless pipeline for medical claims*. Run the following notebook cell to execute this function:

```
def calltextract(documentName):
    client = boto3.client(service_name='textract',
        region_name= 'us-east-1',
```

```
        endpoint_url='https://textract.us-east-1.
amazonaws.com')
    with open(documentName, 'rb') as file:
        img_test = file.read()
        bytes_test = bytearray(img_test)
        print('Image loaded', documentName)
    response = client.analyze_document(Document={'Bytes':
bytes_test}, FeatureTypes=['FORMS'])
            return response
```

2. With that, we've defined a Textract function. Now, we will call this function by passing the scanned medical intake form. We will get a Textract response back. Run the following cell:

```
response= calltextract(documentName)
print(response)
```

If the response from Textract is a success, you will get the following message, along with a JSON response with extracted data:

Image loaded validmedicalform.png
{'DocumentMetadata': {'Pages': 1}, 'Blocks': [{'BlockType': 'PAGE', 'Geometry': {'BoundingBox': {'Width': 1.0, 'Hei
ght': 1.0, 'Left': 0.0, 'Top': 0.0}, 'Polygon': [{'X': 1.2692531957743554e-16, 'Y': 0.0}, {'X': 1.0, 'Y': 1.1816080
497439928e-16}, {'X': 1.0, 'Y': 1.0}, {'X': 0.0, 'Y': 1.0}]}, 'Id': '4af9d333-866f-4e3f-ab3b-74b4c6924970', 'Relati
onships': [{'Type': 'CHILD', 'Ids': ['ede5028d-ed05-40e0-94d0-b5515ecda492', '99bad1eb-479b-4e26-840c-d4eeb1a6c2a1
', 'e1d79e29-d4b5-491c-ad7d-a1df5bd37c75', '4d1de960-a208-448c-912b-7a2be7cb0b49', '4d9eb38c-e0de-4e41-835f-9fa8ea1
dd788', '00a69976-330e-490e-9f8d-b4fe17e12ba3', 'd7195ecc-923b-4ce5-9187-f36902256f37', 'd365cbd5-3c1c-4a3f-85e3-e9
36b7ca89d1', '71a46b5c-29af-4470-9480-186c5b907b25', '4a5a9876-458f-4d34-8b15-2ddf19ea067c', '65b32a81-4b40-4152-86
04-09d58f446932', '8d25cf11-9813-4127-9cc7-7434b138ce7f', 'adc55859-866c-4416-bbbe-e71084f3a045', '121899e0-b058-46
f4-94ac-96c19dc162a5', 'b5362726-5bad-440b-afca-9f5ed263e0d4', '18491ae7-b578-4c68-b5b7-a30393d8bd7a', '8cb6d837-d3
91-4814-8fdc-bd85eea1bbc5', '99ed1313-6a06-44d1-8f7a-9b3c7df02a77', 'df91db51-0410-4a0c-8636-7725ea9b02ea', '307a37
50-19e8-474b-a1e0-d167eadd51e3', 'deda6d4d-4f07-4717-99aa-80bd963c241a', 'a7114686-9d77-4b73-9e1c-d1e37d15fd1e', '4
9742fd4-822a-4bf8-a9df-cf9f4932fe42', '49b7b800-ba01-4cf8-86e4-b0a816395a7f', '2cc368ce-afe9-4705-aa16-105e2980b473
', '295591ac-2bb4-42d5-beca-5a060a7ccec2', 'ab39abad-c866-4bc2-b161-1e8aa5e3a117', 'ceb116b4-e8df-4dba-8af5-5ee2932
79475', '829691d9-0336-41e5-8433-29d6d699a168', 'f1f640c1-70da-46b5-90a2-35d3e53bafe4', '74273f3f-cb47-47a8-8d91-3f
5c4afc0586', 'e4c5530d-9e57-4b45-a8a6-48d13f741bde', '5d7d491d-7c47-4d2f-82da-dfdc86fa949c', '2e1caa52-7f91-402a-b7
09-d52323e44a61', '14c5937f-d62f-461f-9271-afb9ca9917e5', 'f1b2117b-8d4e-4609-9b8c-ed33cfc08980', '287fa619-0a2f-4b
11-85e5-6c5844491574', '1337f531-c99e-4a80-ace1-93d1f096530d', '6f989a73-3bc5-4169-b54c-09ae935d618e', '78c02bb6-93
a8-42b3-b865-8b1167514993', '63f2a3b9-2694-4e54-946c-afc7a7337039', '74bc3196-59e7-4903-bf43-5dfc745c7a53', '31f6a7
```

Figure 12.3 – Textract JSON response for the medical form

The preceding response contains a lot of information, such as geometry, pages, and text in document metadata.

3.  Now, we will create a function to parse form data or key-value text responses from this JSON response. We are using a Textract parser to parse this JSON response. Here, we have created a method that accepts a JSON response and uses a Textract parser to parse the form key values and return a key-value pair:

```
from trp import Document
def getformkeyvalue(response):
```
```

```
doc = Document(response)
key_map = {}
for page in doc.pages:
    # Print fields
    for field in page.form.fields:
        if field is None or field.key is None or
field.value is None:
            continue
        key_map[field.key.text] = field.value.text
return key_map
```

4. Now, we will pass the Textract JSON response to the `def`
    `getformkeyvalue(response)` method to get the key-value pairs or form data
    from the Textract JSON response:

```
get_form_keys = getformkeyvalue(response)
print(get_form_keys)
```

You will get the following output:

{'Married': 'SELECTED', 'Other': 'NOT_SELECTED', 'MEDICAID': 'NOT_SELECTED', 'Single': 'NOT_SELECTED', 'TELEPHONE': '
111-111-1111', 'ZIP CODE': '111111', 'STATE': 'MA', 'INSURANCE PLAN NAME': 'myplan1', 'ID NUMBER': 'a-184054-6661', '
ADDRESS': '1 Test St', 'NAME': 'Failed Test', 'DATE': '08-22-2019', 'SIGNED': 'Failed Test', 'MEDICARE': 'SELECTED',
'DIAGONOSIS': 'Allergy', 'BIRTH DATE': '7-22-1979', 'CITY': 'Testcity', 'SYMPTOMDATE': '06-03-2019', 'PROCEDURE': 'Ox
ygen concentrator', 'EMPLOYER': 'MyEmployer'}

Figure 12.4 – Parsed Textract form data from the JSON response

All the form entries are extracted as key-value pairs.

5. Now, we will check whether these key-value or form entries are valid using some
    defined business rules. For this book, we are checking for form validity based on
    a valid ZIP Code and Claim ID. You can also modify the validation code based on
    your business needs. We have created a method that accepts key-value pairs and
    checks whether the ZIP Code or ID Number information that has been extracted
    from Textract is valid. If it is valid, it will return the required ID, while if it is not
    valid, it will return a message stating that Claim ID and ZIP Code are not valid:

```
def validate(body):
    json_acceptable_string = body.replace("'", "\"")
    json_data = json.loads(json_acceptable_string)
    print(json_data)
    zip = json_data['ZIP CODE']
    id = json_data['ID NUMBER']
    if(not zip.strip().isdigit()):
```

```
        return False, id, "Zip code invalid"
    length = len(id.strip())
    if(length != 12):
        return False, id, "Invalid claim Id"
    return True, id, "Ok"
```

6. Now, we will test this validation method for a valid medical form by sending the key-value pair we extracted from the `getformdata(response)` method:

```
textract_json= json.dumps(get_form_keys,indent=2)
res, formid, result = validate(textract_json)
print(result)
print(formid)
```

7. Since it's a valid claim, both ZIP code and Claim ID are valid, and this method returns a true response (a valid response):

```
{'MEDICAID': 'NOT_SELECTED', 'Single': 'NOT_SELECTED', 'TELEPHONE': '712-674-3619', 'Other': 'NOT_SELECTED', 'Married
': 'SELECTED', 'ADDRESS': '1 Test1 St', 'ZIP CODE': '01742', 'ID NUMBER': 'a-184054-222', 'STATE': 'MA', 'INSURANCE P
LAN NAME': 'myplan1', 'DATE': '07-25-2019', 'MEDICARE': 'SELECTED', 'NAME': 'Test1 Name1', 'CITY': 'Testcity1', 'PROC
EDURE': 'Blood glucose/reagent strips', 'SIGNED': 'Test1 Name1', 'BIRTH DATE': '7-20-1975', 'DIAGONOSIS': 'Diabetic',
'SYMPTOM.DATE': '06-03-2019', 'EMPLOYER': 'MyEmployer'}
Ok
a-184054-222
```

Figure 12.5 – Valid claim response

As you can see, we get an Ok response, along with the valid claim ID.

Now, going back to the architecture, two things can happen:

- If the form is valid or the response from this method is Ok, we will send this data to Comprehend Medical to gain insights, as we will cover in the next section.

- If the form is invalid, we will notify the customer, using Amazon **Simple Notification Service (SNS)**, that this service is used to send email or phone notifications. We will cover this in the last section, *Understanding how to create a serverless pipeline for medical claims*.

In this section, we covered how you can use the Amazon Textract Analyze Document API to extract the form values from a medical intake form. We also covered how you can validate a Textract response.

Since the response is valid for the medical intake form, in the next section, we will show you how you can use Amazon Comprehend Medical to extract medical insights.

Understanding clinical data with Amazon Comprehend Medical

In this section, we will talk about how you can use **Amazon Comprehend Medical** to gain insights from a valid medical intake form. We covered Amazon Comprehend's features in *Chapter 3, Introducing Amazon Comprehend*. In this chapter, we will learn how to use the Amazon Comprehend Medical Entity API to extract entities such as *patient diagnosis* and PHI data types such as *claim ID* from the medical intake form. Let's get started:

1. Go back to your notebook and run the following cell to use the Comprehend Medical `boto3` API:

    ```
    comprehend = boto3.client(service_
    name='comprehendmedical')
    ```

2. Now, we will use the `comprehend.detect_entities_v2` API (https://docs.aws.amazon.com/comprehend/latest/dg/API_medical_DetectEntitiesV2.html) to analyze the clinical text data from medical intake forms and return entities specific to the medical text, such as type or diagnosis. Run the following cell to see what entities we are going to get from the valid medical intake form:

    ```
    cm_json_data =  comprehend.detect_entities_
    v2(Text=textract_json)
    print("\nMedical Entities\n========")
    for entity in cm_json_data["Entities"]:
        print("- {}".format(entity["Text"]))
        print ("   Type: {}".format(entity["Type"]))
        print ("   Category: {}".format(entity["Category"]))
        if(entity["Traits"]):
            print("   Traits:")
            for trait in entity["Traits"]:
                print ("    - {}".format(trait["Name"]))
        print("\n")
    ```

You will get the following medical insights by using this API:

```
Medical Entities
========
- 111-111-1111
    Type: PHONE_OR_FAX
    Category: PROTECTED_HEALTH_INFORMATION

- 111111
    Type: ID
    Category: PROTECTED_HEALTH_INFORMATION

- MA
    Type: NAME
    Category: PROTECTED_HEALTH_INFORMATION

- myplan1
    Type: NAME
    Category: PROTECTED_HEALTH_INFORMATION

- a-184054-6661
    Type: ID
    Category: PROTECTED_HEALTH_INFORMATION

- 08-22-2019
    Type: DATE
    Category: PROTECTED_HEALTH_INFORMATION

- Allergy
    Type: DX_NAME
    Category: MEDICAL_CONDITION
```

Figure 12.6 – Medical entities

It was able to determine the phone number and medical ID as PHI. If you have regulatory requirements, you can mask or redact these entity types easily as they have been correctly identified by this API.

3. Now that we have extracted the entities, we will save this extracted data in Amazon S3 in a CSV file. For large-scale medical intake form processing, you would want to save all these insights in a CSV file, in an S3 bucket, and analyze them by using an analytics service such as *Amazon Athena*, which we covered in *Chapter 8, Leveraging NLP to Monetize Your Media Content*. We have created a function that takes Comprehend Medical's response and validated ID from the medical intake form and saves it in Amazon S3. Run the following code:

```
def printtocsv(cm_json_data,formid):
        entities = cm_json_data['Entities']
        with open(TEMP_FILE, 'w') as csvfile: # 'w' will
truncate the file
            filewriter = csv.writer(csvfile,
delimiter=',',
                            quotechar='|', quoting=csv.
QUOTE_MINIMAL)
            filewriter.writerow([ 'ID','Category',
'Type', 'Text'])
```

```
                for entity in entities:
                    filewriter.writerow([formid,
    entity['Category'], entity['Type'], entity['Text']])
    filename = "procedureresult/" + formid + ".csv"
        S3Uploader.upload(TEMP_FILE, 's3://{}/{}'.format(bucket,
    prefix))
```

4. Now, we will call the `printtocsv(cm_json_data,formid)` method by passing the JSON response from the Comprehend Medical Entity API and `formid` from the validation logic:

```
printtocsv(cm_json_data,formid)
```

You will get the following response:

```
"successfully parsed:procedureresult/a-184054-6661.csv"
```

In this section, we covered how you can extract medical insights or entities using the Amazon Comprehend Medical API for valid claims from Amazon Textract. In the next section, we will take an invalid claim form and extract data using Amazon Textract and postprocess this data to check for validation. If it's not valid, we will show you how you can set up SNs to notify the stakeholder via email.

Understanding invalid medical form processing with notifications

In this section, we will walk through the architecture specified in *Figure 12.1* when the claim is identified as invalid by Textract postprocessing. We will send the message to the stakeholder via Amazon SNS. Let's go back to the notebook:

1. In the notebook, we will start by loading the scanned medical intake form by running the following code:

```
InvalidDocument = "invalidmedicalform.png"
display(Image(filename=InvalidDocument))
```

You will get the following sample medical form, which we will check for invalid use cases:

MEDICARE ✓	MEDICAID ☐	
NAME Failed Test		**BIRTH DATE** 7-22-1979
ADDRESS 1 Test St		
CITY Testcity	**STATE** MA	Single ☐ Married ✓ Other ☐
ZIP CODE 111111	**TELEPHONE** 111-111-1111	
ID NUMBER a-184054-6661		
INSURANCE PLAN NAME myplan1		
PROCEDURE Oxygen concentrator		
EMPLOYER MyEmployer		

READ BACK OF FORM BEFORE COMPLETING & SIGNING THIS FORM.
PATIENT'S OR AUTHORIZED PERSON'S SIGNATURE I authorize the release of any medical or other information necessary to process this claim. I also request payment of government benefits either to myself or to the party who accepts assignment below.

SIGNED _____ Failed Test _____   DATE   08-22-2019

SYMPTOM DATE 06-03-2019	
DIAGONOSIS Allergy	
RESERVED FOR LOCAL USE	

Figure 12.7 – Medical intake invalid claim form

In this form, **ZIP CODE** and **ID NUMBER** have been entered incorrectly.

2. Now, we will call the `calltextract(document)` function that we created in the previous section and pass this document to extract the text or data using the Amazon Textract Sync API. To do so, run the following code:

```
response = calltextract(InvalidDocument)
```

3. After this, we will call the `getformdata(response)` method that we defined in the previous sections, which takes Textract's response as input and returns the form's key-value data:

```
get_form_keys = getformkeyvalue(response)
print(get_form_keys)
```

You will get the following output:

{'Married': 'SELECTED', 'Other': 'NOT_SELECTED', 'MEDICAID': 'NOT_SELECTED', 'Single': 'NOT_SELECTED', 'TELEPHONE': '
111-111-1111', 'ZIP CODE': '111111', 'STATE': 'MA', 'INSURANCE PLAN NAME': 'myplan1', 'ID NUMBER': 'a-184054-6661', '
ADDRESS': '1 Test St', 'NAME': 'Failed Test', 'DATE': '08-22-2019', 'SIGNED': 'Failed Test', 'MEDICARE': 'SELECTED',
'DIAGONOSIS': 'Allergy', 'BIRTH DATE': '7-22-1979', 'CITY': 'Testcity', 'SYMPTOMDATE': '06-03-2019', 'PROCEDURE': 'Ox
ygen concentrator', 'EMPLOYER': 'MyEmployer'}

Figure 12.8 – Extracted form data using Textract

Here, we get all the key-value pairs or form data.

4.   Now, we will check whether the extracted key-value pairs, such as ZIP CODE and
     ID NUMBER, are valid by sending this as input to the validate(body) method
     that we defined in the previous section. This method returns true if the content is
     valid but will return false if invalid claim data is submitted concerning ZIP CODE
     and ID NUMBER:

```
textract_json= json.dumps(get_form_keys,indent=2)

res, formid, result = validate(textract_json)

print(result)

print(formid)

print(res)
```

You will get the following response:

{'Married': 'SELECTED', 'Other': 'NOT_SELECTED', 'MEDICAID': 'NOT_SELECTED', 'Single': 'NOT_SELECTED', 'TELEPHONE': '
111-111-1111', 'ZIP CODE': '111111', 'STATE'. 'MA', 'INSURANCE PLAN NAME': 'myplan1', 'ID NUMBER': 'a-184054-6661', '
ADDRESS': '1 Test St', 'NAME': 'Failed Test', 'DATE': '08-22-2019', 'SIGNED': 'Failed Test', 'MEDICARE': 'SELECTED',
'DIAGONOSIS': 'Allergy', 'BIRTH DATE': '7-22-1979', 'CITY': 'Testcity', 'SYMPTOMDATE': '06-03-2019', 'PROCEDURE': 'Ox
ygen concentrator', 'EMPLOYER': 'MyEmployer'}
Invalid claim Id
a-184054-6661
False

Figure 12.9 – Invalid claim response

The valid method returns an invalid claim and false, along with the invalid
claim ID.

5.   Now, we want to notify the users that this claim is invalid. To do this, we will walk
     you through how you can set up **Amazon SNS** through the Amazon SNS console.
     Go to this link to create a topic where you will publish this invalid message:
     https://console.aws.amazon.com/sns/v3/home?region=us-
     east-1#/create-topic.

6.   For **Name**, enter invalid-claims-notify, as shown in the following screenshot:

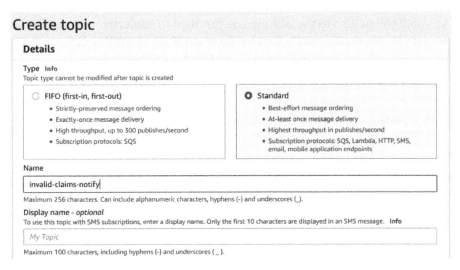

Figure 12.10 – Creating a topic in the SNS AWS console

Make sure you choose the **Standard** topic type.

7. Scroll down and click on the **Create topic** button.

8. After creating a topic, we must add subscribers or people who are going to subscribe to this topic for notifications by going to `https://console.aws.amazon.com/sns/v3/home?region=us-east-1#/create-subscription`.

9. Select your **topic ARN** from the drop-down menu, set **Email** for **Protocol**, and enter your email ID in the **Endpoint** box, as shown in the following screenshot:

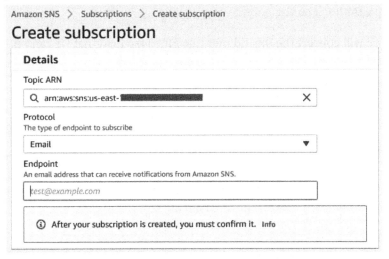

Figure 12.11 – Subscribing to the topic via email

Scroll down and click on **Create Subscription**.

10. An email will be sent to the address you just used to subscribe. Check your email or spam for an email from SNS with a form email ID of **AWS Notification - Subscription Confirmation** and click on **Confirm Subscription**.

> **Note:**
>
> It's important to confirm the subscription; otherwise, you will not be notified.

11. Now, go back to `https://console.aws.amazon.com/sns/v3/home?region=us-east-1#/topics` to copy the **ARN** topic we just created called `invalid-claims-notify`:

Figure 12.12 – Copying the topic's ARN from the AWS console

12. After copying this ARN, go back to the notebook and paste it into the following notebook cell to load the SNS `boto3` client. Here, enter a topic:

```
sns = boto3.client('sns')
topicARN="<Enter your topic arn>"
```

13. Now, we will convert the invalid message into a payload that we can publish to this topic:

```
snsbody = "Content:" + str(textract_json) + "Reason:" +
str(result)
print(snsbody)
```

14. Next, we will use the `sns.publish` Python `boto3` API (`https://boto3.amazonaws.com/v1/documentation/api/latest/reference/services/sns.html#SNS.Client.publish`) to send an invalid email message in the body to the registered email:

```
try:
    response = sns.publish(
                TargetArn = topicARN,
                Message= snsbody
```

```
        )
    print(response)
except Exception as e:
        print("Failed while doing validation")
        print(e.message)
```

You will get the following response:

{'MessageId': '767633de-0fe1-5614-8c34-6aa0cdcdcbd8', 'ResponseMetadata': {'RequestId': 'ec96366c-d9c1-53f8-9ca7-6f12
1bed3e34', 'HTTPStatusCode': 200, 'HTTPHeaders': {'x-amzn-requestid': 'ec96366c-d9c1-53f8-9ca7-6f121bed3e34', 'conten
t-type': 'text/xml', 'content-length': '294', 'date': 'Sat, 31 Jul 2021 03:13:47 GMT'}, 'RetryAttempts': 0}}

Figure 12.13 – Pushing the invalid claim message to the topic

15. Check the email address you subscribed with for an email notifying you of invalid medical claims:

Reply   Reply All   Forward

AN   AWS Notifications <no-reply@sns.amazonaws.com>

AWS Notification Message

"ADDRESS": "1 Test St",
"NAME": "Failed Test",
"DATE": "08-22-2019",
"SIGNED": "Failed Test",
"MEDICARE": "SELECTED",
"DIAGONOSIS": "Allergy",
"BIRTH DATE": "7-22-1979",
"CITY": "Testcity",
"SYMPTOMDATE": "06-03-2019",
"PROCEDURE": "Oxygen concentrator",
"EMPLOYER": "MyEmployer"
}Reason:Invalid claim Id

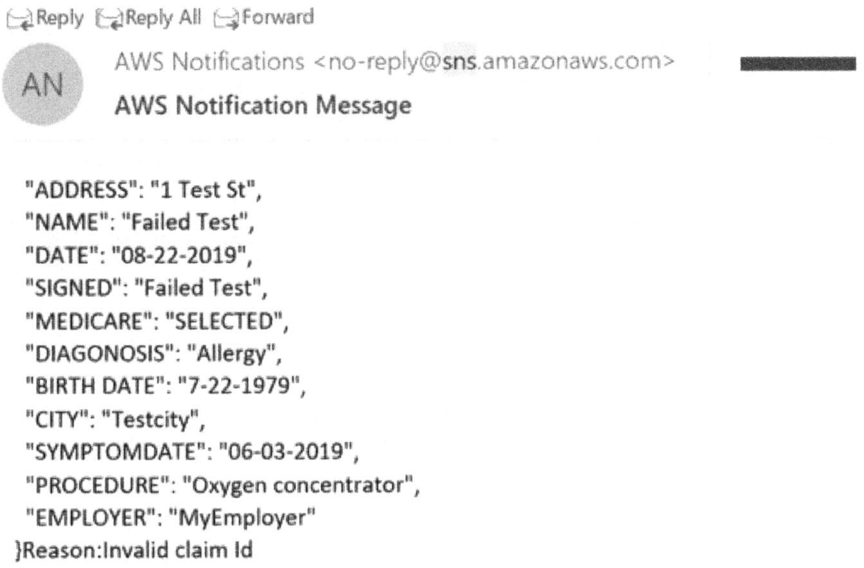

Figure 12.14 – Email notification sent

You can always opt out of the topic you have created.

In this section, we covered how to process a medical claim using Amazon Textract, check for invalid medical claims, and notify the stakeholders about this. Next, we'll learn how to create a serverless pipeline for medical claims.

Understanding how to create a serverless pipeline for medical claims

In the previous sections, we covered the building blocks of the architecture by using the Amazon Textract Sync API, the Amazon Comprehend Medical Detect Entities Sync API, and Amazon SNS to send invalid claims. We defined functions for this workflow and called the text extraction and validation functions to showcase the use case or workflow with both a valid and invalid medical claim form. These functions can be moved into lambda code and, along with **S3 event notifications**, can be invoked to create a scalable pipeline for medical claims processing. We can do this by using the following architecture:

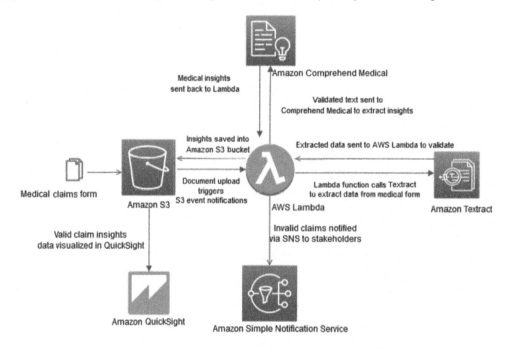

Figure 12.15 – Automating an architecture for scale with AWS Lambda

We walked through a Jupyter notebook showing individual code components for processing medical claims using a single intake form. We created Python functions to extract data, validate data, gather insights, and convert those insights into CSV files. To process millions of such documents, we will learn how to make the code functions AWS Lambda functions to create an end-to-end automated serverless architecture using the preceding diagram. The medical claims form we'll be using has been dropped into an Amazon S3 bucket by payers of *AwakenLife Ltd*:

- Amazon S3 claims that the upload creates an Amazon S3 event notification, which triggers the lambda function.

- In this lambda, you can call the `textract` function we defined in the *Understanding how to extract and validate data from medical intake forms* section and call Amazon Textract by passing this image as input.

- You get a text response back. This extracted text can be sent to the `validation` function we defined in the previous section.

- For valid claims, valid claim data is sent to Amazon Comprehend Medical to extract insights. Extracted insights are sent back to AWS Lambda.

- You can move the code for the `printtocsv` (`cm_json_data, formid`) function, which we defined in the *Understanding clinical data with Amazon Comprehend Medical* section, to this lambda function to convert this extracted insight into a CSV file and save it to Amazon S3.

- For invalid claims, you can use SNS to notify the stakeholders.

We can use scale and process medical claims documents at a large scale with just a few lines of code. This architecture can be quickly automated and deployed in the form of a *CloudFormation template*, which lets you set up **Infrastructure as Code (IaC)**. We have provided a similar scalable implementation in the form of a blog in the *Further reading* section if you're interested.

In this section, we covered how to use the code we defined in the previous sections and move that to an AWS Lambda section to architect an end-to-end automated workflow using a walkthrough architecture. Now, let's summarize this chapter.

Summary

In this chapter, we introduced the medical claim processing use case. We then covered how you can use AWS AI services such as Amazon Textract to extract form data from these scanned medical forms. Then, we spoke about how you can perform some postprocessing on the extracted text based on your business rules to validate their form data. Once the form data had been validated, we showed you how to use Amazon Comprehend Medical, as covered in *Chapter 3, Introducing Amazon Comprehend*, to extract medical insights. Once you have medical insights, this data can be converted into a CSV file and saved in Amazon S3. Once you've done this, you can analyze this data for population health analytics by using **Amazon Athena** or **Amazon QuickSight**. We also discussed how to handle invalid claims processing by showing how to quickly configure Amazon SNS through the AWS console and add subscribers. You can notify your subscribers by email regarding the medical claims that have been submitted as invalid.

Lastly, we showed you how to architect a serverless scalable solution using AWS Lambda to call these Textract Sync and Amazon Comprehend Medical Sync APIs. This ensures that you have an end-to-end working automated architecture with the claim documents you uploaded in Amazon S3.

In the next chapter, we will cover how to improve the accuracy of your existing document processing workflows using *Amazon Augmented AI* with the human-in-the-loop process. We will also deep dive into aspects of why you need a human-in-the-loop process and how it helps improve the accuracy of your existing AI predictions.

Further reading

To learn more about the topics that were covered in this chapter, take a look at the following resource:

- *Automating claims adjudication workflows using Amazon Textract and Amazon Comprehend Medical*, by Sonali Sahu and Ujjwal Ratan (`https://aws.amazon.com/blogs/industries/automating-claims-adjudication-workflows-using-amazon-textract-and-amazon-comprehend-medical/`)

Section 3: Improving NLP Models in Production

In this section, we will dive deep into some strategies for how to include a human in the loop for different purposes in a document processing workflow and cover best practices on how to autoscale your NLP inference for enterprise traffic.

This section comprises the following chapters:

13
Improving the Accuracy of Document Processing Workflows

In the last chapter, we covered how AWS AI services such as **Amazon Textract** and **Amazon Comprehend Medical** can help automate healthcare workflows quickly. In this chapter, we will talk about why we need humans in the loop in document processing workflows, and how setting up **human-in-the-loop** (HITL) processes with **Amazon Augmented AI** (**Amazon A2I**) can help improve accuracy in your existing document processing workflows with **Amazon Textract**.

Amazon A2I is a managed service that makes it easy to build the workflows required for the human review of **machine learning (ML)** predictions. In this chapter, we will cover the following topics:

- The need for setting up HITL processes with document processing
- Seeing the benefits of using Amazon A2I for HITL workflows
- Adding human reviews to your document processing pipelines

Technical requirements

For this chapter, you will need access to an **AWS Account**. Please make sure to follow the instructions specified in the *Technical requirements* section in *Chapter 2, Introducing Amazon Textract,* to create your AWS Account, and log in to the **AWS Management Console** before trying the steps in *Improving the accuracy of document processing workflows*.

The **Python** code and sample datasets for our solution can be found at the following link: https://github.com/PacktPublishing/Natural-Language-Processing-with-AWS-AI-Services/tree/main/Chapter%2013.

Check out the following video to see the Code in Action at https://bit.ly/3jBxBQq.

Please use the instructions in the following sections along with the code in the repository to build the solution.

The need for setting up HITL processes with document processing

In the previous chapters, we have discussed how you can use Amazon Textract and Amazon Comprehend to automate your existing document processing workflows with AWS AI services. We covered some of the key use cases such as using Comprehend to analyze SEC filing reports and using Textract to extract text from any document or quickly digitize any document. We also spoke about how these AI services provide a confidence score with each predicted text, word, line, or entity. Now, the questions that customers often ask are about how to improve these predictions and to make sure they are highly accurate. In most AI systems, it's either AI doing the automation process or it's only humans or manual processes.

The ideal scenario would be both humans and AI working together so that the results predicted by these AI systems can be reviewed by humans to make sure they are highly accurate. This applies to scenarios where we are processing highly critical information in our document processing workflows, for example, processing loan applications, invoice processing, mortgage processing, or legal documents reviews, and so on. In all of these scenarios, you would want a human to validate or review whether the loan amount or invoice amount predicted by the ML or AI systems was accurate because if it was not, one zero could change your life! It could lead to millions in losses for the organization. Also, in the case of low-confidence predictions, you would also want to have the AI-predicted information checked over by a human reviewer. For example, in the case of claims processing, if your ML system has predicted a low confidence score for a claim, you would want to reject or approve the claim based on a human review. This working of humans and AI/ML together builds trust with the process and it also reduces the time to market for the overall document processing solution.

In this section, we covered why you would need to set up a human review loop with your existing document processing workflows – that is, it helps to improve accuracy and build trust with AI systems. In the next section, we will talk about some of the key benefits of using Amazon A2I when setting up HITL workflows.

Seeing the benefits of using Amazon A2I for HITL workflows

Amazon A2I is a managed service that makes it easy to build and manage human reviews with any ML application. It integrates directly with Amazon Textract and **Amazon Rekognition** to set up human workflows for use cases such as content moderation or document processing. You can also create custom workflows with any Sagemaker model. Some of the benefits of using Amazon A2I are as follows:

- It comes with 70+ UI templates to get started quickly with setting up UIs for human reviews. Check them out here: `https://github.com/aws-samples/amazon-a2i-sample-task-uis`.

- It reduces the time to market for your AI systems, as you know that there is a human backstop to catch low confidence scores.

- It provides you with options to choose a workforce. By *workforce*, we mean who is going to review the human loop tasks created. There are three choices with A2I – a private workforce, **Amazon Mechanical Turk**, and third-party vendors. Amazon Mechanical Turk is a globally districted workforce option available for you to use. In case you have sensitive data, you can onboard your own employees and use the private workforce option. In this chapter, we will show you how you can create a private workforce and use it in Amazon A2I.

We have discussed some of the benefits, now, let's deep dive into how Amazon A2I works with any AWS AI service, your custom model, or Sagemaker-deployed models through the following architecture:

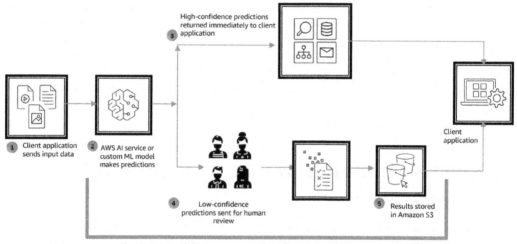

Figure 13.1 – Amazon A2I architecture

Let's understand the diagram by going through each step:

1. Your client application sends the data or documents to your AWS AI service or any custom model.

2. The AWS AI service, such as Amazon Textract, or any custom ML model, makes a prediction.

3. You create criteria or threshold conditions with your ML models to trigger an Amazon A2I human loop. In the previous architecture, the threshold is a high-confidence prediction, which is returned immediately to a client application. This threshold can be set by your business needs and use case, for example, invoices amount detected at 99% and above can be considered high confidence since it's highly critical and needs to be highly accurate. In cases where you are extracting some entity such as the location you may consider 90% as the high confidence level, below which to trigger a human review loop.

4. Low confidence predictions, which are anything below your defined threshold limit, can be sent for human review, where a human or your workforce will be presented with a UI managed by Amazon A2I. The low confidence data will be presented in that UI to the human reviewers where they review the low confidence prediction and augment, correct, or validate it.

5. The human-reviewed results are saved in Amazon S3, consisting of both what the AI predicted and what the humans augmented or modified. This data can be considered the *ground truth* and can be used to retrain the model if you are using a custom model. You can improve the accuracy of your custom models by retraining them from an augmented dataset. See the *Further reading* section for a blog reference on how you can achieve this.

From Amazon S3, your corrected or human augmented/validated AI/ML predictions can be sent to client applications.

> **Note**
>
> With Amazon Textract, you can only augment or validate your predictions. The model retraining feature is not supported yet, as Amazon Textract does not support custom models. However, with Amazon Comprehend's custom classification and the custom entity you can use Amazon A2I to retrain your custom models and improve accuracy.

In this section, we covered the benefits of using Amazon A2I and saw how it works to improve the accuracy of your AI/ML system. In the next section, we will walk you through how you can set up HITL workflows with document processing workflows using Amazon Textract and Amazon A2I.

Adding human reviews to your document processing pipelines

We covered how A2I works in general with any AWS AI service using an architecture. In this section, we will talk specifically about how Amazon A2I integrates with Amazon Textract so that you can automate your existing document workflows with a HITL. We will also show you a walkthrough on how to set up a human review workflow using the AWS Console.

Let's start by walking through how Amazon A2I works with Amazon Textract:

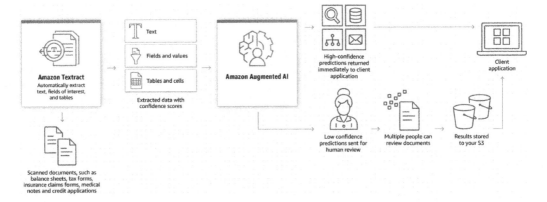

Figure 13.2 – Amazon A2I with Amazon Textract

Your scanned documents are sent to Amazon Textract. Amazon Textract extracts text, key-value pairs, and tables from the document. Now for this extracted text, key-value pairs, and tables, you also get confidence scores. You can set up a threshold that Amazon A2I triggers to create human review loops. You can set up a threshold with Amazon Textract for three things:

- For any missing keys in case of *key-value pair detection*, for example, the mailing address is an important key in a form you are reviewing and it's missing in what the AI predicted.

- You can define a threshold for predictions that can be considered high-confidence.

- You can send predictions for **Quality Assurance (QA)** auditing.

> **Note**
> Amazon Textract and Amazon A2I have a native integration in the API only for the key-value or form data extraction should you want to set up human reviews for text or tabular data detected by Amazon Textract.

You can use a custom A2I UI template and set up a loop using the `starthumanloop` A2I API rather than the Textract API. We will add examples on how you can set up a custom loop (in the *Further reading* section) when Amazon A2I starts a human loop API: `https://docs.aws.amazon.com/sagemaker/latest/dg/a2i-start-human-loop.html#a2i-instructions-starthumanloop`.

Let's go back to our fictitious company use case. This bank, LiveRight, wants to digitize its check processing system. The current system is a manual review of the check amount and date, which is time-consuming and error-prone. We will show you how LiveRight can use Amazon Textract and Amazon A2I to automate their current check processing system. We will use this sample check document:

Figure 13.3 – Sample check

We will use the check to validate the dollar value and date to make sure it's accurate before we issue it to the payee. To do this, we will walk through the following steps:

- Creating an Amazon S3 bucket
- Creating a private work team in the AWS Console
- Creating a human review workflow in the AWS Console
- Sending the document to Amazon Textract and Amazon A2I by calling the Amazon Textract API
- Completing a human review of your document in the A2I Console
- Seeing the results in your S3 bucket

So, let's get started!

Creating an Amazon S3 bucket

First, we will talk about how you can create an Amazon S3 bucket and upload the sample document for Textract A2I processing. Amazon A2I needs an Amazon S3 bucket to store the human-annotated results, as we covered in the architecture in *Figure 13.1*. We will also enable the **Cross-Origin Resource Sharing** (**CORS**) configuration needed to set up the A2I loop in this S3 bucket.

This configuration allows the A2I browser permission to download resources from this S3 bucket. To do this, follow the next steps:

1. Go to the Amazon S3 link: `https://s3.console.aws.amazon.com/s3/bucket/create?region=us-east-1`.

    Then, create a bucket with `a2i-demos` as the bucket name, using the instructions in *Chapter 2, Introducing Amazon Textract*.

2. After creating the bucket, upload the sample check from the following link to the bucket: `https://github.com/PacktPublishing/Natural-Language-Processing-with-AWS-AI-Services/blob/main/Chapter%2013/samplecheck.PNG`.

3. After uploading the sample check, go to **Amazon S3 bucket | Permissions** and scroll down to **CORS**, then copy and paste the following CORS configuration:

```
[
    {
        "AllowedHeaders": [],
        "AllowedMethods": [
            "GET"
        ],
        "AllowedOrigins": [
            "*"
        ],
        "ExposeHeaders": []
    }
]
```

Your CORS configuration should look like this:

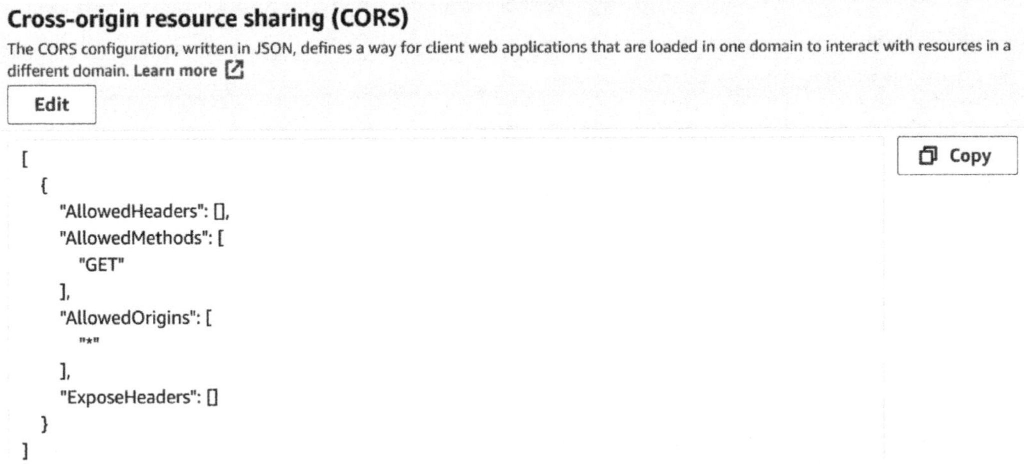

Cross-origin resource sharing (CORS)

The CORS configuration, written in JSON, defines a way for client web applications that are loaded in one domain to interact with resources in a different domain. **Learn more** ⤷

Edit   ⧉ Copy

```
[
  {
    "AllowedHeaders": [],
    "AllowedMethods": [
      "GET"
    ],
    "AllowedOrigins": [
      "*"
    ],
    "ExposeHeaders": []
  }
]
```

Figure 13.4 – CORS configuration for our S3 A2I output bucket

In this section, we covered creating an S3 bucket, uploading the sample check, and setting up the CORS configuration. Now, we will set up a private work team.

Creating a private work team in the AWS Console

In this section, we will walk you through how to create a private work team and add yourself as a worker using your email:

1. Go to the following link and choose **private**: `https://console.aws.amazon.com/sagemaker/groundtruth?region=us-east-1#/labeling-workforces`.

2. Click on **Create private team**, enter `demo-team` as team name, scroll down to **Add workers**, enter your own valid email address as the email address and your own organization in the **Organization name field**:

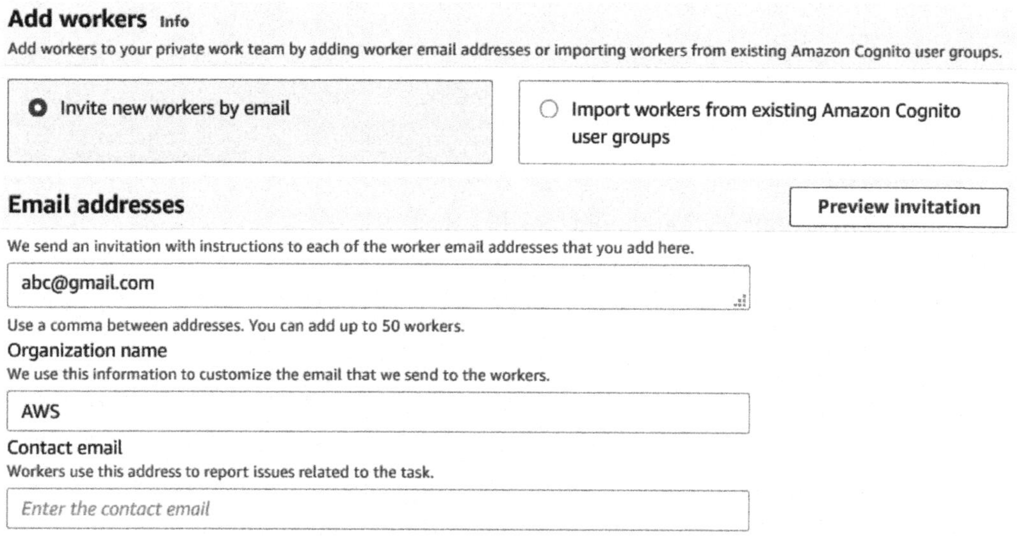

Add workers Info

Add workers to your private work team by adding worker email addresses or importing workers from existing Amazon Cognito user groups.

⦿ Invite new workers by email	◯ Import workers from existing Amazon Cognito user groups

Email addresses   Preview invitation

We send an invitation with instructions to each of the worker email addresses that you add here.

abc@gmail.com

Use a comma between addresses. You can add up to 50 workers.

Organization name

We use this information to customize the email that we send to the workers.

AWS

Contact email

Workers use this address to report issues related to the task.

Enter the contact email

Figure 13.5 – Creating private team and adding workers

3. Scroll down and click **Create private team**.

You will receive an email after adding a worker to the private team you created. This email will have a link to sign in to your A2I task UI portal, along with your username and password.

In this section, we covered how you can create a private workforce. Now, let's move on to the next section to set up a human review workflow.

Creating a human review workflow in the AWS Console

In this section, we will show you how you can create a human review workflow with Amazon Textract. You need the Amazon S3 bucket and private workforce created in previous sections, and a UI where the reviews and options ot set the threshold conditions for triggering the human review loop will appear:

1. Go to this link to create a human review workflow: `https://console.aws. amazon.com/a2i/home?region=us-east-1#/create-human-review- workflows`.

   In the **Workflow setting**s screen, enter `Textract-check` in the **Name** field. In **S3 bucket** enter the name of the bucket you created: `<s3://a2i-demos/>`. For **IAM role**, click **Create new role** and choose any S3 bucket. Your settings should look like following:

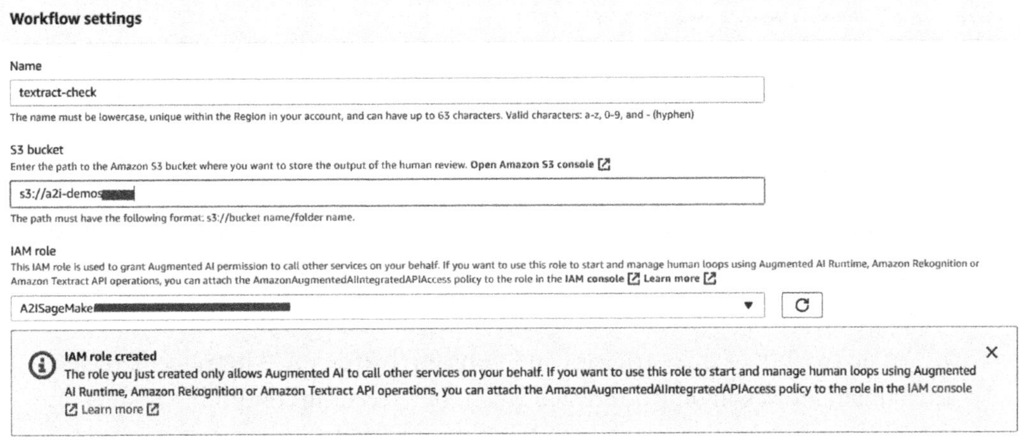

Workflow settings

Name

textract-check

The name must be lowercase, unique within the Region in your account, and can have up to 63 characters. Valid characters: a-z, 0-9, and - (hyphen)

S3 bucket
Enter the path to the Amazon S3 bucket where you want to store the output of the human review. **Open Amazon S3 console** [↗]

s3://a2i-demos▮▮▮

The path must have the following format: s3://bucket name/folder name.

IAM role
This IAM role is used to grant Augmented AI permission to call other services on your behalf. If you want to use this role to start and manage human loops using Augmented AI Runtime, Amazon Rekognition or Amazon Textract API operations, you can attach the AmazonAugmentedAIIntegratedAPIAccess policy to the role in the **IAM console** [↗] **Learn more** [↗]

A2ISageMake▮▮▮▮▮▮▮▮▮▮▮▮▮▮▮▮▮▮▮▮▮▮   ▼ | C |

ⓘ **IAM role created**   ✕
The role you just created only allows Augmented AI to call other services on your behalf. If you want to use this role to start and manage human loops using Augmented AI Runtime, Amazon Rekognition or Amazon Textract API operations, you can attach the AmazonAugmentedAIIntegratedAPIAccess policy to the role in the IAM console
[↗] Learn more [↗]

Figure 13.6 – Creating flow definition with A2I

2. Scroll down and choose **Textract-key-value pair extraction** in **Task type**.

3. For triggers to invoke the human review, you can choose at least one condition or all three. In missing **form key**, enter $ and **add key** and enter **Date**. Enter the range 0 to 90 for the confidence threshold, as shown in the following screenshot:

Amazon Textract form extraction - Conditions for invoking human review

ⓘ When Amazon Textract extracts information from a document, it returns a confidence score. You can use these confidence scores to define business conditions that trigger human review.

Identification confidence
The confidence score for key-value pairs detected within a form.

Qualification confidence
The confidence score for text contained within key and value in a form.

You can define a range for Identification confidence and Qualification confidence thresholds. A human review will be triggered when the confidence score falls within the defined range.

Learn more about using Amazon Augmented AI with Amazon Textract ⧉

☑ Trigger a human review for specific form keys based on the form key confidence score or when specific form keys are missing.
The form key and value will be sent for human review.

Key name

| $ |

Trigger human review when this form key is missing,

or when its identification confidence threshold is between 0 ⬍ and 90 ⬍

or when its qualification confidence threshold is between 0 ⬍ and 90 ⬍

| Add key |

☐ Trigger human review for all form keys identified by Amazon Textract with confidence scores in a specified range.
The form key and value will be sent for human review.

☐ Randomly send a sample of forms to humans for review.
For each form sent, all key-value pairs identified by Amazon Textract for that form will be sent for human review.

Figure 13.7 – Setting the threshold to trigger the A2I loop with Textract

4. Now, click the checkmark the second condition to review all form keys with confidence scores in a specified range and enter 0 to 90.

    We set up two out of three trigger conditions for Textract A2I to trigger a review. The human loops will only be created when the preceding conditions are met – that is, if any key is missing, such as dollar amount and date, or any form key has a confidence score less than 90%.

5. In **Worker task template creation**, enter `textract-check-ui`. This is the default UI for Textract forms with A2I integration. You can bring your own custom UI and add it with APIs, which we will cover in the next chapter.

6. In **Worker task template design**, enter `label the data`.

7. Scroll down to **Workers** and choose **Private**, then click on the **Private** team you just created:

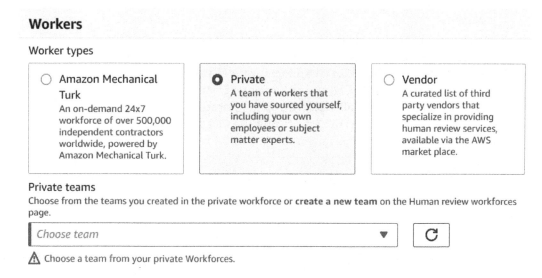

Figure 13.8 – Choosing your private team in the human review workflow setup

8.   Click **Create**. This will create a human flow definition. Copy the ARN of this flow definition, which we will use to invoke the human loop in the Textract API when the conditions defined in this flow definition are met.

In this section, we showed how you can create a flow definition for the human review loop. In the next section, we will show you how you can trigger this flow definition in the Textract Analyze document API while passing documents.

Sending the document to Amazon Textract and Amazon A2I by calling the Amazon Textract API

In this section, we will show you how you can trigger the A2I flow definition you just created in the Textract Analyze document API with forms.

If you have not done so in the previous chapters, you will first have to create an **Amazon SageMaker Jupyter Notebook** and set up **Identity and Access Management (IAM)** permissions for that notebook role to access the AWS services we will use in this notebook. After that, you will need to clone the GitHub repository (`https://github.com/PacktPublishing/Natural-Language-Processing-with-AWS-AI-Services`), go to the `Chapter 13` folder, and open the `chapter13 Improving accuracy of document processing .ipynb` notebook:

> **Note**
> Make sure the IAM role in the notebook has permissions for
> **AmazonTextractFullAccess** (https://console.aws.amazon.
> com/iam/home?#/policies/arn:aws:iam::aws:policy/
> AmazonTextractFullAccess$jsonEditor) and
> **AmazonAugmentedAIFullAccess** (https://console.aws.amazon.
> com/iam/home?#/policies/arn%3Aaws%3Aiam%3A%3Aaws%
> 3Apolicy%2FAmazonAugmentedAIFullAccess).

1. To get started, go to this notebook and enter the S3 bucket name you created in the following notebook cell:

```
bucket="<your s3 bucket name>"
```

2. In humanLoopConfig, paste the flow definition ARN copied from the previous setup:

```
humanLoopConfig = {
    'FlowDefinitionArn':"<enter flow definition arn
created> ",
    'HumanLoopName':"textract-10",
    'DataAttributes': { 'ContentClassifiers': [
'FreeOfPersonallyIdentifiableInformation' ]}
}
```

3. Run the following notebook cell to start the HITL configuration with the A2I Analyze document API by passing the humanloopconfig json, which has the flow definition we created in the console:

```
response = textract.analyze_document(
        Document={'S3Object': {'Bucket': bucket,'Name':
"samplecheck.PNG"}},
        FeatureTypes=["FORMS"],
        HumanLoopConfig=humanLoopConfig
    )
```

4. After running this command, you will get a response that has **HumanLoopActivationConditionsEvaluationResults** in the Textract response, as shown in the following screenshot:

```
print(response)

tionships': [{'Type': 'VALUE', 'Ids': ['9f84a49c-210e-4371-8832-3959dcf0ef50']}, {'Type': 'CHILD', 'Ids': ['6d365fd
2-e381-48a5-8eeb-60b82b61272c']}], 'EntityTypes': ['KEY']}, {'BlockType': 'KEY_VALUE_SET', 'Confidence': 77.0, 'Geo
metry': {'BoundingBox': {'Width': 0.5739195346832275, 'Height': 0.06345107406377792, 'Left': 0.044734030961990356,
'Top': 0.5416923761367798}, 'Polygon': [{'X': 0.044734030961990356, 'Y': 0.5416923761367798}, {'X': 0.6186535954475
403, 'Y': 0.5416923761367798}, {'X': 0.6186535954475403, 'Y': 0.6051434278488159}, {'X': 0.044734030961990356, 'Y':
0.6051434278488159}]}, 'Id': '9f84a49c-210e-4371-8832-3959dcf0ef50', 'Relationships': [{'Type': 'CHILD', 'Ids': ['8
2b39d45-6779-4099-ac4f-2a6d55e8bc2d', 'cf4510f9-6cfd-413b-8898-ee00ff209f1e', '144192d5-a534-4aad-aa56-ab14391b231d
', 'bf27afd9-7163-4a8e-9505-6a9b70e0c2ec', '378cbde0-47e4-4e2b-9b18-9285ef364c93', '703cee3c-47dd-43cf-b0c2-8d90302
6fca4', '3e7ef823-ecfc-48f6-98fa-a0a338f00837']}], 'EntityTypes': ['VALUE']}], 'HumanLoopActivationOutput': {'Human
LoopArn': 'arn:aws:sagemaker:us-east-1:186389221476:human-loop/textract-10', 'HumanLoopActivationReasons': ['Condit
ionsEvaluation'], 'HumanLoopActivationConditionsEvaluationResults': '{"Conditions":[{"And":[{"ConditionType":"Impor
tantFormKeyConfidenceCheck","ConditionParameters":{"ImportantFormKey":"*","ImportantFormKeyAliases":[],"KeyValueBlo
ckConfidenceLessThan":99.0,"WordBlockConfidenceLessThan":99.0},"EvaluationResult":true},{"ConditionType":"Important
FormKeyConfidenceCheck","ConditionParameters":{"ImportantFormKey":"*","ImportantFormKeyAliases":[],"KeyValueBlockCo
nfidenceGreaterThan":0.0,"WordBlockConfidenceGreaterThan":0.0},"EvaluationResult":true}],"EvaluationResult":tru
e}]}'}, 'AnalyzeDocumentModelVersion': '1.0', 'ResponseMetadata': {'RequestId': '67ae6246-bcb1-4ef2-89d4-2c4cb2890d
88', 'HTTPStatusCode': 200, 'HTTPHeaders': {'x-amzn-requestid': '67ae6246-bcb1-4ef2-89d4-2c4cb2890d88', 'content-ty
pe': 'application/x-amz-json-1.1', 'content-length': '38256', 'date': 'Sun, 18 Jul 2021 18:00:41 GMT'}, 'RetryAttem
pts': 0}}
```

Figure 13.9 – Output of the JSON response of Textract Analyze document API with A2I settings

5. Go to the private workteam you created: `https://console.aws.amazon.com/sagemaker/groundtruth?region=us-east-1#/labeling-workforces`

   Copy the workteam ARN and paste it in the notebook cell as follows:

   ```
   WORKTEAM_ARN= "enter your private workteam arn"
   ```

6. Run the following code block to navigate to your workteam or A2I Console:

   ```
   workteamName = WORKTEAM_ARN[WORKTEAM_ARN.rfind('/') + 1:]
   ```

7. You will get a link. Click on the link and sign in with the username and password you received when creating a worker team with your email ID. You will see your A2I tasks, as shown in the following screenshot. Click on **Start working**:

Figure 13.10 – Amazon A2I Console screen with worker tasks

8. You will be redirected to the task created when the Textract A2I loop was invoked:

Figure 13.11 – A2I Console with Textract-detected key-values from sample check

9. You are shown the original sample check on the left side of this UI portal and the extracted key-value pair on the right. Feel free to validate the data and enter the changes if needed. Make sure the **$** amount and date are correct and click **Submit**. You can see that the Textract-detected output is mapped to the original document (bounding box mapping) when you click on a specific key-value:

Figure 13.12 – Reviewing and correcting the Textract response in the A2I Console

10. After augmenting and validating the values and clicking **Submit**, your output is saved in the same S3 bucket you created. Run the following notebook cell to get the JSON results from S3 and see the annotated results:

```
for resp in completed_human_loops:
    splitted_string = re.split('s3://' + bucket  + '/',
resp['HumanLoopOutput']['OutputS3Uri'])
    output_bucket_key = splitted_string[1]
    print(output_bucket_key)
    response = s3.get_object(Bucket= bucket, Key=output_
bucket_key)
    content = response["Body"].read()
    json_output = json.loads(content)
    pp.pprint(json_output)
    print('\n')
```

You will get the output with the human-annotated answers in the following screenshot:

```
textarct-check/2021/07/18/23/29/16/7ecedc0b-d80c-4918-acfc-3b53e3b09326/output.json
{   'awsManagedHumanLoopRequestSource': 'AWS/Textract/AnalyzeDocument/Forms/V1',
    'flowDefinitionArn': 'arn:aws:sagemaker:us-east-1:▓▓▓▓▓▓▓▓▓:flow-definition/textarct-check',
    'humanAnswers': [   {   'acceptanceTime': '2021-07-18T23:30:47.742Z',
                            'answerContent': {   'AWS/Textract/AnalyzeDocument/Forms/V1': {   'blocks': [   {   'bl
ockType': 'WORD',
                                                                                                               'id
': '242eb680-49a8-4262-bc06-4493934af2e2',
                                                                                                               'te
xt': 'THE'},
                                                                                                           {   'bl
ockType': 'KEY_VALUE_SET',
                                                                                                               'co
nfidence': 77,
                                                                                                               'en
tityTypes': [   'KEY'],
                                                                                                               'id
': '74bc7b7c-88fe-4430-9997-94018fb6974a',
                                                                                                               're
```

Figure 13.13 – Human-corrected A2I JSON output

In this section, we gave you a notebook walkthrough of invoking the Textract Analyze document API with a HITL following definition configuration for key-value pair or Forms detection.

Summary

In this chapter, we covered how you can improve the accuracy of your current document processing workflows when using Amazon Textract for automating these document workflows. We introduced Amazon A2I and how it can help improve the accuracy of your text predictions and can be integrated with Amazon Textract to set up a human review workflow. We also discussed how A2I can be used for model retraining with custom models to improve accuracy, which we will cover in the next chapter.

To further demonstrate how A2I works in action, we have also provided a 10-minute **YouTube** video tutorial by one of the authors cited in the *Further reading* section.

Further reading

- *Using Amazon Textract with Amazon A2I for processing critical documents* by Anuj Gupta, Talia Chopra, and Pranav Sachdeva: https://aws.amazon.com/blogs/machine-learning/using-amazon-textract-with-amazon-augmented-ai-for-processing-critical-documents//

- *Learn how to add human reviews to your document processing pipelines* by Mona Mona: https://www.youtube.com/watch?v=U2J_pq17POA

14
Auditing Named Entity Recognition Workflows

In the previous chapter, we were introduced to an approach for improving the accuracy of the results we wanted to extract from documents using **Amazon Augmented AI** (**Amazon A2I**). We saw that Amazon A2I can be added to a document processing workflow to review model prediction accuracy. This enabled us to include human reviews in LiveRight's check processing system.

In this chapter, we will walk through an extension of the previous approach by including **Amazon Comprehend** for text-based insights thereby demonstrating an end-to-end process for setting up an auditing workflow for your custom named entity recognition use cases. We put together this solution based on our collective experience and the usage trends we have observed in our careers. We expect to be hands-on throughout the course of this chapter, but we have all the code samples we need to get going.

With **machine learning (ML)**, companies can set up automated document processing solutions that can be trained to recognize and extract custom entities from your documents. This helps you derive unique insights from your text corpus. These insights can help drive strategic decisions. However, there are certain challenges that need to be navigated first. Typically, companies receive large volumes of incoming documents of different templates, with varying contents, in multiple languages. Also, as businesses grow, the type and volume of documents evolve, and very soon you get into a maintenance overhead situation trying to keep the various templates, formats, and rules synchronized with how you are trying to use these documents for your operational needs. Furthermore, you will have to ensure your infrastructure is able to scale to support your processing needs.

To solve these challenges, we will show you how you can use the ready-made ML capabilities of **Amazon Textract**, leveraging transfer learning to create a custom entity recognition model with **Amazon Comprehend**, and auditing the predictions with a human reviewer loop using A2I. We introduced Amazon A2I in detail in *Chapter 13, Improving the Accuracy of Document Processing Workflows*. In this chapter, we will navigate through the following sections:

- Authenticating loan applications
- Building the loan authentication solution

Technical requirements

For this chapter, you will need access to an **AWS account** at https://aws.amazon. com/console/. Please refer to the *Signing up for an AWS account* subsection within the *Setting up your AWS environment* section in *Chapter 2, Introducing Amazon Textract,* for detailed instructions on how you can sign up for an AWS account and sign in to the **AWS Management Console**.

The **Python** code and sample datasets for the solution discussed in this chapter can be found at the following link: https://github.com/PacktPublishing/Natural-Language-Processing-with-AWS-AI-Services/tree/main/Chapter%20 14.

Check out the following video to see the Code in Action at https://bit. ly/3GoBh1B.

Authenticating loan applications

Financial organizations receive significant volumes of loan applications every day. While the major organizations have switched to fully digital processing, there are still many banks and institutions across the world that rely on paper documents. To illustrate our example, let's go back to our fictitious banking corporation, *LiveRight Holdings Private Limited*, and review the requirements for this use case:

- LiveRight offers a number of lending products to its customers, which are primarily small-to-medium businesses and individual consumers. To apply for a loan, consumers fill out a paper-based loan/mortgage application form that is validated by a team of experts to determine the authenticity of the application (called the *authenticity-check* process). If found to be a valid applicant, LiveRight's loan processors will request supporting documentation from the consumers for pre-approval qualification.

- LiveRight receives anywhere from 8,000 to 10,000 loan applications a day from potential customers. These applications are forwarded nightly from its various branches to the document inlet center at the company's **headquarters (HQ)**. Today, their authenticity-check process takes approximately 2 to 4 weeks for the team to scan all the applications and determine whether they are good enough to be forwarded to the loan processors, causing significant delays even at the pre-approval stage. This has irked many customers who are taking their business elsewhere. LiveRight has hired you to automate the authenticity-check process with a target to reduce the processing time to 24 hours within the first 3 months of the solution being implemented.

As the enterprise architect for the project, you decide to use Amazon Textract to leverage its pre-trained ML model for text extraction, the **Custom Entity Recognizer** feature of Amazon Comprehend to incrementally create your own entity recognizer for loan application checks without the need to build complex **natural language processing (NLP)** algorithms, and A2I to set up a human review workflow to monitor predictions from your entity recognizer and send feedback to the recognizer to improve its detection capabilities for entities unique to the use case.

You plan to have the private human workflow available for the first 2 to 3 months and subsequently disable it, at which point the document processing workflow will become fully automated. As the human team checks and updates the entity labels, you need to determine the authenticity check decision to be either *APPROVE*, *SUMMARY APPROVE*, or *REJECT*. This decision, along with the relevant content from the loan application, should be stored in an **Amazon DynamoDB** (a fully managed, low-latency **NoSQL** database service) table for loan processors to access the content and enable pre-approval qualification. The components of the solution we will build are shown in the following figure:

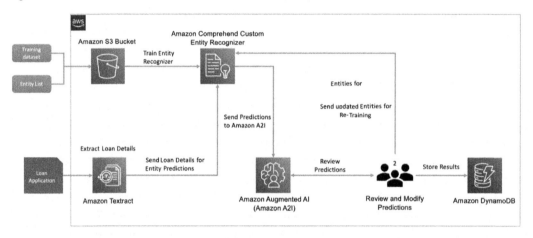

Figure 14.1 – Loan approval document processing solution architecture

We will be walking through our solution using an **Amazon SageMaker Jupyter notebook** that will allow us to review the code and results as we execute it step by step. The solution build includes the following tasks:

1. As a first step, we will create an Amazon Comprehend custom entity recognizer based on the training dataset provided in our GitHub repository.

2. We will then create a private labeling workforce and add a team member who will be responsible for reviewing predictions from the Amazon Comprehend custom entity recognizer, using the Amazon A2I service. We will create the private workforce using the *labeling* workforces feature available in the Amazon SageMaker console. For more details, please refer to this link: `https://docs.aws.amazon.com/sagemaker/latest/dg/sms-workforce-private.html`.

3. We start the solution workflow by inspecting our sample input loan application available in our GitHub repository. We display the image of the loan application in our notebook and look at the contents.

4. Next, we use Amazon Textract to extract the key-value pairs from our input document.

5. We then create an inference request string from the key-value pairs and prepare it to send to Amazon Comprehend custom entity detection.

6. Next, we set up an Amazon Comprehend real-time endpoint and invoke it to detect entities from our inference request string.

7. We will set up an Amazon A2I human review loop using the entity recognition task UI template and send the results of the custom entity detection to an Amazon A2I human loop.

8. Logging in as a private worker, we will review the detected entities and modify the labels as required.

9. We will then check whether a new entity detection event occurred or whether an existing entity detection was modified, update the entity list, and send it back to Amazon Comprehend for retraining our entity detection model.

10. Based on the output from the human loop review, we will also determine a decision for the loan application and upload this to a **DynamoDB** table for downstream processing.

Now that we've got the context for the exercise and gone over our intended process, let's start building the solution.

Building the loan authentication solution

In the previous section, we introduced the loan application approval use case, covered the architecture of the solution we will be building, and briefly walked through the solution components and workflow steps. In this section, we will get right down to action and start executing the tasks to build our solution. But first, there are pre-requisites we will have to take care of.

Setting up to solve the use case

If you have not done so in the previous chapters, you will first have to create a Jupyter notebook and set up **Identity and Access Management (IAM)** permissions for that notebook role to access the AWS services we will use in this notebook. After that, you will need to clone the GitHub repository (`https://github.com/PacktPublishing/Natural-Language-Processing-with-AWS-AI-Services`), create an **Amazon S3** bucket (`https://aws.amazon.com/s3/`), and provide the bucket name in the notebook to start execution. Please follow the next steps to complete these tasks before we can execute the cells from our notebook:

> **Note:**
> Please ensure you have completed the tasks mentioned in the *Technical requirements* section.

1. To create your Jupyter Notebook instance, follow the instructions in the *Create an Amazon SageMaker Jupyter Notebook instance* section in the *Setting up your AWS environment* section in *Chapter 2, Introducing Amazon Textract*.

   > **IAM role permissions while creating Amazon SageMaker Jupyter notebooks**
   > Accept the default for the IAM role at the notebook creation time to allow access to any S3 bucket.

2. Once you create the notebook instance and its status is **InService**, click on **Open Jupyter** in the **Actions** menu, heading for the notebook instance.

3. This will take you to the **home** folder of your notebook instance.

4. Click on **New** and select **Terminal**.

5. In the **Terminal window**, first, type cd SageMaker, and then, type git clone `https://github.com/PacktPublishing/Natural-Language-Processing-with-AWS-AI-Services`.

6. Now, exit the Terminal window and go back to the **home** folder, and you will see a folder called Natural-Language-Processing-with-AWS-AI-Services. Click this folder to bring up the chapter folders and click Chapter 14. Open this folder by clicking. You should see a notebook called chapter14-auditing-workflows-named-entity-detection-forGitHub.ipynb.

7. Open this notebook by clicking it.

Follow through the steps in this notebook that correspond to the next few subheadings in this section by executing one cell at a time. Please do read the descriptions provided preceding each notebook cell.

Additional IAM pre-requisites

To train the Comprehend custom entity recognizer, to set up real-time endpoints, we have to enable additional policies and also update the trust relationships for our SageMaker notebook role. Please refer to *Changing IAM permissions and trust relationships for the Amazon SageMaker Notebook execution role* in the *Setting up your AWS environment* section in *Chapter 2, Introducing Amazon Textract,* for more detailed instructions on how to execute the following steps:

1. Please attach `TextractFullAccess`, `ComprehendFullAccess`, and `AmazonAugmentedAIFullAccess` policies to your Amazon SageMaker Notebook IAM role.

2. Add an `IAM:PassRole` permission as an inline policy to your SageMaker Notebook execution role:

```
{ "Version": "2012-10-17", "Statement": [ {
  "Action": [
      "iam:PassRole"
  ],
  "Effect": "Allow",
  "Resource": "<your sagemaker notebook execution role
ARN">
   }
  ]
}
```

3. Finally, update the trust relationships:

```
{ "Version": "2012-10-17", "Statement": [
  { "Effect": "Allow",
   "Principal":
    { "Service":
      [ "sagemaker.amazonaws.com",
        "s3.amazonaws.com",
        "comprehend.amazonaws.com" ]
    },
```

```
        "Action": "sts:AssumeRole" }
    ]
}
```

Now that we have set up our notebook and set up the IAM role to run the walkthrough notebook, in the next section, we will train an Amazon Comprehend entity recognizer.

Training an Amazon Comprehend custom entity recognizer

Let's begin by training a custom entity recognizer to detect entities unique to this solution. Amazon Comprehend offers pre-trained entity recognition features that we learned about in the previous chapter. For this solution, we will use the **Custom Entity Recognition** feature of Amazon Comprehend that allows you to train a recognizer for custom needs using incremental training. All we have to do is provide a list of entities we want it to recognize, and a raw dataset containing the lines of text comprising the context that will be detected as entities. Open the notebook and execute the steps as follows:

1. Execute the cell under **Step 0 – Import Libraries** to ensure we have the libraries we need for the notebook. Note that in this cell you are getting the Amazon SageMaker execution role for the notebook, along with the SageMaker session. Please ensure you create an Amazon S3 bucket (https://docs.aws.amazon.com/AmazonS3/latest/userguide/create-bucket-overview.html) and provide the bucket name in the following line:

    ```
    bucket = '<bucket-name>'
    ```

2. Execute the cells under **Step 1 – Train an Amazon Comprehend Custom Entity Recognizer**:

    a) First, initialize the boto3 handle for Amazon Comprehend:

    ```
    comprehend = boto3.client('comprehend')
    ```

    b) Then, define the variables for the S3 prefixes and upload the training dataset and the entity list to the S3 bucket:

    ```
    s3_raw_key = prefix + "/train/raw_txt.csv"
    s3_entity_key = prefix + "/train/entitylist.csv"
    s3.upload_file('train/raw_txt.csv',bucket,s3_raw_key)
    s3.upload_file('train/entitylist.csv',bucket,s3_entity_key)
    ```

c) Continue executing the rest of the cells in the notebook to declare the variables with the full S3 **URIs** for our input documents, define the input object for the entity recognizer, and finally, call the Comprehend API to create the custom entity recognizer. This will start the training job:

```
import datetime
cer_name = "loan-app-recognizer"+str(datetime.datetime.
now().strftime("%s"))
cer_response = comprehend.create_entity_recognizer(
        RecognizerName = cer_name,
        DataAccessRoleArn = role,
        InputDataConfig = cer_input_object,
        LanguageCode = "en"
)
```

d) Print the results of the custom entity recognizer training job:

```
import pprint
pp = pprint.PrettyPrinter(indent=4)
response = comprehend.describe_entity_recognizer(
    EntityRecognizerArn=cer_
response['EntityRecognizerArn']
)
pp.pprint(response)
```

3. Check the status of the training job periodically by visiting the Amazon Comprehend AWS console (https://console.aws.amazon.com/ comprehend/v2/home?region=us-east-1#entity-recognition). The training should take approximately 15 to 30 minutes. Time for a coffee/snack break.

Creating a private team for the human loop

Refer to *Step 2* in the notebook (https://github.com/PacktPublishing/ Natural-Language-Processing-with-AWS-AI-Services/blob/main/ Chapter%2014/chapter14-auditing-workflows-named-entity- detection-forGitHub.ipynb) for the instructions we will execute now.

In this step, we will create a private team using the Amazon SageMaker labeling workforce console, and we will add ourselves to the private team as a worker. This is required so we can log in to the labeling task UI when we reach the Amazon A2I step in this solution. Please execute the following tasks:

1. Log in to the AWS Management Console if not already done (please refer to the *Technical requirements* section at the start of this chapter for more details), type `amazon sagemaker` in the **Services** search bar, and go to the Amazon SageMaker console. Once there, on the left of the UI, click on **Ground Truth** and then **Labeling workforces**. On this screen, select **Private** from the tab at the top and click on **Create private team**.

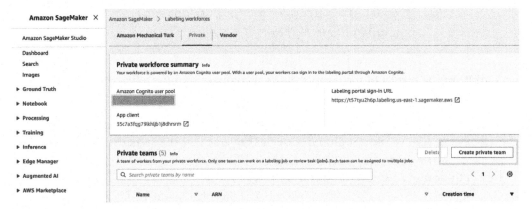

Figure 14.2 – SageMaker labeling workforces

2. Enter a name for your private team in the **Team name** field and leave the default selection of **Create a new Amazon Cognito user group** in the **Add workers** section. Scroll down and click **Create private team**.

3. You will now be returned to the **Labeling workforces** screen. The private team, `nlp-doc-team`, should be visible under **Private teams**. Next to that, you will see an ARN, which is a long string that looks like `arn:aws:sagemaker:region-name-123456:workteam/private-crowd/team-name`. Please copy the ARN from the screen and provide this in the notebook cell:

```
WORKTEAM_ARN= '<workteam-arn>'
```

4. Next, scroll down in the previous screen, go to the **Workers** section, and click on **Invite new workers**. Provide your email address and click **Invite new workers**. You will receive an email from `no-reply@verificationemail.com`. Follow the instructions to complete the sign-up process.

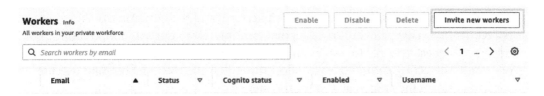

Figure 14.3 – Inviting new workers

5. Now, add yourself to the private team by clicking on **nlp-doc-team** and then clicking on **Add workers to team**. Select your email address from the list and click on **Add workers to team**.

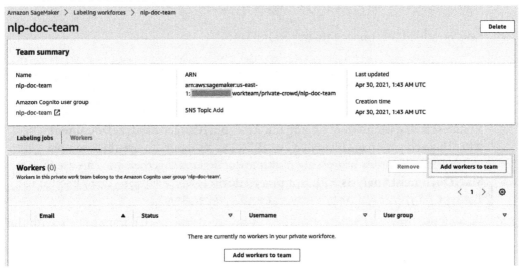

Figure 14.4 – Adding workers to team

Now that we have added the private team, let's review our loan application by extracting the contents using Amazon Textract.

Extracting sample document contents using Amazon Textract

This section corresponds to *Step 3* in the notebook: `https://github.com/PacktPublishing/Natural-Language-Processing-with-AWS-AI-Services/blob/main/Chapter%2014/chapter14-auditing-workflows-named-entity-detection-forGitHub.ipynb`.

In this step, we will review the sample loan application, and then use Amazon Textract to extract the key-value pairs or form data that is of interest to our solution, creating an inference request CSV file to pass as an input to our Comprehend custom entity recognizer for detecting entities. Please follow through using the notebook and execute the cells to perform the tasks required for this step:

1. Review the input document by executing the code in the notebook cell, as shown here:

    ```
    documentName = "input/sample-loan-application.png"
    display(Image(filename=documentName))
    ```

2. Let's now load this image into our S3 bucket:

    ```
    s3.upload_
    file(documentName,bucket,prefix+'/'+documentName)
    ```

3. We will extract the key-value pair data from this document to transform and create a request string for inference using the Amazon Textract **AnalyzeDocument** API. This accepts image files (PNG or JPEG) as an input. To use this example with a PDF file, or for processing multiple documents together, you can use the **StartDocumentAnalysis** API: https://docs.aws.amazon.com/textract/latest/dg/API_StartDocumentAnalysis.html.

4. We will use the amazon-textract-response-parser library to help with the JSON response from Textract. Install it by typing the following:

    ```
    !pip install amazon-textract-response-parser
    ```

5. Now, let's use the Textract boto3 Python SDK to retrieve the contents of the document, as shown here:

    ```
    textract = boto3.client('textract')
    response = textract.analyze_document(Document={'S3Object':
    {
                'Bucket': bucket,
                'Name': prefix+'/'+documentName
            }}, FeatureTypes=['FORMS'])
    ```

6. We will now extract the key-value pairs we need for our solution. We will not use the checkbox fields but only those fields with values in them. Also, we will filter out the fields that we actually need in the next few steps:

```
from trp import Document
doc = Document(response)
df = pd.DataFrame()
# Iterate over elements in the document
x = 0
for page in doc.pages:
    for field in page.form.fields:
        if field.key is not None and field.value is not
None:
            if field.value.text not in ('SELECTED','NOT_
SELECTED'):
                df.at[x,'key'] = field.key.text
                df.at[x,'value'] = field.value.text
                x+=1
df
```

7. Now that we have loaded the results from Textract into a **pandas DataFrame** (https://pandas.pydata.org/docs/reference/api/pandas.DataFrame.html), we will run a series of operations to filter the columns we are interested in from the loan application. Execute all the cells under the *Extract contents for sending to Comprehend CER* section in the notebook. We should see the final filtered list of fields as follows:

key	Cell Phone	Name	Years	Social Security Number	Country	Date of Birth	TOTAL $
0	(555) 0200 1234	Kwaku Mensah	18	123 - 45 - 6789	US	01 / 01 / 1953	8000.00/month

Figure 14.5 – Finalized list of fields we will use for Comprehend entity recognition

Now, let's cover detecting entities using the Amazon Comprehend custom entity recognizer.

Detecting entities using the Amazon Comprehend custom entity recognizer

Now that we have what we need from the loan application, let's construct a string that will become our inference request to the Comprehend custom entity recognizer we trained at the beginning of this walkthrough (*Step 1* in the notebook). Before we can detect the entities, we need to create a real-time endpoint and associate that with our entity recognizer. When you deploy this solution in batch mode or use it for processing multiple documents, you will use the Amazon Comprehend **StartEntitiesDetection** API: https://docs.aws.amazon.com/comprehend/latest/dg/API_StartEntitiesDetectionJob.html.

Please follow the instructions in this section by executing the cells in *Step 4* in the notebook: https://github.com/PacktPublishing/Natural-Language-Processing-with-AWS-AI-Services/blob/main/Chapter%2014/chapter14-auditing-workflows-named-entity-detection-forGitHub.ipynb:

1. We will now create a request string that will be sent to the Amazon Comprehend custom entity recognizer model to detect the entities we trained it on. This string comprises data that we extracted from our loan application document using Amazon Textract in the previous step. We will transpose our pandas DataFrame, add a document number column, and use it to prepare the inference request string:

    ```python
    df_T.columns = df_T.columns.str.rstrip()
    df_T['doc'] = 1
    df_T
    for idx, row in df_T.iterrows():
            entry = 'Country'+':'+str(row['Country']).
    strip()+" "+'Years'+':'+str(row['Years']).strip()+"
    "+'Cell Phone'+':'+str(row['Cell Phone']).strip()+"
    "+'Name'+':'+str(row['Name']).strip()+" "+'Social
    Security Number'+':'+str(row['Social Security Number']).
    strip()+" "+'TOTAL $'+':'+str(row['TOTAL $']).strip()+"
    "+'Date of Birth'+':'+str(row['Date of Birth']).strip()
    ```

2. Next, let's create a real-time endpoint for Comprehend:

    ```python
    custom_recognizer_arn=cer_response['EntityRecognizerArn']
    endpoint_response = comprehend.create_endpoint(
        EndpointName='nlp-chapter4-cer-endpoint',
        ModelArn=custom_recognizer_arn,
    ```

```
        DesiredInferenceUnits=2,
        DataAccessRoleArn=role
    )
endpoint_response['EndpointArn']
```

3. We see the endpoint Arn printed as follows:

```
arn:aws:comprehend:us-east-1:<aws-account-nr>:entity-
recognizer-endpoint/nlp-chapter4-cer-endpoint
```

4. Check the status of the endpoint by navigating to the **Amazon Comprehend** console, go to **custom entity recognition** in the left menu, click on your recognizer, and scroll down to verify your real-time endpoint has been created successfully. If the endpoint is not active, the code in the next cell in the notebook will fail. It may take about *15 minutes* for the endpoint to be ready:

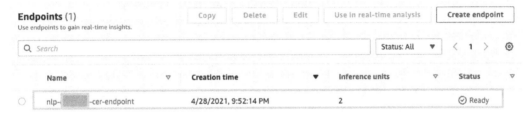

Figure 14.6 – Waiting for an endpoint to be ready

5. When the endpoint is **Ready**, execute the code in the notebook cell to send the inference request to the custom entity recognizer, as shown here:

```
response = comprehend.detect_entities(Text=entry,
                    LanguageCode='en',
EndpointArn=endpoint_response['EndpointArn']
            )
print(response)
```

6. We see the output as shown in the following code block. This display shows that our Comprehend entity recognition has identified all these attributes that represent a valid person:

```
{'Entities': [{'Score': 0.9999999403953552, 'Type':
'PERSON', 'Text': 'Years:18', 'BeginOffset': 11,
'EndOffset': 19}, {'Score': 0.9999998211860657,
'Type': 'PERSON', 'Text': 'Cell Phone:(555 ) 0200
1234', 'BeginOffset': 20, 'EndOffset': 47}, {'Score':
```

```
1.0, 'Type': 'PERSON', 'Text': 'Name:Kwaku Mensah',
'BeginOffset': 48, 'EndOffset': 65}, {'Score': 1.0,
'Type': 'PERSON', 'Text': 'Social Security Number:123
- 45 - 6789', 'BeginOffset': 66, 'EndOffset': 104},
{'Score': 1.0, 'Type': 'PERSON', 'Text': 'TOTAL
$:8000.00/month', 'BeginOffset': 105, 'EndOffset':
126}, {'Score': 1.0, 'Type': 'PERSON', 'Text': 'Date of
Birth:01 / 01 / 1953', 'BeginOffset': 127, 'EndOffset':
155}], 'ResponseMetadata': {'RequestId': 'ecbd75fd-
22bc-4dca-9aa0-73f58f6784e4', 'HTTPStatusCode': 200,
'HTTPHeaders': {'x-amzn-requestid': 'ecbd75fd-22bc-4dca-
9aa0-73f58f6784e4', 'content-type': 'application/x-amz-
json-1.1', 'content-length': '620', 'date': 'Tue, 06 Jul
2021 22:26:11 GMT'}, 'RetryAttempts': 0}}
```

7. The last task in *Step 4* is to prepare a `human_loop_input` list to be used with the Amazon A2I human workflow that we will create in the next step:

```python
import json
human_loop_input = []
data = {}
ent = response['Entities']
existing_entities = []
if ent != None and len(ent) > 0:
    for entity in ent:
        current_entity = {}
        current_entity['label'] = entity['Type']
        current_entity['text'] = entity['Text']
        current_entity['startOffset'] =
entity['BeginOffset']
        current_entity['endOffset'] = entity['EndOffset']
        existing_entities.append(current_entity)
    data['ORIGINAL_TEXT'] = entry
    data['ENTITIES'] = existing_entities
    human_loop_input.append(data)
print(human_loop_input)
126}, {'label': 'PERSON', 'text': 'Date of Birth:01 / 01
/ 1953', 'startOffset': 127, 'endOffset': 155}]}]
```

In this section, we were able to detect entities with the Amazon Comprehend entity recognizer. In the next section, we will walk through how you can use Amazon A2I to review the predictions and make changes to the predicted versus actual entity.

Setting up an Amazon A2I human workflow loop

For the code blocks discussed here, refer to *Step 5* in the notebook: `https://github.com/PacktPublishing/Natural-Language-Processing-with-AWS-AI-Services/blob/main/Chapter%2014/chapter14-auditing-workflows-named-entity-detection-forGitHub.ipynb`.

Now that we have the detected entities from our Comprehend custom entity recognizer, it's time to set up a human workflow using the *private team* we created in *Step 2* and send the results to the Amazon A2I human loop for review, and any modifications/augmentation as required. Subsequently, we will update the `entitylist.csv` file that we originally used to train our Comprehend custom entity recognizer so we can prepare it for retraining based on the human feedback:

1. Let's start by initializing some variables we will need for the next few tasks:

    ```
    timestamp = time.strftime("%Y-%m-%d-%H-%M-%S", time.gmtime())
    # Amazon SageMaker client
    sagemaker = boto3.client('sagemaker')
    # Amazon Augment AI (A2I) client
    a2i = boto3.client('sagemaker-a2i-runtime')
    # Flow definition name
    flowDefinition = 'fd-nlp-chapter14-' + timestamp
    # Task UI name - this value is unique per account and
    region. You can also provide your own value here.
    taskUIName = 'ui-nlp-chapter14-' + timestamp
    # Flow definition outputs
    OUTPUT_PATH = f's3://' + bucket + '/' + prefix + '/a2i-results'
    ```

2. Now, we will create the human task UI by executing the next cell in the notebook (refer to *Step 5* in the notebook). We selected the task template for named entity recognition from the Amazon A2I Sample Task UI GitHub repository (`https://github.com/aws-samples/amazon-a2i-sample-task-uis`) and customized it for our needs.

3. Create the task UI based on the template:

```
def create_task_ui():
    '''
    Creates a Human Task UI resource.
    Returns:
    struct: HumanTaskUiArn
    '''
    response = sagemaker.create_human_task_ui(
        HumanTaskUiName=taskUIName,
        UiTemplate={'Content': template})
    return response
# Create task UI
humanTaskUiResponse = create_task_ui()
humanTaskUiArn = humanTaskUiResponse['HumanTaskUiArn']
print(humanTaskUiArn)
```

4. We get the output as shown:

```
arn:aws:sagemaker:us-east-1:<aws-account-nr>:human-
task-ui/ui-nlp-chapter14-<timestamp>
```

5. Execute the next couple of cells in the notebook to create the **Amazon A2I flow definition** that manages the orchestration of tasks to workforces and the collection of the output data. We are now ready to start the human workflow loop. Execute the next code block in the notebook to start the human loop.

6. Check the status of your human loop by executing the code block in the next cell in the notebook – it should be InProgress:

```
completed_human_loops = []
a2i_resp = a2i.describe_human_
loop(HumanLoopName=humanLoopName)
print(f'HumanLoop Name: {humanLoopName}')
print(f'HumanLoop Status: {a2i_resp["HumanLoopStatus"]}')
print(f'HumanLoop Output Destination: {a2i_
resp["HumanLoopOutput"]}')
print('\n')
if a2i_resp["HumanLoopStatus"] == "Completed":
    completed_human_loops.append(resp)
```

7. We get the output as shown:

```
HumanLoop Name: 0fe076a4-b6eb-49ea-83bf-78f953a71c89
HumanLoop Status: InProgress
HumanLoop Output Destination: {'OutputS3Uri': 's3://<your-
bucket-name>/chapter4/a2i-results/fd-nlp-chapter4-2021-
07-06-22-32-21/2021/07/06/22/33/08/<hashnr>/output.json'
```

In the next section, we will walk through how your private reviewers can log in to the console and review the entities detected by Amazon Comprehend.

Reviewing and modifying detected entities

Now, we will log in to the **Amazon A2I Task UI** to review, change, and re-label the detected entities from our Comprehend custom entity recognizer. Execute the cells in the notebook based on the instructions discussed in this sectio:.

1. Let's log in to the worker portal to review the predictions and modify them as required. Execute the following code to get the URL to our Task UI:

```
workteamName = WORKTEAM_ARN[WORKTEAM_ARN.rfind('/') + 1:]
print("Navigate to the private worker portal and do
the tasks. Make sure you've invited yourself to your
workteam!")
print('https://' + sagemaker.describe_
workteam(WorkteamName=workteamName)['Workteam']
['SubDomain'])
```

2. Once you log in you will see a **LOAN APPLICATION REVIEW** task. Select it and click on **Start working**:

Figure 14.7 – Amazon A2I task list

3. You should see the Amazon A2I labeling UI with the list of entities detected by Comprehend custom entity recognition highlighted along with the labels, as shown in the following screenshot:

Figure 14.8 – Amazon A2I labeling UI ready for human review

4. Now, select the **GHOST** label from the labels on the right then assign this to the unlabeled **Country:US** entry in the UI and click **Submit**.

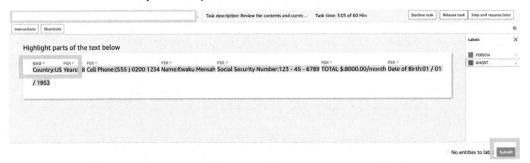

Figure 14.9 – Adding/modifying labels to the detected entities and clicking Submit

5. Continue executing the cells in the notebook to check the status of the human loop again (this should show a status of **Completed**) and print the Amazon A2I output JSON object. If there is a difference in entities, we will update the `entitylist.csv` file and trigger a retraining of our Comprehend custom entity recognizer. Let's verify whether new entities are present:

```
retrain='N'
el = open('train/entitylist.csv','r').read()
for annotated_entity in a2i_entities:
    if original_text[annotated_
entity['startOffset']:annotated_entity['endOffset']] not
in el:
        retrain='Y'
        word = '\n'+original_text[annotated_
entity['startOffset']:annotated_
```

```
entity['endOffset']]+','+annotated_entity['label'].
upper()
        print("Updating Entity List with: " + word)
        open('train/entitylist.csv','a').write(word)
if retrain == 'Y':
    print("Entity list updated, model to be retrained")
```

6. We see the output as shown in the following code block. Though Comprehend detected Years and Cell Phone to be a PERSON entity, it was not present in the original entitylist.csv file, and so it will be updated with these values and the Comprehend entity recognition will be re-trained:

```
Updating Entity List with:
Country:US,GHOST
Updating Entity List with:
Years:18,PERSON
Updating Entity List with:
Cell Phone:(555 ) 0200 1234,PERSON
Entity list updated, model to be retrained
```

This response is saved automatically in the Amazon S3 bucket JSON file in the form of labels. In the next section, we will use these modified or reviewed labels to retrain our custom entity recognizer model.

Retraining Comprehend custom entity recognizer

We will now retrain our Comprehend custom entity recognizer. The cells to be executed are similar to what we did when we originally trained our recognizer:

1. Execute the cells in *Step 7* of the notebook: https://github.com/PacktPublishing/Natural-Language-Processing-with-AWS-AI-Services/blob/main/Chapter%2014/chapter14-auditing-workflows-named-entity-detection-forGitHub.ipynb.

   After declaring variables, we execute the following code block to start the training:

```
Import datetime
cer_name = "retrain-loan-recognizer"+str(datetime.
datetime.now().strftime("%s"))
cer_response = comprehend.create_entity_recognizer(
        RecognizerName = cer_name,
        DataAccessRoleArn = role,
```

```
            InputDataConfig = cer_input_object,
            LanguageCode = "en"
)
```

2. We see the output shown that indicates the retraining job has been submitted. The metadata has been removed from the response for clarity:

```
{    'EntityRecognizerProperties': {
'DataAccessRoleArn': 'arn:aws:iam::<aws-account-nr>:role/
service-role/<execution-role>',

'EntityRecognizerArn': 'arn:aws:comprehend:us-east-
1:<aws-account-nr>:entity-recognizer/retrain-loan-
recognizer1625612436',
                                        'InputDataConfig':
{    'DataFormat': 'COMPREHEND_CSV',

'Documents': {    'S3Uri': 's3://<s3-bucket>/chapter4/
train/raw_txt.csv'},

'EntityList': {    'S3Uri': 's3://<s3-bucket>/chapter4/
train/entitylist.csv'},

'EntityTypes': [    {    'Type': 'PERSON'},

{    'Type': 'GHOST'}]},
                                        'LanguageCode':
'en',
                                        'Status':
'SUBMITTED',
                                        'SubmitTime':
datetime.datetime(2021, 7, 6, 23, 0, 36, 759000,
tzinfo=tzlocal())}}
```

3. As before, go to the Amazon Comprehend console to check the status of the entity recognizer, and verify that the status has changed to **Trained**.

4. Please repeat *Steps 3* to *5* from the notebook to test the newly retrained recognizer.

Let's now execute the steps to store the results of the authentication check for access by applications downstream.

Storing decisions for downstream processing

Now we understand how to set up an auditing workflow, let's execute the steps needed to persist the results from our entity detection so we can send them to a downstream application. If the majority or all of the entities are of the GHOST type, we will send a *rejection* decision, if the majority is of the PERSON type, we will send a *summary approval*, if all of them are PERSON, we will send *approval*, and if they are evenly distributed, we will send a *rejection* decisio:.

1. First, let's check how many entities were detected to be of the PERSON or GHOST type from A2I. Execute the first cell in *Step 8* from the notebook. We get the output as shown:

```
[{'endOffset': 10, 'label': 'GHOST', 'startOffset': 0},
 {'endOffset': 19, 'label': 'PERSON', 'startOffset': 11},
 {'endOffset': 47, 'label': 'PERSON', 'startOffset': 20},
 {'endOffset': 65, 'label': 'PERSON', 'startOffset': 48},
 {'endOffset': 104, 'label': 'PERSON', 'startOffset':
66},
 {'endOffset': 126, 'label': 'PERSON', 'startOffset':
105},
 {'endOffset': 155, 'label': 'PERSON', 'startOffset':
127}]
```

2. Let's apply the preceding rules to determine the decision for this loan application:

```
from collections import Counter
docstatus = ''
ghost = float(Counter(labellist)['GHOST'])
person = float(Counter(labellist)['PERSON'])
if ghost >= len(labellist)*.5:
    docstatus = 'REJECT'
elif min(len(labellist)*.5, len(labellist)*.8) < person <
max(len(labellist)*.5, len(labellist)*.8):
    docstatus = 'SUMMARY APPROVE'
elif person > len(labellist)*.8:
    docstatus = 'APPROVE'
print(docstatus)
```

3. We get the output APPROVE.

4. Store the decision in an Amazon DynamoDB table (reminder: a managed database service for storing and accessing key-value pairs with very low latency). Loan processors can use this data to start the pre-qualification process. Execute the next cell in the notebook to create the DynamoDB table.

5. Now, execute the next cell in the notebook to insert the contents of the loan application and the decision into the table. We see the values inserted into the DynamoDB table as follows:

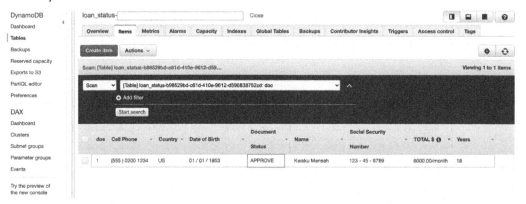

Figure 14.10 – Loan authenticity check status in DynamoDB

That concludes the solution build. Please refer to the *Further reading* section for more examples of approaches for this use case, as well as the code sample for building a similar solution using **AWS Lambda** and **CloudFormation**.

Summary

In this chapter, we learned how to build an auditing workflow for named entity recognition to solve real-world challenges that many organizations face today with document processing, using Amazon Textract, Amazon Comprehend, and Amazon A2I. We reviewed the loan authentication use case to validate the documents before they can be passed to a loan processor. We considered an architecture based on conditions such as reducing the validation time from 2 to 4 weeks to 24 hours within the first 3 months of solution implementation. We assumed that you, the reader, are the solution architect assigned to this project, and we reviewed an overview of the solution components along with an architectural illustration in *Figure 4.1*.

We then went through the pre-requisites for the solution build, set up an Amazon SageMaker Notebook instance, cloned our GitHub repository, and started executing the code in the notebook based on instructions from this chapter. We covered training an Amazon Comprehend custom entity recognizer, setting up our private work team using Amazon SageMaker labeling workforces, extracting the relevant content from the loan application using Amazon Textract, sending it to the Comprehend custom entity recognizer for detecting entities, forwarding the detection results to an Amazon A2I human review loop, completing the human task steps using the UI, reviewing the results of the review, updating the entities list to retrain the custom entity recognizer, and finally, storing the document contents and the loan validation decision to an Amazon DynamoDB table for downstream processing.

In the next chapter, we will be building a classical use case that's tailor-made for NLP – namely, the active learning workflow for text classification. We will be training a text classification model using Amazon Comprehend custom for labeling documents into classes, review predictions using Amazon A2I, and retrain the classifier based on feedback from the Amazon A2I human review loop. We will demonstrate how the solution evolves in intelligence in being able to improve classification accuracy because of the feedback loop.

Further reading

- *Building an end-to-end intelligent document processing solution using AWS* by Purnesh Tripathi: https://aws.amazon.com/blogs/machine-learning/building-an-end-to-end-intelligent-document-processing-solution-using-aws/

- *Setting up human review of your NLP-based entity recognition models with Amazon SageMaker Ground Truth, Amazon Comprehend, and Amazon A2I* by Mona Mona and Prem Ranga: https://aws.amazon.com/blogs/machine-learning/setting-up-human-review-of-your-nlp-based-entity-recognition-models-with-amazon-sagemaker-ground-truth-amazon-comprehend-and-amazon-a2i/

- *Announcing model improvements and lower annotation limits for Amazon Comprehend custom entity recognition* by Prem Ranga, Chethan Krishna, and Mona Mona: https://aws.amazon.com/blogs/machine-learning/announcing-model-improvements-and-lower-annotation-limits-for-amazon-comprehend-custom-entity-recognition/

15

Classifying Documents and Setting up Human in the Loop for Active Learning

In the last chapter, we covered how you can use **Amazon Comprehend Custom Entity** to extract business entities from your documents, and we showed you how you can use humans in the loop with Amazon Augmented AI (A2I) to augment or improve entity predictions. Lastly, we showed you how you can retrain the Comprehend custom entity model with an augmented dataset to improve accuracy using Amazon A2I.

In this chapter, we will talk about how you can use **Amazon Comprehend** custom classification to classify documents and then how you can set up active learning feedback with your custom classification model using Amazon A2I.

We will be covering the following topics in this chapter:

- Using comprehend custom classification with human in the loop for active learning
- Building the document classification workflow

Technical requirements

For this chapter, you will need access to an AWS account. Please make sure to follow the instructions specified in the *Technical requirements* section in *Chapter 2, Introducing Amazon Textract*, to create your AWS account, and log in to the AWS Management Console before trying the steps in this chapter.

The Python code and sample datasets for setting up Comprehend custom classification with a human-in-the-loop solution are in the following link: https://github. com/PacktPublishing/Natural-Language-Processing-with-AWS-AI-Services/tree/main/Chapter%2015.

Check out the following video to see the Code in Action at https://bit. ly/3BiOjKt.

Please use the instructions in the following sections along with the code in the repository to build the solution.

Using Comprehend custom classification with human in the loop for active learning

Amazon Comprehend provides the capability to classify the data using Amazon Comprehend AutoML and bring your own custom training dataset. You can easily accomplish a lot with the Amazon Comprehend custom classification feature as it requires fewer documents to train Comprehend AutoML models. You are spending less time labeling the dataset and then worrying about setting up infrastructure or choosing the right algorithm.

You can use Amazon Comprehend custom classification for a variety of use cases, such as classifying documents based on type, classifying news articles, or classifying movies based on type.

The fictitious company *LiveRight pvt ltd* wants to classify the documents submitted by the customers, such as whether the document submitted is an ID or a bank statement, even before analyzing the data inside the document. Moreover, if you are using a classification model to classify the documents based on the type of submitted document, you would also want to improve the accuracy of your predicted outcome in real time, based on the confidence score predicted by the Comprehend custom classification model. This is where humans in the loop with Amazon Augmented AI is going to help.

We covered Amazon A2I in *Chapter 13, Improving the Accuracy of Document Processing Workflows*. In this chapter, we will walk you through some reference architecture on how you can easily set up a custom classification model using Amazon Comprehend and have a feedback loop set up with Amazon A2I for active learning on your Comprehend custom model.

First, we will walk you through the following architecture on how you can train a custom classification model and create a real-time endpoint for inferencing or classifying documents in near real time.

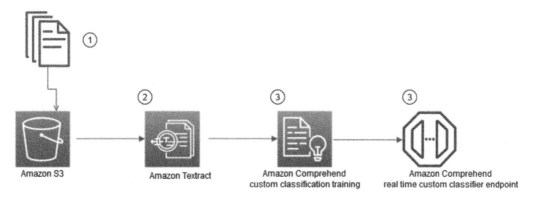

Figure 15.1 – Comprehend custom classification training workflow

This architecture walks through the following steps:

1. Training documents, such as bank statements or pay stubs, are uploaded to Amazon S3.

2. Amazon Textract extracts text from these documents and then some post-processing is done to create a labeled training file for Comprehend custom classification training.

3. Using the training file, an Amazon Comprehend job is created to classify documents, such as bank statements or pay stubs.

4. After training is completed, you have two options with Amazon Comprehend: either you can do batch inferencing on a batch of documents to classify them or you can create real-time endpoints. In the architecture, we are showing how you can set up a real-time endpoint to classify a document type.

We are going to walk you through the preceding conceptual architecture using Jupyter Notebook and a few lines of Python code in the *Setting up to solve the use case* section.

Now, we have a near real-time document classification endpoint. We will show you how you can set up humans in the loop with this Amazon Comprehend custom classification endpoint and set up a model retraining or active-learning loop to improve your model accuracy using the following architecture:

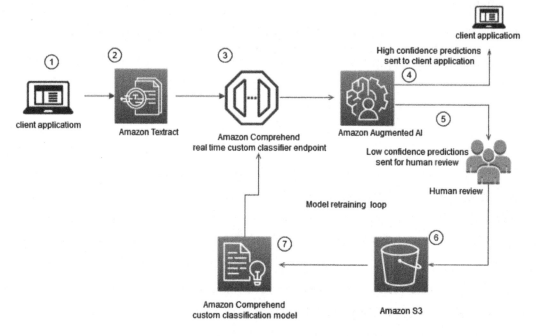

Figure 15.2 – Real-time classification with model retraining

In this architecture, we will walk you through the following steps:

1. **Client application** sends the document to Amazon Textract.

2. **Amazon Textract** extracts the data or text in real-time API and extracted data is passed on to the Amazon Comprehend real-time classifier endpoint.

3. The Amazon Comprehend custom classification endpoint classifies this document type.

4. This classification endpoint is configured with Amazon A2I human in the loop. If the prediction of classification is **high confidence** based on your business threshold, which you can configure, the high-confidence predictions are directly sent to client applications.

5. For low-confidence predictions, such as anything below the 95% confidence, the score predicted is low confidence for you. A human loop is created, and these predictions are sent for human review. Refer to *Chapter 3*, *Introducing Amazon Comprehend*, to understand what a confidence score is and Comprehend custom features.

6. The augmented or corrected data from human labelers are saved in an Amazon S3 bucket as a **JSON** file.

7. This data is then combined with the original training dataset and the Amazon Comprehend custom model is retrained for active learning using human feedback.

We will walk you through *steps 1 to 6* using Jupyter Notebook in the *Setting up the use case section*. Feel free to combine the augmented classified labels with the original dataset and try retraining for your understanding. You can automate this architecture using step functions and Lambda functions. We will share with you the blogs that can help you set up this architecture using Lambda functions in the *Further reading* section.

In this section, we covered the architecture for both model training and retraining or active learning. Now, let's move on to the next section to see these concepts with code.

Building the document classification workflow

In this section, we will get right down to action and start executing the tasks to build our solution. But first, there are prerequisites we will have to take care of.

Setting up to solve the use case

If you have not done so in the previous chapters, you will first have to create an Amazon SageMaker Jupyter notebook and set up **Identity and Access Management** (**IAM**) permissions for that notebook role to access the AWS services we will use in this notebook. After that, you will need to clone the GitHub repository (`https://github.com/PacktPublishing/Natural-Language-Processing-with-AWS-AI-Services`), go to the `Chapter 15` folder, and open the `chapter15 classify documents with human in the loop.ipynb` notebook.

Now, let's move to the next section to show you how you can set up the libraries and upload training data to Amazon S3 using this notebook.

Setting up and uploading sample documents to Amazon S3

In this step, we will follow instructions to set up an S3 bucket and upload documents:

1. Go to the notebook and run the cells below **Step 1: Set up and upload sample documents to Amazon S3** in the notebook to install libraries such as boto 3 for setup.

2. Move on to the next cell and enter a bucket name to create an S3 bucket in your account. Make sure you add the current month and date in MMDD for data_bucket, as shown in the following code block, before executing this cell:

```
data_bucket = "doc-processing-bucket-MMDD"
region = boto3.session.Session().region_name
                os.environ["BUCKET"] = data_bucket
os.environ["REGION"] = region
if region=='us-east-1':
    !aws s3api create-bucket --bucket $BUCKET
else:
    !aws s3api create-bucket --bucket $BUCKET --create-
bucket-configuration LocationConstraint=$REGION
```

3. Now run the following cell to upload or copy a sample bank statement or pay stub image as a training file from your local notebook to the S3 bucket that you just created:

```
!aws s3 cp documents/train s3://{data_bucket}/train -
recursive
```

4. Now run the next two cells in the notebook to list the training images we just copied in Amazon S3. We created a function named get_s3_bucket_items. We are getting the image objects from S3 and saving them as images for Textract processing in future steps. Refer to the notebook to execute these steps.

5. Run the following step to define a path or local directory structure to store data extracted from Amazon Textract:

```
word_prefix=os.getcwd()+'/SAMPLE8/WORDS/'
box_prefix=os.getcwd()+'/SAMPLE8/BBOX/'
```

We've covered how to create an S3 bucket and we have loaded training data. Now, let's move on to the next section to extract text.

Extracting text from sample documents using Amazon Textract

Go to the notebook and run the calls in **Step 2: Extract text from sample documents using Amazon Textract** to define a function using Amazon Textract to extract data from the sample images in Amazon S3. We are using the DetectDocumentText sync API to do this extraction; you can also use *AsyncAPI* or *Textract batch APIs* to perform data extraction. Refer to *Chapter 4, Automating Document Processing Workflows*, to dive deep into these APIs:

```python
def data_retriever_from_path(path):
    mapping={}
    for i in names:
        if os.path.isdir(path+i):
            mapping[i] = sorted(os.listdir(path+i))
    label_compre = []
    text_compre = []
    for i, j in mapping.items():
            for k in j:
            label_compre.append(i)
            text_compre.append(open(path+i+"/"+k,
encoding="utf-8").read().replace('\n',' '))
    return label_compre, text_compre
```

This function takes the *image's* path and returns the text and labels for the images.

Let's call this function by passing the scanned document's images by running the following cell in the notebook:

```python
tic = time.time()
pool = mp.Pool(mp.cpu_count())
pool.map(textract_store_train_LM, [table for table in images ])
print("--- %s seconds for extracting ---" % (time.time() -
tic))
pool.close()
```

The preceding function extracts the data and saves it in the local directory structure you defined in the **Set up and Upload Sample Documents** step. The following is the output:

```
/home/ec2-user/SageMaker/SAMPLE8/WORDS/
train/Pay Stubs
/home/ec2-user/SageMaker/SAMPLE8/WORDS/
train/Pay Stubs
/home/ec2-user/SageMaker/SAMPLE8/WORDS/
train/Pay Stubs
/home/ec2-user/SageMaker/SAMPLE8/WORDS/
train/Pay Stubs
/home/ec2-user/SageMaker/SAMPLE8/WORDS/
train/Pay Stubs
/home/ec2-user/SageMaker/SAMPLE8/WORDS/
train/Pay Stubs
/home/ec2-user/SageMaker/SAMPLE8/WORDS/
train/Pay Stubs
/home/ec2-user/SageMaker/SAMPLE8/WORDS/
train/Pay Stubs
/home/ec2-user/SageMaker/SAMPLE8/WORDS/
train/Pay Stubs
--- 74.77762579917908 seconds for extracting ---
```

Figure 15.3 – Textract output

Now, we have extracted the text and associated labels, for example, *0* for a bank statement and *1* for pay stubs. Now, let's move to the next section for Comprehend training.

Creating an Amazon Comprehend classification training job

We have extracted the data and labels in the previous step from our sample of scanned documents in Amazon S3. Now, let's understand how to set up a Comprehend classification training job using **Step 3: Create Amazon Comprehend Classification training job** in the notebook:

1. We will first create a function to map the extracted data and labels into a pandas DataFrame so that we can convert that into a CSV training file in the next step. Run the following code to define the function, which takes the extracted data location and returns labels and text from it:

```
def data_retriever_from_path(path):
    mapping={}
    for i in names:
        if os.path.isdir(path+i):
```

```
            mapping[i] = sorted(os.listdir(path+i))
        # label or class or target list
        label_compre = []
        # text file data list
        text_compre = []
        # unpacking and iterating through dictionary
        for i, j in mapping.items():
            # iterating through list of files for each class
            for k in j:
                # appending labels/class/target
                label_compre.append(i)
                # reading the file and appending to data list
                text_compre.append(open(path+i+"/"+k,
  encoding="utf-8").read().replace('\n',' '))
        return label_compre, text_compre
```

2. Now, we will call the function we defined in the previous step by running the following cell:

```
label_compre, text_compre=[],[]
path=word_prefix+'train/'
label_compre_train, text_compre_train=data_retriever_
from_path(path)
label_compre.append(label_compre_train)
text_compre.append(text_compre_train)
if type(label_compre[0]) is list:
        label_compre=[item for sublist in label_compre
for item in sublist]
        #print(label_compre)
        text_compre=[item for sublist in text_compre for
item in sublist]
        #print(text_compre)
data_compre= pd.DataFrame()
data_compre["label"] =label_compre
data_compre["document"] = text_compre
data_compre
```

You will get a pandas DataFrame with labels and documents, shown as follows:

Out[39]:

	label	document
0	Pay Stubs	CO FILE DEPT. CLOCK VCHR NO. 046 LV3 000342 00...
1	Pay Stubs	Acme LLC Earnings Statement 555 Woolworth Driv...
2	Pay Stubs	Acme LLC Earnings Statement 555 Woolworth Driv...
3	Pay Stubs	Acme LLC Earnings Statement 555 Woolworth Driv...
4	Pay Stubs	Acme LLC Earnings Statement 555 Woolworth Driv...
...	...	...
72	Bank Statements	This is a sample checking account bank stateme...
73	Bank Statements	Bank name COMPANY NAME AND Address 1 Address 2...
74	Bank Statements	CHASE July 1, 2008 through July 31, 2008 Prima...
75	Bank Statements	CHASE July 1, 2008 through July 31, 2008 Prima...
76	Bank Statements	CHASE July 1, 2008 through July 31, 2008 Prima...

77 rows × 2 columns

Figure 15.4 – Labeled training DataFrame

3. Now, we will save this DataFrame as a CSV and upload it to Amazon S3 using S3. Put the `boto3` API object as the Comprehend training file for Amazon Comprehend training:

```
csv_compre=io.StringIO()
data_compre.to_csv(csv_compre,index=False, header=False)
key='comprehend_train_data.csv'
input_bucket=data_bucket
output_bucket= data_bucket
response2 = s3.put_object(
        Body=csv_compre.getvalue(),
        Bucket=input_bucket,
        Key=key)
```

4. Now, go to the Amazon Comprehend console link (`https://console.aws.amazon.com/comprehend/v2/home?region=us-east-1#classification`) to create a classification job. Click on **Train Classifier**.

5. In **Model name**, enter `doc-classifier`, and in **Version name**, enter `1`, and scroll down to select **Using Single-label model** for **Classifier mode**. Also, make sure the data format is `csv file`.

> **Important Note**
>
> We have the choice to add versions for Amazon Comprehend custom models. To learn more about this feature, refer to this link: `https://docs.aws.amazon.com/comprehend/latest/dg/model-versioning.html`.

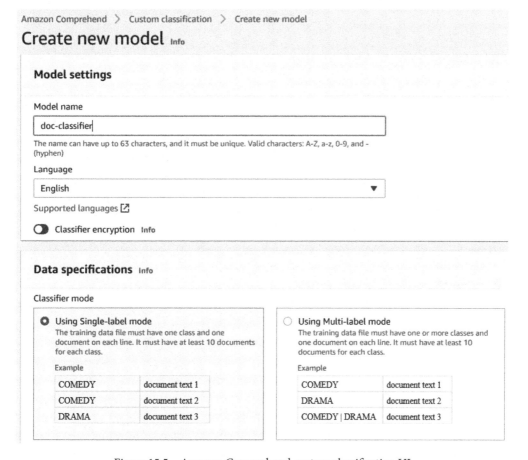

Figure 15.5 – Amazon Comprehend custom classification UI

6. For the training data location, browse to the `doc-processing-bucket-MMDD` S3 bucket created in the **Set up and upload sample documents to Amazon S3** step or enter `s3://doc-processing-bucket-MMDD/comprehend_train_data.csv`.

7. For **Test Dataset**, go with the default `Autosplit`, which means Amazon Comprehend will automatically split the test data for you. You also have the choice to tune your model by bringing your own test dataset here.

8. For output data, enter the `s3://doc-processing-bucket-MMDD` S3 bucket.

9. For access permissions, select **Create an IAM Role** and enter `classifydoc` in **NameSuffix**.

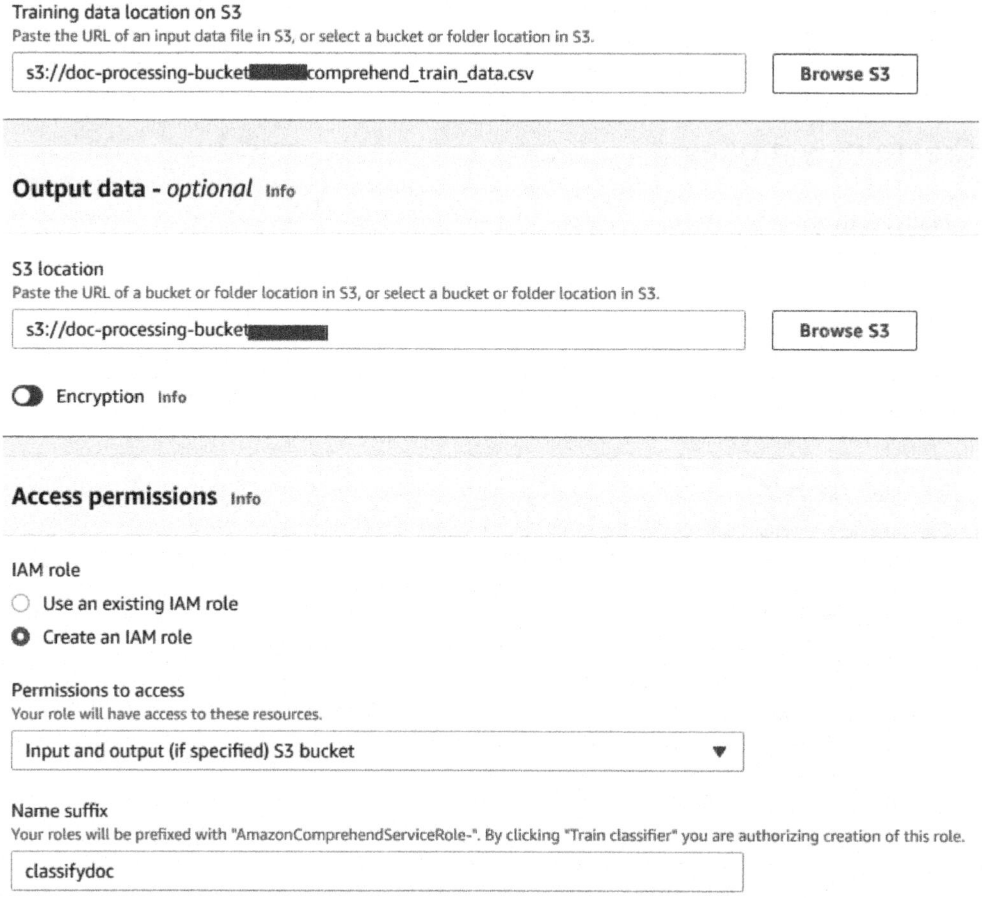

Training data location on S3
Paste the URL of an input data file in S3, or select a bucket or folder location in S3.

s3://doc-processing-bucket████comprehend_train_data.csv   Browse S3

Output data - *optional* Info

S3 location
Paste the URL of a bucket or folder location in S3, or select a bucket or folder location in S3.

s3://doc-processing-bucket██████   Browse S3

Encryption Info

Access permissions Info

IAM role
○ Use an existing IAM role
● Create an IAM role

Permissions to access
Your role will have access to these resources.

Input and output (if specified) S3 bucket   ▼

Name suffix
Your roles will be prefixed with "AmazonComprehendServiceRole-". By clicking "Train classifier" you are authorizing creation of this role.

classifydoc

Figure 15.6 – Amazon Comprehend custom classification IAM setting

10. Scroll down and click on the **Train Classifier** button to start training.

> **Important Note**
> This training will take 30 minutes to complete as we have a large number of documents to train with in this chapter. You can use this time to set up a private workforce for setting up humans in the loop, which we did in *Chapter 13, Improving the Accuracy of Document Processing Workflows*.

Once your job is completed, move on to the next step.

Creating Amazon Comprehend real-time endpoints and testing a sample document

In this section, we will show you how you can create a real-time endpoint with the trained model in the **AWS Management Console**. Comprehend uses the **Inference Unit (IU)** to analyze how many characters can be analyzed in real time per second. IU is a measure of the endpoint's throughput. You can adjust the IU of an endpoint anytime. After creating the endpoint, we will then show you how you can call this endpoint to test a sample bank statement using the Jupyter Notebook:

1. Go to this link, `https://console.aws.amazon.com/comprehend/v2/home?region=us-east-1#endpoints`, and click on **Create Endpoint.**

2. Enter `classify-doc` as the endpoint name, set **Custom model** as `doc-classifier`, which we trained in the previous step, and set **Inference units** to **1**.

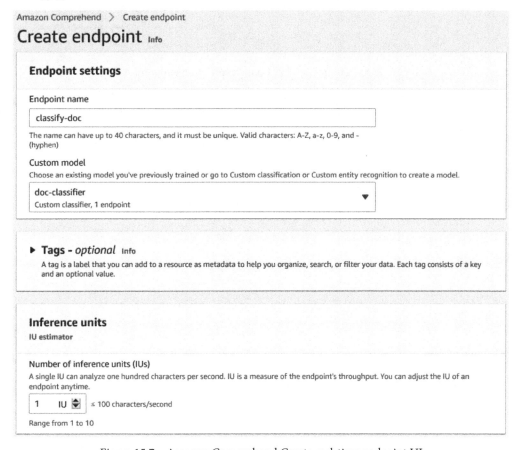

Figure 15.7 – Amazon Comprehend Create real-time endpoint UI

3. Scroll down and select **I Acknowledge** and click on **Create Endpoint**.

    Delete this endpoint at the cleanup section in the notebook to avoid incurring a cost.

4. Now, copy the **ARN** of the endpoint, as shown in the next screenshot, and move to the Jupyter Notebook link:

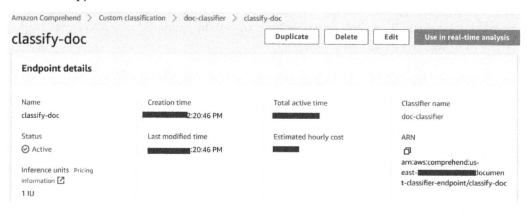

Figure 15.8 – Comprehend custom classification endpoint ARN

5. In the notebook, enter the preceding copied endpoint arn in the notebook cell as follows:

```
ENDPOINT_ARN='your endpoint arn paste here'
```

6. Now, we will take a sample test document or any pay stub not used in training for real-time classification. Run the following code to see the sample pay statement:

```
documentName = "paystubsample.png"
display(Image(filename=documentName))
```

You will get the following output:

ABC Company

Earnings Statement

123 Main Street,
Anytown, NY 10000.
EIN: 51-2322286

Pay Period: May 15, 2020 to May 16, 2020
Pay Date: May 16, 2020

SSN: XXX-XXX-1425

Peter Sims

Stub No.: 1112

Emp.ID: 263
102 Main Street, Anytown, NY 10000.

Earnings	Rate	Hours	This Period	YTD
Regular Earnings	$100.00	40.00 hrs	$4,000.00	$20,000.00
Gross Pay			$4,000.00	$20,000.00

Taxes / Deductions	Type	This Period	YTD
	Federal Withholding	$339.54	$1,697.70
	FICA - Social Security	$248.00	$1,240.00
	FICA - Medicare	$58.00	$290.00
	State Withholding	$264.00	$1,320.00
	Employer Taxes		
	FUTA	$1.00	$11.00

Figure 15.9 – Sample pay stub document

7. Run the next two cells in the notebook under **Extract Text from this sample doc using Textract** to extract text from this sample document.

8. Run the following cell, which calls a Comprehend ClassifyDocument API. This method takes the extracted text and custom classification endpoint and returns a response:

```
response = comprehend.classify_document(
    Text= page_string,
    EndpointArn=ENDPOINT_ARN
)
print(response)
```

You will get the following response:

```
{'Classes': [{'Name': 'Pay Stubs', 'Score': 0.9994999766349792}, {'Name': 'Bank Statements', 'Score': 0.0005000000237
487257}], 'ResponseMetadata': {'RequestId': '60d202a0-0fce-4185-a96a-e9bbfc53a81f', 'HTTPStatusCode': 200, 'HTTPHeade
rs': {'x-amzn-requestid': '60d202a0-0fce-4185-a96a-e9bbfc53a81f', 'content-type': 'application/x-amz-json-1.1', 'cont
ent-length': '117', 'date': 'Wed, ███████████████████████}, 'RetryAttempts': 0}}
```

Figure 15.10 – ClassifyDocument response

As per the response, the model endpoint has classified the document as a pay stub with 99% confidence. We tested this endpoint, so now let's move on to the next section to set up a human loop.

Setting up active learning with a Comprehend real-time endpoint using human in the loop

In this section, we are going to show you a custom integration with a Comprehend classifier endpoint, which you can invoke using the A2I StartHumanLoop API. You can pass any type of AI/ML prediction response to this API to trigger a human loop. In *Chapter 13*, *Improving the Accuracy of Document Processing Workflows*, we showed you a native integration with the Textract Analyze document API by passing a human loop workflow ARN to the AnalyzeDocument API. Setting up a custom workflow includes the following steps:

1. Create a **worker task template**.

2. Create a **human review workflow**.

3. Create and start an A2I human loop.

4. Check the human loop status and start labeling.

To get started, you need to create a private workforce and copy the private ARN in the *Environment setup* step in the Jupyter Notebook:

1. To create a private workforce, refer to the *Creating a private work team in AWS Console* section in *Chapter 13*, *Improving the Accuracy of Document Processing Workflows*:

```
REGION = 'enter your region'
WORKTEAM_ARN= "enter your private workforce arn "
BUCKET = data_bucket
ENDPOINT_ARN= ENDPOINT_ARN
role = sagemaker.get_execution_role()
region = boto3.session.Session().region_name
prefix = "custom-classify" + str(uuid.uuid1())
```

2. Run the next cell and move to the `Create worker task` template. This is the UI that the workers are going to view while labeling. We will show the prediction results in the UI and the original document data. We have used a pre-built classification template (`https://github.com/aws-samples/amazon-a2i-sample-task-uis/blob/master/text/document-classification.liquid.html`) for this use case. Run the notebook cell to define the HTML template.

> **Important Note**
>
> You can create a custom UI HTML template based on what type of data you want to show to your labelers. For example, you can show the actual document on the right and entities highlighted on the left using custom UIs.

3. We have defined or chosen the HTML template in the preceding step, in which we will create a function to create a UI task using the `create_human_task_ui` API by running the following code:

```
def create_task_ui():
    response = sagemaker.create_human_task_ui(
        HumanTaskUiName=taskUIName,
        UiTemplate={'Content': template})
return response
```

4. Run the next cell to invoke the function to create the UI task defined in the previous step. You will get a `human task arn` response.

5. Now, we will define a human review workflow. This human review workflow needs the private workforce you created, the UI template task you created, and a data bucket where you want the output of human review. We will use the `sagemaker.create_flow_definition` API to create a flow definition or human review workflow by running the following code:

```
create_workflow_definition_response = sagemaker.create_
flow_definition(
        FlowDefinitionName= flowDefinitionName,
        RoleArn= role,
        HumanLoopConfig= {
            "WorkteamArn": WORKTEAM_ARN,
            "HumanTaskUiArn": humanTaskUiArn,
            "TaskCount": 1,
            "TaskDescription": "Read the instructions",
```

```
            "TaskTitle": "Classify the text"
        },
        OutputConfig={
            "S3OutputPath" : "s3://"+BUCKET+"/output"
        }

flowDefinitionArn = create_workflow_definition_
response['FlowDefinitionArn']
```

6. Now, we will get the response from the Comprehend custom classifier endpoint for the sample document for pay stubs on the sample data and parse this response for the human loop setup:

```
response = comprehend.classify_document(
    Text= page_string,
    EndpointArn=ENDPOINT_ARN
)
print(response)
p = response['Classes'][0]['Name']
score = response['Classes'][0]['Score']
        #print(f»S:{sentence}, Score:{score}»)
response = {}
response['utterance']=page_string
response['prediction']=p
response['confidence'] = score
print(response)
```

7. Now, using this preceding JSON response, we will set a confidence threshold. This StartHumanloop API needs the workflow ARN or flow definition ARN created in the previous step and the JSON response from the Comprehend classification to create a human loop. We are triggering this loop based on the confidence score threshold, as shown in the next code block:

```
human_loops_started = []
CONFIDENCE_SCORE_THRESHOLD = .90
if(response['confidence'] > CONFIDENCE_SCORE_THRESHOLD):
        humanLoopName = str(uuid.uuid4())
        human_loop_input = {}
```

```
            human_loop_input['taskObject'] =
response['utterance']

            start_loop_response = a2i_runtime_client.start_
human_loop(

            HumanLoopName=humanLoopName,

            FlowDefinitionArn=flowDefinitionArn,

            HumanLoopInput={

                    "InputContent": json.dumps(human_loop_
input)

                 }

            )

            print(human_loop_input)

            human_loops_started.append(humanLoopName)

            print(f'Score is less than the threshold of
{CONFIDENCE_SCORE_THRESHOLD}')

            print(f'Starting human loop with name:
{humanLoopName}   \n')

else:

            print('No human loop created. \n')
```

> **Important Note**
>
> The preceding condition states anything greater than 90% confidence from your model endpoint will trigger a loop. This threshold is for demo purposes and needs to be changed for real use cases, such as anything below 90% that would trigger a human loop.

8. Now, run the following code to get the link to your private work team to start labeling:

```
workteamName = WORKTEAM_ARN[WORKTEAM_ARN.rfind('/') + 1:]

print("Navigate to the private worker portal and do
the tasks. Make sure you've invited yourself to your
workteam!")

print('https://' + sagemaker.describe_
workteam(WorkteamName=workteamName)['Workteam']
['SubDomain'])
```

You will get a link to the following A2I portal:

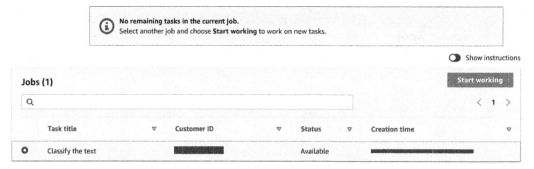

Figure 15.11 – Amazon A2I login console

9. Select **Task title** and click on **Start working**; you will be redirected to the classification task UI.

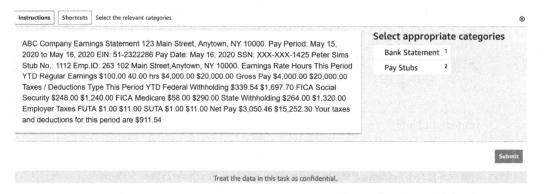

Figure 15.12 – Amazon A2I sample classification task UI

Review the data on the left in the previous screenshot and classify it by selecting the **Pay Stubs** category, and then click **Submit**.

10. After submitting this classification task as a human reviewer, go back to the notebook and run the following code to get the completed tasks:

```
completed_human_loops = []
resp = a2i_runtime_client.describe_human_
loop(HumanLoopName=humanLoopName)
```

11. Now, we will review the human-reviewed results from completed human reviews, which are stored automatically as a JSON file in Amazon S3 by running the following code:

```
for resp in completed_human_loops:
    splitted_string = re.split('s3://' + data_bucket +
'/', resp['HumanLoopOutput']['OutputS3Uri'])
    output_bucket_key = splitted_string[1]
    response = s3.get_object(Bucket=data_bucket,
Key=output_bucket_key)
    content = response["Body"].read()
    json_output = json.loads(content)
    pp.pprint(json_output)
```

You get the following response:

```
output/custom-classify4d1a13be-0ad3-11ec-a906-06c3864a6c5f-fd-a2i/                        /1ac1e472-572b-4167-ae34-f8d139f
08dc7/output.json
doc-processing-bucket-
{   'flowDefinitionArn': 'arn:aws:sagemaker:us-east-1:              :flow-definition/custom-classify4d1a13be-0ad3-11ec-
a906-06c3864a6c5f-fd-a2i',
    'humanAnswers': [   {   'acceptanceTime': '2021-09-01T03:51:17.363Z',
                            'answerContent': {   'category': {   'labels': [   'Pay '
                                                                               'Stubs']}},
                            'submissionTime': '2021-09-01T03:52:49.959Z',
                            'timeSpentInSeconds': 92.596,
                            'workerId': 'a4d8700afb91b37f',
                            'workerMetadata': {   'identityData': {   'identityProviderType': 'Cognito',
                                                                      'issuer': 'https://cognito-idp.us-east-1.amazon
aws.com/us-east-1_VHJkg7Dra',
                                                                      'sub': 'd0b307cb-3a7d-483f-9933-e6bb2f2a2aec
'}}}],
    'humanLoopName': '1ac1e472-572b-4167-ae34-f8d139f08dc7',
    'inputContent': {   'taskObject': 'ABC Company\n'
                                      'Earnings Statement\n'
                                      '123 Main Street,\n'
                                      'Anytown, NY 10000.\n'
                                      'Pay Period: May 15, 2020 to May 16, '
                                      '2020\n'
                                      'EIN: 51-2322286\n'
                                      'Pay Date: May 16, 2020\n'
                                      'SSN: XXX-XXX-1425\n'
                                      'Peter Sims\n'
```

Figure 5.13 – Human-reviewed JSON response

Using this data, you can augment or enrich your existing dataset used for training. Try combining this data with the Comprehend training data we created and try retraining your model to improve accuracy. We will point you to some blogs to accomplish this step in the *Further reading* section.

> **Important Note**
> Please delete the model and the Comprehend endpoints created for the steps we did in this notebook.

Summary

In this chapter, we covered two things using a reference architecture as well as a code walkthrough. Firstly, we covered how you can extract data from various types of documents, such as pay stubs, bank statements, or identification cards using Amazon Textract. Then, we learned how you can perform some post-processing to create a labeled training file for Amazon Comprehend custom classification training.

We showed you that even with 36 bank statement documents and 24 pay stubs as a training sample, you can achieve really good accuracy using Amazon Comprehend transfer-learning capabilities and AutoML with document or text classification. Obviously, the accuracy improves with more data.

Then, you learned how to set up a training job in the AWS Management Console and how to set up a real-time classification endpoint using the AWS Management Console.

Secondly, you learned how you can set up humans in the loop with the real-time classification endpoint to review/verify and validate what the model has classified. We then also discussed how you can retrain your existing model by adding this data with your existing training data and set up a retraining or active-learning loop. Please refer to the *Further reading* section to automate this workflow using Lambda functions.

In the next chapter, we will cover how you can improve the accuracy of **PDF batch processing** with Amazon Textract and humans in the loop. So, stay tuned!

Further reading

- *Active learning workflow for Amazon Comprehend custom classification models – Part 2, Shanthan Kesharaju, Joyson Neville Lewis, and Mona Mona* (https://aws.amazon.com/blogs/machine-learning/active-learning-workflow-for-amazon-comprehend-custom-classification-part-2/)

- *Creating and Using Custom Classifiers* (https://docs.aws.amazon.com/comprehend/latest/dg/getting-started-document-classification.html)

16
Improving the Accuracy of PDF Batch Processing

Congratulations on getting so far in this book! At this point, you are an advanced builder of real-world applications that harness the power of NLP and AI to deliver tangible business benefits. You may not have realized it but the topics we've covered so far – and will continue to cover – address some of the most popular, in-demand business challenges that we have helped our customers with. **Intelligent Document Processing (IDP)** is a very hot requirement today and is something prevalent across almost every industry type. We started reading about advanced concepts from *Chapter 13, Improving the Accuracy of Document Processing Workflows* onward, and we saw how **Amazon A2I** (`https://aws.amazon.com/augmented-ai/`) plays a key role in making human reviews of your ML workflows easier and more accurate, enabling active learning in the process.

In this chapter, we will tackle an operational need that has been around for a while, is ubiquitous, and yet organizations struggle to address it efficiently. This is known as **PDF batch processing**. Think of this as setting up an automated document processing workflow (similar to what we built in the previous chapters) but with the added flexibility of bulk processing PDF documents, combined with the intelligence to automatically route specific text passages in the document for human reviews due to low - confidence detection caused by illegible or erroneous text.

By now, due to your diligent efforts in implementing advanced AI solutions, **LiveRight Holdings** has seen its profitability go through the roof. This growth has resulted in LiveRight spinning up a couple of subsidiaries as independent organizations in their own right, and the board has decided that all three companies will go public in the mid-term. You have been promoted to Chief Architect of Operations at LiveRight, and the CIO has tasked you with building the necessary components to automate the registration process for the three companies with the **Securities and Exchanges Commission (SEC)** as publicly traded companies.

In this chapter, we will cover the following topics:

- Introducing the PDF batch processing use case
- Building the solution

Technical requirements

For this chapter, you will need access to an AWS account, which you can get by going to `https://aws.amazon.com/console/`. Please refer to the *Signing up for an AWS account* subsection within the *Setting up your AWS environment* section of *Chapter 2, Introducing Amazon Textract*, for detailed instructions on how to sign up for an AWS account and sign into the **AWS Management Console**.

The Python code and sample datasets for the solution discussed in this chapter can be found in this book's GitHub repository: `https://github.com/PacktPublishing/Natural-Language-Processing-with-AWS-AI-Services/tree/main/Chapter%2016`.

Check out the following video to see the Code in Action at `https://bit.ly/3nobrCo`.

Introducing the PDF batch processing use case

To determine what the architecture will look like, you talk to your accounting department to understand the process for registering companies with the SEC. As per the process, the accounting department will generate PDF documents using the SEC's template for registration, also known as *Form S20* (`https://www.sec.gov/files/forms-20.pdf`). The process also involves creating all the supporting documentation, along with the registration, which will be sent together to the SEC using an API call. LiveRight's **Partner Integration** team has the handshake with SEC in place, and they need the form data to be available in an **Amazon DynamoDB** (`https://aws.amazon.com/dynamodb/`) table that they will consume to create the message call to the SEC API.

However, before making the data available to the Partner Integration team, the accounting team mentioned that they need to review a collection of text lines that have been detected in the PDF document, specifically the ones that may not have been interpreted correctly due to document quality issues.

With this input, you realize that you need to add a batch component to your document processing solution. This will enable bulk detection of text from PDF documents and routing of those text lines that fall below a confidence threshold to a human review loop comprised of the accounting team members. You decide to use the asynchronous document text detection API from **Amazon Textract** to leverage its pre-trained ML model for text extraction from PDF documents, **Amazon A2I**, to set up a human workflow to review and modify text detected with a confidence of less than 95%, and Amazon DynamoDB to store the original detected text, along with the corrections for consumption by the Partner Integration team.

We will be building our solution using an Amazon SageMaker Jupyter notebook that will allow us to review the code and results as we execute it step by step. We will be performing the following tasks:

1. As a first step, we will create a private labeling workforce for human review using the Amazon SageMaker Console. For more details, please refer to `https://docs.aws.amazon.com/sagemaker/latest/dg/sms-workforce-private.html`.

2. We will start the solution workflow by inspecting the sample registration forms available to us when we clone the GitHub repository for this chapter. We will use Amazon Textract to start an asynchronous text detection job.

3. Then, we will get the results for the text detection job, select specific lines from the document, and inspect the detection confidence scores.

4. We will set up an Amazon A2I human review loop using the tabular task UI template and send the text lines from each document for all the documents to the human loop.

5. Logging in as a private worker, we will work on the allocated review task, making changes to the text lines with low - confidence detection scores for all the documents.

6. We will upload the detected and corrected text lines to a DynamoDB table for downstream processing.

Now that we've got the context for the exercise and gone over our intended process, let's start building the solution.

Building the solution

In the previous section, we introduced our use case, which is to submit company registrations for public trading to the SEC, covered the architecture of the solution we will be building, and briefly walked through the solution components and workflow steps. In this section, we will get right down to business and start executing the tasks that will build our solution. But first, there are some prerequisites we have to take care of.

Setting up for the solution build

If you have not done so in the previous chapters, you will have to create an Amazon SageMaker Jupyter notebook, as well as setting up **Identity and Access Management (IAM)** permissions for that notebook role to access the AWS services we will use in this notebook. After that, you will need to clone this book's GitHub repository (`https://github.com/PacktPublishing/Natural-Language-Processing-with-AWS-AI-Services`), create an Amazon S3 (`https://aws.amazon.com/s3/`) bucket, and provide the bucket's name in the notebook to start execution.

> **Note**
> Please ensure that you have completed the tasks mentioned in the *Technical requirements* section.

Follow these steps to complete these tasks before we execute the cells from our notebook:

1. Follow the instructions documented in the *Creating an Amazon SageMaker Jupyter notebook instance* subsection in the *Setting up your AWS environment* section of *Chapter 2*, *Introducing Amazon Textract*, to create your Jupyter notebook instance.

> **IAM role Permissions While Creating Amazon SageMaker Jupyter Notebooks**
> Accept the default for the IAM role at notebook creation time to allow access for any S3 bucket.

2. Once you have created the notebook instance and its status is **InService**, click on **Open Jupyter** in the **Actions** menu heading for the notebook instance.

3. This will take you to the **home** folder of your notebook instance.

4. Click on **New** and select **Terminal**.

5. In the terminal window, type `cd SageMaker` and then `git clone https://github.com/PacktPublishing/Natural-Language-Processing-with-AWS-AI-Services`.

6. Now, exit the terminal window, go back to the home folder, and you will see a folder called `Natural-Language-Processing-with-AWS-AI-Services`. Click this folder to bring up the chapter folders and click `Chapter 16`.

7. Open this folder by clicking on it. You should see a notebook called `Improve-accuracy-of-pdf-processing-with-Amazon-Textract-and-Amazon-A2I-forGitHub.ipynb`.

8. Open this notebook by clicking on it.

9. Follow the steps in this notebook that correspond to the next few subheadings in this section by executing one cell at a time. Please read the descriptions that were added to each notebook cell.

Next, we'll cover some additional IAM prerequisites.

Additional IAM prerequisites

We have to enable additional policies for our SageMaker Notebook role. Please refer to the *Changing IAM permissions and trust relationships for the Amazon SageMaker Notebook execution role* subsection in the *Setting up your AWS environment* section in *Chapter 2, Introducing Amazon Textract*, for detailed instructions on how to execute the following steps:

1. Please attach the `TextractFullAccess` and `AmazonAugmentedAIFullAccess` policies to your Amazon SageMaker Notebook IAM role if you've not already done so.

2. Add an `iam:PassRole` permission as an inline policy to your SageMaker Notebook execution role:

```
{ "Version": "2012-10-17", "Statement": [ {
    "Action": [
        "iam:PassRole"
    ],
    "Effect": "Allow",
    "Resource": "<your sagemaker notebook execution role
ARN">
    }
  ]
}
```

Now that we have set up our notebook and set up an IAM role to run the walkthrough notebook, we will create the private labeling workforce.

Creating a private team for the human loop

Refer to *Step 0* in the notebook (`https://github.com/PacktPublishing/Natural-Language-Processing-with-AWS-AI-Services/blob/main/Chapter%2016/Improve-accuracy-of-pdf-processing-with-Amazon-Textract-and-Amazon-A2I-forGitHub.ipynb`) for the instructions we will execute now. In this section, we will create a private team using the Amazon SageMaker labeling workforce console, and we will add ourselves to the private team as a worker. This is required so that we can log in to the labeling task UI when we reach the Amazon A2I step in this solution. Please execute the following steps:

1. Log in to the AWS Management Console if you've not already done so (please refer to the *Technical requirements* section at the beginning of this chapter for more details), type Amazon SageMaker in the **Services** search bar, and go to the Amazon SageMaker console. Once there, on the left of the UI, click on **Ground Truth** and then **Labelling workforces**. On the screen, select the **Private** tab at the top and click on **Create private team**.

2. Enter a name for your private team in the **Team Name** field and leave the default selection of **Create a new Amazon Cognito user group** as-is in the **Add Workers** section. Scroll down and click **Create private team**.

3. You will be returned to the **Labelling workforces** screen. The private `nlp-doc-team` team should be visible under **Private teams**. Next to that, you will see an ARN, which is a long string that looks like `arn:aws:sagemaker:region-name-123456:workteam/private-crowd/team-name`. Please copy this ARN and provide it in the notebook in **Step 1 – Cell 1**:

   ```
   WORKTEAM_ARN= '<your-private-workteam-arn>'
   ```

4. Next, scroll down the previous screen, go to the **Workers** section, and click on **Invite new workers**. Provide your email address and click **Invite new workers**. You will receive an email from `no-reply@verificationemail.com`. Follow the instructions provided to complete the signup process.

5. Now, add yourself to the private team by clicking on **nlp-doc-team** and then **Add workers to team**. Select your email address from the list and click on **Add workers to team**.

Now that we have added the private team, let's create an Amazon S3 bucket.

Creating an Amazon S3 bucket

Follow the instructions documented in the *Creating an Amazon S3 bucket, a folder, and uploading objects* subsection in the *Setting up your AWS environment* section of *Chapter 2, Introducing Amazon Textract*, to create your Amazon S3 bucket. If you created an S3 bucket in the previous sections, please reuse that bucket. For this chapter, you just need to create the S3 bucket. We will create the folders and upload the objects directly from the notebook:

1. Once you have the bucket's name, please type it in **Step 1 – Cell 1** of the notebook:

    ```
    bucket = "<S3-bucket-name>"
    ```

2. Execute **Step 1 – Cell 1** of the notebook by clicking the **Run** button in the top menu of the notebook UI. This will import the libraries we need, initialize the variables, and get our kernel ready for the next set of steps.

3. Finally, execute **Step 1 – Cell 2** in the notebook to upload the registration documents to our S3 bucket:

    ```
    s3_client = boto3.client('s3')
    for secfile in os.listdir():
        if secfile.endswith('pdf'):
            response = s3_client.upload_file(secfile, bucket,
    prefix+'/'+secfile)
            print("Uploaded {} to S3 bucket {} in folder {}".
    format(secfile, bucket, prefix))
    ```

Now that we have created the S3 bucket, imported the libraries we need, and uploaded the documents to our S3 bucket, let's extract the contents using **Amazon Textract**.

Extracting the registration document's contents using Amazon Textract

This section corresponds to *Steps 2* and *3* in the notebook (`https://github.com/PacktPublishing/Natural-Language-Processing-with-AWS-AI-Services/blob/main/Chapter%2016/Improve-accuracy-of-pdf-processing-with-Amazon-Textract-and-Amazon-A2I-forGitHub.ipynb`). In this section, we will submit an asynchronous text detection job using Amazon Textract. Once the job completes, we will get the results of the text detection and load them into a **pandas DataFrame** (`https://pandas.pydata.org/docs/reference/api/pandas.DataFrame.html`), select the text lines we need, and review the results. Follow these steps using the aforementioned notebook and execute the cells to perform the tasks required:

1. Execute **Step 2 – Cell 1** to define the bucket handle and declare a dictionary for storing Textract Job IDs for each of our documents:

    ```
    input_bucket = s3.Bucket(bucket)
    jobids = {}
    ```

2. Execute **Step 2 – Cell 2** to submit the three text detection jobs, one for each registration document:

    ```
    for doc in input_bucket.objects.all():
        if doc.key.startswith(prefix) and doc.key.endswith('pdf'):
            tres = textract.start_document_text_detection(
                DocumentLocation={
                    "S3Object": {
                        "Bucket": bucket,
                        "Name": doc.key
                    }
                }
            )
            jobids[doc.key.split('/')[2]] = tres['JobId']
    ```

> **Note**
>
> When you build this solution in an event-driven architecture using AWS Lambda (https://aws.amazon.com/lambda/), an event-driven serverless compute service, you can pass the NotificationChannel attribute as input to the Textract StartDocumentTextDetection API (https://docs.aws.amazon.com/textract/latest/dg/API_StartDocumentTextDetection.html) to indicate the Amazon SNS (https://aws.amazon.com/sns) topic that the message will be sent to when the job completes. You can set up AWS Lambda to subscribe to the topic, and on receipt of the message, you can call the Textract GetDocumentTextDetection API (https://docs.aws.amazon.com/textract/latest/dg/API_GetDocumentTextDetection.html) to retrieve the extracted text. We will execute this API in the notebook in **Step 3 – Cell 1** here.

3. Finally, execute **Step 2 – Cell 3** to print the Job IDs for each of the documents:

```
for j in jobids:
    print("Textract detection Job ID for {} is {}".
format(j,str(jobids[j])))
```

4. Now, we must go to *Step 3* in the notebook. Here, we will define the helper classes to parse the JSON response from Textract. Then, we will load the text lines we need into a dictionary that we will use in the subsequent steps. Click **Run** in the notebook to execute **Step 3 – Cell 1**.

5. Execute **Step 3 – Cell 2** to call the helper class we defined in the previous section and extract the text for each of our registration documents. The extracted text will be loaded into a DataFrame called df_indoc:

```
text_extractor = TextExtractor()
indoc = {}
df_indoc = pd.DataFrame(columns =
['DocName','LineNr','DetectedText','Confidence',
'CorrectedText', 'Comments'])
for x in jobids:
    pages = text_extractor.extract_text(jobids[x])
    contdict =pages[1]['Content']
    for row in range(1,(int(len(contdict)/2))+1):
        df_indoc.loc[len(df_indoc.index)]
= [x, row, contdict['Text'+str(row)],
round(contdict['Confidence'+str(row)],1),'','']
```

6. Execute **Step 3 – Cell 3** in the notebook to define the filter criteria for what text lines are important to us when reviewing the registration documents. Finally, execute **Step 3 – Cell 4** to create a new DataFrame that only contains the text lines we are interested in:

```
df_newdoc = pd.DataFrame(columns =
['DocName','LineNr','DetectedText','Confidence',
'CorrectedText','Comments'])

for idx, row in df_indoc.iterrows():

    if str(row['LineNr']) in bounding_dict['lines'].
split(':'):

        df_newdoc.loc[len(df_newdoc.index)] =
[row['DocName'],row['LineNr'], row['DetectedText'],
row['Confidence'], row['CorrectedText'],row['Comments']]

df_newdoc
```

7. The DataFrame's results are shown in the following screenshot. Some of the low - confidence entries are highlighted here:

	DocName	LineNr	DetectedText	Confidence	CorrectedText	Comments
0	form-s20-LRHL-registration.pdf	9	Holdings	99.5		
1	form-s20-LRHL-registration.pdf	11	123	99.7		
2	form-s20-LRHL-registration.pdf	12	Unicoumstleet Supernova City, NY 99999 and Pho...	91.9		
3	form-s20-LRHL-registration.pdf	13	(Address, including zip code, and telephone nu...	99.8		
4	form-s20-LRHL-registration.pdf	15	@###	96.4		
5	form-s20-LRHL-registration.pdf	16	(Name, address, including zip code, and teleph...	99.5		
6	form-s20-LRHL-registration.pdf	17	Approximate date of commencement of proposed s...	99.9		
7	form-s20-LRHL-registration.pdf	18	October 20th, 2022	99.8		
8	form-s20-LRHL-registration.pdf	19	Calculation of Registration Fee	99.8		
9	form-s20-LRHL-registration.pdf	20	Title: LfRHL	76.1		
10	form-s20-LRHL-registration.pdf	21	Amount: 1000033	72.4		
11	form-s20-LRHL-registration.pdf	22	Fee per unit:	99.6		
12	form-s20-LRHL-registration.pdf	23	Maximum Fee:	99.6		
13	form-s20-LRHL-registration.pdf	24	Registration Fee:	99.7		
14	form-s20-LRHL-registration.pdf	25	$130	99.0		
15	form-s20-SUBS1-registration.pdf	9	LiveRight Holdings Subsidiary. 1	90.1		
16	form-s20-SUBS1-registration.pdf	11	123-Unicorn Street, Supemovar City; NY.99999 a...	68.1		

Figure 16.1 – Text lines from the SEC registration documents

> **Note**
> The text entries appear garbled because these were intentionally introduced in the PDF documents for our use case to trigger low - confidence predictions.

Now that we have digitized the text we need from the registration documents, let's cover setting up our human review workflow using Amazon A2I.

Setting up an Amazon A2I human workflow loop

For the code blocks discussed here, please refer to *Steps 4, 5,* and *6* in the notebook (https://github.com/PacktPublishing/Natural-Language-Processing-with-AWS-AI-Services/blob/main/Chapter%2016/Improve-accuracy-of-pdf-processing-with-Amazon-Textract-and-Amazon-A2I-forGitHub.ipynb). It is time to set up a human workflow using the Private Team we created in *Step 0* and send the results to the **Amazon A2I** human loop for review and modifications, as required:

1. Let's start by initializing some variables we will need for the next few tasks. Please execute **Step 4 – Cell 1** in the notebook.

2. Execute **Step 4 – Cell 2** in the notebook to define the human task UI template that we will use for the human review activity. We selected the task template for tabular data from the Amazon A2I Sample task UI GitHub repository (https://github.com/aws-samples/amazon-a2i-sample-task-uis) and customized it for our needs.

3. Execute **Step 4 – Cell 3** to create the task UI based on the template:

```
def create_task_ui():
        response = sagemaker.create_human_task_ui(
        HumanTaskUiName=taskUIName,
        UiTemplate={'Content': template})
    return response
# Create task UI
humanTaskUiResponse = create_task_ui()
humanTaskUiArn = humanTaskUiResponse['HumanTaskUiArn']
print(humanTaskUiArn)
```

4. We will get the following output:

```
arn:aws:sagemaker:us-east-1:<aws-account-nr>:human-
task-ui
/ui-pdf-docs-<timestamp>
```

5. Now, execute **Step 5 – Cell 1** in the notebook to create an **Amazon A2I Flow Definition** that orchestrates tasks to workforces and collects output data:

```
create_workflow_definition_response = sagemaker_client.
create_flow_definition(
        FlowDefinitionName=flowDefinitionName,
        RoleArn=role,
        HumanLoopConfig= {
            "WorkteamArn": WORKTEAM_ARN,
            "HumanTaskUiArn": humanTaskUiArn,
            "TaskCount": 1,
            "TaskDescription": "Review the contents and
correct values as indicated",
            "TaskTitle": "SEC Registration Form Review"
        },
        OutputConfig={
            "S3OutputPath" : OUTPUT_PATH
        }
    )
flowDefinitionArn = create_workflow_definition_
response['FlowDefinitionArn'] # let's save this ARN for
future use
```

6. Execute **Step 5 – Cell 2** to start the human workflow loop:

```
for x in range(60):
    describeFlowDefinitionResponse = sagemaker_client.
describe_flow_definition(FlowDefinitionName=
flowDefinitionName)
    print(describeFlowDefinitionResponse
['FlowDefinitionStatus'])
    if (describeFlowDefinitionResponse
['FlowDefinitionStatus'] == 'Active'):
```

```
            print("Flow Definition is active")
            break
        time.sleep(2)
```

7. We will get the following results:

```
Initializing
Active
Flow Definition is active
```

8. Execute **Step 6 – Cell 1** to upload the scanned images for the first page of the registration documents to our S3 bucket. We will refer to these images from within the Amazon A2I task UI:

```
reg_images = {}
for image in os.listdir():
    if image.endswith('png'):
        reg_images[image.split('_')[0]] = S3Uploader.
upload(image, 's3://{}/{}'.format(bucket, prefix))
```

9. Execute **Step 6 – Cell 2** to start the human loop for all three registration documents in our use case. In this cell, we will create a random name for each human loop, select specific lines from each document that fall below the confidence threshold of 95%, and send those inputs to an Amazon A2I **StartHumanLoop** API call (https://docs.aws.amazon.com/augmented-ai/2019-11-07/APIReference/API_StartHumanLoop.html):

```
humanLoopName = {}
docs = df_newdoc.DocName.unique()
# confidence threshold
confidence_threshold = 95
for doc in docs:
    doc_list = []
    humanLoopName[doc] = str(uuid.uuid4())
    for idx, line in df_newdoc.iterrows():
        # Send only those lines whose confidence score is
less than threshold
        if line['DocName'] == doc and line['Confidence']
<= confidence_threshold:
```

```
            doc_list.append({'linenr':
line['LineNr'], 'detectedtext': line['DetectedText'],
'confidence':line['Confidence']})
    ip_content = {"document": doc_list,
            'image': reg_images[doc.split('.')[0]]
        }
    start_loop_response = a2i.start_human_loop(
        HumanLoopName=humanLoopName[doc],
        FlowDefinitionArn=flowDefinitionArn,
        HumanLoopInput={
            "InputContent": json.dumps(ip_content)
        }
    )
```

10. Execute **Step 6 – Cell 3** to check the status of our human loops; the status should be **InProgress**:

```
completed_human_loops = []
for doc in humanLoopName:
    resp = a2i.describe_human_
loop(HumanLoopName=humanLoopName[doc])
    print(f'HumanLoop Name: {humanLoopName[doc]}')
    print(f'HumanLoop Status: {resp["HumanLoopStatus"]}')
    print(f'HumanLoop Output Destination:
{resp["HumanLoopOutput"]}')
    print('\n')
```

11. Now, we will log in to the Amazon A2I task UI to review and modify the text lines. Let's log in to the worker portal to review the predictions and modify them as required. Execute **Step 6 – Cell 4** to get the URL to our Task UI:

```
workteamName = WORKTEAM_ARN[WORKTEAM_ARN.rfind('/') + 1:]
print("Navigate to the private worker portal and do
the tasks. Make sure you've invited yourself to your
workteam!")
print('https://' + sagemaker.describe_
workteam(WorkteamName=workteamName)['Workteam']
['SubDomain'])
```

12. Use the credentials you set up in *Step 0* when creating the labeling workforce to log in to the task UI. You will see a task called **SEC Registration Form Review**. Select it and click on **Start working**.

13. The first page of the original registration form will be displayed:

| Hello, | | Customer ID: | Task description: Review the contents and co... | Task time: 22:06 of 59 Min 17 Sec |

Instructions

Please review the SEC registration form inputs, and make corrections where appropriate.

Original Registration Form - Page 1

UNITED STATES
SECURITIES AND EXCHANGE COMMISSION
Washington, D.C. 20549

OMB APPROVAL
Not subject to -
P.L. 96-511

FORM S-20

REGISTRATION STATEMENT UNDER THE SECURITIES ACT OF 1933

LiveRight Holdings
_____
(Exact name of registrant as specified in its charter)

123 Unicorn Street, Supernova City, NY 99999 and Phone: 999-123-4567
_____
(Address, including zip code, and telephone number, including area code, of registrant's principal executive offices)

LiveRight Brokerage, 456, Pathless Road, Lightness City, NY 88888 and Phone: 888-456-7890   @###
_____
(Name , address, including zip code, and telephone number, including area code, of agent for service)

Approximate date of commencement of proposed sale to the public October 20th, 2022
_____

Calculation of Registration Fee

Title: LRHL	Amount: 1000000	Fee per unit: $10	Maximum Fee: $100M	Registration Fee: $100K

Note: Specific details relating to the fee calculation shall be furnished in notes to the table, including references to provisions of Rule 457 (§230.457 of this chapter) relied upon, if the basis of the calculation is not otherwise evident from the information presented in the table.

Figure 16.2 – Task UI displaying an image of the registration form with illegible text

14. Scroll down the page to find a table that displays what Textract detected, the confidence score of the text line, a radio button to check if we think the detected text is correct or incorrect, an input area for us to modify the detected text, and a comments field. Make changes to the table and click the **Submit** button at the lower left of the page:

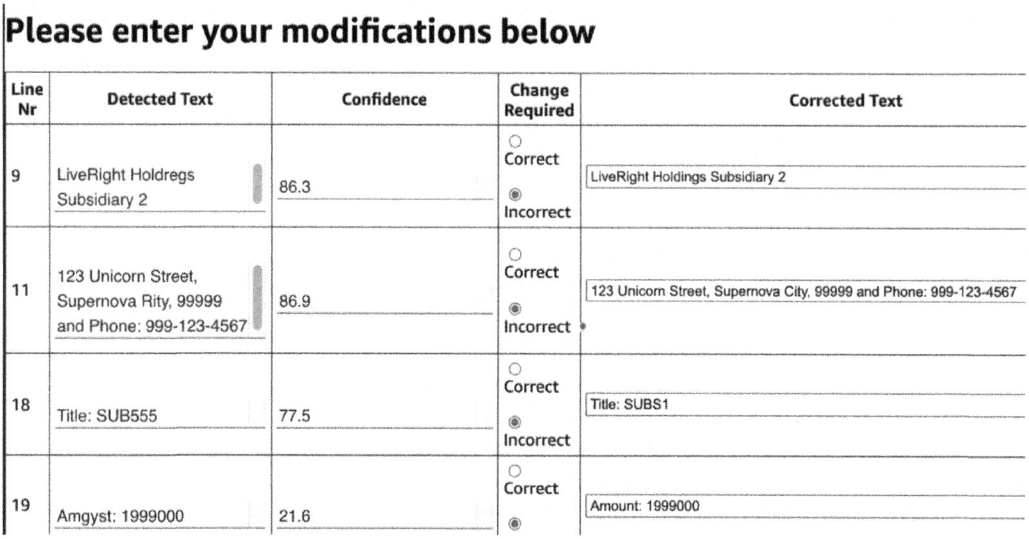

Please enter your modifications below

Line Nr	Detected Text	Confidence	Change Required	Corrected Text
9	LiveRight Holdregs Subsidiary 2	86.3	○ Correct ◉ Incorrect	LiveRight Holdings Subsidiary 2
11	123 Unicorn Street, Supernova Rity, 99999 and Phone: 999-123-4567	86.9	○ Correct ◉ Incorrect	123 Unicorn Street, Supernova City, 99999 and Phone: 999-123-4567
18	Title: SUB555	77.5	○ Correct ◉ Incorrect	Title: SUBS1
19	Amgyst: 1999000	21.6	○ Correct ◉	Amount: 1999000

Figure 16.3 – The document modifications page in Amazon A2I

15. Now, the task UI will be refreshed to show the next document from the three we sent to Amazon A2I for human review. Repeat the preceding two steps to review the image, scroll down to make changes in the table, and click **Submit**. You will have to repeat this for the last document as well.

16. Once you have made your changes and submitted the task for all three documents, go back to the notebook and execute **Step 6 – Cell 5** to check the status of the human loops. All three human loops will have a status of **Completed**.

17. Finally, execute **Step 6 – Cell 7** in the notebook to retrieve the changes that were made by the human reviewers and add this to our DataFrame. When inspecting the DataFrame, we will see the following result:

	DocName	LineNr	DetectedText	Confidence	CorrectedText	Comments
0	form-s20-LRHL-registration.pdf	9	Holdings	99.5		
1	form-s20-LRHL-registration.pdf	11	123	99.7		
2	form-s20-LRHL-registration.pdf	12	Unicoumstleet Supernova City, NY 99999 and Pho...	91.9	123 Unicorn Street, Supernova City, NY 99999 a...	Street name was missing
3	form-s20-LRHL-registration.pdf	13	(Address, including zip code, and telephone nu...	99.8		
4	form-s20-LRHL-registration.pdf	15	@###	96.4		
5	form-s20-LRHL-registration.pdf	16	(Name, address, including zip code, and teleph...	99.5		
6	form-s20-LRHL-registration.pdf	17	Approximate date of commencement of proposed s...	99.9		
7	form-s20-LRHL-registration.pdf	18	October 20th, 2022	99.8		
8	form-s20-LRHL-registration.pdf	19	Calculation of Registration Fee	99.8		
9	form-s20-LRHL-registration.pdf	20	Title: LfRHL	76.1	Title: LRHL	typo in title
10	form-s20-LRHL-registration.pdf	21	Amount: 1000033	72.4	Amount: 100000	incorrect amount

Figure 16.4 – A2I human review results updated

In this section, we covered the majority of the processing needs for this solution by using Amazon Textract asynchronous APIs to extract text from multiple PDF documents. After that, we used Amazon A2I to set up a human loop to review and correct low - confidence text detections. As the final step in our solution, we will persist the results of our activity.

Storing results for downstream processing

Now that we understand how to set up a review workflow, let's persist the results for consumption by downstream applications. We will be executing the cells in *Step 7* of the notebook for this section:

1. Execute **Step 7 – Cell 1** to create an **Amazon DynamoDB** table, a managed database service for storing and accessing key-value pairs with very low latency.

2. Execute **Step 7 – Cell 2** to upload the contents of our DataFrame to the DynamoDB table:

```
for idx, row in df_newdoc.iterrows():
    table.put_item(
        Item={
            'row_nr': idx,
```

```
            'doc_name': str(row['DocName']) ,

            'line_nr': str(row['LineNr']),

            'detected_line': str(row['DetectedText']),

            'confidence': str(row['Confidence']),

            'corrected_line': str(row['CorrectedText']),

            'change_comments': str(row['Comments'])

            }

    )

print("Items were successfully created in DynamoDB
table")
```

3.   The values will be inserted into the DynamoDB table, as follows:

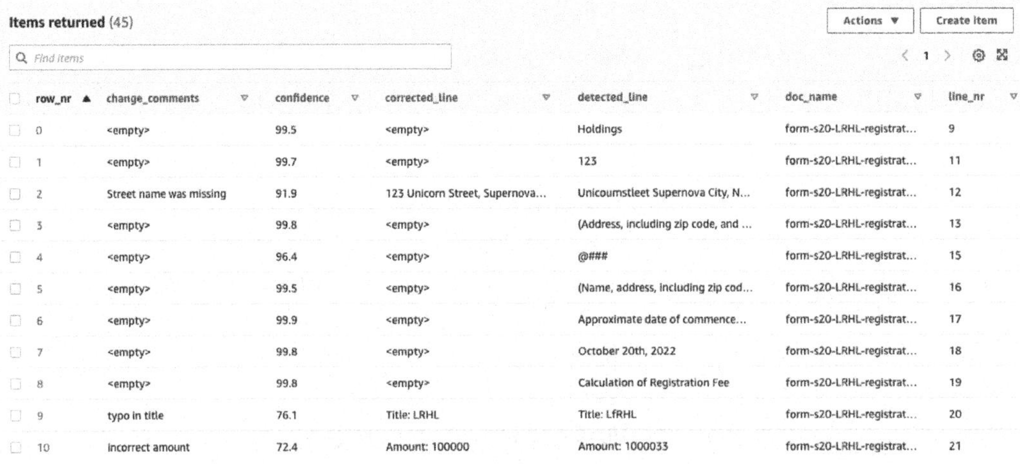

	row_nr ▲	change_comments ▽	confidence ▽	corrected_line ▽	detected_line ▽	doc_name ▽	line_nr ▽
☐	0	<empty>	99.5	<empty>	Holdings	form-s20-LRHL-registrat...	9
☐	1	<empty>	99.7	<empty>	123	form-s20-LRHL-registrat...	11
☐	2	Street name was missing	91.9	123 Unicorn Street, Supernova...	Unicoumstleet Supernova City, N...	form-s20-LRHL-registrat...	12
☐	3	<empty>	99.8	<empty>	(Address, including zip code, and ...	form-s20-LRHL-registrat...	13
☐	4	<empty>	96.4	<empty>	@###	form-s20-LRHL-registrat...	15
☐	5	<empty>	99.5	<empty>	(Name, address, including zip cod...	form-s20-LRHL-registrat...	16
☐	6	<empty>	99.9	<empty>	Approximate date of commence...	form-s20-LRHL-registrat...	17
☐	7	<empty>	99.8	<empty>	October 20th, 2022	form-s20-LRHL-registrat...	18
☐	8	<empty>	99.8	<empty>	Calculation of Registration Fee	form-s20-LRHL-registrat...	19
☐	9	typo in title	76.1	Title: LRHL	Title: LfRHL	form-s20-LRHL-registrat...	20
☐	10	incorrect amount	72.4	Amount: 100000	Amount: 1000033	form-s20-LRHL-registrat...	21

Items returned (45)   Actions ▼   Create item

Figure 16.5 – Corrected registration document entries in DynamoDB

That concludes the solution build. Please refer to the *Further reading* section for a code sample for building a similar solution using AWS Lambda and CloudFormation.

Summary

In this chapter, we continued building advanced NLP solutions to address real-world requirements. We focused on asynchronously processing PDF documents and improving their accuracy by reviewing and modifying low - confidence detections using Amazon Textract and Amazon A2I.

We learned how to register companies to the SEC use case with a need to extract text, and then validate and modify specific text lines in the documents before they could be passed to the Partner Integration team for submission to SEC. We considered an architecture built for scale and ease of setup. We assumed that you are the chief architect overseeing this project, and we then proceeded to provide an overview of the solution components in the *Introducing the PDF batch processing use case* section.

We then went through the prerequisites for the solution build, set up an Amazon SageMaker Notebook instance, cloned our GitHub repository, and started executing the code in the notebook based on the instructions provided in this chapter. We covered setting up our private work team using Amazon SageMaker labeling workforces, extracting the relevant content from the PDF documents in batch mode using Amazon Textract, forwarding the detection results to an Amazon A2I human review loop, completing the human task steps using the UI, reviewing the results, and storing the document's contents, along with the corrections, in an Amazon DynamoDB table for downstream processing.

In the next chapter, we will be addressing one more interesting feature in Amazon Textract, namely handwriting detection, and how to set up a solution to detect handwritten content for review, modification, and consumption.

Further reading

Please refer to the following resources for more information:

- *Deriving conversational insights from invoices with Amazon Textract, Amazon Comprehend and Amazon Lex*, by Mona Mona, Prem Ranga, and Saida Chanda (`https://aws.amazon.com/blogs/machine-learning/deriving-conversational-insights-from-invoices-with-amazon-textract-amazon-comprehend-and-amazon-lex/`).

- *Amazon Textract documentation for asynchronous operations* (`https://docs.aws.amazon.com/textract/latest/dg/async.html`).

17
Visualizing Insights from Handwritten Content

In the previous chapters, we talked about and learned how to build **Intelligent Document Processing (IDP)** pipelines using **Amazon Textract**, **Amazon Comprehend**, and **Amazon A2I**. The advantage of setting up such pipelines is that you introduce automation into your operational processes and unlock insights that were previously not so evident. Speaking of insights, what are they exactly and why is everyone so interested in mining text, and of what use can they be?

To answer this, let's summon *Doc Brown* and *Marty McFly's* time-traveling car, the *DeLorean* from the movie *Back to the Future*, and travel back to *Chapter 1, NLP in the Business Context and Introduction to AWS AI Services*, to re-read the *Understanding why NLP is becoming mainstream* section. Remember now? Maybe this will help: according to *Webster's dictionary* (`https://www.merriam-webster.com/`), the word "*insight*" is defined as "*the act or result of apprehending the inner nature of things or of seeing intuitively.*" You got it – it is all about uncovering useful information from seemingly vague or even mundane data. Simply put, it means to "*see with clarity.*"

This chapter is all about how to visualize insights from text – that is, handwritten text – and make use of it to drive decision-making. According to Wikipedia, the earliest known handwritten script was **Cuneiform** (`https://en.wikipedia.org/wiki/Cuneiform`), which was prevalent almost 5,500 years ago. Equally old in spoken and written form is the native language of one of the authors, the Tamil language. That said, let's now head back to our favorite fictional organization, **LiveRight Holdings**, to solve a new challenge they seem to be having.

You have been given the task of running the Founder's Day for the firm, which is touted to be a spectacular gala, considering how popular LiveRight has become. To keep up with LiveRight's culture of benefiting the community, you will have to work with several local vendors to source what you need, such as furniture, food, and other items, for the event. You have been told that the management needs aggregated reports of all expenditure, so you decide to use your existing Document Processing pipeline to process their receipts. However, to your chagrin, you discover that the local vendors only provide handwritten receipts. You remember from a previous solution you built that Amazon Textract supports handwritten content, so you start thinking about how best to design for the situation.

In this chapter, we will cover the following topics:

- Extracting text from handwritten images
- Visualizing insights using Amazon QuickSight

Technical requirements

For this chapter, you will need access to an AWS account, which you can do at `https://aws.amazon.com/console/`. Please refer to the *Signing up for an AWS account* sub-section within the *Setting up your AWS environment* section of *Chapter 2, Introducing Amazon Textract*, for detailed instructions on how you can signup for an AWS account and sign into the **AWS Management Console**.

The Python code and sample datasets for the solution discussed in this chapter can be found at `https://github.com/PacktPublishing/Natural-Language-Processing-with-AWS-AI-Services/tree/main/Chapter%2017`.

Check out the following video to see the Code in Action at `https://bit.ly/3vLX5j0`.

Extracting text from handwritten images

At this point, you are ready to start designing and building the approach. You realize that what will you build for this use case will become an extension of the existing Document Processing solution, so it will have long-term usage within the organization. So, you need to design for future scalability. With this in mind, you decide to use **Amazon S3** (`https://aws.amazon.com/s3/`) for object storage, **Amazon Textract** (`https://aws.amazon.com/textract/`) for handwriting detection, and **Amazon QuickSight** (`https://aws.amazon.com/quicksight/`), a serverless ML-powered business intelligence service, for visualizing the insights from the handwritten content. We will be using an Amazon SageMaker Jupyter notebook for text extraction, followed by the AWS Management Console to set up the QuickSight visualizations. Let's get started.

Creating the SageMaker Jupyter notebook

If you have not done so in the previous chapters, you will have to create an Amazon SageMaker Jupyter notebook and set up **Identity and Access Management** (**IAM**) permissions for that Notebook Role to access the AWS services we will use in this notebook. After that, you will need to clone this book's GitHub repository (`https://github.com/PacktPublishing/Natural-Language-Processing-with-AWS-AI-Services`), create an Amazon S3 bucket (`https://aws.amazon.com/s3/`), and provide the bucket name in the notebook to start execution.

> **Note**
> Please ensure you have completed the tasks mentioned in the *Technical requirements* section.

Follow these steps to complete these tasks before we execute the cells from our notebook:

1. Follow the instructions documented in the *Creating an Amazon SageMaker Jupyter notebook instance* sub-section in the *Setting up your AWS environment* section of *Chapter 2, Introducing Amazon Textract*, to create your Jupyter notebook instance.

> **IAM Role Permissions While Creating Amazon SageMaker Jupyter Notebooks**
> Accept the default for the IAM Role at notebook creation time to allow access to an S3 bucket.

2. Once you have created the notebook instance and its status is **InService**, click on **Open Jupyter** from the **Actions** menu heading to get the notebook instance.

3. This will take you to the home folder of your notebook instance.

4. Click on **New** and select **Terminal**.

5. If you've not done so already, in the terminal window, type `cd SageMaker`, followed by `git clone https://github.com/PacktPublishing/Natural-Language-Processing-with-AWS-AI-Services`.

6. Now, exit the terminal window and go back to the home folder; you will see a folder called `Natural-Language-Processing-with-AWS-AI-Services`. Click this folder to bring up the chapter folders and click on **Chapter 17**.

7. Open this folder by clicking on it. You should see a notebook called `chapter17-deriving-insights-from-handwritten-content-forGitHub.ipynb`. Open this notebook by clicking on it. We will need this notebook in the upcoming sections. For now, leave this window open.

Next, we'll cover some additional IAM prerequisites.

Additional IAM prerequisites

We have to enable additional policies for our SageMaker notebook role. Please refer to the *Changing IAM permissions and trust relationships for the Amazon SageMaker notebook execution role* sub-section in the *Setting up your AWS environment* section of *Chapter 2, Introducing Amazon Textract*, for detailed instructions for executing the following steps:

1. Please attach all the `TextractFullAccess` policies to your Amazon SageMaker Notebook IAM Role if you haven't done so already.

2. Add an `iam:PassRole` permission as an inline policy to your SageMaker Notebook Execution Role:

```
{ "Version": "2012-10-17", "Statement": [ {
  "Action": [
      "iam:PassRole"
  ],
  "Effect": "Allow",
  "Resource": "<your sagemaker notebook execution role
ARN">
  }
```

```
    ]
  }
```

Now that we have set up our Notebook and set up an IAM Role to run the walkthrough notebook, in the next section, we will create an Amazon S3 bucket.

Creating an Amazon S3 bucket

Follow the instructions documented in the *Creating an Amazon S3 bucket, a folder, and uploading objects* sub-section in the *Setting up your AWS environment* section of *Chapter 2, Introducing Amazon Textract*, to create your Amazon S3 bucket. If you created an S3 bucket in the previous sections, please reuse that bucket. For this chapter, you just need to create the S3 bucket; we will create the folders and upload the necessary objects directly from the notebook. Let's get started:

1. Once you have the bucket's name, please type it in *STEP 0 – CELL 1* of the notebook:

```
bucket = "<enter-S3-bucket-name>"
```

2. Execute *STEP 0 – CELL 1* of the notebook by clicking the **Run** button at the top menu of the notebook UI. Alternatively, you can press **Shift + Enter** to execute the cell. This will import the libraries we need, initialize their variables, and get our kernel ready for the next set of steps.

Now that we have created the S3 bucket and imported the libraries we need, let's extract the contents using **Amazon Textract**.

Extracting text using Amazon Textract

We will now continue executing the rest of the cells in the notebook to update the QuickSight manifest file with our bucket and prefix entries. The manifest file provides metadata for the QuickSight dataset to correctly import the content for visualization. Please see the documentation (https://docs.aws.amazon.com/quicksight/latest/user/create-a-data-set-s3.html) for more details. Let's get started:

1. Execute *STEP 1 – CELL 1* in the notebook to format the manifest file with the bucket and prefix names.
2. Now, execute *STEP 1 – CELL 2* to upload the formatted manifest file to the S3 bucket:

```
s3 = boto3.client('s3')
s3.upload_file(outfile,bucket,prefix+'/'+outfile)
```

3. We will get the following output. Take a copy of the S3 location that is printed here as we will need it when we set up QuickSight:

```
Manifest file uploaded to: s3://<your-bucket-name>/
chapter17/qsmani-formatted.json
```

4. Now, execute *STEP 2 – CELL 1* to install the **Amazon Textract Response Parser (TRP)** (`https://github.com/aws-samples/amazon-textract-response-parser/blob/master/src-python/README.md`), a helper library that provides you with an easy way to parse the JSON response from Textract:

```
!python -m pip install amazon-textract-response-parser
```

5. Execute *STEP 2 – CELL 2* to import the parser's Document class, which we need to initialize the boto3 handle for Textract.

6. *STEP 2 – CELL 3* does a few things, so let's examine it in parts. First, it searches the current directory for the presence of files ending with a *.jpg* extension. These are our input image files of the receipts. The following is one of these receipts:

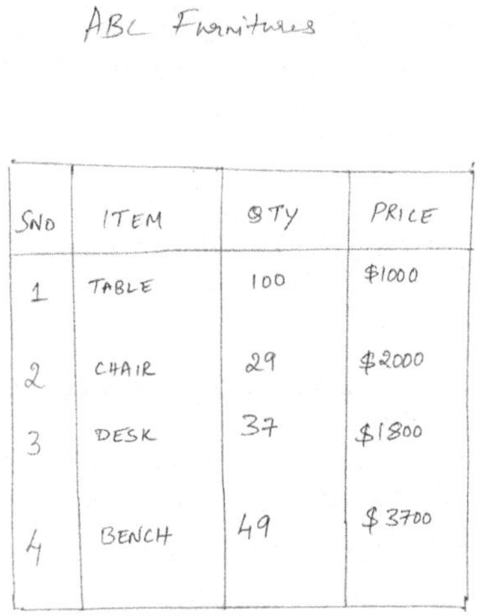

ABC Furnitures

SNO	ITEM	QTY	PRICE
1	TABLE	100	$1000
2	CHAIR	29	$2000
3	DESK	37	$1800
4	BENCH	49	$3700

Figure 17.1 – A sample handwritten receipt

7. When they're found, the files are read one at a time and converted into bytearrays:

```
for docs in os.listdir('.'):
    if docs.endswith('jpg'):
        with open(docs, 'rb') as img:
            img_test = img.read()
            bytes_test = bytearray(img_test)
```

8. Next, it calls the `AnalyzeDocument` Textract API and passes `bytearray` as an input, specifically looking for tables and forms from the input image. The Textract response is then parsed by the Textract Response Parser library and the results are stored in a variable. Then, we must loop through the results to get to the table and initialize a variable denoting the CSV file we will write to:

```
response = textract.analyze_document(Document={'Bytes':
bytes_test}, FeatureTypes=['TABLES','FORMS'])
        text = Document(response)
        for page in text.pages:
            for table in page.tables:
                csvout = docs.replace('jpg','csv')
                with open(csvout, 'w', newline='') as
csvf:
```

9. Finally, the individual cell values are written to the CSV file, along with the column headings by stripping spaces, if any, as well as the $ symbol, denoting the currency. Finally, the newly created CSV files are uploaded to the S3 bucket. This is repeated for each image file that's found in the input folder:

```
tab = csv.writer(csvf, delimiter=',')
                    for r, row in enumerate(table.rows):
                        csvrow = []
                        for c, cell in enumerate(row.
cells):
                            if cell.text:
                                csvrow.append(cell.text.
replace('$','').rstrip())
                        tab.writerow(csvrow)
            s3.upload_file(csvout,bucket,prefix+'/
dashboard/'+csvout)
```

10. Execute *STEP 2 – CELL 3* to complete the tasks outlined in the preceding steps. We will get the following output. Please make a note of the S3 location of the CSV files. The manifest file we formatted earlier contains these locations to allow QuickSight to upload these CSV files:

```
Extracted text from hw-receipt2.jpg
CSV file for document hw-receipt2.jpg uploaded to:
s3://<s3-bucket-name>/chapter17/dashboard/hw-receipt2.csv
```

```
Extracted text from hw-receipt1.jpg
CSV file for document hw-receipt1.jpg uploaded to:
s3://<s3-bucket-name>/chapter17/dashboard/hw-receipt1.csv
```

> **Note**
>
> You can also use **Amazon A2I** in this solution to set up a human loop to review the Textract outputs, as well as to make changes to the content as required, before creating the CSV files. For more details, please refer to *Chapter 13, Improving the Accuracy of Document Processing Workflows*, onward.

This concludes the steps from the notebook. Now, we will log into the AWS Management Console to set up QuickSight for visualization.

Visualizing insights using Amazon QuickSight

First, we need to enable QuickSight for your AWS account before we can import the data and run the visualizations. Please execute the following steps to proceed:

1. Log into AWS Management Console (refer to the *Technical requirements* section if you don't have access to the AWS Management Console) and type QuickSight in the services search bar at the top center of the page. Click **QuickSight** from the results to be navigated to the **QuickSight registration** page.

2. Enter your email address and click **Continue**:

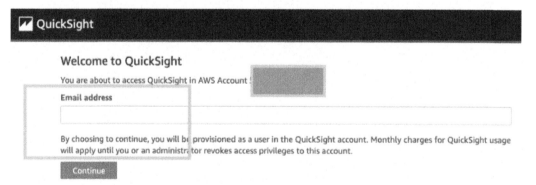

Figure 17.2 – Registering for QuickSight

3. Once you've logged in, click **Datasets** on the left pane and click the **New dataset** button at the top right:

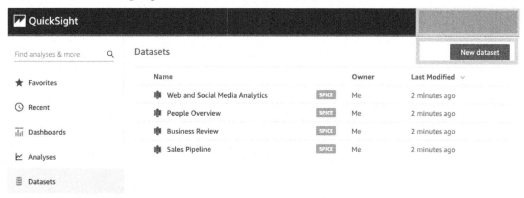

Figure 17.3 – New dataset

4. Click on **S3** on the **Datasets** page:

Figure 17.4 – S3

5. In the popup that appears, for **Data source name**, type `handwritten-receipts`. In the **Upload a manifest file** input area, copy and paste the S3 location that was printed in the Jupyter notebook in *STEP 1 – CELL 2*. Then, click on **Connect**:

Figure 17.5 – Specifying the S3 manifest file

6. Once the dataset has been imported, click the **Visualize** button at the bottom right of the popup to open the QuickSight console. In the console, you should see a small popup that displays the import status. Verify that the import was successful. If you see errors at this stage, verify the contents of the CSV file to ensure there are no issues. These should be available in the S3 bucket in the `Chapter17/dashboard` prefix:

Import complete:

100% success
9 rows were imported to SPICE
0 rows were skipped

Figure 17.6 – Dataset import successful

7. You should see the column names from the CSV file displayed to the left, under **Fields list**. You should see a center pane with space for a graph named **AutoGraph**. When you add fields from the list on the left, QuickSight automatically creates the appropriate graph based on your data.

8. For our use case, we will create a pie chart and a donut chart to visualize the quantity of furniture that's been ordered and how much it cost us. Under the **Visual types** section on the left, click on the symbol for the pie chart and add fields from **Fields list** to the chart, as shown here:

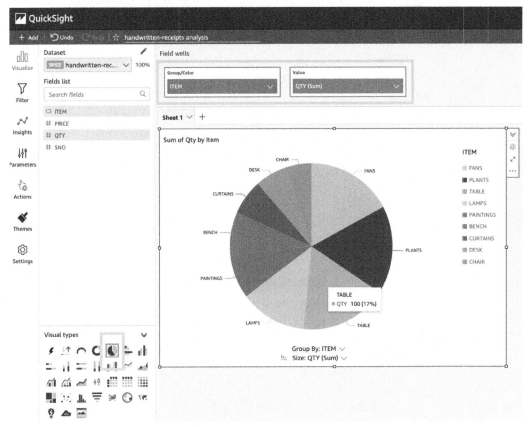

Figure 17.7 – Visualizing furniture quantities across types

9. Now, let's add a new visual to this dashboard. Click on **Add** at the top left and select **Add visual**:

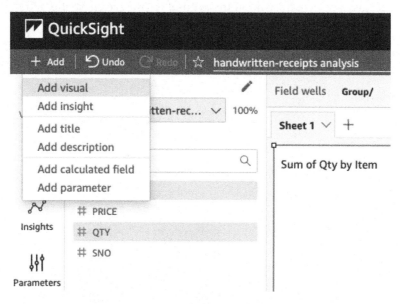

Figure 17.8 – Add visual

10. Now, add a donut chart to display the total costs and cost by furniture type, as shown in the following screenshot. Begin by selecting the donut visual in the **Visual types** section on the left, select **ITEM** and **PRICE**, and then add them to the **Group/Color** and **Value** fields:

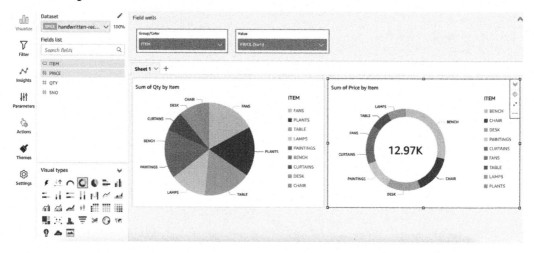

Figure 17.9 – Donut chart for visualizing the total costs and cost by furniture type

11. Click on the **Insights** option on the middle left of the console to display the insights that QuickSight was able to gather from our data:

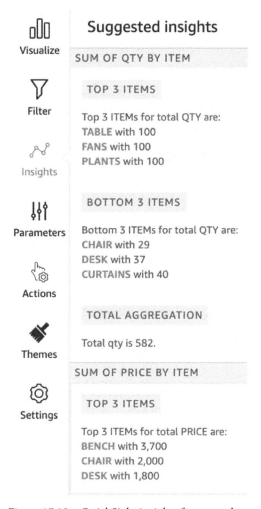

Figure 17.10 – QuickSight insights from our data

It is as simple as that. Feel free to try out the other visual types, as well as ML-powered forecasting and insights. For more details, please refer to the following documentation: `https://docs.aws.amazon.com/quicksight/latest/user/making-data-driven-decisions-with-ml-in-quicksight.html`. You can set up, share, publish, or export your dashboard for consumption by your management and other stakeholders. And that concludes the solution build for this use case.

Summary

We have just scratched the surface with what we can do with written text with this use case – the possibilities are truly endless! With just a few steps, by leveraging the advanced AI capabilities offered by services such as Amazon Textract, and the serverless scalable visualization offered by Amazon QuickSight, we were able to create powerful visuals from content scribbled on a piece of paper.

We began by creating the SageMaker Jupyter notebook instance we needed for this solution, cloned the GitHub repository for this chapter, created an S3 bucket, and executed the steps in the notebook to format the QuickSight S3 manifest file. Then, we used Amazon Textract and the Textract Response Parser library to read the contents of the handwritten receipts before creating CSV files that were uploaded to the S3 bucket. We concluded the notebook after executing these steps and then logged into the AWS Management Console and registered to use Amazon QuickSight.

In QuickSight, we imported the S3 dataset, which comprised our CSV files, and created two visuals and an insight. The first visual was a pie chart that showed the items that have been ordered against their quantities, while the second visual was a donut chart that showed the total cost of the two receipts, along with the cost per item. Finally, we displayed the insights that QuickSight had automatically generated, giving us a summary of what it was able to read from our content. We briefly discussed how we can export or share the dashboard and QuickSight's ML-based insights. And that concluded our solution build for this chapter.

Based on the myriad of use cases we have covered in this book so far, you know how to solve mainstream challenges in NLP for you and your customers, and we did all this without the need to tune a hyperparameter or train a model from the ground up. Granted, we trained a few custom Comprehend models, but that was without the overhead of a traditional ML workflow.

In the next chapter, we will conclude this book, so we thought we would leave you with some best practices, techniques, and guidelines to keep in your back pocket as you navigate your career as an NLP and AI expert. We will talk about document pre-processing, post-processing, and other items to consider during solution design. We are almost there!

18

Building Secure, Reliable, and Efficient NLP Solutions

Thank you, dear reader, for staying with us through this (hopefully informative) journey in building best-in-class **Natural Language Processing** (**NLP**) solutions for organizations looking to uncover insights from their text data. Our aim in writing this book was to create awareness that **Artificial Intelligence** (**AI**) is mainstream and that we are at the cusp of a huge tidal wave of AI adoption that many enterprises are moving toward. This exciting technology not only helps you advance your career but also provides opportunities to explore new avenues of innovation that were not possible previously. For example, according to a BBC article (https://www.bbc.com/future/article/20181129-the-ai-transforming-the-way-aircraft-are-built), **Autodesk** (https://www.autodesk.com/), a global leader in designing and making technology, uses **Generative AI** (https://www.amazon.com/Generative-AI-Python-TensorFlow-Transformer/dp/1800200889) to help aircraft manufacturers design more efficient airframes, a key requirement to reduce fuel consumption.

Throughout this book, we reviewed several types of use cases that enterprises deal with today to garner useful information from text-based data. This information will either directly help them derive insights or serve as a precursor to driving downstream decision-making, with operational implications in both cases. We read through different business scenarios and discussed different solution design approaches, architecture implementation frameworks', and real-time and batch solutions that met these requirements.

We now understand how to design, architect, and build NLP solutions with **AWS AI services**, but we are still missing an important step. How do we ensure our solution is production-ready? What are the operational requirements to ensure our solution works as expected when dealing with real-world data? What are the non-functional requirements that the architecture needs to adhere to? And how do we build this into the solution as we go along? To answer these questions, we will review the best practices, techniques, and guidance on what makes a good NLP solution great.

In this chapter, we will discuss the following topics:

- Defining best practices for NLP solutions
- Applying best practices for optimization

Technical requirements

For this chapter, you will need access to an AWS account (`https://aws.amazon.com/console/`).

Please refer to the *Signing up for an AWS account* sub-section within the *Setting up your AWS environment* section in *Chapter 2, Introducing Amazon Textract*, for detailed instructions on how you can sign up for an AWS account and sign in to the **AWS Management Console**.

Defining best practices for NLP solutions

If you have done DIY (do-it-yourself) projects in the past, you know how important your tools are for your work. When building an NLP solution, or any solution for that matter, you need to keep the following in mind:

- You need to know your requirements (the "*what*").
- You need to know the problem that you are trying to solve by building the solution (the "*why*").
- You need to know the tools and techniques required to build the solution (the "*how*").

- You need to estimate the time you require to build the solution (the "*when*").

- Finally, you need to determine the required skills for the team (the "*who*").

But with this approach, you haven't necessarily addressed the needs that will make your solution reliable, scalable, efficient, secure, or cost-effective. And these are equally important (if not more so) to building long-lasting solutions that will delight your customers.

When building with AWS, you have access to prescriptive guidance and valuable insights garnered from decades of building and operating highly performant, massive-scale applications such as **Amazon**, along with the expertise that comes from helping some of the world's largest enterprises with running their cloud workloads on AWS. All of this experience and knowledge has been curated into a collection of architectural guidelines and best practices called the **AWS Well-Architected Framework**.

Think of *well-architected* as a comprehensive checklist of questions that is defined by five pillars, as follows:

- **Operational excellence**: The operational excellence pillar recommends automating infrastructure provisioning and management (if applicable), modularizing the solution architecture into components that can be managed independently, enabling agility, implementing CI/CD-based DevOps practices, simulating operational failures, and preparing for and learning from it.

- **Security**: The security pillar recommends making security the top priority by implementing least privilege governance measures and associated guardrails from the ground up with a focus on identity and access management, compute and network security, data protection in transit and at rest, automation, simulation, and incident response.

- **Reliability**: The reliability pillar requires the setting up of highly resilient architectures with the ability to self-heal from failures, with a focus on fail-fast and recovery testing, elastic capacity with auto scale-in/scale-out, and a high degree of automation.

- **Performance efficiency**: The performance efficiency pillar recommends the use of **AWS Managed Services** (**AMS**) to remove the undifferentiated heavy lifting associated with managing infrastructure, using the global AWS network to reduce latency for your end users and remove the need for repeated experimentation and decoupling resource interactions by means of APIs.

- **Cost optimization**: The cost optimization pillar provides recommendations on measures you can take to track and minimize usage costs.

For more details on the *Well-Architected Framework*, along with the resources to get you started, please go to the Amazon documentation: `https://docs.aws.amazon.com/wellarchitected/latest/framework/welcome.html`

Taken together, the Well-Architected questions from the various pillars guide you through your architecture design, build, and implementation. This enables you to include critical design principles, resulting in solutions that are built for secure, reliable, cost-effective, and efficient operations (and hence the term Well-Architected). So, what does Well-Architected mean in our case with regard to NLP solutions and AI services? To help you understand this clearly, we will create a matrix of the Well-Architected pillars, aligned with NLP development stages such as document preprocessing, prediction, and post-processing, from the perspective of the major AWS AI services we used in this book (**Amazon Textract** and **Amazon Comprehend**). We will also look at the application of principles for NLP solution builds in general. In each cell of this matrix, we will summarize how to apply the Well-Architected principles for design and implementation using best practices.

AWS Well-Architected Framework Pillars					
Stages of NLP development	Operational excellence	Security	Reliability	Performance efficiency	Cost optimization
Document pre-processing	1.1a – Collect data from disparate sources into an S3 Data Lake.	1.2a – Use S3 Object Lambda Access Points for PII. 1.2b – Encrypt data at rest. 1.2c – Enforce least privilege access.	1.3a – Use an S3 Data Lake.	1.4a – Use AWS Glue for pre-processing. 1.4b – Use SageMaker Ground Truth for annotations. 1.4c – Use Amazon Comprehend with PDF, Word directly.	1.5a – Save costs with serverless pre-processing using AWS Glue.
Prediction	2.1a – Use API Gateway for throttling requests to Amazon Comprehend custom real-time endpoints.	2.2a – Encrypt data in transit.	2.3a – Set up Auto Scaling for Amazon Comprehend real-time endpoints. 2.3b – Use Amazon A2I to review predictions.	2.4a – Use async batch for bulk predictions.	2.5a – Save on training costs with pre-trained Textract and Amazon Comprehend models for common NLP tasks.
Document post-processing	3.1a – Use AWS Glue for transformation.	3.2a – Encrypt data at rest. 3.2b – Enforce least privilege access.	3.3a – Persist results.	3.4a – Use Textract Response Parser Library. 3.4b – Use AWS Glue for serverless transformation.	3.5a – Save costs with AWS Glue for serverless transformation.
Overall NLP solution build	4.1a – Use CloudFormation templates. 4.1b – Use AWS Step Function for orchestration.	4.2a – Use least privilege IAM policies. 4.2b – Obfuscate sensitive data. 4.3b – Protect data at rest and in transit.	4.3a – Automate monitoring of custom training metrics.	4.4a – Use more async APIs to build a loosely coupled architecture.	4.5a – Save costs using managed services when available, such as Amazon Textract and Amazon Comprehend for NLP.

Figure 18.1 – Well-Architected NLP solutions matrix

As you can see from the preceding matrix, there are a number of design principles you can adopt during your solution development to build efficient and secure NLP applications. For the sake of clarity, we separated these principles based on the Well-Architected Framework pillars and the NLP development stages. However, as you might have noticed, some of these principles are repetitive across the cells. This is because an application of a principle for a particular pillar may automatically also address the needs of a different pillar based on what principle we refer to. For example, when using **AWS Glue ETL** jobs for document pre-processing and post-processing tasks, our Well-Architected needs for operational excellence, cost optimization, and performance efficiency are addressed without the need to do anything else.

We will explain the reason for this in more detail in the next section. We introduced the AWS Well-Architected Framework in this section and reviewed a matrix of how the Well-Architected principles can be applied to the AWS AI services we used throughout this book. In the next section, we will delve deeper and discuss how to implement some of the principles from the matrix.

Applying best practices for optimization

In this section, we will dive a bit deeper into what each of the design principles that we documented in the Well-Architected NLP solutions matrix means, and how to implement them for your requirements. Since the scope of this book is primarily about AWS AI services, we already have the advantage of using serverless managed services, and this addresses a number of suggestions that the Well-Architected Framework alludes to. Additionally, as mentioned previously, some of the best practices documented in the matrix may appear to be repetitive – this is not a mistake but intentional, as the application of one design pattern may have a cascading benefit across multiple pillars of the Well-Architected Framework. We will highlight these as we come across them. Without further ado, let's dig in.

Using an AWS S3 data lake

This section addresses principles *1.1a* and *1.3a* from the Well-Architected NLP solutions matrix (*Figure 18.1*).

A **data lake** is a repository for structured, semi-structured, and unstructured data. Initially, it is a collection of data from disparate sources within the enterprise and it serves as the data source for downstream analytics, business intelligence, **machine learning** (**ML**), and operational needs. However, since the data hydrated into a data lake retains its source format (data is not transformed before loading into the data lake), the data needs to undergo transformation at the time of consumption from the data lake. Building a data lake using **Amazon S3** (a fully managed object storage solution in the AWS cloud) makes a lot of sense because it scales as much as you want, and data stored in S3 is highly durable (for more information, see the section on the *"11 9s"* of durability at (`https://aws.amazon.com/s3/faqs/`).

Furthermore, AWS provides a number of ways in which you can get your data into S3, and several options to read data from S3, transform it, and feed it to your consumers for whatever needs you have, and all of these steps are carried out in a highly secure manner. To read in detail about creating a data lake on S3, hydrating it with your data sources, creating a data catalog, and securing, managing, and transforming the data, please refer to the *Building Big Data Storage Solutions* white paper (`https://docs.aws.amazon.com/whitepapers/latest/building-data-lakes/building-data-lake-aws.html`). For instructions on how to set up your data lake using **AWS Lake Formation** (a fully managed service to build and manage data lakes), please refer to the getting started guide (`https://docs.aws.amazon.com/lake-formation/latest/dg/getting-started.html`).

Let's now discuss how to use AWS Glue for data processing.

Using AWS Glue for data processing and transformation tasks

This section addresses principles *1.4a*, *1.5a*, *3.1a*, *3.4b*, and *3.5a* from the Well-Architected NLP solutions matrix (*Figure 18.1*).

AWS Glue is a fully managed and serverless data cataloging, processing, and transformation service that enables you to build end-to-end ETL pipelines providing ready-made connections to data stores both on-premises and on AWS. The serverless, managed nature of AWS Glue removes the costs associated with infrastructure management and undifferentiated heavy lifting. AWS Glue enables you to configure connections to your data stores and your S3 data lake to directly pull this data for document pre-processing. You can use Glue ETL jobs to deliver this data after transformation (as required) to an NLP solution pipeline, both for training your custom NLP models and for predictions at inference time. This makes your solution more elegant and efficient, avoiding the need to create multiple solution components to take care of these tasks.

AWS Glue ETL jobs can be triggered on-demand or scheduled based on your requirements. You can also use it for document post-processing after your NLP solution has completed its recognition or classification tasks, for persisting to downstream data stores, or for consumption by operational processes that need this data. For a detailed demonstration of how AWS Glue can help you, please refer to the following tutorial using **AWS Glue Studio**, a graphical interface to make it easy to interact with Glue when creating and running ETL jobs: `https://docs.aws.amazon.com/glue/latest/ug/tutorial-create-job.html`

In the next section, we will review how to use **Amazon SageMaker Ground Truth** for our text labeling tasks.

Using Amazon SageMaker Ground Truth for annotations

This section addresses principle *1.4b* from the Well-Architected NLP solutions matrix (*Figure 18.1*).

The accuracy of an NLP model is directly proportional to the quality of the labeled data it is based on. Though we primarily use AWS AI services that are pre-trained models, we saw quite a few use cases that needed Amazon Comprehend custom models for entity recognition and classification tasks. Amazon Comprehend custom models use **transfer learning** to train a custom model incrementally from its own pre-trained models with data that we provide (that is, data that is unique to our business). And so, for these custom training requirements, we need to provide high-quality labeled data that influences the accuracy of our models. As a best practice, we recommend using Amazon SageMaker Ground Truth (`https://aws.amazon.com/sagemaker/groundtruth/`) for these labeling tasks. Ground Truth is directly integrated with Amazon Comprehend, and all you need to do is point to the location of the Ground Truth manifest when you set up your Amazon Comprehend job.

Ground Truth is a fully managed service, providing easy-to-use capabilities for data labeling with options to either use your own private workforce, third-party data labelers that you can source from **AWS Marketplace**, or with crowdsourced public data labelers using **Amazon Mechanical Turk**.

Ground Truth provides data encryption by default, and it automatically learns from the labeling activities conducted by the human labelers by training an ML model behind the scenes. This ML model will be applied to automate the labeling tasks once a confidence threshold has been reached. Ground Truth provides pre-built task templates for various data formats, such as image, text, and video files. You can also create custom templates for your own requirements by selecting the **Custom** task type when creating a labeling job. Please see the following screenshot for different types of text-based labeling tasks supported by Ground Truth:

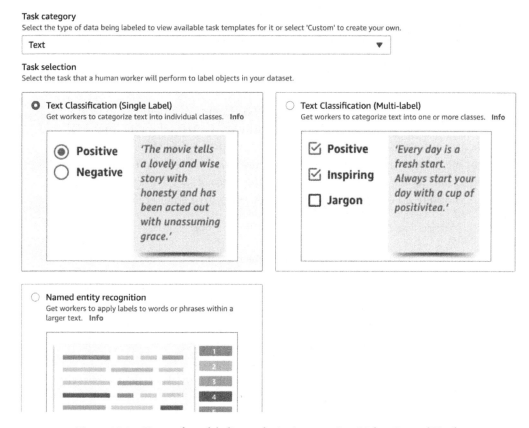

Figure 18.2 – Types of text labeling tasks in Amazon SageMaker Ground Truth

To get started, you create a labeling job, select an S3 location for your dataset, specify an **IAM** role (or ask Ground Truth to create one for you), select the task category from a list of pre-built templates (or you can select **Custom** for your own template), and choose the labeling workforce who will work on your request. Please refer to the following documentation for more details on how to get started: `https://docs.aws.amazon.com/sagemaker/latest/dg/sms-label-text.html`

Now that we know how to use Ground Truth for annotations, let's review a new feature that was launched recently to enable **custom entity recognizer training** directly from **PDF** or **Microsoft Word** documents.

Using Amazon Comprehend with PDF and Word formats directly

This section addresses principle *1.4c* from the Well-Architected NLP solutions matrix (*Figure 18.1*).

> **Note:**
> Amazon Comprehend updated the custom entity recognition feature in
> September 2021 to support training and inference with PDF and Word
> documents directly.

To improve the performance efficiency of your NLP solution pipeline, Amazon
Comprehend now supports training custom entity recognizers directly from PDF and
Word document formats, without having to run pre-processing steps to flatten the
document into a machine-readable format. To use this feature, you follow the same steps
we specified in *Chapter 14, Auditing Named Entity Recognition Workflows,* to train an
Amazon Comprehend custom entity recognizer, but with a small difference.

> **Note:**
> You still need to annotate your entities in the training document and create
> an augmented manifest using Ground Truth. For more details, please refer to
> the instructions in this blog: `https://aws.amazon.com/blogs/`
> `machine-learning/custom-document-annotation-for-`
> `extracting-named-entities-in-documents-using-`
> `amazon-comprehend/`

Please use the following steps to train and infer from PDF or Word documents directly
with Amazon Comprehend:

1. Log in to your AWS Management Console (please refer to the *Technical
    requirements* section for more details) and navigate to the **Amazon Comprehend**
    Console by typing `comprehend` in the **Services** search bar.

2. Click on **Custom entity recognition** on the left pane and then click on **Create
    new model**.

3. In the **Model settings** section, provide the name for your model and scroll down
    to the **Data specifications** section to select the **Augmented manifest** and **PDF,
    Word documents** formats for training. Provide the S3 location for your augmented
    manifest. Scroll down to select or create an IAM role and click on **Create** to start the
    training. Once the model is trained, you can run an inference using the same steps
    we discussed in *Chapter 14, Auditing Named Entity Recognition Workflows.* But,
    provide a PDF or Word document as an input instead of a CSV file.

Annotation and data format

Configure how you are providing your data.

Data format

To train your custom model, you must provide training data. This data must be formatted as either a CSV file or as one or more augmented manifest files.

○ **CSV file** Info

The CSV file that contains either the annotations or the entity lists for your training data. The required format depends on the type of CSV file that you provide.

⦿ **Augmented manifest** Info

A labeled training dataset that is produced by Amazon SageMaker Ground Truth. You can provide up to 5 augmented manifest files. To create an augmented manifest file, you can create a labeling job in Amazon SageMaker Ground Truth.

Training and test dataset

Training model type

○ **Plain text documents**	⦿ **PDF, Word documents**
Choose this option if your augmented manifest labeling job was used to label plain text documents.	Choose this option if your augmented manifest labeling job was used to label PDF documents.

Augmented manifest locations and attribute names   Collapse all

You can provide up to 5 augmented manifest files. Each file can reside in a separate location. For each file, you can name up to 5 attributes to use as training data.

▼ **Input location**   Remove

SageMaker Ground Truth augmented manifest file S3 location

Paste the URL of an input data file in S3, or select a bucket or folder location in S3.

s3://MyBucketName/output.manifest	**Browse S3**

Figure 18.3 – Amazon Comprehend custom entity recognizer training using PDF, Word documents

This feature update improves pre-processing efficiency and reduces upfront time investments in setting up our NLP solution pipelines. In the next section, we will review how to enforce access control when building NLP solutions.

Enforcing least privilege access

This section addresses principles *1.2c*, *3.2b*, and *4.2a* from the Well-Architected NLP solutions matrix (*Figure 18.1*).

One of the core tenets of a highly secure architecture is enforcing what is called the *least privilege for access to resources*. **AWS Identity and Access Management (IAM)** is a security service that enables defining and implementing your authentication and authorization strategy for secured access to your AWS infrastructure for your users. With IAM, you can create permissions policies that are attached to roles or users (*identities*) that define what (*actions*) the identity can or cannot do with AWS services (*resources*). Least privilege, as the name indicates, is all about defining highly restrictive permissions policies for your users and roles. The default permission in AWS is a *deny*.

If no policies are specified for a user, the user does not have permission to do anything in AWS. So, you add policy statements that allow a user or a role to perform specific tasks using AWS services or resources. In our examples in this book, due to the nature of our use cases and for the sake of simplicity and ease of configuration, we suggest you add managed permissions policies such as *TextractFullAccess* or *ComprehendFullAccess* to your **SageMaker execution IAM role** for your notebook. When you build your NLP solution and promote it to production, as a best practice, you should enforce least privilege access. Let's discuss what this means through an example. The *ComprehendFullAccess* permissions policy is defined by the following **JSON** statement:

```json
{
    "Version": "2012-10-17",
    "Statement": [
        {
            "Action": [
                "comprehend:*",
                "s3:ListAllMyBuckets",
                "s3:ListBucket",
                "s3:GetBucketLocation",
                "iam:ListRoles",
                "iam:GetRole"
            ],
            "Effect": "Allow",
            "Resource": "*"
        }
    ]
}
```

If you refer to the highlighted section in the preceding JSON code, the wildcard (*) attached to `"comprehend"` indicates that all Amazon Comprehend API actions are allowed for the role or the user that wields this policy. This is not a restrictive policy but rather provides a broad set of permissions.

To enforce least privilege access, a new policy should be created that should be changed as shown in the following JSON statement:

```json
{
    "Version": "2012-10-17",
    "Statement": [
        {
            "Action": [
                "comprehend:DetectEntities",
                "comprehend:BatchDetectEntities",
                "comprehend:DetectPiiEntities",
                "comprehend:ContainsPiiEntities",
                "s3:ListAllMyBuckets",
                "s3:ListBucket",
                "s3:GetBucketLocation",
                "iam:ListRoles",
                "iam:GetRole"
            ],
            "Effect": "Allow",
            "Resource": "*"
        }
    ]
}
```

In this changed JSON statement, we provide restrictive permissions that allow a user or a role to only use the **entities detection** feature in Amazon Comprehend. A good approach would be to only provide those permissions that are absolutely needed for a user or role to perform a task. Also, you will have to ensure that you monitor IAM roles and policy assignments to ensure that you clean up the permissions once the user or role has completed the task. This way, you avoid the situation of an old permission granting a user more access than they need. AWS provides a feature called **IAM Access Analyzer** to proactively monitor permissions and take actions as required. For a detailed introduction to Access Analyzer, please refer to the following documentation: https://docs.aws.amazon.com/IAM/latest/UserGuide/what-is-access-analyzer.html.

In the next section, we will review how to protect sensitive data during our NLP solution building task.

Obfuscating sensitive data

This section addresses principles *1.2a* and *4.2b* from the Well-Architected NLP solutions matrix (*Figure 18.1*).

Protecting the confidentiality of your data is highly important. Enterprises typically classify their data into categories such as *public*, *confidential*, *secret*, and *top-secret*, and apply controls and guardrails based on these classifications. If you are unsure of how to classify your data, please refer to an existing data classification model such as the **US National Classification Scheme**. More details on this model, as well as best practices for data classification as recommended by AWS, can be found in the following documentation: https://docs.aws.amazon.com/whitepapers/latest/ data-classification/welcome.html.

Once you have classified your data, the next step is to determine the type of confidentiality your data contains. Data can be **personally Identifiable Information (PII)**, for example, it may contain social security numbers, credit card numbers, bank account numbers, and so on. Or, if your data contains your customers' private health records, it is called **protected health information (PHI)**. If you are in the legal industry, the *Attorney-Client Privileged Information* is protected data and must be kept confidential.

So, as we can see, data protection is vitally important and must be a key consideration in our NLP solution development. When building on AWS, there are multiple ways in which you can protect your confidential data, including data encryption at rest and in transit, which we cover in subsequent sections in this chapter. For details on how AWS supports the highest privacy standards, and information about the resources to help you protect your customers' data, please refer to the following link: https://aws.amazon.com/ compliance/data-privacy/

The following screenshot shows the results of an Amazon Comprehend PII detection in real time.

Figure 18.4 – Amazon Comprehend PII detection

In *Chapter 4, Automating Document Processing Workflows*, we reviewed how Amazon Comprehend provides support for detecting PII entities from your data. You can use this capability as part of your document pre-processing stage by means of the **AWS S3 Object Access Lambda**. This service can be used to detect and redact PII data from your S3 bucket before using them in your NLP pipelines, if that is your requirement. The S3 Object Access Lambda allows you to execute an AWS `Lambda` function automatically to either process or transform your data when you fetch it from Amazon S3. For PII detection, two `Lambda` functions are made available to be used with S3 Object Access Lambda. The Amazon Comprehend `ContainsPiiEntites` API is used to classify documents that contain PII data and the `DetectPiiEntities` API is used to identify the actual PII data within the document for the purposes of redaction. For a tutorial on how to detect and redact PII data from your documents using the S3 Object Access Lambda, please refer to this GitHub repository: `https://github.com/aws-samples/amazon-comprehend-s3-object-lambda-functions`

In the next section, we will review how to implement data protection at rest and in transit.

Protecting data at rest and in transit

This section addresses principles *1.2b*, *2.2a*, *3.2a*, and *4.3b* from the Well-Architected NLP solutions matrix (*Figure 18.1*).

Now that we have discussed least privilege and data confidentiality, let's review the best practices for protecting your data *at rest* and *in transit* (that is, when it resides in a data store and during transit, for example, as a result of service API calls). When we talk about data protection at rest, we refer to encrypting your data during storage in AWS. Your data can reside in an Amazon S3 data lake, a relational database in **Amazon RDS** (a managed AWS service for relational databases), in **Amazon Redshift** (an exabyte-scale, cloud-based data warehouse), in **Amazon DynamoDB**, or in one of the other purpose-built databases such as **Amazon DocumentDB** (a managed AWS service for **MongoDB**), or **Amazon Neptune** (a managed AWS service for **Graph** databases), and many more.

With AWS, the advantage is that you can enable encryption to protect your data at rest easily using **AWS Key Management Service** (**KMS**) (a reliable and secure service to create, manage, and protect your encryption keys, and for applying the encryption of data across many services in AWS). Encryption is supported using the **AES-256** standard (`https://en.wikipedia.org/wiki/Advanced_Encryption_Standard`).

For example, when you store objects in Amazon S3, you can request **Server-side encryption** (encrypting data at the destination as it is stored in S3) by selecting to either use S3-managed encryption keys (that is, keys you create in KMS at the bucket level) or your own encryption keys (which you provide when you upload the objects to your S3 bucket).

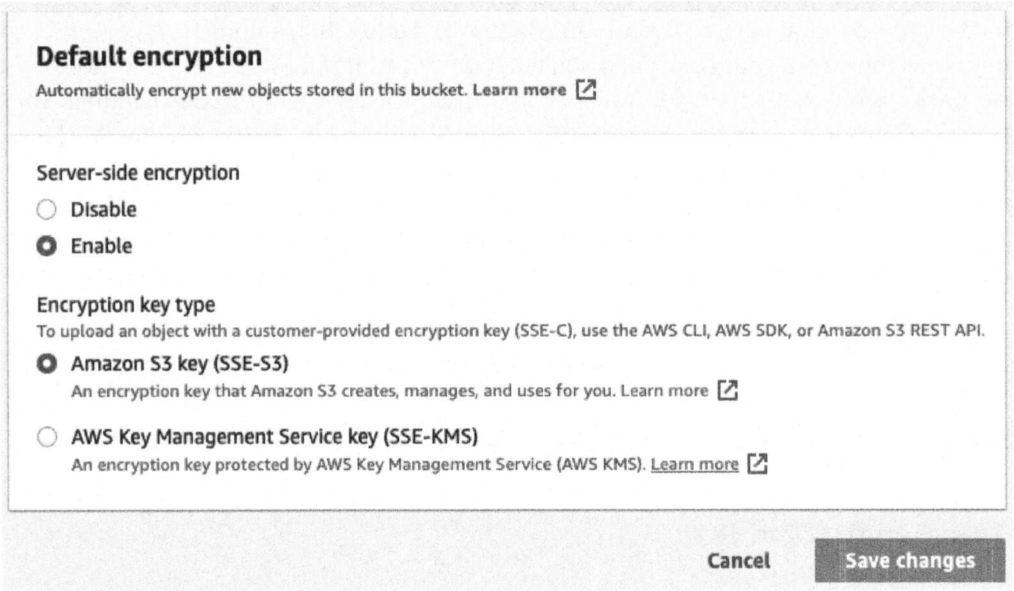

Figure 18.5 – Enabling encryption for your S3 bucket

Amazon Redshift provides similar options at cluster creation time to encrypt your data (`https://docs.aws.amazon.com/redshift/latest/mgmt/security-server-side-encryption.html`).

Amazon DynamoDB encrypts all your data by default using AWS KMS (`https://docs.aws.amazon.com/amazondynamodb/latest/developerguide/EncryptionAtRest.html`).

You can enable encryption for your Amazon RDS databases (`https://docs.aws.amazon.com/AmazonRDS/latest/UserGuide/Overview.Encryption.html`).

You can also enable encryption for any purpose-built AWS databases, such as Amazon DocumentDB (`https://docs.aws.amazon.com/documentdb/latest/developerguide/encryption-at-rest.html`).

All AWS services that handle customer data support encryption. Please refer to this blog for more details: `https://aws.amazon.com/blogs/security/importance-of-encryption-and-how-aws-can-help/`

To protect data in transit, you secure your API endpoints using a protocol such as **Transport Layer Security** (**TLS**): `https://en.wikipedia.org/wiki/Transport_Layer_Security`

Similar to protecting data at rest, AWS provides the means to secure your data in transit using **AWS Certificate Manager** (a managed service to provision and manage TLS certificates) to secure communications, verify identities, and implement **HTTPS** endpoints for application interactions. All AWS services that handle customer data are secured using TLS with HTTPS.

Using Amazon API Gateway for request throttling

This section addresses principle *2.1a* from the Well-Architected NLP solutions matrix (*Figure 18.1*).

When we build Amazon Comprehend custom entity recognizers or classifiers, we host these models by creating Comprehend real-time endpoints, as shown in the following screenshot:

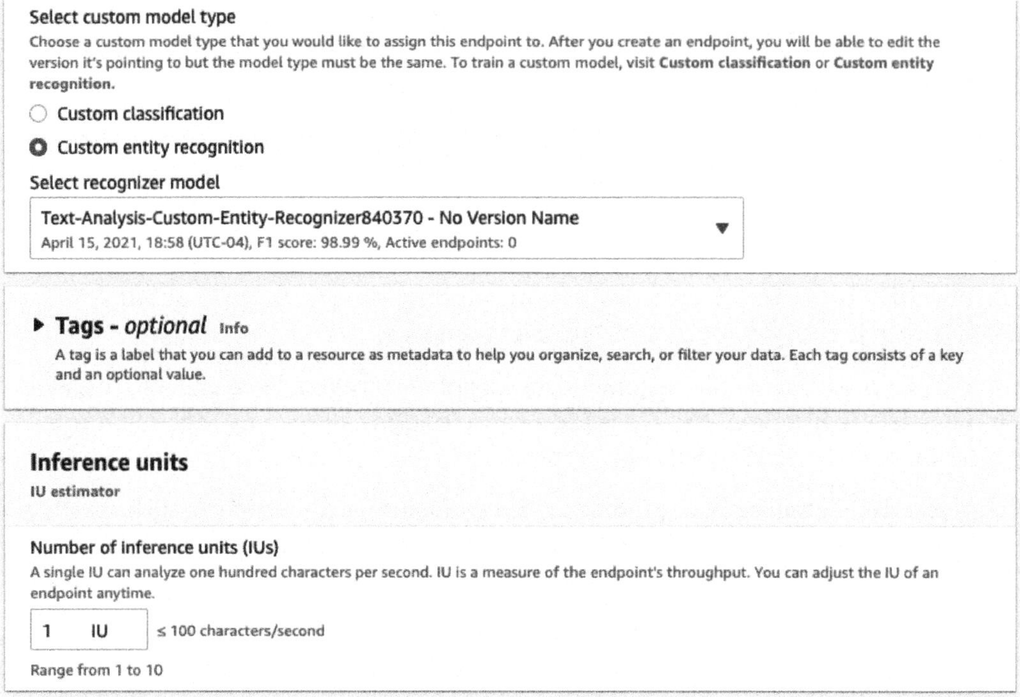

Select custom model type

Choose a custom model type that you would like to assign this endpoint to. After you create an endpoint, you will be able to edit the version it's pointing to but the model type must be the same. To train a custom model, visit **Custom classification** or **Custom entity recognition**.

○ Custom classification

● Custom entity recognition

Select recognizer model

Text-Analysis-Custom-Entity-Recognizer840370 - No Version Name	▼
April 15, 2021, 18:58 (UTC-04), F1 score: 98.99 %, Active endpoints: 0	

▶ **Tags - *optional*** Info

A tag is a label that you can add to a resource as metadata to help you organize, search, or filter your data. Each tag consists of a key and an optional value.

Inference units

IU estimator

Number of inference units (IUs)

A single IU can analyze one hundred characters per second. IU is a measure of the endpoint's throughput. You can adjust the IU of an endpoint anytime.

1 IU	≤ 100 characters/second

Range from 1 to 10

Figure 18.6 – Creating Amazon Comprehend real-time endpoints

You can call these endpoints directly from your code to detect entities or for text classification needs, as shown in the following code snippet:

```
response = comprehend.detect_entities(Text=entry,
                LanguageCode='en',
                EndpointArn='endpoint-arn'
        )
```

We will talk about how to set up auto scaling for your Amazon Comprehend real-time endpoints in a subsequent section, but you are billed by the second for your inference endpoints (https://aws.amazon.com/comprehend/pricing/), and the capacity is measured in inference units that represent a throughput of 100 characters per second. Throttling requests to the endpoint will allow for a more managed use of capacity. **Amazon API Gateway** (https://aws.amazon.com/api-gateway/) is a fully managed, secure, and scalable service for API management that can be used to create an API to abstract the calls to the Amazon Comprehend endpoint by using an AWS Lambda function, as demonstrated in the tutorial in the following link: https://github.com/aws-samples/amazon-comprehend-custom-entity-recognizer-api-example

Apart from throttling, API Gateway also supports traffic management, access control, monitoring, and version management, which can help implement a robust approach for handling requests for our solution. For more details, please refer to the following documentation: https://docs.aws.amazon.com/apigateway/latest/developerguide/api-gateway-create-api-as-simple-proxy-for-lambda.html

In the next section, we will cover how to set up auto scaling for your Amazon Comprehend real-time endpoints.

Setting up auto scaling for Amazon Comprehend endpoints

This section addresses principle *2.3a* from the Well-Architected NLP solutions matrix (*Figure 18.1*).

In the previous section, we discussed that you need endpoints to enable real-time predictions from your Amazon Comprehend custom models. The endpoint inference capacity is denoted as an **Inference Unit** (**IU**), which represents a throughput of 100 characters per second. When you create an endpoint, you specify the number of IUs you need, which helps Amazon Comprehend determine the resources to allocate to your endpoint. You calculate IUs based on the output throughput you need from the endpoint in terms of characters per second, and you are charged for the duration of when the endpoint is active, irrespective of whether it is receiving requests or not. So, you need to manage the IUs carefully to ensure you receive the required capacity when needed (for performance) but can also discard the capacity when not needed (to save costs). You can do this using Amazon Comprehend auto scaling: https://docs.aws.amazon.com/comprehend/latest/dg/comprehend-autoscaling.html

You can set up auto scaling only by using the **AWS Command Line Interface** (**AWS CLI**). The following example shows how to enable auto scaling for custom entity recognition:

1. Register a scalable target by running the following code snippet in the AWS CLI. Here `scalable-dimension` refers to the Amazon Comprehend resource type along with the unit of measurement for capacity (IUs):

```
aws application-autoscaling register-scalable-target \
--service-namespace comprehend \
--region <region> \
--resource-id <your-comprehend-custom-endpoint> \
--scalable-dimension comprehend:entity-recognizer-
endpoint:DesiredInferenceUnits \
--min-capacity 1 \
--max-capacity 2
```

2. You then create a JSON configuration for what target you would like to track, as shown in the following code snippet:

```
{
"TargetValue": 90,
"PredefinedMetricSpecification":
{
"PredefinedMetricType": "ComprehendInferenceUtilization"
}
}
```

3. Finally, you put this scaling policy into action, as shown in the following code snippet:

```
aws application-autoscaling put-scaling-policy \
--service-namespace comprehend \
--region <region> \
--scalable-dimension comprehend:entity-recognizer-
endpoint:DesiredInferenceUnits \
--resource-id <your-comprehend-custom-endpoint> \
--policy-name CERPolicy \
--policy-type TargetTrackingScaling \
--target-tracking-scaling-policy-configuration file://
config.json
```

In the next section, we will review how to monitor training metrics for our custom models to enable proactive actions.

Automating monitoring of custom training metrics

This section addresses principle *4.3a* from the Well-Architected NLP solutions matrix (*Figure 18.1*).

When training your custom classification or entity recognition models, Amazon Comprehend generates **metrics** (`https://docs.aws.amazon.com/comprehend/latest/dg/cer-metrics.html`), such as F1 score, precision, recall, and more, based on the evaluation it performed with the trained model. You can use the `DescribeEntityRecognizer` API (for entity recognition) or `DescribeDocumentClassifier` API (for classification) to get the evaluation metrics for your custom model.

The following is a code snippet of how to use the `DescribeEntityRecognizer` API:

```
comprehend = boto3.client('comprehend')
response = comprehend.describe_entity_recognizer(
    EntityRecognizerArn='<arn-of-your-entity-recognizer>'
)
```

To monitor for the completion of the Amazon Comprehend custom training job, you can use **Amazon EventBridge** (a managed serverless event bus) to create an event that is enabled when a training job is submitted, and which runs an AWS Lambda function to monitor the status of the training job in periodic intervals. When training completes, this AWS Lambda function will use the `DescribeEntityRecognizer` or `DescribeDocumentClassifier` APIs to retrieve the evaluation metrics. If the metrics are below a threshold, this function can send alerts or notifications using **Amazon Simple Notification Service (SNS)**. For details on how to schedule an event using Amazon EventBridge, please refer to the documentation: `https://docs.aws.amazon.com/eventbridge/latest/userguide/eb-run-lambda-schedule.html`.

In the next section, we will look at using Amazon A2I to set up human loops to review predictions.

Using Amazon A2I to review predictions

This section addresses principle *2.3b* from the Well-Architected NLP solutions matrix (*Figure 18.1*).

We covered using **Amazon Augmented AI (Amazon A2I)** (a managed service to set up human reviews of ML predictions) in great detail in many of the previous chapters in this book, starting with *Chapter 13, Improving the Accuracy of Document Processing Workflows*. When your solution is newly developed, it is a best practice to set up a human loop for prediction reviews, auditing, and making corrections as needed. Your solution should also include a feedback loop with model re-training based on human-reviewed data. We recommend having a human loop with Amazon A2I for the first three to six months to allow your solution to evolve based on direct feedback. Subsequently, you can disable the human loop.

In the next section, we will cover how to build modular, loosely coupled solutions using **Async APIs**.

Using Async APIs for loose coupling

This section addresses principles *2.4a* and *4.4a* from the Well-Architected NLP solutions matrix (*Figure 18.1*).

When we set up an NLP solution pipeline that is required to scale to processing millions of documents, it is a good idea to use the **Asynchronous Batch APIs** to implement this architecture. Synchronous APIs follow the request-response paradigm, meaning the requesting application will wait for a response and will be held up until a response is received. This approach works well when the need is to process a few documents quickly for a real-time or near-real-time, mission-critical requirement. However, when the document volume increases, a synchronous approach will hold compute resources, and slow down the process. Typically, organizations implement two separate NLP solution pipelines: one for real-time processing, and a second for batch processing. For batch processing, depending on the number of documents to be processed, the inference results are available after a few minutes to a few hours, depending on how the architecture is set up.

With Amazon Comprehend, once the entity recognizer or classifier training is completed, use the `Batch` API when you need to run `inference` for large document volumes, as shown in the following code snippets for entity recognition.

1. First, we submit an `entities detection` job (if we provide the endpoint ARN, it will use our custom entity recognizer). The response returns a `JobId`, a `Job ARN`, and a `job status`. Once the job is completed, the results are sent to the S3 location you specify in the `OutputDataConfig`:

```
response = comprehend.start_entities_detection_job(
    InputDataConfig={
        'S3Uri': '<s3-location-input-documents>',
```

```
            'InputFormat': 'ONE_DOC_PER_FILE'|'ONE_DOC_PER_
    LINE'
        },
        OutputDataConfig={
            'S3Uri': '<s3-location-output-results>'
        },
        DataAccessRoleArn='<IAM-role>',
        JobName='<provide a job name>',
        EntityRecognizerArn='<ARN of your custom entity
    recognizer>')
```

When using Amazon Textract for processing large document volumes, you can use the Batch APIs to first submit a text analysis or detection job, and then subsequently get the extraction results once the analysis job is completed. The following steps show how you can use the Amazon Textract Batch APIs.

Let's assume our use case is to process documents that contain tables and form data along with text. In this case, we will use the StartDocumentAnalysis API (https://docs.aws.amazon.com/textract/latest/dg/API_ StartDocumentAnalysis.html) as a first step, and ask it to look for table and form contents. Text in paragraphs is extracted by default. We also pass an Amazon SNS topic and an IAM role that provides permissions for Amazon Textract to publish a message to the SNS topic. This API returns a JobId that we will use in the next step:

```
textract = boto3.client('textract')
job = textract.start_document_analysis(
    DocumentLocation={
        'S3Object': {
            'Bucket': '<s3-bucket-name>',
            'Name': '<file-name>'
        }
    },
    FeatureTypes=[
        'TABLES'|'FORMS',
    ],
    NotificationChannel={
        'SNSTopicArn': '<SNS-topic-arn>',
        'RoleArn': '<IAM-role-arn>'
```

```
        }
    )
```

2. When the job completes, Amazon Textract sends a message to the SNS topic indicating the job status. You can attach an AWS Lambda function to this SNS topic as an event trigger. This Lambda function will call the GetDocumentAnalysis API (https://docs.aws.amazon.com/textract/latest/dg/API_ GetDocumentAnalysis.html) to retrieve the results from the Amazon Textract job, as shown in the following code snippet:

```
textract_results = textract.get_document_analysis(
    JobId='<JobID that was returned in the previous
step>',
    NextToken='<pagination-token>'
)
```

The response is a JSON object of blocks of text data that include both tabular and form content. In the next section, we will discuss how we can simplify the parsing of the JSON response object using Amazon Textract Response Parser.

Using Amazon Textract Response Parser

This section addresses principle *3.4a* from the Well-Architected NLP solutions matrix (*Figure 18.1*).

The JSON documents returned by the Amazon Textract APIs are comprehensive, with document contents categorized as blocks that encapsulate information for pages, lines, words, tables, forms, and the relationships between them. When using Amazon Textract to process complex or descriptive documents, it can seem time-consuming to understand the JSON results and parse them to obtain the data we need from the various ways text is contained in the document. The following code snippet shows the JSON response for a line that Amazon Textract extracted from the document we used in *Chapter 14*, *Auditing Named Entity Recognition Workflows*:

```
{'BlockType': 'LINE',
    'Confidence': 98.13241577148438,
    'Text': 'Lender Loan No./Universal Loan Identifier',
    'Geometry': {'BoundingBox': {'Width': 0.1989699900150299,
      'Height': 0.008062363602221012,
      'Left': 0.06528056412935257,
      'Top': 0.06330667436122894},
```

```
    'Polygon': [{'X': 0.06528056412935257, 'Y':
0.06330667436122894},
      {'X': 0.2642505466938019, 'Y': 0.06330667436122894},
      {'X': 0.2642505466938019, 'Y': 0.07136903703212738},
      {'X': 0.06528056412935257, 'Y': 0.07136903703212738}]},
    'Id': '678695ec-6c9c-4943-9dad-2d64fc5acc44',
    'Relationships': [{'Type': 'CHILD',
      'Ids': ['2600b0dc-ee1b-421b-a7f6-49de293c7b20',
        '70e20616-32b6-45f6-970d-e1a268ee97ec',
        '69792a6d-5df6-4729-8d25-b1f3b05a8cd5',
        'dfc16ed6-a526-46ac-98f3-f50453354c03',
        '71a1f5a2-3ff3-40de-9e58-3288f2ac83ee']}]},
```

So, in order to make the process of retrieving the content we need from the JSON output simpler, the **Amazon Textract Response Parser** library (or **TRP**) (https://github.com/aws-samples/amazon-textract-response-parser) was created. TRP makes it easy to get all the data we need with very few lines of code and improves the efficiency of our overall solution. We have already used TRP in this book, for example, in *Chapter 14, Auditing Named Entity Recognition Workflows*, and *Chapter 17, Visualizing Insights from Handwritten Content*.

The following code snippets show how to install and use the TRP library:

1. To install the TRP library, use the following code snippet:

    ```
    !python -m pip install amazon-textract-response-parser
    ```

2. Import the library, call the Textract API to analyze a document, and use TRP to parse the results:

    ```
    from trp import Document
    textract = boto3.client('textract')
    response = textract.analyze_document(Document={'Bytes':
    bytes_test}, FeatureTypes=['TABLES','FORMS'])
    text = Document(response)
    ```

3. Now, we can loop through the results to extract data from pages, tables, and more. For a **Python** example of how to use TRP, please refer to the code sample: `https://github.com/aws-samples/amazon-textract-response-parser/tree/master/src-python#parse-json-response-from-textract`

```
for page in text.pages:
            for table in page.tables:
for r, row in enumerate(table.rows):
for c, cell in enumerate(row.cells):
```

In the next section, we will review why it is important to persist the prediction results from our NLP solution, and how we can make use of this data.

Persisting prediction results

During the course of this book, we have seen examples where the results of an entity recognition or classification task are sent to an **Amazon Elasticsearch** instance (for metadata extraction) or to Amazon DynamoDB (for persistence). We also saw examples where these results are used to inform decisions that impact downstream systems. The reason for this is because we often see with organizations that document processing provides important inputs to their mainstream operations. So, when you design and build NLP solutions, you have to keep in mind how your prediction results are going to be consumed, by whom, and for what purpose. Depending on the consumption use case, there are different options available for us to use. Let's review some of these options:

- If the need is for real-time access to inference results, set up an API Gateway and AWS Lambda function to abstract the Amazon Comprehend real-time endpoint. Persist the inference request and response in an Amazon S3 bucket or Amazon DynamoDB for future reference. Please refer to the *Using API Gateway for request throttling* section for more details.

- If the results are to be sent to downstream applications that need these inputs for decision-making or functional requirements, you can persist the results to Amazon S3, or an Amazon RDS database, or any of the purpose-built data stores in AWS. To notify the applications that new results are available, you can publish a message to an Amazon SNS topic or use an event trigger in the data stores. For more information, please refer to the following: `https://docs.aws.amazon.com/lambda/latest/dg/services-rds-tutorial.html`

- If you need the results to populate a knowledge repository or make it available for user search, send it to an Amazon Elasticsearch (now called **OpenSearch**) index. For more information, please refer to the following: `https://docs.aws.amazon.com/opensearch-service/latest/developerguide/search-example.html`

- If you would like to use the results for business intelligence or visualization, you can send the results to an Amazon S3 bucket and use **Amazon QuickSight** with the data in Amazon S3. For more information, please refer to the following: `https://docs.aws.amazon.com/quicksight/latest/user/getting-started-create-analysis-s3.html`

- If you would like to transform the results before sending them to the data stores, use AWS Glue ETL jobs. For more details, please refer to the *Using AWS Glue for data processing and transformation* section.

Let's now review how to automate the NLP solution development using **AWS Step Function**.

Using AWS Step Function for orchestration

In a previous section, we read how using Batch APIs can help scale the architecture to handle large volumes of documents. We reviewed Amazon Comprehend and Textract APIs that can help us implement a batch-processing pipeline. When we start designing a batch solution, it may take the shape of an Amazon S3 bucket, to which an AWS Lambda event trigger is attached that will call the Amazon Textract API to start document analysis. To this, an Amazon SNS topic would be provided, a message will be sent by Amazon Textract to this topic, to which an AWS Lambda is attached, and so on. You get the point. It can get really difficult to manage all of these moving parts in our solution. To design an elegant and efficient NLP solution, you can use AWS Step Function to manage the orchestration of your entire pipeline (`https://aws.amazon.com/step-functions/`).

AWS Step Function is a serverless, event-driven orchestration service that can help tie together several steps in a process and manage it end to end. Error handling is built in, so you can configure retries, branching, and compensation logic into the orchestration. An example of a Step Function orchestration from the samples available in the AWS Console is shown in the following screenshot:

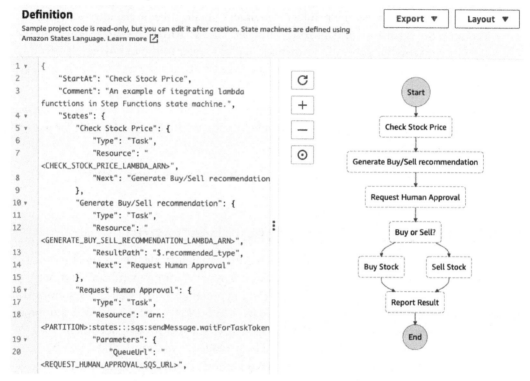

Figure 18.7 – A sample Step Function orchestration

To get started, you can run a sample orchestration in your Step Function Console in the AWS Management Console by selecting **Run a sample project** in the **State Machines** option on the left of the console. You can also try the Step Function tutorials available here: https://aws.amazon.com/getting-started/hands-on/create-a-serverless-workflow-step-functions-lambda/

In the next section, let's discuss how to automate our deployment process using AWS CloudFormation.

Using AWS CloudFormation templates

AWS CloudFormation (`https://aws.amazon.com/cloudformation/`) is an infrastructure-as-code service that helps you automate and manage your resource provisioning tasks in AWS. When building NLP solutions using AWS AI services, we primarily deal with managed services, but, depending on how our operational architecture looks, it makes a lot of sense to use AWS CloudFormation to automate our deployment process. This is mainly because it removes a lot of overhead related to the setup, makes change management easier, and helps us achieve operational excellence. Every solution topology is different, but if your NLP architecture includes Amazon S3 buckets and other types of AWS data stores, AWS Step Function, AWS Lambda functions, Amazon SNS topics, and so on, you will benefit from using AWS CloudFormation. Templates can be written in JSON or **YAML**, and there are lots of resources available to help you get started.

For an example CloudFormation template with AWS Step Function and AWS Lambda functions, please refer to the following: `https://docs.aws.amazon.com/step-functions/latest/dg/tutorial-lambda-state-machine-cloudformation.html`

For template snippet code examples for a variety of AWS services, please refer to the following: `https://docs.aws.amazon.com/AWSCloudFormation/latest/UserGuide/CHAP_TemplateQuickRef.html`

As we saw in detail in the preceding sections, these are some of the principles and best practices you can adopt to design and build long-lasting NLP solutions that are cost-effective, resilient, scalable, secure, and performance-efficient. These are the characteristics that make great solutions.

Summary

After having learned how to build NLP solutions for a number of real-world use cases in the previous chapters, we spent this chapter reading about how to build secure, reliable, and efficient architectures using the AWS Well-Architected Framework. We first introduced what the Well-Architected Framework is, and reviewed the five pillars it is comprised of: operational excellence, security, reliability, performance efficiency, and cost optimization. We read about each of the pillars in brief, and then discussed how the Well-Architected Framework can help us build better and more efficient NLP solutions by using a matrix of best practices aligned with the Well-Architected principles and the different stages of NLP solution development.

We followed this summary of the best practices by diving deep into each one, learning how to implement them using the AWS Management Console, AWS documentation references, and some code snippets.

That brings us to the end of this book. It is with a heavy heart that we bid adieu to you, our wonderful readers. We hope that you had as much fun reading this book as we had writing it. Please don't forget to check out the *Further reading* section for a few references we have included to continue your learning journey in the exciting space that is NLP.

Further reading

- AWS Well-Architected Labs (`https://www.wellarchitectedlabs.com/`)

- Amazon Textract blogs (`https://aws.amazon.com/blogs/machine-learning/category/artificial-intelligence/amazon-textract/`)

- Amazon Comprehend blogs (`https://aws.amazon.com/blogs/machine-learning/category/artificial-intelligence/amazon-comprehend/`)

- Amazon Comprehend workshops (`https://comprehend-immersionday.workshop.aws/`)

- AWS Automating data processing from documents (`https://aws.amazon.com/machine-learning/ml-use-cases/document-processing/`)

`Packt.com`

Subscribe to our online digital library for full access to over 7,000 books and videos, as well as industry leading tools to help you plan your personal development and advance your career. For more information, please visit our website.

Why subscribe?

- Spend less time learning and more time coding with practical eBooks and Videos from over 4,000 industry professionals

- Improve your learning with Skill Plans built especially for you

- Get a free eBook or video every month

- Fully searchable for easy access to vital information

- Copy and paste, print, and bookmark content

Did you know that Packt offers eBook versions of every book published, with PDF and ePub files available? You can upgrade to the eBook version at `packt.com` and as a print book customer, you are entitled to a discount on the eBook copy. Get in touch with us at `customercare@packtpub.com` for more details.

At `www.packt.com`, you can also read a collection of free technical articles, sign up for a range of free newsletters, and receive exclusive discounts and offers on Packt books and eBooks.

Other Books You May Enjoy

If you enjoyed this book, you may be interested in these other books by Packt:

Machine Learning with Amazon SageMaker Cookbook

Joshua Arvin Lat

ISBN: 978-1-80056-703-0

- Train and deploy NLP, time series forecasting, and computer vision models to solve different business problems
- Push the limits of customization in SageMaker using custom container images
- Use AutoML capabilities with SageMaker Autopilot to create high-quality models
- Work with effective data analysis and preparation techniques
- Explore solutions for debugging and managing ML experiments and deployments
- Deal with bias detection and ML explainability requirements using SageMaker Clarify
- Automate intermediate and complex deployments and workflows using a variety of solutions

Amazon SageMaker Best Practices

Sireesha Muppala , Randy DeFauw , Shelbee Eigenbrode

ISBN: 978-1-80107-052-2

- Perform data bias detection with AWS Data Wrangler and SageMaker Clarify
- Speed up data processing with SageMaker Feature Store
- Overcome labeling bias with SageMaker Ground Truth
- Improve training time with the monitoring and profiling capabilities of SageMaker Debugger
- Address the challenge of model deployment automation with CI/CD using the SageMaker model registry
- Explore SageMaker Neo for model optimization
- Implement data and model quality monitoring with Amazon Model Monitor
- Improve training time and reduce costs with SageMaker data and model parallelism

Packt is searching for authors like you

If you're interested in becoming an author for Packt, please visit authors. packtpub.com and apply today. We have worked with thousands of developers and tech professionals, just like you, to help them share their insight with the global tech community. You can make a general application, apply for a specific hot topic that we are recruiting an author for, or submit your own idea.

Share Your Thoughts

Now you've finished *Natural Language Processing with AWS AI Services*, we'd love to hear your thoughts! Scan the QR code below to go straight to the Amazon review page for this book and share your feedback or leave a review on the site that you purchased it from.

https://packt.link/r/1-801-81253-5

Your review is important to us and the tech community and will help us make sure we're delivering excellent quality content.

Index

C

D

Made in the USA
Las Vegas, NV
08 December 2021